AN ANTHOLOGY OF WESTERN MARXISM

AN ANTHOLOGY OF WESTERN MARXISM

From Lukács and Gramsci to Socialist-Feminism

Edited by

ROGER S. GOTTLIEB

New York Oxford

OXFORD UNIVERSITY PRESS

1989

Oxford University Press

Oxford New York Toronto
Delhi Bombay Calcutta Madras Karachi
Petaling Jaya Singapore Hong Kong Tokyo
Nairobi Dar es Salaam Cape Town
Melbourne Auckland

and associated companies in
Berlin Ibadan

Published by Oxford University Press, Inc.,
200 Madison Avenue, New York 10016

Library of Congress Cataloging-in-Publication Data
An anthology of western Marxism: from Lukács and Gramsci to socialist-feminism/edited by Roger S. Gottlieb.
p. 3 cm. Bibliography: p.
ISBN 0-19-505568-3
ISBN 0-19-505569-1 (pbk.)
1. Philosophy, Marxist. 2. Feminism. I. Gottlieb, Roger S.
B809.8.A644 1989
335.4--dc19 8-10121 CIP

3 5 7 9 8 6 4

Printed in the United States of America

To the women and men
who created this tradition
and fought for its ideals

Preface

Dozens of writers could have been included in the collection. Why have I chosen the ones that are here? These selections show the central contributions of Western Marxism: its *general philosophical orientation, understanding of historical materialism, model of socialist political practice,* and *conceptions of human liberation*. Although some readers might wonder why certain authors were not included, I do not believe anyone can question the importance of the ones already in this collection.

My commitment to making this a quality anthology of substantive selections—rather than a collection of snippets from a larger number of authors—dictated that some important authors be left out. As it now stands, however, the anthology brings together material that will give the reader a detailed and comprehensive introduction to the crucial contributions of Western Marxism. I have also searched among these authors' voluminous writings to find selections that speak as clearly as possible to the critical issues.

Moreover, I believe that this collection constitutes a coherent theoretical statement. Despite their enormous inherent value, the detailed studies of Marxist economists or historians do not really belong in a volume focusing on the basic philosophical and political orientation of a Marxism both anti-Stalinist and anticapitalist. Nor is there a place here for the "analytic Marxism" of contemporary writers such as G. A. Cohen, for the philosophical sophistication of these writers masks a view of social life that has not absorbed the insights of Western Marxism. Although the ideas of many Eastern European anti-Soviet leftists (for example, the Praxis school of Yugoslavia) are compatible with the theoretical tendencies represented here, I believe most of those ideas were anticipated by Lukacs and Gramsci. Conversely, the most liberating and creative of the pre-Western Marxists (for example, Rosa Luxemburg and Leon Trotsky) are really on the edge of traditional Marxism rather than in the same camp as the theoreticians gathered here; and they are well represented in other anthologies.

More controversial is my decision to join familiar Western Marxists with socialist-feminists, which reveals my own theoretical, political, and personal understanding of leftist thought in this century. It is not a viewpoint that everyone will share. I argue for it in the Introduction to this anthology (and at greater length in my own *History and Subjectivity: The Transformation of Marxist Theory* [Philadelphia: Temple Univ. Press, 1987]).

Finally, this book would surely have benefited from writings of socialists expressing the viewpoints of racial, ethnic, or national groups (for example, blacks, Jews, and anti-imperialists). Space constraints—as well as the belief that the writings of such socialists, however important, may not directly relate to this tradition—led me to make the difficult decision to exclude them.

To any critic who finds my reasons for selecting individual contributions for this anthology inadequate I can only suggest the course of creating another one. Let a thousand anthologies bloom, and let us move from better books to a more just and humane society in which to read, write, edit, and forget them.

A generous grant from the Research Development Council of Worcester Polytechnic Institute helped support the publication of this book.

R.S.G.

Worcester, Mass.
April 1988

Contents

AN ANTHOLOGY OF WESTERN MARXISM

Introduction

Can Marxist theory help us create a free and liberating society? Most people in the United States would say "no," for in this country "Marxism" is usually considered synonymous with the world's communist governments and political parties. As such, "Marxism" describes totalitarianism, brutal repression of dissent, single-minded dogmatism, state control of all aspects of social life, and an affinity for violence.

Since the 1960s, however, political life in Western Europe and North America has included activist movements that use aspects of Marxist theory yet oppose traditional communism, movements that are as critical of Eastern bloc repression as they are of capitalist exploitation.

What kind of Marxism, one might ask, has helped shape groups such as the New Left, Euro-Communism, socialist-feminists, America's democratic socialists, and anticapitalist groups of racial or religious minorities? The selections in this book answer that question. Along with their intrinsic theoretical value, the writings of Western Marxists are important because they have foreshadowed, influenced, and expressed a new and liberating political practice in Western Europe and North America.

The authors included in this anthology have responded to three major influences: (1) the content, ambiguities, and limitations of traditional Marxist theory; (2) the failures of traditional Marxist practice, especially those of the German Social Democratic party, the Second International, Leninism, and the Communist International; and (3) social change and the resurgence of radical political movements after World War II.

Problems with Marx's Theory

The limitations and ambiguities of Marx's writings provide a starting point for the theoretical accomplishments of Western Marxism. Marx's original theory of society and history can be summarized briefly. "Human nature" is not a fixed essence that belongs to each person as an individual. Rather, personhood is constituted by historically specific and historically evolving social relations. Not all social relations, however, are equally important. The forces and relations of production are central in determining the structure of a given society and the transformation of a particular society into a different one. Technical resources and the social organization of labor determine history by creating economic classes—collective social agents who act on interests derived from their roles in the production and control of material wealth. Intellectual, political, and cultural life are, therefore, not autonomous but dependent. They reflect and support a particular level of historical development and a particular set of class interests.

More concretely, the prospects for human liberation stem from the contradictions of capitalist society. Capitalist development necessarily leads to increasingly severe economic crises and an ever-larger industrial proletariat, thereby creating a politically radical working class that will replace capitalism with socialism. Thus, the capitalist creation of modern forces of production, combined with the appropriation of those forces by organized workers, will form the basis for communism. Communists will serve as organizers, catalysts, and educators to accomplish this task. With the end of capitalist wage exploitation, virtually all other forms of oppression and alienation will be overcome. After the revolution, communism will provide both freedom from material want and the fullest possible development of human abilities.

Despite its brilliance and influence, Marx's theory is plagued by serious problems. Its own inherent weaknesses, subsequent historical developments in capitalist society, and the actions of purportedly socialist and communist political parties and governments have led Western Marxists to transform the theory they inherited.

From Laws of History to Class Consciousness and Subjectivity

Since the 1920s, Western Marxists have faced the failure or absence of socialist revolutions. The conditions that Marx thought would lead to revolution—economic and social crises in advanced capitalism—existed, yet power and authority remained with the state and capitalists. Also, Marxist political parties rigidified into oppressive state powers or dogmatic and self-serving cliques.

In response, Western Marxists have tried to explain the coexistence of the social structure of advanced capitalism and the political passivity of the working class by stressing the critical importance of class consciousness, subjectivity, and personal experience. It is to these factors, rather than what traditional Marxism saw as "laws of history," that our authors turned to explain the failures of Marxist politics and to direct the struggle for socialism.

One basic problem is that occasionally both Marx and some of his followers claimed the structure of a society's economy would guarantee its future social development. Marx wrote that his analysis of capitalism's development, tendency to crisis, and eventual breakdown showed "natural laws of capitalist production . . . working with iron necessity towards inevitable results."[1] He also compared his theory of capitalist development to the laws governing planetary motion, implying that society is governed by economic "laws" which, like those of the natural world, are both universal and essentially independent of human consciousness and will. Similarly, certain passages in Marx's writings and in those of subsequent Marxists assert that politics and culture have no independent role in social life. Both within a society and in the transformation from one type of society to another, the economy is seen as socially primary. On this view, economic development and class structure determine the basic form of all other aspects of social life and are the only segments of social life to possess a "real" or independent history.

Western Marxists rejected traditional Marxism's belief in historical laws and in the power of the economy to determine all aspects of social life. Korsch and Lukacs initiated the argument that the structure of social life is essentially different from that of the natural world and we should therefore not expect social theories to produce universal laws. Social reality, unlike nature, is partly constituted by human beliefs and attitudes. Also, a belief in theories about society and an awareness of past social regularities can motivate actions to change social life. Thus, social life and historical change do not flow from abstract "laws of history." Rather, human beings make themselves through their consciousness, actions, and institutional life.

For Western Marxists historical change is inseparable from human consciousness, not something distinct from and causally determining it. Social life cannot be understood without reference to the conscious and unconscious, comprehended and misunderstood, experiences and activities of collectively organized human beings. Western Marxist theory began by stressing the importance of beliefs and attitudes in constituting the mode of production (Korsch) and of class consciousness and culture in the revolutionary process (Lukacs, Gramsci). In this theoretical development, interestingly, we may see the influence of (though clearly not a return to) Hegel's belief that human development proceeds through stages of consciousness.

Western Marxists have also rejected Marx's confidence that massive industrial organization and recurrent economic crises would necessarily create a revolutionary class consciousness among workers. Marx's rudimentary social psychology was rendered suspect by the failure of revolutionary movements and the rise of fascism, rather than socialism, as a result of the economic crisis of the 1930s. These events led Western Marxists to focus on how personal experience in capitalist society obstructs the emergence of revolutionary class consciousness. In their investigations Western Marxists integrated non-Marxist social sciences, especially psychoanalysis, with Marxist economic and political theory. The failures of working-class politics in the 1930s made it necessary to extend Lukacs's and Gramsci's concepts of class consciousness and cultural hegemony. Reich, Horkheimer, and Adorno thus developed a notion of political subjectivity by applying psychoanalysis and the critique of culture to bourgeois society. The rise of fascism compelled these writers to investigate the social forces that seemed to make the working class not only politically passive but psychically attached to bourgeois or Stalinist authority. These forces included not just conscious beliefs but unconscious personality structures, not just the experiences of work but those of sexuality and family life as well. Finally, the notion of subjectivity was further developed and extended to the realm of gender by socialist-feminism (Mitchell, Rowbotham, Hartmann, Ehrenreich, Ferguson), which argued that working-class subjectivity is constituted by sexual politics as well as class power.

Complementing their denial of mechanical "laws of history," Western Marxists believe that social structure and historical change are not determined solely by the economy. For instance, the mode of production cannot simply be the "cause" of the worker's consciousness because that consciousness (as Korsch argues) is an essential element in the mode of production itself. At most, objective economic developments can create a range of historical possibilities. Which of those possibilities becomes real is determined by class consciousness and political struggle.

The capitalist exploitation of labor is also reinforced by areas of social life that create and sustain workers in the world of paid labor. Workers are *reproduced* by specific social practices and institutions, a process as essential to the mode of production as technological development or the accumulation of wealth. Gender relations and the nuclear family, as Reich in the 1930s and socialist-feminists in the 1970s were to argue, create a personal psychology congenial to capitalism. Further, as Ferguson shows, the concept of labor must be expanded to include socially female, unpaid "sex-affective" labor—housework, child care, and emotional nurturance—which is essential in reproducing the working class, both physically and psychically.

Western Marxists thus believe that society appears to be governed by "historical laws" only because capitalism makes social life seem objective and immutable. Radical class consciousness, Lukacs suggests, develops when the oppressed start to see through this reification and understand society as the product of human action. Moreover, Western Marxists (starting with Korsch and continuing with Reich and Sartre) have criticized leftist groups for using Marxism's supposedly scientific status as an excuse for their own domination of the working class. When social processes are represented as objective, quasinatural, mechanical processes, our authors argue, the "masters" of Marxist theory can arrogate to themselves the right to order political struggle and social life according to their self-proclaimed "scientific" knowledge of those processes. Workers in particular and society at large are then reduced to the status of passive objects and the theoretical basis for totalitarianism is established. The brutalities of Stalinism or the dogmatism and bureaucracy of Western communism then set in. Habermas (following Horkheimer, Adorno, and Marcuse) develops this position into a critique of science and technology as ideology. When we identify social theory with natural science, he suggests we end up treating people like things; and we fail to distinguish between science's goal of *controlling nature* and social theory's goal of *understanding and liberating human beings*. The fundamental moral and political dilemmas of social life—which should be settled by a free and enlightened population—are represented as the province of engineers and managers. Further, as Rowbotham argues, seeing revolutionary theory and practice as a matter of science and expertise reflects and reproduces the politics of gender. Communist leaders, we might say, "feminized" the working class, manifesting a culturally male bias toward the division of all groups into the active experts and the passive followers.

From Exploitation to Domination

Although Marx recognized the existence of oppression not specifically economic in character (e.g., the oppression of women), he believed that class oppression was the necessary condition for these other forms—at least since the advent of capitalism. Just as capitalism "homogenized" the life experiences and interests of all workers, so the elimination of capitalist class structure would lead to the phasing out of sexism, racism, and national oppression.

For Western Marxists, by contrast, the interrelation among different forms of oppression is much more problematic. Self-proclaimed "socialisms" in China, Cuba, and Vietnam, for example, as well as socialist movements in the West, have manifested bureaucratic privilege, sexism, nationalism, ethnic chauvinism, homophobia, and racism. In bourgeois society at large there is a painful legacy of different oppressions—men over women, whites over blacks—which blocks the creation of socialist class consciousness.

Moreover, the widespread affluence of the West after World War II, as Gorz and Marcuse observe, makes it unlikely that a homogeneous working class will unite in a militant struggle simply to win a higher standard of living. New needs and values, ones not rooted in an expansion of material consumption, must be found and cultivated. Further, ecological crises and nuclear terror raise the issue of the domination of nature and of a generally human interest in ending that domination.

Many writers have shown that traditional Marxists find it very hard to deal with these issues. And Western Marxists have supplemented traditional Marxism's focus on an economically exploited working class with concern for all those (including, for some, nature itself) dominated by unjust power relations. Although class power might be central in determining long-term historical developments, the oppressions of race and sex, to name but two, are now recognized as both critical and in some ways independent of class: they are embedded in Western culture and rooted within the working class itself. Further, it is crucial to recognize that the male industrial working class—the "vanguard" of traditional Marxist theory—has colluded in the oppression of other groups (especially women; see Hartmann).

These theoretical changes also reflect the post–World War II political passivity of industrial workers in the United States and northern Europe. During this period radicalism has often been led by students, racial minorities, or women. Accordingly, post–World War II Western Marxists have seen the political experiences and needs of these oppressed groups—as well as the traditional working class—as essential to any socialist strategy. Gorz and Marcuse suggest that the political problem is no longer how to organize a homogeneous working class around a simple and unified set of political demands. Rather, socialists face the much more complex task of organizing coalitions of different oppressed groups against the common enemy of capitalist economic power, the capitalist state, and embedded antagonisms among the oppressed themselves.

From the Party to Consciousness-Raising

For Western Marxists the relationship between communists and the working class is a central problem of revolutionary strategy. The problem arises because they believe that both "reformist" social democrats and "revolutionary" communists have betrayed the struggle for socialism. For Marx the possibility that communists themselves might be enemies of the revolution does not arise. For Western Marxism this possibility is a reality. Korsch criticized Leninism for producing a "dictatorship over, not of, the proletariat." Reich claimed that socialists practiced "bourgeois politics" when they ignored workers' class consciousness. Socialist-feminists reject male domination and its associated elitism. In these and other ways Western Marxists have consistently struggled to formulate an open, democratic, and progressive relationship between self-conscious radicals and the majority of the population. Our authors have stressed that intellectualized Marxist theory is less significant in the revolutionary process than the self-creation of a radical subjectivity and consciousness. Thus Reich's account of class consciousness and the stress on consciousness-raising within the women's movement highlight the attempt to find a form of radical thought, feeling, and action that is not subject to the betrayals and domination of a revolutionary elite.

The Failures of Traditional Marxist Practice

Marx wanted to change the world, not just understand it. Similarly, numerous political parties, international organizations, and governments have claimed to put Marx's theory into practice. It is *against* these groups—especially the German Social Democratic party, the Second International, and the Soviet Communist party—that Western Marxists have formed themselves.

The Mechanical Marxism of European Social Democracy

In 1875 German socialists created the German Social Democratic party (SPD). The SPD affirmed the central political role of the industrial proletariat; the need to overthrow rather than reform the state; the desirability of a broad, democratic party rather than a small, conspiratorial one; and the necessity for the workers' movement to be independent from the progressive middle classes. By 1890 the SPD controlled thirty-five seats in the legislature and close to 1.5 million (almost 20 percent of the total) votes. Its size and influence made it a model for the smaller and less influential social democratic parties of Europe. With the exception of France, continental socialism looked to Germany for leadership (see Joll, Novack et al., and Lichtheim).

The Second International was founded in 1889. More than four hundred representatives from twenty countries began an organization that would be the center of European socialism for the next twenty-five years. Two major issues dominated. First, most members chose a revolutionary strategy based on mass parties and parliamentary victories rather than one that stressed direct action, strikes, and revolutionary violence. Second, it was assumed that a European war would be prevented because the interests of the proletariat transcended national boundaries and workers would not support their governments' militarism. The failure of the SPD-led Second International was shown most clearly in August 1914, when most of its leaders endorsed their countries' entry into World War I.

This failure was directly connected to the Second International's political strategy. While its leaders claimed that social democracy sought the overthrow of capitalism, the SPD's politics were essentially reformist. In the Preface to an 1895 reprinting of Marx's *Class Struggles in France,* Engels proposed to replace revolutionary violence of the 1848 or 1871 variety with electoral activity by a mass party. Although Engels recommended such activity as a temporary tactic, for the Second International it became a long-term strategy.

This strategy was consistent with the Second International's understanding of Marxist theory. Social democratic leaders expected the economic contradictions of capitalism to pave the way for an easy socialist victory. Seeing the breakdown of capitalism as an inevitable consequence of its systematic laws of development, the SPD could reasonably trust in democracy, the increasing size of the proletariat, and its own well-protected organization. Cultivating a politically conscious and militant mass movement was unnecessary.

Eduard Bernstein, editor of the SPD's main theoretical journal, sought to rectify this contradiction between radical theory and reformist politics by demanding a fundamental revision of Marxism. He argued that capitalism's self-regulation disproved Marx's prediction of inevitable economic crisis and proletarian immisseration. Capitalism had stabilized itself and was providing a steadily increasing standard of living. Socialism would follow the slow increment of socialist parliamentary power and the increased strength of trade unions and consumer cooperatives. Given a climate of political democracy, these institutions would erode capitalist profits to the vanishing point. Gradual progress, not economic crisis and revolution, would lead to socialism.

The SPD formally rejected revisionism. But Bernstein's position reflected the actual practice of the party. As an experienced Bavarian socialist wrote to him, "one doesn't formally decide to do what you ask, one doesn't say it, one *does* it. Our whole activity . . . was the activity of a Social Democratic reforming Party."[2] Bernstein's revisionism reflected crucial changes in European society, not just the reformism of the Second International. The extended economic crisis of 1873–95 fundamentally altered world capitalism. Competitive capitalism was giving way to trusts and monopolies and there was a resurgence of colonization. The state's role in the economy was increasing and social welfare legislation was introduced to contain working-class dissent.

These changes from competitive to monopoly and imperialist capitalism led to temporary political stability and economic affluence in Europe and the United States. A comparatively privileged sector of craft labor won (after bitter struggle in some cases) improvements in wages, working conditions, and political rights. Social democracy functioned in the service of the limited interests of these workers and their leaders. Cultivating their organizations and trusting their deterministic version of Marxism, leaders of the Second International were unprepared for the catastrophic social effects of a world war motivated by the pursuit of third-world markets and resources. Nor could they understand that workers, despite Marxist theory, identified with their nationality as much as, or more than, with their class.

Perhaps most important, the Second International's acceptance of the most mechanical version of Marxist theory ignored the essential role of class consciousness and subjectivity in political change.[3] On the one hand, the SPD's leaders did not see that the ruling class could learn from the past and modify capitalism toward greater organization and stability. On the other hand, they were blind to the critical importance of the fact that workers were socialized to accept relations of authority and could continue in that acceptance even during economic crises.

The beginnings of Western Marxism are found in the wave of theoretical and political criticism of the Second International which arose after World War I. Korsch, Lukacs, and Gramsci rejected the Second International's lack of concern with class consciousness and dogmatic trust in the inevitability of socialism. Korsch argued against any "scientific" understanding of Marxist theory and claimed that any theory unconnected to a mass movement inevitably became (as in the Second International) an ideology. Lukacs tried to show how the radical class consciousness essential for socialist revolution could emerge from the workers' daily experience of capitalist exploitation. Gramsci developed the notion of hegemony to describe forms of class power based on consent rather than violence.

Leninism, the Bolshevik Revolution, and Comintern

Russian socialists faced an economically and politically undeveloped country. They therefore could not successfully employ an SPD strategy dependent on bourgeois democracy. Instead, they had to adapt Marxism to Russia: an overwhelmingly rural society that also possessed a few centers of large-scale industry and militant workers' organizations. The small and weak Russian bourgeoisie was heir to enough political experience to know some of the dangers of allying itself to a now potentially revolutionary proletariat. Just because of historical developments since the events generalized on by Marx—including proletariat uprisings in 1848 and 1871 and the rise of socialist parties—Marx's generalizations no longer held. The political strategy of the Second International could have little place in Russia.

Of the various competing socialists who attempted to synthesize Marxism for Russia, Lenin was the most successful. Lenin began by combining the legal Marxists' stress on state reform with the economists' concentration on trade unions. However, he joined both tactics with a more militant struggle for the overthrow of both Czarism and capitalism. This process, he argued, required the leadership not of a mass but of a "vanguard" party. The model of such a party was Lenin's most dramatic contribution to Marxism, the one still most closely identified with the term *Marxism-Leninism*. In a series of polemics written in 1901–7 Lenin defined the vanguard party as a group of disciplined, highly trained, professional revolutionaries. Only such a party, he believed, could coordinate diverse struggle in the face of state repression and inject socialist class consciousness into a working class dominated by bourgeois ideology (Lenin 1943, 1960, 1970).

My concern here is not with Lenin's vast and not always consistent writings.[4] Rather, I wish only to summarize what Leninism came to mean in the context of the Russian revolution: faith in the vanguard party, alliance between peasants and proletariat under the latter's leadership, and a belief that political consciousness and action directed by the party could create a revolution.

Some weaknesses of Leninism are indicated even in this capsule summary. First, Lenin held that a working class and peasant alliance could hold power and begin to build socialism in Russia only with aid from a postrevolutionary Europe. What would happen, however, if an uprising by the tiny but politically advanced Russian proletariat and both the commune-dwelling and the land-hungry peasants did not spark a European upheaval? How long, for instance, would the alliance between the proletariat and the peasantry last, especially since many peasants wished to retain their own communal institutions, institutions that had no place in Lenin's model of proletarian social dictatorship?

Also, what if the small, professionalized party were to become a power elite, a privileged bureaucracy rather than a selfless revolutionary leadership? This last possibility was anticipated by Trotsky's prophetic critique of Lenin at the 1903 Russian Social Democratic Congress. Trotsky warned of a situation in which, after having substituted the party for the class, "the party organization is substituted for the party, the Central committee is substituted for the party organization, and finally a single 'dictator' is substituted for the Central Committee."[5] Similarly, Rosa Luxemburg, one of the SPD's radicals, criticized Lenin for confusing "the corpselike obedience of a dominated class and the organized rebellion of a class struggling for its liberation."[6]

Although Lenin's vanguardism was in some ways an improvement over the mechanical Marxism of the Second International, his faith in the knowledge and virtue of "the party" sowed the seeds of future dictatorship.[7] After its seizure of power in 1917, the Russian Communist party came to dominate Russian political and social life. Other political parties were eliminated while local councils, trade unions, and peasant cooperatives were destroyed or turned into puppets of party power. All independent political expression was made impossible.

The party claimed its repression was justified by the existence of both internal and external problems. First among these was Russia's economic underdevelopment, which worsened after a civil war crippled both agricultural and industrial production and distribution. Far from inheriting an economically and socially modernized country, as Marxist theory forecast, Lenin's party had to modernize, industrialize, and demand that their citizens sacrifice immediate consumption for future productive capacity.

Second, internal political relations occurred in the complete absence of democratic traditions. The outlawing of opposition parties is often taken as evidence of Leninist dictatorship. Yet it should be remembered that opposition members attempted to kill Lenin and negotiated with hostile foreign powers.

Third, the international revolution did not occur. After a series of uprisings, the postwar tide of radicalism ebbed in 1923. Instead of sparking—and receiving aid from—European revolutions, Russian communists found themselves surrounded by antagonistic capitalist powers. They had become the lonely vanguard of history instead of the inspiration of a new world order.

Finally, the original social base of the Bolsheviks, the peasant–worker alliance, collapsed. By 1921 the Russian working class, as an organized group capable of exercising some control over its political representatives, had ceased to exist. Workers had been killed in the civil war, had returned to the countryside as industry broke down, or had risen into the ranks of the new bureaucracy. By 1921 even Lenin had to admit that the Russian proletariat no longer existed.[8]

With the absence of a self-active proletariat, then, the Communist party became an autonomous force. To the extent that the peasants supported revolutionary aims, they sought to develop their historic communes into autonomous rural institutions, not serve a centralized Communist party (CP). The party allied with the peasantry during the New Economic Policy of 1921–28, but it would not permit independent political institutions for long. For Leninism the majority of Russia's population was to be subordinate to the (supposed) representatives of the tiny working class. With the stabilization of communist rule by the late 1920s, the CP–peasant alliance turned into a violent struggle, as some variously estimated 5 million to 15 million peasants were killed or allowed to starve and noncommunist peasant leadership was killed. Although some efforts were made to win the poorer peasants to socialist ideology, no serious consideration was given to sharing power with progressive peasant forces (see Kingston-Mann).

In 1921, with the end of the civil war, the "Workers' Opposition" demanded increased power for community and workers' councils (the soviets). True to its belief in the role of the party, the Communist party responded that

> only the political party of the working class, i.e., the Communist Party, is in a position to unite, educate and organize such a vanguard of the proletariat and all the laboring masses as will be able to counteract the inevitable petit-bourgeois wavering of the masses, to counteract tradition and unavoidable lapses of trade union narrowness . . . to direct all sides of the proletarian movements . . .[9]

Responding to an uprising of the usually supportive sailors of Kronstadt, the party passed a resolution demanding strict unity and banning factions.

The democratic reforms of 1920 were curtailed and greater power was accorded to the party's organizational structure. By 1928 the defeat of the joint opposition marked the end of serious inner-party struggles. Justifying its dictatorship by appeals to security, the Russian CP modernized agriculture and initiated the fastest industrialization in world history. It also created a new class of privileged bureaucrats and technical experts.

Far from imbuing the working class with socialist consciousness, this ruling class took Russian society as an object to be controlled. Unlike in the early years of the revolution, the rights of women and homosexuals, progressive education, and collective childrearing were attacked. There was a resurgence of narrow nationalism, anti-Semitism, and support for traditional family structure (even as women were increasingly entering the work force). In the 1930s a Stalinist reign of terror led to the often completely random killing of millions, including many (perhaps most) of the most dedicated party members. False confessions were extracted by torture, and history was intentionally distorted (see Medvedev).

At the same time, Soviet citizens and the world at large were assured that communists were creating "socialism in one country." Just as traditional Marxism had been unprepared for revolution in backward Russia, so Marxism–Leninism could equate socialism with central planning and nationalization of the means of production. Believing that the mode of production determined all aspects of social life, traditional Marxists could not see how the failure to change socialization processes and the absence of political activity within the mass of Russia's population made the Soviet Union a new form of class society rather than a socialist republic.

The "success" of Leninism led to the formation of communist parties throughout the world. All of these parties accepted Soviet leadership. Affiliating together in the Third or Communist International (Comintern), these parties agreed to unconditional support of the Soviet Union, obedience to the Executive of the Comintern subject to expulsion, splitting of previously existing parties along lines defined by the Executive, and acceptance of the Soviet model of revolutionary strategy and organization.[10]

As European revolutionary movements faded, Soviet—and hence Comintern—policy shifted. Waiting for a breakdown of capitalism, once again seen as "inevitable," communists were instructed to protect the Soviet Union. Not only a shifting theory, but self-interested Russian nationalism motivated this strategy. In a sense Comintern was the SPD on a world scale. A poverty of theory combined with an unfortunate "wealth" of narrow national and bureaucratic self-interest masquerading as universal revolutionary morality. Consequently, communist parties justified opportunistic deals between the Soviet Union and capitalist nations, allowed themselves to be pushed into catastrophic alliances with bourgeois nationalist forces in colonial countries and rejected cooperation with social democratic forces during the rise of fascism. On the level of theory, independent ideas and creative Marxist scholarship were replaced by dogmatic justifications of Soviet policies.

As it had initially rejected the Second International, Western Marxism later defined itself in opposition to Comintern. In Korsch's later writings, and in those of Reich, Horkheimer, and Adorno, we find attempts by isolated radicals to create a Marxist theory opposing both bourgeois thought and a worldwide communist movement. This theory had to explain the failures of traditional Marxism, workers' continuing acceptance of capitalism, and the differences between a truly radical theory and both bourgeois and Stalinist apologies for domination. Decades later, Sartre, Marcuse, Gorz, and socialist-feminists took it for granted that organized communism has little to offer any movement to overthrow capitalism in the direction of human freedom. Somehow, all of these thinkers believed, it is possible to transform Marxist theory so that it no longer views society as a law-governed mechanism—or workers as raw materials to be manipulated by bureaucrats. Conversely, it is also necessary to build a critique of bourgeois social relations into a theory of capitalist society. Thus Reich, Horkheimer, and Adorno initiated an understanding of the cultural mechanisms that perpetuate the workers' attachment to authority; Gorz and Marcuse offer a new vision of the structure of revolutionary intentions; and Sartre attempts to reconcile Marxism's social understanding with the existentialist conception of individual choice.

On the Edge of the Present

The Collapse of World Communism

Pre–World War II Western Marxists were isolated in their rejection of Comintern, but the postwar period saw increasing numbers of leftists abandon any allegiance to Soviet and Soviet-supporting communist parties. The discovery of the enormity of Stalinist terror, the opportunist and reformist practices of communist parties, and the dogmatic and unthinking quality of communist ideology all contributed to this action. Orthodox communism's wait for the "inevitable" breakdown of capitalism seemed a little unrealistic during the postwar economic boom; so did the reiterated assertion of the leading role of the industrial proletariat in the face of working-class prosperity and trade union conservatism. Finally, the claim that revolution required a Leninist vanguard was refuted—or at least made highly questionable—by the failures and brutalities of Soviet communism. (In the 1970s the previously traditional communist parties of France, Spain, and Italy rejected obedience to Moscow and stressed their support of democracy.)

Internationally, communist-led or influenced popular victories in China, Vietnam, Laos, Cambodia, Algeria, Cuba, Angola, Yemen, and Nicaragua have made the Soviet Union only one of a number of socialist countries and ended the ideological and political unity of world communism. Minor border clashes and major ideological battles have occurred between China and Russia, while communist political independence from Soviet domination has been a possibility in Eastern Europe since Yugoslavia rebelled in 1948. Soviet armed intervention in Hungary (1956) and Czechoslovakia (1967), as well as conflicts between Vietnam and both China and Cambodia, have shown that nations that define themselves as communist, reject capitalism, and oppose Western imperialism can still be in conflict with each other.

Admiring the courage and determination of anti-imperialist movements, Western Marxists nevertheless tend to doubt the applicability of their strategies—or of the policies of anti-imperialist governments—to the West. Our authors have recognized that all "socialist" revolutions have faced the tasks of industrialization and modernization and have had to defend themselves against imperialism. These tasks have precluded the development of socialist social relations: democracy, self-management, community control, overcoming racial and gender antagonisms, and the flowering of human creativity. Instead, increases in consumption, health care, literacy, and so forth generally combine with the creation of a new ruling class of technocrats and managers who benefit from an authoritarian social structure. Thus, postwar Western Marxists have been increasingly free to define their own Marxist theory, unconcerned with the political or ideological consequences of rejecting orthodoxy.

The Revival of Radicalism

The 1960s saw a dramatic revival of radicalism in the West. This revival was inspired by many factors: the threat of nuclear war; the failure of U.S. society to grant economic or civil equality to blacks; an increasing resistance to imperialist foreign policies in places like Algeria, Vietnam, the Middle East, and Central America; and a general revulsion for the irrational and inhuman character of affluent societies managed by profit-minded efficiency experts.

The new radicalism emerged from a cold war setting of anticommunist hysteria and communist totalitarianism. In this context, movements based on moral idealism and the actions of small, unconnected groups developed. Most participants in the civil rights and peace movements of the 1950s and early 1960s, for instance, lacked developed political theories or long-term strategies. Activists believed that their just demands and moral example would stimulate social reform. These movements—along with the early student power and antiwar groups—sought neither socialism nor revolution. Often unstable coalitions of white liberals, students, blacks, pacifists, and radical clergy, they were neither capable of nor particularly interested in mobilizing a radical working class. They relegated Marxism to the dustbin of outworn formulas used by Communist functionaries to justify Moscow's latest line.

But the dialectic of social experience could not rest with morally oriented, reformist politics. In Europe, where Marxism had always been a more living tradition than in the United States, the New Left marched from the first under an anticapitalist (though also anti-Soviet) banner. In the United States the limitations of the civil rights movement and the escalation of U.S. involvement in the Vietnam War drove activists to the left. By the late 1960s members of the New Left saw themselves not as loyal citizens out to reform a viable system, but as revolutionaries bent on an overall transformation of society. They identified with an international movement of radicals and peoples of color against imperialism and totalitarianism, a movement that stretched from the National Liberation Front in Vietnam to the sugar fields of Cuba, from the attempt to create "socialism with a human face" in Czechoslovakia to the bureaucracy-challenging Cultural Revolution in China. This movement against capitalism and the Soviet system would succeed, most of the New Left believed, without the pacified and privileged white working class.

The New Left was neither ideologically nor institutionally unified. Although the organizational expertise guiding massive antiwar demonstrations often came from anti-Soviet Trotskyist groups, the demonstrations themselves united hippies celebrating the joys of LSD with Maoists demanding a "worker–student" alliance. Ex-members of the American Communist party came out of political retirement to work with pacifists and anti-Soviet social democrats. Radicalized black civil rights activists joined with affluent whites from elite universities. Despite its heterogeneity, late 1960s radicalism became a mass movement in Europe and

North America: an independent struggle posing a radical critique of capitalist society and imperialism.

The New Marxism of the New Left (and Beyond)

The shift from moral reformism to anticapitalist radicalism necessarily led in the direction of Marxism. If the enemy was a system, rather than a few bad leaders or mistaken policies, then a comprehensive theory of that system was needed. Moral outrage, moral example, and media coverage were not enough. Yet the rediscovery of Marxism was combined with a persistent distrust of orthodox communist versions of the theory. Orthodox communism seemed consistently out of joint with the experience of the New Left—for instance, when it denied the political relevance of college students or claimed vanguard status for industrial workers. Traditional Marxist theory (as Sartre argues) simply obscured social realities with tired abstractions. Likewise, the New Left rejected the communists' unending attempts to channel dissent through their organizations, as in the French Communist party's reformist and bureaucratic response to the student and worker upheaval of May 1968.

From a mass movement, much of the New Left degenerated into fringe groups preoccupied with violence, or posturing radicals who aped the worst features of Third World or traditional Stalinist politics. These tendencies burned themselves out, or were destroyed by state repression, by the early 1970s. It eventually became clear that any revolutionary force not tied to a working-class movement would fail. Radicals also began to see the need to design political institutions for the realities of the advanced industrial world, rather than take those of Cuba, Vietnam, or China as models.

Echoing the ideas of Gramsci and Reich, many radicals since the 1970s have tried to produce an original and more inclusive definition of the revolutionary process, and in so doing have turned for help to the Western Marxist tradition. The enemy, these radicals realized, was not only economic exploitation, but also a large variety of social relations and cultural forms. Authoritarianism, sexual repression, and intellectual elitism, for example, were identified as aspects of the class power, unjust privilege, and alienation essential to capitalist society. Yet cultural and psychic domination could not be dismissed as simple products of class structure, which would necessarily evaporate once the structure was changed. Not only did culture and subjectivity obstruct the development of class consciousness: their present, oppressive nature could duplicate the oppressive elements of the dominant society in any purportedly radical political movement. An entire culture had to be overcome through the social transformation of virtually all aspects of modern Western society.

Thus, we find Marcuse, for instance, seeking the roots of a truly radical culture of resistance in groups marginalized by the affluent society. He also elaborates the need for a total transformation of social values, not simply an alteration of economic control and political power. Material poverty is only a limited issue in this critique of capitalism. At least as much stress is placed on the moral and spiritual failures of a culture based on mindless and deadening material consumption. Furthermore, as Habermas argues, any tendency to claim scientific status for Marxism simply reproduces the dominant ideology that defines human beings and social relations as "objects" to dominate as modern science and technology dominate nature. Taken as the only form of knowledge, technology—the hallmark of modernized societies—becomes an ideology.

Recent radicalism's stress on cultural and social as well as economic and political issues reflects fundamental changes in the class structure of advanced capitalist society. In the last thirty years there has been an enormous growth of a "new working class" of teachers, technicians, engineers, nurses, and so forth, tremendous increases in the number of government employees and service workers, and a dramatic shrinking of the number of industrial workers. As Gorz argues, it is quite unlikely that a radical social movement could appeal to this new working class (or to well-paid unionized workers) solely on the basis of economic interests. Simultaneously, increased government intervention in the economy has rendered cataclysmic economic crisis unlikely. The state has become a key social actor. Economic interests are significant among the nonunionized, people of color, and the unemployed, of course, and in times of high unemployment, inflation, and fading industries. But activist movements have also been built around less obviously economic interests such as job satisfaction, environmental pollution, sexual preference, and respect for the cultural identity of minorities. Finally, pollution, nuclear weapons, and the general unhappiness and alienation of our high-technology society have created a profound distrust of science's capacity to meet human needs.

The Advent of Feminism

The most dramatic social change in recent decades has been the enormous influx of women into the labor market. The corresponding pressure on the nuclear family and traditional sex roles set the stage for a reemergence of feminism, which took a radical turn for New Left women who were active in the civil rights, student power, and antiwar movements. In the mid-1960s female activists came to see that they themselves were oppressed, both in society at large and within revolutionary groups. Most aspects of this oppression were not comprehended by revolutionary theory—nor were they of much interest to male revolutionary leaders. Thus, the genesis of socialist-feminism: the attempt to merge modernized Marxist accounts of class domination with a newly formulated theory of male domination.

Building on Western Marxism, socialist-feminists deny that sex roles are simple products of the economic system, or that ending wage exploitation will unproblematically end all other types of oppression. To understand women's experiences and needs, it is necessary to analyze the interaction of the public mode of production with the private realm of human *reproduction;* the gender-based structures of family life, sexuality, emotional attachment, and child-raising. Furthermore, virtually all aspects of society have become gender-based and women's oppression shapes public life as well as private. Thus, our feminist authors describe the interaction between economic exploitation and class structure, on the one hand, and sexism and the sexual division of labor, on the other. In practice, socialist-feminists have combined the traditional Marxist concern with economic power with issues such as violence against women, child care, and women's specific economic inequality, and they have demanded that women's needs and experiences be made part of the socialist agenda.

Socialist-feminists also defined politics in a new way and struggled for the liberation of women against newly identified forms of oppression. The feminist assertion that "the personal is political" indicated women's concern with resistance to oppression acted out in everyday personal habits, feelings, and attitudes. Feminists have shown that the factory and the state are not the only arenas of political action and that "the revolution" must transform attitudes toward sexuality, marriage, and child raising. In these and other areas, acceptance of the gender-based personality structures of bourgeois society simply perpetuates both the oppression of women and other forms of social domination.

Finally, socialist-feminists have led the struggle against the recapitulation of social domination in revolutionary organizations themselves, criticizing and fighting against male elitism, one-upmanship, and careerism. Women have demanded recognition of the "personal" work of dealing with the feelings and human needs of revolutionaries as well as with finding the right line or strategy—and rejected the sexual division of labor that relegated women to this "labor of relationships." In a struggle that has united political principle with personal experiences, socialist-feminists have helped make the Western Marxist theoretical critique of uncritical trust in revolutionary expertise concrete. They have demonstrated that revolutionaries must be aware not only of working-class consciousness and subjectivity, but also of their own victimization by and participation in the oppression and alienation of modern society. In this way, socialist-feminism is the fulfillment of the Western Marxist project. Conversely, socialist-feminists have argued for the centrality of capitalism in women's oppression (thus opposing the liberal feminists who ignore class issues) and have maintained (in opposition to many radical feminists) that political alliances with men are necessary.

Feminist concerns and insights have helped inspire a number of contemporary radical movements—movements expressing the interests of a variety of oppressed groups: gay men and lesbians; racial, ethnic, and religious minorities; the elderly; and the physically challenged. In their most radical versions, these movements connect the generalities of capitalist exploitation with the specifics of their particular social experience. They thus join with Western Marxists in transforming Marxism, from a purportedly universalistic doctrine which actually justifies bureaucratic repression to a living theory that shapes the struggle for a rational, free, and liberating society.

Marcuse, Gorz, Sartre, Habermas, Rowbotham, Mitchell, Hartmann, Ehrenreich, and Ferguson reflect the concerns, experiences, and goals of the postwar struggle for noncommunist revolutionary Marxism. In their words this struggle is writ large. We can also see how far they have come from Marx's original theory. Although Western Marxists take that theory as a starting point, they have adapted its insights and abandoned many of its limitations. They share Marx's goal of creating a society in which human capacities can freely unfold and his belief that such a society is incompatible with capitalism. Yet Western Marxists have rejected belief in the sole social primacy of the economy, in the historical laws that make socialist revolution inevitable, and in the leading political role of a homogeneous working class.

A definitive history of the theory and practice of Western Marxism cannot be written. As a structured vision of a liberated social order, it can be fully understood only when that vision is implemented, or proved to be impossible. Although political radicals of all kinds are again marginalized in the United States, Western Marxists think and act, organize, and communicate. In so doing they seek to keep alive the human image of liberating socialism in the midst of brutal and deadening societies whose contradictions brought their tradition into existence.

Notes

1. Karl Marx, *Capital* (New York, 1967), I, 8.

2. Quoted in James Joll, *The Second International, 1889–1914* (New York, 1966), 94.

3. Engel's "dialectical materialism" represented both social life and the natural world as following universal "laws" of dialectics. Kautsky's commentary on the SPD's important Erfurt Program of 1891 speaks of the "natural necessity" of an "inevitable" breakdown of capitalism. Colletti's essay on the Second International (pp. 45–110) forms the basis of much of my interpretation. See also Lichtheim (pp. 203–304). For a detailed account of the last years of the SPD before World War I, see Schorske.

4. He justified the vanguard party, but during times of mass insurgency he also criticized the Bolsheviks for lagging behind the masses. Although he spent much of his energy seeking to purify party doctrine to justify its vanguard role, during the last year of his life he struggled against the bureaucratic and totalitarian behavior of the party. While he sought rigid discipline in the party, his vision of socialism in *State and Revolution* emphasized the withering away of the state and the possibility of all administrative tasks being shared by the majority of the population (see Harding; Cliff; Carr 1964, 134–50; Lichtheim, 325–80; Leonhard, 47–94; Menashe; and Siranni).

5. Quoted in Robert V. Daniels, *A Documentary History of Communism* (New York, 1960), I, 31.

6. Quoted in Rosa Luxemburg, *Selected Political Writings* (New York, 1971), 191.

7. My interpretation of the Russian Revolution and Soviet Marxism is based in the sources listed in note 4 and the following: Deutscher 1959, 1963, 1965; Carr 1966, Lichtheim, 355–380; Trotsky; Daniels 1960, 1969; Kingston-Mann; Rowbotham 1974, 134–79; and Marcuse 1958.

8. In 1921 Lenin argued against self-described "representatives of the proletariat": "[W]hat do you describe as proletariat? That class of labourers which is employed in large-scale industry. But where is [your] large-scale industry? What sort of proletariat is this? Where is your industry?" At the party congress in 1922 he claimed:

> Since the war it is not at all working-class people but malingerers that have gone to the factories. And are our social and economic conditions at present such that genuine proletarians go to the factories? No. They should go, according to Marx. But Marx wrote not about Russia—he wrote about capitalism in general, capitalism as it has developed since the fifteenth century. All this has been correct for 600 years, but it is incorrect in present-day Russia.

A representative of the Workers' Opposition later argued: "Vladimir Illich said yesterday that the proletariat as a class, in the Marxian sense, did not exist [in Russia]. Permit me to congratulate you on being the vanguard of a non-existing class." (All quotations are from Deutscher, *The Prophet Unarmed* [New York, 1959], 14–15 n.)

9. Daniels, *Documentary History,* II, 210.

10. For accounts of Comintern, see: Deutscher 1959; Borkenau; Gruber; Daniels 1960, vol. 2 and Novack et al.

References

Borkenau, Franz. 1962. *World Communism*. Ann Arbor: University of Michigan Press.

Carr, E. H. 1964. *Studies in Revolution*. New York: Grosset & Dunlap.

———. 1966. *The Bolshevik Revolution*. 3 vols. 1966. London: Pelican.

Cliff, Tony. 1980. *Lenin*. 2 vols. London: Pluto Press.

Colletti, Lucio. 1972. *From Rousseau to Lenin*. New York: Monthly Review Press.

Daniels, Robert V. 1960. *A Documentary History of Communism*. 2 vols. New York: Vintage.

———. 1969. *The Conscience of the Revolution*. New York: Simon & Schuster.

Deutscher, Isaac. 1959. *The Prophet Unarmed*. New York: Vintage.

———. 1963. *The Prophet Outcast*. New York: Vintage.

———. 1965. *The Prophet Armed*. New York: Vintage.

Gruber, Helmut, ed. 1972. *International Communism in the Era of Lenin*. New York: Anchor.

Harding, Neil. 1977. *Lenin's Political Thought: Theory and Practice in the Democratic Revolution*. New York: Columbia University Press.

Joll, James. 1966. *The Second International, 1889–1914*. New York: Harper & Row.

Kingston-Mann, Esther. 1983. *Lenin and the Problem of Marxist Peasant Revolution*. New York: Oxford University Press.

Lenin, V. I. 1943. *What Is to Be Done?* New York: International Publishers.

———. 1960. *Lenin on Proletarian Revolution and Proletarian Dictatorship*. Peking: Foreign Languages Press.

———. 1970. *Two Tactics of Social-Democracy in the Democratic Revolution*. Peking: Foreign Languages Press.

Leonhard, Wolfgang. 1974. *Three Faces of Marxism*. New York: Putnam.

Lichtheim, George. 1965. *Marxism*. New York: Praeger.

Luxemburg, Rosa. 1971. *Selected Political Writings*. Dick Howard. New York: Monthly Review Press.

Marcuse, Herbert. 1958. *Soviet Marxism*. New York: Vintage.

Marx, Karl. 1967. *Capital*. Vol. 1. Trans. Samuel Moore and Edward Avelins. New York: International Publishers.

Medvedeu, Roy. *Let History Judge. 1971*. Trans. Colleen Taylor. New York: Random House.

Menashe, Louis. 1973. "An Essay on Lenin." *Socialist Revolution*, no. 18 (Nov.–Dec.).

Novack, George, Dave Frankel, and Fred Feldman. 1974. *The First Three Internationals*. New York: Pathfinder Press.

Rowbotham, Sheila. 1974. *Women, Resistance and Revolution*. New York: Vintage.

Schorske, Carl E. 1965. *German Social Democracy, 1905–1917*. New York: Wiley.

Siranni, Carman. 1975. "Rereading Lenin." *Socialist Revolution*, no. 23 (April).

Trotsky, Leon. 1970. *The Revolution Betrayed*. Trans. New York: Pathfinder.

I

THE REVOLUTIONARY INTELLECTUAL AND THE BREAKDOWN OF SOCIAL DEMOCRACY

1

Karl Korsch (1896–1961)

Born in Germany, Korsch received a doctorate in law in 1910. In 1917 he joined the Independent Social Democratic party of Germany. Korsch worked in the newly formed Communist party of Germany (KPD) in 1920 and in 1923 served briefly as Minister of Justice in the short-lived Thuringen workers' government. When the postwar uprisings in Germany failed, the KPD was brought under direct control of Comintern. Korsch resisted this trend and by 1926 was attacking Comintern and "Soviet Imperialism." Later that year he was expelled from the party and condemned to a political isolation that lasted the rest of his life.

In these selections from Marxism and Philosophy *(1923) and "The Present State of the Problem of* Marxism and Philosophy*" (1930) Korsch is criticizing the Second International and Soviet communism, respectively. The earlier essay (explicitly criticized by Comintern in 1924) is the first Marxist analysis of Marxist theory and practice. Responding to the failures of the Second International, Korsch finds that its version of Marxism consistently underestimated the roles of ideology, subjectivity, and culture. In the second selection Korsch attacks the Leninist dictatorship* over, *not* of, *the proletariat. This dictatorship is supported, he claims, by a positivist attempt to treat Marxism as a natural science.*

Marxism and Philosophy

. . . . .

If we thus apply Marx's principle of dialectical materialism to the whole history of Marxism, we can distinguish three major stages of development through which Marxist theory has passed *since* its birth—inevitably so in the context of the concrete social development of this epoch. The first phase begins around 1843, and corresponds in the history of ideas to the *Critique of Hegel's Philosophy of Right*. It ends with the Revolution of 1848—corresponding to the *Communist Manifesto*. The second phase begins with the bloody suppression of the Parisian proletariat in the battle of June 1848 and the resultant crushing of all the working class' organizations and dreams of emancipation "in a period of feverish industrial activity, moral degeneration and political reaction," as Marx masterfully describes it in his *Inaugural Address* of 1864. We are not concerned here with the social history of the working-class as a whole, but only with the internal development of Marxist theory in its relation to the general class history of the proletariat. Hence the second period may be said to last approximately to the end of the century, leaving out all the less important divisions (the foundation and collapse of the First International; the interlude of the Commune; the struggle between Marxists and Lassalleaner; the Anti-socialist laws in Germany; trade unions; the founding of the Second International). The third phase extends from the start of this century to the present and into an indefinite future.

Arranged in this way, the historical development of Marxist theory presents the following picture. The first manifestation of it naturally remained essentially unchanged in the minds of Marx and Engels themselves throughout the later period, although in their *writings* it did not stay entirely unaltered. In spite of all their denials of philosophy, this first version of the theory is permeated through and through with philosophical thought. It is a theory of *social development* seen and comprehended as a living totality; or, more precisely, it is a theory of *social revolution* comprehended and practised as a living totality. At this stage there is no question whatever of dividing the economic, political and intellectual moments of this totality into separate branches of knowledge, even while every concrete peculiarity of each separate moment is comprehended, analyzed and criticized with historical fidelity. Of course, it is not only economics, politics and ideology, but also the historical process and conscious social action that continue to make up the living unity of "revolutionary practice" (*Theses on Feuerbach*). The best example of this early and youthful form of Marxist theory as the theory of social revolution is obviously the *Communist Manifesto*.

It is wholly understandable from the viewpoint of the materialist dialectic that this original form of Marxist theory could not subsist unaltered throughout the long years of the second half of the nineteenth century (which was in practice quite unrevolutionary). Marx's remark in the *Pref-*

ace to the Critique of Political Economy on mankind as a whole is necessarily also true for the working class, which was then slowly and antagonistically maturing toward its own liberation: "It always sets itself only such problems as it can solve; since, looking at the matter more closely it will always be found that the problem itself arises only when the material conditions for its solution are already present or are at least understood to be in the process of emergence." This dictum is not affected by the fact that a problem which supersedes present relations may have been formulated in an anterior epoch. To accord theory an autonomous existence outside the objective movement of history would obviously be neither materialist, nor dialectical in the Hegelian sense; it would simply be an idealist metaphysic. A dialectical conception comprehends every form without exception in terms of the flow of this movement, and it necessarily follows from it that Marx's and Engels's theory of social revolution inevitably underwent considerable changes in the course of its further development. When Marx in 1864 drafted the *Inaugural Address* and the *Statutes of the First International* he was perfectly conscious of the fact that "time was needed for the reawakened movement to permit the old audacity of language."[1] This is of course true not only for language but for all the other components of the theory of the movement. Therefore the scientific socialism of the *Capital* of 1867–94 and the other later writings of Marx and Engels represent an expression of the general theory of Marxism, which is in many ways a different and more developed one than that of the direct revolutionary communism of the *Manifesto of 1847–8*—or for that matter, *The Poverty of Philosophy, The Class Struggles in France* and *The Eighteenth Brumaire*. Nevertheless, the central characteristic of Marxist theory remains essentially unaltered even in the later writings of Marx and Engels. For in its later version, as scientific socialism, the Marxism of Marx and Engels remains the inclusive whole of a theory of social revolution. The difference is only that in the later phase the various components of this whole, its economic, political and ideological elements, scientific theory and social practice, are further separated out. We can use an expression of Marx's and say that the umbilical cord of its natural combination has been broken. In Marx and Engels, however, this never produces a multiplicity of independent elements instead of the whole. It is merely that another combination of the components of the system emerges developed with greater scientific precision and built on the infrastructure of the critique of political economy. In the writings of its creators, the Marxist system itself never dissolves into a sum of separate branches of knowledge, in spite of a practical and outward employment of its results that suggests such a conclusion. For example, many bourgeois interpreters of Marx and some later Marxists thought they were able to distinguish between the historical and the theoreticoeconomic material in Marx's major work *Capital;* but all they proved by this is that they understood nothing of the real method of Marx's critique of political economy. For it is one of the essential signs of his dialectical materialist method that this distinction does not exist for it; it is indeed precisely a theoretical comprehension of history. Moreover, the unbreakable interconnection of theory and practice, which formed the most characteristic sign of the first communist version of Marx's materialism, was in no way abolished in the later form of his system. It is only to the superficial glance that a pure theory of thought seems to have displaced the practice of the revolutionary will. This revolutionary will is latent, yet present, in every sentence of Marx's work and erupts again and again in every decisive passage, especially in the first volume of *Capital*. One need only think of the famous seventh section of Chapter 24 on the historical tendency of capital accumulaton.

On the other hand, it has to be said that the supporters and followers of Marx, despite all their theoretical and methodological avowals of historical materialism, in fact divided the theory of social revolution into fragments. The correct materialist conception of history, understood theoretically in a dialectical way and practically in a revolutionary way, is incompatible with separate branches of knowledge that are isolated and autonomous, and with purely theoretical investigations that are scientifically objective in dissociation from revolutionary practice. Yet later Marxists came to regard scientific socialism more and more as a set of purely scientific observations, without any *immediate* connection to the political or other practices of class struggle. Sufficient proof of this is one writer's account of the relation between Marxist science and politics, who was in the best sense a representative Marxist theoretician of the Second International. In December 1909, Rudolph Hilferding published his *Finance Capital* which attempts to "understand scientifically" the economic aspects of the most recent development of capitalism "by inserting these phenomena into the theoretical system of classical political economy." In the introduction he wrote: "Here it need only be said that for Marxism the study of politics itself aims only at the discovery of causal connections. Knowledge of the laws governing a society of commodity production reveals at once the determinants of the will of the classes of this society. For a Marxist, the task of scientific politics—a politics which describes causal connections—is to discover these determinants of the will of classes. Marxist politics, like Marxist theory, is free of value-judgments. It is therefore false simply to identify Marxism with socialism, although it is very common for Marxists and non-Marxists to do so. Logically Marxism, seen only as a scientific system and therefore apart from its historical effects, is only a theory of the laws of motion of society, which the Marxist conception of history formulated in general, while Marxist economics has applied it to the age of commodity production. The advent of socialism is a result of tendencies that develop in a society that produces commodities. But insight into the correctness of Marxism, which includes insight into the necessity of socialism, is in no way a result of value judgments and has no implications for practical behavior. It is one thing to acknowledge a necessity and quite another to place oneself at the service of this necessity. It is more than possible that a man may be convinced of the final victory of socialism, and yet decides to fight against it. The insight into the laws of motion of society provided by Marxism ensures superiority to whoever has mastered them. The most dangerous opponents of socialism are undoubtedly those who have profited most from its experience." According to Hilferding, Marxism is a theory which is logically "a scientific, objective and free science, without value judgments." He has no difficulty in explaining the remarkable fact that people so often identify it with the struggle for socialism by invoking the "insuperable reluctance of the ruling class to accept the results of Marxism" and therefore to take the "trouble" to study such a "complicated system." "Only in this sense is it the science of the proletariat and the opponent of bourgeois economics, since it otherwise holds unflinchingly to the claim made by every science of the objective and general validity of its conclusions." Thus the materialist conception of history, which in Marx and Engels was essentially a dialectical one, eventually became something quite undialectical in their epigones. For one tendency, it has changed into a kind of heuristic principle of specialized theoretical investigation. For another, the fluid methodology of Marx's materialist dialectic freezes into a number of theoretical formulations about the causal interconnection of historical phenomena in different areas of society—in other words it became something that could best be described as a general systematic sociology. The former school treated Marx's materialist principle as merely a "subjective basis for reflective judgement" in Kant's sense, while the latter dogmatically regarded the teachings of Marxist "sociology" primarily as an economic system, or even a geographical and biological one. All these deformations and a row of other less important ones were inflicted on Marxism by its epigones in the second phase of its development, and they can be summarized in one all-inclusive formulation: a unified general theory of social revolution was changed into criticisms of the bourgeois economic order, of the bourgeois

State, of the bourgeois system of education, of bourgeois religion, art, science and culture. These criticisms no longer necessarily develop by their very nature into revolutionary practice, they can equally well develop, into all kinds of attempts at *reform,* which fundamentally remain within the limits of bourgeois society and the bourgeois State, and in actual practice usually did so. This distortion of the revolutionary doctrine of Marxism itself—into a purely theoretical critique that no longer leads to practical revolutionary action, or does so only haphazardly—is very clear if one compares the *Communist Manifesto* or even the 1864 *Statutes of the First International* drawn up by Marx, to the programs of the Socialist Parties of Central and Western Europe in the second half of the nineteenth century, and especially to that of the German Social Democratic Party. It is well known how bitterly critical Marx and Engels were of the fact that German Social Democracy made almost entirely *reformist* demands in the political as well as cultural and ideological fields in their Gotha (1875) and Erfurt (1891) programs. These documents contained not a whiff of the genuine materialist and revolutionary principle in Marxism. Indeed, toward the end of the century this situation led to the assaults of revisionism on orthodox Marxism. Eventually, at the start of the twentieth century, the first signs of the approaching storm heralded a new period of conflicts and revolutionary battles, and thereby led to the decisive crisis of Marxism in which we still find ourselves today.

Both processes may be seen as necessary phases of a total ideological and material development—once it is understood that the decline of the original Marxist theory of social revolution into a theoretical critique of society without any revolutionary consequences is for dialectical materialism a necessary expression of parallel changes in the social practice of the proletarian struggle. Revisionism appears as an attempt to express in the form of a coherent theory the reformist character acquired by the economic struggles of the trade unions and the political struggles of the working class parties, under the influence of altered historical conditions. The so-called orthodox Marxism of this period (now a mere vulgar-marxism) appears largely as an attempt by theoreticians, weighed down by tradition, to maintain the theory of social revolution which formed the first version of Marxism, in the shape of pure theory. This theory was wholly abstract and had no practical consequences—it merely sought to reject the new reformist theories, in which the real character of the historical movement was then expressed as un-Marxist. This is precisely why, in a new revolutionary period, it was the orthodox Marxists of the Second International who were inevitably the least able to cope with such questions as the relation between the State and proletarian revolution. The revisionists at least possessed a theory of the relationship of the "working people" to the State, although this theory was in no way a Marxist one. Their theory and practice had long since substituted political, social and cultural reforms within the bourgeois State for a social revolution that would seize, smash and replace it by the dictatorship of the proletariat. The orthodox Marxists were content to reject this solution to the problems of the transitional period as a violation of the principles of Marxism. Yet with all their orthodox obsession with the abstract letter of Marxist theory they were unable to preserve its original revolutionary character. Their scientific socialism itself had inevitably ceased to be a theory of social revolution. Over a long period, when Marxism was slowly spreading throughout Europe, it had in fact no practical revolutionary task to accomplish. Therefore problems of revolution had ceased, even in theory, to exist as problems of the real world for the great majority of Marxists, orthodox as well as revisionist. As far as the reformists were concerned, these problems had disappeared completely. But even for the orthodox Marxists they had wholly lost the immediacy with which the authors of the *Manifesto* had confronted them, and receded into a distant and eventually quite transcendental *future*. In this period people became used to pursuing here and now policies of which revisionism may be seen as the theoretical expression. Officially condemned by party congresses, this revisionism was in the end accepted no less officially by the trade unions. At the beginning of the century, a new period of development put the question of social revolution back on the agenda as a realistic and terrestrial question in all its vital dimensions. Therewith purely theoretical orthodox Marxism—till the outbreak of the World War the officially established version of Marxism in the Second International—collapsed completely and disintegrated. This was, of course, an inevitable result of its long internal decay. It is in this epoch that we can see in many countries the beginnings of the *third period of development,* above all represented by Russian Marxists, and often described by its major representatives as a "restoration" of Marxism.

This transformation and development of Marxist theory has been effected under the peculiar ideological guise of a return to the pure teaching of original or true Marxism. Yet it is easy to understand both the reasons for this guise and the real character of the process which is concealed by it. What theoreticians like Rosa Luxemburg in Germany and Lenin in Russia have done, and are doing, in the field of Marxist theory is to liberate it from the inhibiting traditions of the Social Democracy of the second period. They thereby answer the practical needs of the new revolutionary stage of proletarian class struggle, for these traditions weighed "like a nightmare" on the brain of the working masses whose objectively revolutionary socioeconomic position no longer corresponded to these evolutionary doctrines. The apparent revival of original Marxist theory in the Third International is simply a result of the fact that in a new revolutionary period not only the workers' movement itself, but the theoretical conceptions of communists which express it, must assume an explicitly revolutionary form. This is why large sections of the Marxist system, which seemed virtually forgotten in the final decades of the nineteenth century, have now come to life again. It also explains why the leader of the Russian Revolution could write a book a few months before October in which he stated that his aim was "in the first place to *restore* the correct Marxist theory of the State." Events themselves placed the question of the dictatorship of the proletariat on the agenda as a practical problem. When Lenin placed the same question theoretically on the agenda at a decisive moment, this was an early indication that the internal connection of theory and practice within revolutionary Marxism had been consciously reestablished.

A fresh examination of the problem of Marxism and philosophy would also seem to be an important part of this restoration. A negative judgment is clear from the start. The minimization of philosophical problems by most Marxist theoreticians of the Second International was only a *partial expression* of the loss of the practical, revolutionary character of the Marxist movement which found its *general expression* in the simultaneous decay of the living principles of dialectical materialism in the vulgar-marxism of the epigones. We have already mentioned that Marx and Engels themselves always denied that scientific socialism was any longer a philosophy. But it is easy to show irrefutably, by reference to the sources, that what the revolutionary dialecticians Marx and Engels meant by the opposite of philosophy was something very different from what it meant to later vulgar-marxism. Nothing was further from them than the claim to impartial, pure, theoretical study, above class differences, made by Hilferding and most of the other Marxists of the Second International. The scientific socialism of Marx and Engels, correctly understood, stands in far greater contrast to these pure sciences of bourgeois society (economics, history or sociology) than it does to the philosophy in which the revolutionary movement of the Third Estate once found its highest theoretical expression. Consequently, one can only wonder at the insight of more recent Marxists who have been misled by a few of Marx's well-known expressions and by a few of the later Engels, into interpreting the Marxist abolition of philosophy as the replacement of this philosophy by a system of abstract and undialectical positive sciences. The real contradiction between Marx's scientific socialism and all bourgeois philosophy *and sciences* consists entirely in the fact that scientific socialism is the theoretical expression of a revolutionary process, which will end with the total abolition of these bourgeois philosophies and sciences, together with the abolition of the material relations that find their ideological expression in them.

. . . . .

This dialectical conception of the relationship of economics to politics became such an unalterable part of Marxist theory that even the vulgar-marxists of the Second International were unable to deny that the problem of the revolutionary transition existed, at least *in theory,* although they ignored the problem *in practice*. No orthodox Marxist could even in principle have claimed that a theoretical and practical concern with politics was unnecessary for Marxism. This was left to the syndicalists, some of whom invoke Marx, but none of whom have ever claimed to be orthodox Marxists. However, many good Marxists did adopt a theoretical and practical position on the reality of ideology which was identical to that of the syndicalists. These materialists are with Marx in condemning the syndicalist refusal of political action and in declaring that the social movement must include the political movement. They often argue against anarchists that even after the victorious proletarian revolution, and in spite of all the changes undergone by the bourgeois State, politics will long continue to be a reality. Yet these very people fall straight into the anarchosyndicalist "transcendental underestimation" of ideology when they are told that *intellectual* struggle in the ideological field cannot be replaced or eliminated by the social movement of the proletariat alone, or by its social and political movements combined. Even today most Marxist theoreticians conceive of the efficacy of so-called intellectual phenomena in a purely negative, abstract and undialectical sense, when they should analyze this domain of social reality with the materialist and scientific method molded by Marx and Engels. Intellectual life should be conceived in union with social and political life, and social being and becoming (in the widest sense, as economics, politics or law) should be studied in union with social consciousness in its many different manifestations, as a real yet also ideal (or "ideological") component of the historical process in general. Instead, all consciousness is approached with totally abstract and basically metaphysical dualism, and declared to be a reflection of the one really concrete and material developmental process, on which it is completely dependent (even if relatively independent, still dependent in the last instance).

Given this situation, any theoretical attempt to restore what Marx regarded as the only scientific, dialectical materialist conception and treatment of *ideological* realities, inevitably encounters even greater theoretical obstacles than an attempt to restore the correct Marxist theory of the State. The distortion of Marxism by the epigones in the question of the *State* and *politics* merely consisted in the fact that the most prominent theoreticians of the Second International never dealt concretely enough with the most vital political problems of the revolutionary transition. However, they at least agreed in abstract, and emphasized strongly in their long struggles against anarchists and syndicalists that, for materialism, not only the economic structure of society, which underlay all other sociohistorical phenomena, but also the juridical and political superstructure of Law and the State were *realities*. Consequently, they could not be ignored or dismissed in an anarchosyndicalist fashion: they had to be overthrown in reality by a political revolution. In spite of this, many vulgar-marxists to this day have never, even in theory, admitted that intellectual life and forms of social consciousness are comparable realities. Quoting certain statements by Marx and especially Engels they simply explain away the *intellectual (ideological) structures of society* as a mere *pseudoreality* which only exists in the minds of ideologues—as error, imagination and illusion, devoid of a genuine object. At any rate, this is supposed to be true for all the so-called higher ideologies. For this conception, political and legal representatives may have an ideological and unreal character, but they are at least related to something real—the institutions of Law and the State, which comprise the superstructure of the society in question. On the other hand, the "higher" ideological representations (men's religions, aesthetic and philosophical conceptions) correspond to no real object. This can be formulated concisely, with only a slight caricature, by saying that for vulgar-marxism there are *three degrees of reality:* (1) the economy, which in the last instance is the only objective and totally nonideological reality; (2) Law and the State, which are already somewhat less real because clad in ideology; and (3) pure ideology which is objectless and totally unreal ("pure rubbish").

To restore a genuine dialectically materialist conception of intellectual reality, it is first necessary to make a few mainly terminological points. The key problem to settle here is how in general to approach the relationship of consciousness to its object. Terminologically, it must be said that it never occurred to Marx and Engels to describe social consciousness and intellectual life merely as ideology. Ideology is only a false consciousness, in particular one that mistakenly attributes an autonomous character to a partial phenomena of social life. Legal and political representations which conceive Law and the State to be independent forces above society are cases in point. In the passage where Marx is most precise about his terminology,[2] he says explicitly that within the complex of material relations that Hegel called civil society, the social relations of production—the economic structure of society—forms the real foundation on which arise juridical and political superstructures and to which determinate forms of social consciousness correspond. In particular, these forms of social consciousness, which are no less real than Law and the State, include commodity fetishism, the concept of value, and other economic representations derived from them. Marx and Engels analyzed these in their critique of political economy. What is strikingly characteristic of their treatment is that they never refer to this basic economic ideology of bourgeois society as an ideology. In their terminology only the legal, political, religious, aesthetic or philosophical forms of consciousness are ideological. Even these need not be so in all situations, but become so only under specific conditions which have already been stated. The special position now allotted to forms of economic consciousness marks the new conception of philosophy which distinguishes the fully matured dialectical materialism of the later period from its undeveloped earlier version. The theoretical and practical criticism of philosophy is henceforward relegated to the second, third, fourth or even last but one place in their critique of society. The "critical philosophy" which the Marx of the *Deutsch-Französische Jahrbücher* saw as his essential task[3] became a more radical critique of society, which went to the roots of it[4] through a critique of political economy. Marx once said that a critic could *"start from any form of philosophical and practical consciousness* and develop from the specific forms of existent reality, its true reality and final end."[5] But he later became aware that no juridical relations, constitutional structures or forms of social consciousness can be understood in themselves or even in Hegelian or post-Hegelian terms of the general development of the human Spirit. For they are *rooted* in the material conditions of life that form "the material basis and skeleton" of social organization as a whole.[6] A radical critique of bourgeois society can no longer start from "any" form of theoretical or practical consciousness whatever, as Marx thought as late as 1843. It must start from the particular forms of consciousness which have found their scientific expression in the political economy of bourgeois society. Consequently the critique of political economy is theoretically and practically the first priority. Yet even this deeper and more radical version of Marx's revolutionary critique of society never ceases to be a critique of the *whole* of bourgeois society and so of *all* its forms of consciousness. It may seem as if Marx and Engels were later to criticize philosophy only in an occasional and haphazard manner. In fact, far from neglecting the subject, they actually developed their critique of it in a more profound and radical direction. For proof, it is only necessary to reestablish the full revolutionary meaning of Marx's critique of political economy, as against certain mistaken ideas about it which are common today. This may also serve to clarify both its place in the whole system of Marx's critique of society, and its relation to his critique of ideologies like philosophy.

It is generally accepted that the critique of political economy—the most important theoretical and practical component of the Marxist theory of society—includes not only a critique of the material relations of production of the capitalist epoch but also of its specific forms of social consciousness. Even the pure and impartial "scientific science" of vulgar-marxism acknowledges this. Hilferding admits that scientific knowledge of the economic laws of a society is also a "scientific politics" in so far as it shows "the determinant factors which define the *will of the classes* in this society." Despite this relation of economics to politics, however, in the totally abstract and undialectical conception of vulgar-marxism, the "critique of political economy" has a purely theoretical role as a "science." Its function is to criticize the errors of bourgeois economics, classical or vulgar. By contrast, a proletarian political party uses the results of critical and scientific investigation for its practical ends—ultimately the overthrow of the real economic structure of capitalist society and of its relations of production. (On occasion, the results of this Marxism can also be used against the proletarian party itself, as by Simkhovitch or Paul Lensch.)

The major weakness of vulgar socialism is that, in Marxist terms, it clings quite "unscientifically" to a naïve realism—in which both so-called common sense, which is the "worst metaphysician," and the normal positivist science of bourgeois society, draw a sharp line of division between consciousness and its object. Neither is aware that this distinction had ceased to be completely valid even for the transcendental perspective of critical philosophy, and has been completely superseded in dialectical philosophy. At best, they imagine that something like this might be true of Hegel's idealist dialectic. It is precisely this, they think, that constitutes the "mystification" which the dialectic, according to Marx, "suffered at Hegel's hands." It follows therefore for them that this mystification must be completely eliminated from the rational form of the dialectic: the materialist dialectic of Marx. In fact, we shall show, Marx and Engels were very far from having any such dualistic metaphysical conception of the relationship of consciousness to reality—not only in their first (philosophical) period but also in their second (positive-scientific) period. It never occurred to them that they could be misunderstood in this dangerous way. Precisely because of this, they sometimes did provide considerable pretexts for such misunderstandings in certain of their formulations (although these can easily be corrected by a hundred times as many other formulations). For the *coincidence of consciousness and reality* characterizes every dialectic, including Marx's dialectical materialism. Its consequence is that the material relations of production of the capitalist epoch only are what they are in combination with the forms in which they are reflected in the prescientific and bourgeois-scientific consciousness of the period; and they could not subsist in reality without these forms of consciousness. Setting aside any philosophical considerations, it is therefore clear that *without this coincidence of consciousness and reality, a critique of political economy could never have become the major component of a theory of social revolution.* The converse follows. Those Marxist theoreticians for whom Marxism was no longer essentially a theory of social revolution could see no need for this dialectical conception of the coincidence of reality and consciousness: it was bound to appear to them as theoretically false and unscientific.

. . . . .

We have now shown the real consequences of the dialectical materialist principle for a Marxist conception of the relationship of consciousness to reality. By the same token, we have shown the error of all abstract and undialectical conceptions found among various kinds of vulgar-marxists in their theoretical and practical attitudes to so-called intellectual reality. Marx's dictum is true not just of forms of economic consciousness in the narrower sense, but of *all* forms of social consciousness: they are not mere chimeras, but "highly objective and highly practical" social realities and consequently "must be abolished in a practical and objective manner." The naïvely metaphysical standpoint of sound bourgeois common sense considers thought independent of being and defines truth as the correspondence of thought to an object that is external to it and "mirrored" by it. It is only this outlook that can sustain the view that all forms of economic consciousness (the economic conceptions of a prescientific and unscientific consciousness, as well as scientific economics itself) have an objective meaning because they correspond to a reality (the material relations of production which they comprehend)—whereas all higher forms of representation are merely objectless fantasies which will automatically dissolve into their essential nullity after the overthrow of the economic structure of society, and the abolition of its juridical and political superstructure. Economic ideas themselves only *appear* to be related to the material relations of production of bourgeois society in the way an image is related to the object it reflects. In fact they are related to them in the way that a specific, particularly defined part of a whole is related to the other parts of this whole. Bourgeois economics belongs with the material relations of production to bourgeois society as a totality. This totality also contains political and legal representations and their apparent objects, which bourgeois politicians and jurists—the "ideologues of private property" (Marx)—treat in an ideologically inverted manner as autonomous essences. Finally, it also includes the higher ideologies of the art, religion and philosophy of bourgeois society. If it seems that there are no objects which these representations can reflect, correctly or incorrectly, this is because economic, political or legal representations do not have particular objects which exist independently either, isolated from the other phenomena of bourgeois society. To counterpose such objects to these representations is an abstract and ideological bourgeois procedure. They merely express bourgeois society as a totality in a particular way, just as do art, religion and philosophy. Their ensemble forms the *spiritual structure* of bourgeois society, which corresponds to its economic structure, just as its legal and political superstructure corresponds to this same basis. All these forms must be subjected to the revolutionary social criticism of scientific socialism, which embraces the whole of social reality. They must be criticized in theory and overthrown in practice, together with the economic, legal and political structures of society and at the same time as them. Just as political action is not rendered unnecessary by the economic action of a revolutionary class, so intellectual action is not rendered unnecessary by either political or economic action. On the contrary it must be carried through to the end in theory and practice, as revolutionary scientific criticism and agitational work before the seizure of state power by the working class, and as scientific organization and ideological dictatorship after the seizure of state power. If this is valid for intellectual action against the forms of consciousness which define bourgeois society in general, it is especially true of philosophical action. Bourgeois consciousness necessarily sees itself as apart from the world and independent of it, as pure critical philosophy and impartial science, just as the bourgeois State and bourgeois Law appear to be above society. This consciousness must be philosophically fought by the revolutionary materialistic dialectic, which is the philosophy of the working class. This struggle will only end when the whole of existing society and its economic basis have been totally overthrown in practice, and this consciousness has been totally surpassed and abolished in theory. "Philosophy cannot be abolished without being realized."

Notes

1. Marx and Engels, *Selected Correspondence,* p. 182 [4 November 1864].
2. Cf. the Preface to the *Critique of Political Economy (Selected Works,* vol. II, p. 363).
3. Marx to Ruge, September 1843, *Nachlass,* vol. I, p. 383.
4. This is how Marx defines the word "radical" in his "Introduction to the *Critique of Hegel's Philosophy of Right,*" *On Religion,* p. 50.
5. Marx to Ruge, September 1843, *Nachlass,* p. 381.
6. Introduction to the *Critique of Political Economy* (Chicago, 1904) p. 310; see also the Preface in ibid., and *Selected Works,* vol. I.

"The Present State of the Problem of *Marxism and Philosophy*: An Anti-Critique"

• • • • •

Since *Marxism and Philosophy* I have written a study elsewhere of the real historical nature of the "Marxism of the Second International." What happened was that the socialist movement reawoke and grew stronger as historical conditions changed over the last third of the nineteenth century; yet contrary to what is supposed, it never *adopted Marxism as a total system.* According to the ideology of the orthodox Marxists and of their opponents, who share much the same dogmatic ground, it is to be believed that the *whole of Marxism* was adopted in both theory and practice. In fact all that was even theoretically adopted were some isolated economic, political and social "theories," extracted from the general context of revolutionary Marxism. Their general meaning had thereby been altered, and their specific content usually truncated and falsified. The endless asseverations of *the rigorously "Marxist" character of the program and theory of the movement* do not date from the period in which the practice of the new Social Democratic workers' movement approximated most to the revolutionary and class-combative character of Marxist theory. In this early period the "two old men in London," and after Marx's death in 1883, Friedrich Engels alone, were directly involved in the movement. Paradoxically, these asseverations date from a *later* period when certain other tendencies were gaining ground in both trade union and political practice, which were ultimately to find their ideological expression in "revisionism." In fact, at the time when the practice of the movement was most revolutionary, its theory was essentially "populist" and democratic (under the influence of Lassalle and Dühring) and only sporadically "Marxist." This was the result of the impact of the periods of economic crisis and depression in the 1870s, the political and social reaction following the defeat of the Paris Commune in 1871, the antisocialist laws in Germany, the defeat of the growing socialist movement in Austria in 1884 and the violent suppression of the movement for an eight-hour day in America in 1886. However, the 1890s saw a new industrial boom in Europe, especially in Germany, and therewith the first signs appeared of a "more democratic" use of state power on the continent of Europe. This process included the French amnesty for the Communards in 1880, and the lapsing of the antisocialist laws in Germany in 1890. In this new practical context, *formal avowals of the Marxist system as a whole* emerged as a kind of theoretical defense and metaphysical consolation. In this sense, one can actually invert the generally accepted relationship between Kautskyian "Marxism" and Bernsteinian "revisionism," and define Kautsky's *orthodox Marxism* as the theoretical obverse and symmetrical complement of *Bernstein's revisionism*.

In the light of this real historical situation, the complaints of orthodox Marxist critics against my work are not only unjustified but null and void. I am alleged to have a predilection for the "primitive" form of the first historical version of the theory of Marx and Engels, and to have disregarded its positive development by Marx and Engels themselves, and by other Marxists in the second half of the nineteenth century. It is claimed that the "Marxism of the Second International" represents an advance on original Marxist theory. Yet in fact it was *a new historical form of proletarian class theory,* which emerged from the altered practical context of the class struggle in a new historical epoch. Its relationship to the earlier or later versions of the theory of Marx and Engels is very different from, and essentially more complex than, the way it is presented by those who talk of a *positive development,* or conversely of a *formal stagnation* or *regression and decay* of Marx's theory in the "Marxism of the Second International." Marxism is therefore in no way a socialist theory that has been "superseded" by the present outlook of the workers' movement, as Kautsky maintains (formally he refers only to its earlier version, the "primitive Marxism of the Communist Manifesto," but actually he includes all the later components of Marx and Engels's theory as well). Nor is Marxism what it was claimed to be by the representatives of the revolutionary tendency within orthodox Social Democratic Marxism at the start of the third period toward 1900, or what some Marxists still consider it to be. It is not a theory that has miraculously anticipated the future development of the workers' movement for a long time to come. Consequently it cannot be said that the subsequent practical progress of the proletariat has, as it were, lagged behind its own theory or that it will only gradually come to occupy the framework allotted to it by this theory. When the SPD became a "Marxist" party (a process completed with the Erfurt Programme written by Kautsky and Bernstein in 1891) a gap developed between its highly articulated revolutionary "Marxist" theory and a practice that was far behind this revolutionary theory; in some respects it directly contradicted it. This gap was in fact obvious, and it later came to be felt more and more acutely by all the vital forces in the party (whether on the Left or Right) and its existence was denied only by the orthodox Marxists of the Center. This gap can easily be explained by the fact that in this historical phase "Marxism," while formally accepted by the workers' movement, was from the start not a true *theory*, in the sense of being "nothing other than a general expression of the real historical movement" (Marx). On the contrary it was always an *ideology* that had been adopted "from outside" in a preestablished form.

In this situation such "orthodox Marxists" as Kautsky and Lenin made a permanent virtue out of a temporary necessity. They energetically defended the idea that socialism can only be brought to the workers "from outside," by bourgeois intellectuals who are allied to the workers' movement. This was also true of Left radicals like Rosa Luxemburg who talked of the "stagnation of Marxism" and explained it by contrasting Marx to the proletariat: the one had creative power because he was armed with all the resources of a bourgeois education, while the other remains tied to "the social conditions of existence in our society," which will continue unaltered throughout the capitalist epoch. The truth is that a *historical fact* provides a materialist explanation of this apparent contradiction between theory and practice in the "Marxist" Second International, and a rational solution for all the mysteries which the orthodox Marxists of that time devised to explain it. The fact is this. The workers' movement at that time formally adopted "Marxism" as its ideology; yet although its effective practice was now on a *broader basis* than before, it has in no way reached the *heights* of general and theoretical achievement earlier attained by the revolutionary movement and proletarian class struggle on a *narrower basis*. This height was attained during the final phase of the first major capitalist cycle that came to an end toward 1850. At that time, the workers' movement had achieved a peak of development. But it then came to a temporary yet complete halt, and only revived slowly, as conditions changed. Marx and Engels had initially conceived their revolutionary theory in direct relation to the practical revolutionary movement, but when this died down they could only continue their work as theory. It is true that this later development of Marxist theory was never just the production of "purely theoretical" study; it was always a theoretical reflection of the latest practical experiences of the class struggle which was reawakening in various ways. Nevertheless it is clear that the *theory* of Marx and Engels was progressing toward an ever higher level of theoretical perfection although it was no longer directly related to the *practice* of the worker's movement. Thus two processes unfolded side by side in relative independence of each other. One was the *development under novel conditions of the old theory which had arisen in a previous historical epoch*. The other was the *new practice of the workers' movement*. It is this which explains the literally "anachronistic" height which Marxist theory reached and surpassed in this period, generally and philosophically, in the work of Marx, Engels and some of their disciples. This is also why it was wholly impossible for this highly elaborate Marxist theory to be effectively and not just formally assimilated by the proletarian movement, whose practice reawakened during the last third of the nineteenth century.

. . . . .

Any discussion of Lenin's position on philosophy and ideology must pose one initial question on which a judgment of Lenin's specific "materialist philosophy" has to depend. According to a principle established by Lenin himself, this question is a *historical* one. Lenin argued that there had been a change in the whole intellectual climate which made it necessary when dealing with dialectical materialism to stress *materialism* against certain fashionable tendencies in bourgeois philosophy, rather than to stress *dialectics* against the vulgar, predialectical and in some cases explicitly undialectical and antidialectical materialism of bourgeois science. The question is whether there had been such a change. What I have written elsewhere shows that I do not think this is really the case. There are some superficial aspects of contemporary bourgeois philosophy and science which appear to contradict this, and there certainly are some trends which genuinely do so. Nevertheless the dominant *basic trend* in contemporary bourgeois philosophy, natural science and humanities is the same as it was sixty or seventy years ago. It is inspired not by an idealist outlook but by a *materialist outlook that is colored by the natural sci-*

ences. Lenin's position, which disputes this, is in close ideological relation to his politicoeconomic theory of "imperialism." Both have their *material roots* in the specific economic and social situation of Russia and the specific practical and theoretical political tasks that seemed, and for a short period really were, necessary to accomplish the Russian Revolution. This means that the "Leninist" theory is not theoretically capable of answering the *practical needs of the international class struggle in the present period*. Consequently, Lenin's materialist philosophy, which forms the ideological basis of this theory, cannot constitute the revolutionary proletarian philosophy that will answer the needs of today.

The *theoretical character* of Lenin's materialist philosophy also corresponds to this historical and practical situation. Like Plekhanov, his philosophical master, and L. Axelrod-Orthodox, the latter's other philosophical pupil, Lenin wanted very seriously to be a *Marxist* while remaining a *Hegelian*. He thereby flouted the dialectical materialist outlook that Marx and Engels founded at the start of their revolutionary development. This outlook was by its very nature unavoidably "philosophical," but it pointed toward the complete supersession of philosophy; and it left one single revolutionary task in the philosophical field, which was to develop this outlook by taking it to a higher level of elaboration. Lenin regards the transition from Hegel's idealist dialectic to Marx and Engels's dialectical materialism as nothing more than an *exchange:* the idealist outlook that lies at the basis of Hegel's dialectical method is replaced by a new *philosophical outlook* that is no longer "idealist" but "materialist." He seems to be unaware that *such* a "materialist inversion" of Hegel's idealist philosophy involves at the most a merely terminological change whereby the Absolute instead of being called "Spirit" is called "Matter." There is, however, an even more serious vice in Lenin's materialism. For he not only annuls Marx and Engels's materialist inversion of the Hegelian dialectic; *he drags the whole debate between materialism and idealism back to a historical stage which German idealism from Kant to Hegel had already surpassed*. The dissolution of the metaphysical system of Leibniz and Wolff began with Kant's transcendental philosophy and ended with Hegel's dialectic. Thereafter the "Absolute" was definitively excluded from the *being* of both "*spirit*" and "*matter,*" and was transferred into the dialectical *movement* of the "*idea*." The materialist inversion by Marx and Engels of Hegel's idealist dialectic merely consisted in freeing this dialectic from its final mystifying shell. The *real movement of history* was discovered beneath the dialectical "self-movement of the idea," and this revolutionary movement of history was proclaimed to be the only "Absolute" remaining. Lenin, however, goes back to the absolute polarities of "thought" and "being," "spirit" and "matter," which had formed the basis of the philosophical, and even some of the religious, disputes that had divided the two currents of the Enlightenment in the seventeenth and eighteenth centuries. Hegel, of course, had already surpassed these dialectically.

This kind of materialism is derived from a metaphysical idea of Being that is absolute and given; and despite all its formal claims to the contrary it is no longer fully dialectical let alone dialectically materialist. Lenin and his followers unilaterally transfer the dialectic into Object, Nature and History and they present knowledge merely as the passive mirror and reflection of this objective Being in the subjective Consciousness. In so doing they destroy both the dialectical interrelation of *being* and *consciousness* and, as a necessary consequence, the dialectical interrelation of *theory* and *practice*. They thereby manage to pay an involuntary tribute to the "Kantianism" that they attack so much. Not content with this, they have abandoned the question of the *relationship between the totality of historical being and all historically prevalent forms of consciousness*. This was first posed by Hegel's dialectic and was then given a more comprehensive elaboration by the dialectical materialism of Marx and Engels. Lenin and those like him have revised it in a retrograde way by replacing it with the much narrower epistemological or "gnoseological" question of the *relationship between the subject and the object of knowledge*. Nor is this all. They present knowledge as a fundamentally harmonious *evolutionary progress* and an *infinite progression toward absolute truth*. Their presentation of the relationship between theory and practice in general, and in particular within the revolutionary movement itself, is a complete abandonment of Marx's dialectical materialism and a retreat to a totally abstract opposition of pure *theory,* which discovers truths, to pure *practice,* which applies these laboriously discovered truths to reality. "The real unity of theory and practice is achieved by changing reality in practice, through the revolutionary movement based on the laws of objective development discovered by theory"—these are the words of one of Lenin's philosophical interpreters, and he has not departed one iota from the teachings of the master. With them, the grandiose dialectical materialist unity of Marx's revolutionary practice collapses into a *dualism* comparable to that of the most typical bourgeois *idealists*.

There is another inevitable consequence of this displacement of the accent from the *dialectic* to *materialism*. It prevents materialist philosophy from contributing to the further development of the empirical sciences of nature and society. In the dialectic *method and content are inseparably linked:* in a famous passage Marx says that "form has no value when it is not the form of its content." It it therefore completely against the spirit of the dialectic, and especially of the materialist dialectic, to *counterpose* the dialectical materialist "method" to the substantive results achieved by applying it to philosophy and the sciences. This procedure has become very fashionable in Western Marxism. Nevertheless, behind this exaggeration there lies a correct insight—namely, that dialectical materialism influenced the progress of the empirical study of nature and society in the second half of the nineteenth century above all because of its method.

When the revolutionary movement and its practice came to a halt in the 1850s, there inevitably developed an *increasing gap between the evolution of philosophy and that of the positive sciences, between the evolution of theory and that of practice:* this has already been explained in *Marxism and Philosophy*. The result was that for a long period the new revolutionary conceptions of Marx and Engels survived and developed mainly through their application as a dialectical materialist method to the empirical sciences of society and nature. It is in this period that one finds statements, especially by the later Engels, formally proclaiming individual sciences to be independent of "all philosophy," and asserting that philosophy has been "driven from nature and from history" into the only field of activity left to it: "the theory of thought and its laws—formal logic and dialectics." In reality, this meant that Engels reduced so-called "philosophy" from an individual science *above* others, to an empirical science *among* others. Lenin's later positions might appear at first glance to be like that of Engels, but they are in actual fact as distinct as night and day. Engels considered that it was the crucial task of the materialist dialectic to "rescue the *conscious dialectic* from German idealism and to incorporate it in the materialist conception of nature and of history." Lenin's procedure is the inverse. For him the major task is to uphold and defend the *materialist position* which no one has ever seriously thought of questioning. Engels goes on to make a statement that is in keeping with the progress and development of the sciences; he says that modern materialism whether applied to nature or history "is in both cases essentially dialectical and does not in addition need a philosophy which stands above the other branches of knowledge." Lenin, however, insistently carps at "philosophical deviations" that he has discerned not only among political friends or enemies, or philosophical ideologues, but even among the most creative natural scientists. His "materialist philosophy" becomes a kind of supreme judicial authority for evaluating the findings of individual sciences, past, present or future. This materialist "philosophical" domination covers all the sciences, whether of nature or society, as well as all other cultural developments in literature, drama, plastic arts and so on; and Lenin's epigones have taken it to the most absurd lengths. This has resulted in a specific kind of *ideological dictatorship* which oscillates between revolutionary progress and the blackest reaction. Under the slogan of what is called "Marxism-Leninism," this dictatorship is applied in Russia today to the whole intellectual life not only of the ruling Party, but of the working-class in general. There are now attempts to extend it from Russia to all the Communist Parties in the West, and in the rest of the world. These attempts, however, have precisely shown the inevitable limits to any such artificial extension of this ideological dictatorship into the international arena outside Russia, where it no longer receives the direct coercive support of the State. The Draft Program of the Communist International, of the Fifth Comintern Congress of 1924, called for a "rigorous struggle against idealist philosophy and against all philosophies other than dialectical materialism," whereas at the Sixth Congress, held four years later, the version of the Program that was finally adopted spoke in a much more general way of the struggle against "all manifestations of a bourgeois outlook." It no longer described "the dialectical materialism of Marx and Engels' as a materialist philosophy, but only as a "revolutionary method(!) for understanding reality with the aim of its revolutionary overthrow."

It is only recently that "Marxist-Leninist" ideology has made such claims outside Russia, and the change in Comintern policy I have mentioned may indicate that these claims are now going to be abandoned. Nevertheless, the deeper problem of Lenin's "materialist philosophy" and of Marxism-Leninism has not been resolved. The problem of *Marxism and Philosophy* must be reopened, together with the broader issue of the *relation between the ideology and the practice of the revolutionary workers' movement*. This poses a concrete task in relation to Communist "Marxism-Leninism." A materialist, that is a historical, critical and undogmatic analysis has already been made of the character of the "Kautskyian" orthodox Marxism of the Second International. This must now be unflinchingly extended to the "Leninist" orthodox Marxism of the Third International; and it must be applied to the whole history of Russian Marxism and its relation to international Marxism. For the "Marxism-Leninism" of today is only the latest offshoot of this history. It is not possible to provide a more concrete elaboration here. One can only indicate a very general outline of such a materialist account of the real history of Marxism in Russia and elsewhere. Even so it yields a sobering conclusion. Russian Marxism, which was if possible *even more "orthodox"* than German Marxism, had throughout its history an *even more ideological character* and if possible was in *even greater conflict* with the concrete historical movement of which it was the ideology.

Trotsky's perceptive critical analysis of 1908 showed that this was true of the *first phase of its history*. The Russian intelligentsia had previously been brought up in the Bakuninist "spirit of a simple rejection of capitalist culture," and Marxism served as an ideological instrument to reconcile them to the development of capitalism.[2] It is also valid for the *second phase,* which reached its climax in the first Russian Revolution of 1905. At that time all revolutionary Marxists in Russia, not least Lenin and Trotsky, declared themselves to be part of "the flesh and blood" of international socialism—and for them this meant *orthodox Marxism*. On the other side Karl Kautsky and his *Neue Zeit* were in complete agreement with orthodox Russian Marxism on all theoretical questions. Indeed, as far as the philosophical foundations of its theory were concerned, German orthodox Marxism was more influenced by Russian Marxism than itself influential on it, since the Germans were to a considerable extent under the sway of the Russian theoretician Plekhanov. Thus a great international united front of Marxist orthodoxy was able to sustain itself without major difficulty, because historically it was only necessary for it to exist *in the realm of ideology* and *as ideology*. This was true both in the West and in Russia, and in Russia even more than in Central and Western Europe. Russian Marxism is now in its *third phase* and it still exhibits the same ideological character and the same inevitable concomitant contradiction between a professed "orthodox" theory and the real historical character of the movement. It found its most vivid expression in Lenin's orthodox Marxist theory and his totally unorthodox practice, and it is now caricatured by the glaring contradictions between theory and practice in contemporary "Soviet Marxism."

This general character of Russian Marxism has persisted without fundamental change into the "Soviet Marxism" of today. Involuntary confirmation of this is provided by the position of the above-mentioned Schifrin, a political opponent of the ruling Bolshevik Party, on the general philosophical principles of Soviet Marxism. In an article in *Die Gesellschaft* (IV, 7), he made what looked like a fierce attack on "Soviet Marxism," but from a philosophical point of view this really concealed a *defense* of it. He claims that Soviet Marxism "wants to make a sincere attempt to reinforce Marxism in its most consistent and orthodox form" against degenerate "subjectivist" and "revisionist" tendencies (e.g., "neglect of the master's most important statements"), that have emerged as a result of the insuperable difficulties that it is facing. The same bias is even clearer in another article of Schifrin in *Die Gesellschaft* of August 1929. In this, Schifrin discusses the latest work by Karl Kautsky, the leading representative of German orthodox Marxism, and although he is very critical of most of Kautsky's individual positions, he greets Kautsky's book warmly as the beginning of a "restoration of genuine Marxism." He assigns Kautsky the "ideological mission" of overcoming the various kinds of "subjectivist disintegration of Marxism" that have recently appeared in the West as well as in "Sovietized Russian Marxism," and of overcoming the "ideological crisis" that this has caused throughout Marxism. The article is particularly clear evidence of the *philosophical solidarity of the whole orthodox Marxist movement* down to this day. In his critique of contemporary Soviet Marxist "Leninism" and in his attitudes toward contemporary "Kautskyism," Schifrin completely fails to see that both of these ideological versions of orthodox Marxism have emerged from the traditions of earlier Russian and international Marxism. *Today they only represent evanescent historical forms that date from a previous phase of the workers' movement*. Hence, in this assessment of the character of "Marxism-Leninism" and of "Soviet Marxism," one can see the full and fundamental unity of outlook between the old and the new schools of contemporary orthodox Marxism: Social Democracy and Communism. It has been seen how Communist theoreticians reacted to *Marxism and Philosophy* by defending the positive and progressive character of the Marxism of the Second International. Now, in the periodical of German Social Democracy, one can see a Menshevik theoretician entering the lists to defend the "generally valid" and "compelling" philosophical features of the Marxism of the Third International.

This ends my account of the present state of the problem of *Marxism and Philosophy*—a problem that since 1923 has been changed in many ways by new theoretical and practical developments. The general outlines of my evolution since then are clear enough, and I have therefore refrained from correcting all the details of what I then said in the light of my present position. In only one respect does it appear to be necessary to make an exception. *Marxism and Philosophy* argued that during the social revolution a "dictatorship" was necessary not only in the field of politics, but also that of ideology. This led to many misunderstandings, especially in the case of Kautsky. In his review of my book he showed both that he had misinterpreted my positions and that he had certain illusions about the conditions prevailing in Russia. Thus as late as 1924 he stated that "dictatorship in the realm of ideas" had "never occurred to anyone, not even to Zinoviev and Dzherzhinsky." I now think that the abstract formulation of this demand in my book is genuinely misleading, and I must emphasize that the pursuit of revolutionary struggle by what *Marxism and Philosophy* called an "ideological dictatorship" is in three respects different from the *system of intellectual oppression* established in Russia today in the name of the "dictatorship of the proletariat." First of all, it is a dictatorship *of* the proletariat and not *over* the proletariat. Secondly, it is a dictatorship of a class and not of a party or party leadership. Thirdly, and most importantly, as a revolutionary dictatorship it is one element only of that radical process of social overthrow which by suppressing classes and class contradictions creates the preconditions for a "withering away of the State," and thereby the end of all ideological constraint. The essential purpose of an "ideological dictatorship" in this sense is to abolish its own material and ideological causes and thereby to make its own existence unnecessary and impossible. *From the very first day,* this genuine proletarian dictatorship will be distinguished from every false imitation of it by its creation of the conditions of intellectual freedom not only for "all" workers but for "each individual" worker. Despite the alleged "democracy" and "freedom of thought" in bourgeois society, this freedom has never been enjoyed anywhere by the wage slaves who suffer its physical and spiritual oppression. This is what concretely defines the Marxist concept of the revolutionary *dictatorship of the proletariat*. With it disappears the otherwise apparent contradiction between a call for "ideological dictatorship," and the essentially critical and revolutionary nature of the method and the outlook of Communism. *Socialism, both in its ends and in its means, is a struggle to realize freedom.*

Notes

1. Foreword to the second (1885) edition of *Anti-Dühring*.
2. See Trotsky's article on the 25th anniversary of *Neue Zeit*, *Neue Zeit*, XXVI, I, pp. 7ff.

2

György (Georg) Lukács (1885–1971)

Born in Hungary and for many years a student in Germany, György Lukács was intellectually shaped by German Idealism, Kierkegaard, and classical German sociology. He began writing works in aesthetics before World War I but converted to Marxism in 1918 and joined the Hungarian Communist party. During the Hungarian Commune of 1919 he served as "People's Comissar" of Education and Culture. With the collapse of the Hungarian revolt, he went abroad, living successively in Austria, Germany, and the Soviet Union. During the remainder of his life, periods of political involvement and controversy alternated with periods of political passivity (usually after he was disciplined and criticized by Soviet or Hungarian party leaders). Recognized as one of the most brilliant of twentieth-century Marxists, Lukács left an enormous collection of writings on philosophy, politics, culture, and aesthetics.

In the following excerpts from what some feel is his most important work, the collection of essays entitled History and Class Consciousness *(1923), Lukács explores two basic issues: the nature and critical importance of class consciousness in determining the outcome of revolutionary struggles and how a capitalist society permeated by reification and commodification can be understood—and, as a result of that process, transformed—by the working class.*

History and Class Consciousness

CLASS CONSCIOUSNESS

The question is not what goal is *envisaged* for the time being by this or that member of the proletariat, or even by the proletariat as a

> whole. The question is *what is the proletariat* and what course of action will it be forced historically to take in conformity with its own *nature*.
>
> MARX, *The Holy Family*

Marx's chief work breaks off just as he is about to embark on the definition of class. This omission was to have serious consequences for both the theory and the practice of the proletariat. For on this vital point the later movement was forced to base itself on interpretations, on the collation of occasional utterances by Marx and Engels and on the independent extrapolation and application of their method. In Marxism the division of society into classes is determined by position within the process of production. But what, then, is the meaning of class consciousness? The question at once branches out into a series of closely interrelated problems. First of all, how are we to understand class consciousness (in theory)? Second, what is the (practical) function of class consciousness, so understood, in the context of the class struggle? This leads to the further question: is the problem of class consciousness a "general" sociological problem or does it mean one thing for the proletariat and another for every other class to have emerged hitherto? And lastly, is class consciousness homogeneous in nature and function or can we discern different gradations and levels in it? And if so, what are their practical implications for the class struggle of the proletariat?

1

In his celebrated account of historical materialism[1] Engels proceeds from the assumption that although the essence of history consists in the fact that "nothing happens without a conscious purpose or an intended aim," to understand history it is necessary to go further than this. For on the one hand, "the many individual wills active in history for the most part produce results quite other than those intended—often quite the opposite; *their motives, therefore, in relation to the total result are likewise of only secondary importance*. On the other hand, the further question arises: *what driving forces in turn stand behind these motives?* What are the historical causes which transform themselves into these motives in the brain of the actors?" He goes on to argue that these driving forces ought themselves to be determined, in particular those which "set in motion great masses, whole peoples and again whole classes of the people; and which create *a lasting action resulting in a great transformation.*" The essence of scientific Marxism consists, then, in the realization that the real motor forces of history are independent of man's (psychological) consciousness of them.

At a more primitive stage of knowledge this independence takes the form of the belief that these forces belong, as it were, to nature and that in them and in their causal interactions it is possible to discern the "eternal" laws of nature. As Marx says of bourgeois thought: "Man's reflections on the forms of social life and consequently also his scientific analysis of those forms, take a course directly opposite to that of their actual historical development. He begins post festum, with the results of the process of development ready to hand before him. The characters . . . have already acquired the stability of natural self-understood forms of social life, before man seeks to decipher not their historical character (for in his eyes they are immutable) but their meaning."[2]

This is a dogma whose most important spokesmen can be found in the political theory of classical German philosophy and in the economic theory of Adam Smith and Ricardo. Marx opposes to them a critical philosophy, a theory of theory and a consciousness of consciousness. This critical philosophy implies above all historical criticism. It dissolves the rigid, unhistorical, natural appearance of social institutions; it reveals their historical origins and shows therefore that they are subject to history in every respect including historical decline. Consequently history does not merely unfold *within* the terrain mapped out by these institutions. It does not resolve itself into the evolution of *contents,* of men and situations, etc., while the *principles* of society remain eternally valid. Nor are these institutions the *goal* to which all history aspires, such that when they are realized history will have fulfilled her mission and will then be at an end. On the contrary, history is precisely *the history of these institutions,* of the changes they undergo *as* institutions which bring men together in societies. Such institutions start by controlling economic relations between men and go on to permeate all human relations (and hence also man's relations with himself and with nature, etc.).

At this point bourgeois thought must come up against an insuperable obstacle, for its starting-point and its goal are always, if not always consciously, an apologia for the existing order of things or at least the proof of their immutability.[3] "Thus there has been history, but there is no longer any,"[4] Marx observes with reference to bourgeois economics, a dictum which applies with equal force to all attempts by bourgeois thinkers to understand the process of history. (It has often been pointed out that this is also one of the defects of Hegel's philosophy of history.) As a result, while bourgeois thought is indeed able to conceive of history as a problem, it remains an *intractable* problem. Either it is forced to abolish the process of history and regard the institutions of the present as eternal laws of nature which for "mysterious" reasons and in a manner wholly at odds with the principles of a rational science were held to have failed to establish themselves firmly, or indeed at all, in the past. (This is characteristic of bourgeois sociology.) Or else, everything meaningful or purposive is banished from history. It then becomes impossible to advance beyond the mere "individuality" of the various epochs and their social and human representatives. History must then insist with Ranke that every age is "equally close to God," i.e., has attained an equal degree of perfection and that—for quite different reasons—there is no such thing as historical development.

In the first case it ceases to be possible to understand the *origin* of social institutions.[5] The objects of history appear as the objects of immutable, eternal laws of nature. History becomes fossilized in a *formalism* incapable of comprehending that the real nature of sociohistorical institutions is that they consist of *relations between men*. On the contrary, men become estranged from this, the true source of historical understanding and cut off from it by an unbridgeable gulf. As Marx points out,[6] people fail to realize "that these definite social relations are just as much the products of men as linen, flax, etc."

In the second case, history is transformed into the irrational rule of blind forces which is embodied at best in the "spirit of the people" or in "great men." It can therefore only be described pragmatically but it cannot be rationally understood. Its only possible organization would be aesthetic, as if it were a work of art. Or else, as in the philosophy of history of the Kantians, it must be seen as the instrument, senseless in itself, by means of which timeless, suprahistorical, ethical principles are realized.

Marx resolves this dilemma by exposing it as an illusion. The dilemma means only that the contradictions of the capitalist system of production are reflected in these mutually incompatible accounts of the same object. For in this historiography with its search for "sociological" laws or its formalistic rationale, we find the reflection of man's plight in bourgeois society and of his helpless enslavement by the forces of production. "To them, *their own social action,*" Marx remarks,[7] "takes the form of the action of objects which rule the producers instead of being ruled by them." This law was expressed most clearly and coherently in the purely natural and rational laws of classical economics. Marx retorted with the demand for a historical critique of economics which resolves the totality of the reified objectivities of social and economic life into *relations between men*. Capital and with it every form in which the national economy objectifies itself is, according to Marx, "not a thing but a social relation between persons mediated through things."[8]

However, by reducing the objectivity of the social institutions so hostile to man to relations between men, Marx also does away with the false implications of the irrationalist and individualist principle, i.e., the other side of the dilemma. For to eliminate the objectivity attributed both to social institutions inimical to man and to their historical evolution means the restoration of this objectivity to their underlying basis, to the relations between men; it does not involve the elimination of laws and objectivity independent of the will of man and in particular the wills and thoughts of individual men. It simply means that this objectivity is the self-objectification of human society at a particular stage in its development; its laws hold good only within the framework of the historical context which produced them and which is in turn determined by them.

It might look as though by dissolving the dilemma in this manner we were denying consciousness any decisive role in the process of history. It is true that the conscious reflexes of the different stages of economic growth remain historical facts of great importance; it is true that while dialectical materialism is itself the product of this process, it does not deny that men perform their historical deeds themselves and that they do so consciously. But as Engels emphasizes in a letter to Mehring,[9] this consciousness is false. However, the dialectical method does not permit us simply to proclaim the "falseness" of this consciousness and to persist in an inflexible confrontation of true and false. On the contrary, it requires us to investigate this "false consciousness" concretely as an aspect of the historical totality and as a stage in the historical process.

Of course bourgeois historians also attempt such concrete analyses; indeed they reproach historical materialists with violating the concrete uniqueness of historical events. Where they go wrong is in their belief that the concrete can be located in the empirical individual of history ("individual" here can refer to an individual man, class or people) and in his empirically given (and hence psychological or mass-psychological) consciousness. And just when they imagine that they have discovered the most concrete thing of all—*society as a concrete totality*, the system of production at a given point in history and the resulting division of society into classes—they are in fact at the furthest remove from it. In missing the mark they mistake something wholly abstract for the concrete. "These relations," Marx states, "are not those between one individual and another, but between worker and capitalist, tenant and landlord, etc. Eliminate these relations and you abolish the whole of society; your Prometheus will then be nothing more than a spectre without arms or legs. . . ."[10]

Concrete analysis means, then, the relation to society *as a whole*. For only when this relation is established does the consciousness of their existence that men have at any given time emerge in all its essential characteristics. It appears, on the one hand, as something which is *subjectively* justified in the social and historical situation, as something which can and should be understood, i.e., as "right." At the same time, *objectively,* it bypasses the essence of the evolution of society and fails to pinpoint it and express it adequately. That is to say, objectively, it appears as a "false consciousness." On the other hand, we may see the same consciousness as something which fails *subjectively* to reach its self-appointed goals, while furthering and realizing the *objective* aims of society of which it is ignorant and which it did not choose.

This twofold dialectical determination of "false consciousness" constitutes an analysis far removed from the naïve description of what men *in fact* thought, felt and wanted at any moment in history and from any given point in the class structure. I do not wish to deny the great importance of this, but it remains after all merely the *material* of genuine historical analysis. The relation with concrete totality and the dialectical determinants arising from it transcend pure description and yield the category of objective possibility. By relating consciousness to the whole of society it becomes possible to infer the thoughts and feelings which men would have in a particular situation if they were *able* to assess both it and the interests arising from it in their impact on immediate action and on the whole structure of society. That is to say, it would be possible to infer the thoughts and feelings appropriate to their objective situation. The number of such situations is not unlimited in any society. However much detailed researches are able to refine social typologies there will always be a number of clearly distinguished basic types whose characteristics are determined by the types of position available in the process of production. Now class consciousness consists in fact of the appropriate and rational reactions "imputed" [zugerechnet] to a particular typical position in the process of production.[11] This consciousness is, therefore, neither the sum nor the average of what is thought or felt by the single individuals who make up the class. And yet the historically significant actions of the class as a whole are determined in the last resort by this consciousness and not by the thought of the individual—and these actions can be understood only by reference to this consciousness.

This analysis establishes right from the start the distance that separates class consciousness from the empirically given, and from the psychologically describable and explicable ideas which men form about their situation in life. But it is not enough just to state that this distance exists or even to define its implications in a formal and general way. We must discover, firstly, whether it is a phenomenon that differs according to the manner in which the various classes are related to society as a whole and whether the differences are so great as to produce *qualitative distinctions*. And we must discover, secondly, the *practical* significance of these different possible relations between the objective economic totality, the imputed class consciousness and the real, psychological thoughts of men about their lives. We must discover, in short, the *practical, historical function* of class consciousness.

Only after such preparatory formulations can we begin to exploit the category of objective possibility systematically. The first question we must ask is how far is it *in fact* possible to discern the whole economy of a society from inside it? It is essential to transcend the limitations of particular individuals caught up in their own narrow prejudices. But it is no less vital not to overstep the frontier fixed for them by the economic structure of society and establishing their position in it.[12] Regarded abstractly and formally, then, class consciousness implies a class-conditioned *unconsciousness* of one's own sociohistorical and economic condition.[13] This condition is given as a definite structural relation, a definite formal nexus which appears to govern the whole of life. The "falseness," the illusion implicit in this situation is in no sense arbitrary; it is simply the intellectual reflex of the objective economic structure. Thus, for example, "the value or price of labour-power takes on the appearance of the price or value of labour itself . . ." and "the illusion is created that the totality is paid labour. . . . In contrast to that, under slavery even that portion of labour which is paid for appears unpaid for."[14] Now it requires the most painstaking historical analysis to use the category of objective possibility so as to isolate the conditions in which this illusion can be exposed and a real connection with the totality established. For if from the vantage point of a particular class the totality of existing society is not visible, if a class thinks the thoughts imputable to it and which bear upon its interests right through to their logical conclusion and yet fails to strike at the heart of that totality, then such a class is doomed to play only a subordinate role. It can never influence the course of history in either a conservative or progressive direction. Such classes are normally condemned to passivity, to an unstable oscillation between the ruling and the revolutionary classes, and if perchance they do erupt, then such explosions are purely elemental and aimless. They may win a few battles but they are doomed to ultimate defeat.

For a class to be ripe for hegemony means that its interests and consciousness enable it to organize the whole of society in accordance with those interests. The crucial question in every class struggle is this: which class possesses this capacity and this consciousness at the decisive moment? This does not preclude the use of force. It does not mean that the class-interests destined to prevail and thus to uphold the interests of society as a whole can be guaranteed an automatic victory. On the contrary, such a transfer of power can often only be brought about by the most ruthless use of force (as, e.g., the primitive accumulation of capital). But it often turns out that questions of class consciousness prove to be decisive in just those situations where force is unavoidable and where classes are locked in a life-and-death-struggle. Thus the noted Hungarian Marxist Erwin Szabó is mistaken in criticizing Engels for maintaining that the Great Peasant War (of 1525) was essentially a reactionary movement. Szabó argues that the peasants' revolt was suppressed *only* by the ruthless use of force and that its defeat was not grounded in socioeconomic factors and in the class consciousness of the peasants. He overlooks the fact that the deepest reason for the weakness of the peasantry and the superior strength of the princes is to be sought in class consciousness. Even the most cursory student of the military aspects of the Peasants' War can easily convince himself of this.

It must not be thought, however, that all classes ripe for hegemony have a class consciousness with the same inner structure. Everything hinges on the extent to which they can become conscious of the actions they need to perform in order to obtain and organize power. The question then becomes: how far does the class concerned perform the actions history has imposed on it "consciously" or "unconsciously?" And is that consciousness "true" or "false?" These distinctions are by no means academic. Quite apart from problems of culture where such fissures and dissonances are crucial, in all practical matters too the fate of a class depends on its ability to elucidate and solve the problems with which history confronts it. And here it becomes transparently obvious that class consciousness is concerned neither with the thoughts of individuals, however advanced, nor with the state of scientific knowledge. For example, it is quite clear that ancient society was broken economically by the limitations of a system built on slavery. But it is equally clear that neither the ruling classes nor the classes that rebelled against them in the name of revolution or reform could perceive this. In consequence the practical emergence of these problems meant that the society was necessarily and irremediably doomed.

The situation is even clearer in the case of the modern bourgeoisie, which, armed with its knowledge of the workings of economics, clashed with feudal and absolutist society. For the bourgeoisie was quite unable to perfect its fundamental science, its own science of classes: the reef on which it foundered was its failure to discover even a theoretical solution to the problem of crises. The fact that a scientifically acceptable solution does exist is of no avail. For to accept that solution, even in theory, would be tantamount to observing society *from a class standpoint other than that of the bourgeoisie*. And no class can do that—unless it is willing to abdicate its power freely. Thus the barrier which converts the class consciousness of the bourgeoisie into "false" consciousness is objective; it is the class situation itself. It is the objective result of the economic setup, and is neither arbitary, subjective nor psychological. The class consciousness of the bourgeoisie may well be able to reflect all the problems of organization entailed by its hegemony and by the capitalist transformation and penetration of total production. But it becomes obscured as soon as it is called upon to face problems that remain within its jurisdiction but which point beyond the limits of capitalism. The discovery of the "natural laws" of economics is pure light in comparison with mediaeval feudalism or even the mercantilism of the transitional period, but by an internal dialectical twist they become "natural laws based on the unconsciousness of those who are involved in them."[15]

It would be beyond the scope of these pages to advance further and attempt to construct a historical and systematic typology of the possible degrees of class consciousness. That would require—in the first instance—an exact study of the point in the total process of production at which the interests of the various classes are most immediately and vitally involved. Secondly, we would have to show how far it would be in the interest of any given class to go beyond this immediacy, to annul and transcend its immediate interest by seeing it as a factor within a totality. And lastly, what is the nature of the totality that is then achieved? How far does it really embrace the true totality of production? It is quite evident that the quality and structure of class consciousness must be very different if, e.g., it remains stationary at the separation of consumption from production (as with the Roman *Lumpenproletariat*) or if it represents the formation of the interests of circulation (as with merchant capital). Although we cannot embark on a systematic typology of the various points of view it can be seen from the foregoing that these specimens of "false" consciousness differ from each other both qualitatively, structurally and in a manner that is crucial for the activity of the classes in society.

. . . . .

3

Bourgeoisie and proletariat are the only pure classes in bourgeois society. They are the only classes whose existence and development are entirely dependent on the course taken by the modern evolution of production and only from the vantage point of these classes can a plan for the total organization of society *even be imagined*. The outlook of the other classes (petty bourgeois or peasants) is ambiguous or sterile because their existence is not based exclusively on their role in the capitalist system of production but is indissolubly linked with the vestiges of feudal society. Their aim, therefore, is not to advance capitalism or to transcend it, but to reverse its action or at least to prevent it from developing fully. Their class interest concentrates on *symptoms of development* and not on development itself, and on elements of society rather than on the construction of society as a whole.

The question of consciousness may make its appearance in terms of the objectives chosen or in terms of action, as for instance in the case of the petty bourgeoisie. This class lives at least in part in the capitalist big city and every aspect of its existence is directly exposed to the influence of capitalism. Hence it cannot possibly remain wholly unaffected by the *fact* of class conflict between bourgeoisie and proletariat. But as a "transitional class in which the interests of two other classes become simultaneously blunted . . ." it will imagine itself "to be above all class antagonisms."[16] Accordingly it will search for ways whereby it will "not indeed eliminate the two extremes of capital and wage labour, but will weaken their antagonism and transform it into harmony."[17] In all decisions crucial for society its actions will be irrelevant and it will be forced to fight for both sides in turn but always without consciousness. In so doing its own objectives—which exist exclusively in its own consciousness—must become progressively weakened and increasingly divorced from social action. Ultimately they will assume purely "ideological" forms. The petty bourgeoisie will only be able to play an active role in history as long as these objectives happen to coincide with the real economic interests of capitalism. This was the case with the abolition of the feudal estates during the French Revolution. With the fulfillment of this mission its utterances, which for the most part remain unchanged in form, become more and more remote from real events and turn finally into mere caricatures (this was true, e.g., of the Jacobinism of the Montagne 1848–51).

This isolation from society as a whole has its repercussions on the internal structure of the class and its organizational potential. This can be seen most clearly in the development of the peasantry. Marx says on this point:[18] "The small-holding peasants form a vast mass whose members live in similar conditions but without entering into manifold relations with each other. Their mode of production isolates them from one another instead of bringing them into mutual intercourse. . . . Every single peasant family . . . thus acquires its means of life more through exchange with nature than in intercourse with society. . . . In so far as millions of families live under economic conditions of existence that separate their mode of life, their interests and their culture from those of other classes and place them in opposition to them, they constitute a class. In so far as there is only a local connection between the small-holding peasants, and the identity of their interests begets no community, no national unity and no political organization, they do not constitute a class." Hence *external* upheavals, such as war, revolution in the towns, etc. are needed before these masses can coalesce in a unified movement, and even then they are incapable of organizing it and supplying it with slogans and a positive direction corresponding to their own interests.

Whether these movements will be progressive (as in the French Revolution of 1789 or the Russian Revolution of 1917), or reactionary (as with Napoleon's coup d'état) will depend on the position of the other classes involved in the conflict, and on the level of consciousness of the parties that lead them. For this reason, too, the *ideological* form taken by the class consciousness of the peasants changes its content more frequently than that of other classes: this is because it is always borrowed from elsewhere. Hence parties that base themselves wholly or in part on this class consciousness always lack really firm and secure support in critical situations (as was true of the Socialist Revolutionaries in 1917 and 1918). This explains why it is possible for peasant conflicts to be fought out under opposing flags. Thus it is highly characteristic of both Anarchism and the "class consciousness" of the peasantry that a number of counterrevolutionary rebellions and uprisings of the middle and upper strata of the peasantry in Russia should have found the anarchist view of society to be a satisfying ideology. We cannot really speak of class consciousness in the case of these classes (if, indeed, we can even speak of them as classes in the strict Marxist sense of the term): for a full consciousness of their situation would reveal to them the hopelessness of their particularist strivings in the face of the inevitable course of events. Consciousness and self-interest then are *mutually incompatible* in this instance. And as class consciousness was defined in terms of the problems of imputing class interests the failure of their class consciousness to develop in the immediately given historical reality becomes comprehensible philosophically.

With the bourgeoisie, also, class consciousness stands in opposition to class interest. But here the antagonism is *not contradictory but dialectical*.

The distinction between the two modes of contradiction may be briefly described in this way: in the case of the other classes, a class consciousness is prevented from emerging by their position within the process of production and the interests this generates. In the case of the bourgeoisie, however, these factors combine to produce a class consciousness but one which is cursed by its very nature with the tragic fate of developing an insoluble contradiction at the very zenith of its powers. As a result of this contradiction it must annihilate itself.

The tragedy of the bourgeoisie is reflected historically in the fact that even before it had defeated its predecessor, feudalism, its new enemy, the proletariat, had appeared on the scene. Politically, it became evident when at the moment of victory, the "freedom" in whose name the bourgeoisie had joined battle with feudalism was transformed into a new repressiveness. Sociologically, the bourgeoisie did everything in its power to eradicate the fact of class conflict from the consciousness of society, even though class conflict had only emerged in its purity and became established as an historical fact with the advent of capitalism. Ideologically, we see the same contradiction in the fact that the bourgeoisie endowed the individual with an unprecedented importance, but at the same time that same individuality was annihilated by the economic conditions to which it was subjected, by the reification created by commodity production.

All these contradictions, and the list might be extended indefinitely, are only the reflection of the deepest contradictions in capitalism itself as they appear in the consciousness of the bourgeoisie in accordance with their position in the total system of production. For this reason they appear as dialectical contradictions in the class consciousness of the bourgeoisie. They do not merely reflect the inability of the bourgeoisie to grasp the contradictions inherent in its own social order. For, on the one hand, capitalism is the first system of production able to achieve a total economic penetration of society,[19] and this implies that in theory the bourgeoisie should be able to progress from this central point to the possession of an (imputed) class consciousness of the whole system of production. On the other hand, the position held by the capitalist class and the interests which determine its actions ensure that it will be unable to control its own system of production even in theory.

There are many reasons for this. In the first place, it only seems to be true that for capitalism production occupies the center of class consciousness and hence provides the theoretical starting-point for analysis. With reference to Ricardo "who had been reproached with an exclusive concern with production," Marx emphasized[20] that he "defined distribution as the sole subject of economics." And the detailed analysis of the process by which capital is concretely realized shows in every single instance that the interest of the capitalist (who produces not goods but commodities) is necessarily confined to matters that must be peripheral in terms of production. Moreover, the capitalist, enmeshed in what is for him the decisive process of the expansion of capital, must have a standpoint from which the most important problems become quite invisible.[21]

The discrepancies that result are further exacerbated by the fact that there is an insoluble contradiction running through the internal structure of capitalism between the social and the individual principle, i.e., between the function of capital as private property and its objective economic function. As the *Communist Manifesto* states: "Capital is a social force and not a personal one." But it is a social force whose movements are determined by the individual interests of the owners of capital—who cannot see and who are necessarily indifferent to all the social implications of their activities. Hence the social principle and the social function implicit in capital can only prevail unbeknown to them and, as it were, against their will and behind their backs. Because of this conflict between the individual and the social, Marx rightly characterized the stock companies as the "negation of the capitalist mode of production itself."[22] Of course, it is true that stock companies differ only in inessentials from individual capitalists and even the so-called abolition of the anarchy in production through cartels and trusts only shifts the contradiction elsewhere, without, however, eliminating it. This situation forms one of the decisive factors governing the class consciousness of the bourgeoisie. It is true that the bourgeoisie acts as a class in the objective evolution of society. But it understands the process (which it is itself instigating) as something external which is subject to objective laws which it can only experience passively.

Bourgeois thought observes economic life consistently and necessarily from the standpoint of the individual capitalist and this naturally produces a sharp confrontation between the individual and the overpowering suprapersonal "law of nature" which propels all social phenomena.[23] This leads both to the antagonism between individual and class interests in the event of conflict (which, it is true, rarely becomes as acute among the ruling classes as in the bourgeoisie), and also to the logical impossibility of discovering theoretical and practical solutions to the problems created by the capitalist system of production.

"This sudden reversion from a system of credit to a system of hard cash heaps theoretical fright on top of practical panic; and the dealers by whose agency circulation is effected shudder before the impenetrable mystery in which their own economic relations are shrouded."[24] This terror is not unfounded, that is to say, it is much more than the bafflement felt by the individual capitalist when confronted by his own individual fate. The facts and the situations which induce this panic force something into the consciousness of the bourgeoisie which is too much of a brute fact for its existence to be wholly denied or repressed. But equally it is something that the bourgeoisie can never fully understand. For the recognizable background to this situation is the fact that "the *real barrier* of capitalist production is *capital itself*."[25] And if this insight were to become conscious it would indeed entail the self-negation of the capitalist class.

In this way the objective limits of capitalist production become the limits of the class consciousness of the bourgeoisie. The older "natural" and "conservative" forms of domination had left unmolested the forms of production of whole sections of the people they ruled and therefore exerted by and large a traditional and unrevolutionary influence. Capitalism, by contrast, is a revolutionary form par excellence. *The fact that it must necessarily remain in ignorance of the objective economic limitations of its own system expresses itself as an internal, dialectical contradiction in its class consciousness.*

This means that *formally* the class consciousness of the bourgeoisie is geared to economic consciousness. And indeed the highest degree of unconsciousness, the crassest form of "false consciousness" always manifests itself when the conscious mastery of economic phenomena appears to be at its greatest. From the point of view of the relation of consciousness to society this contradiction is expressed as the *irreconcilable antagonism between ideology and economic base*. Its dialectics are grounded in the irreconcilable antagonism between the (capitalist) individual, i.e., the stereotyped individual of capitalism, and the "natural" and inevitable process of development, i.e., the process not subject to consciousness. In consequence theory and practice are brought into irreconcilable opposition to each other. But the resulting dualism is anything but stable; in fact it constantly strives to harmonize principles that have been wrenched apart and thenceforth oscillate between a new "false" synthesis and its subsequent cataclysmic disruption.

This internal dialectical contradiction in the class consciousness of the bourgeoisie is further aggravated by the fact that the objective limits of capitalism do not remain purely negative. That is to say that capitalism does not merely set "natural" laws in motion that provoke crises which it cannot comprehend. On the contrary, those limits acquire a historical embodiment with its own consciousness and its own actions: the proletariat.

Most "normal" shifts of perspective produced by the capitalist point of view in the image of the economic structure of society tend to "obscure and mystify the true origin of surplus value." In the "normal," purely theoretical view this mystification only attaches to the organic composition of capital, viz., to the place of the employer in the productive system and the economic function of interest, etc., i.e., it does no more than highlight the failure of observers to perceive the true driving forces that lie beneath the surface. But when it comes to practice this mystification touches upon the central fact of capitalist society: the class struggle.

In the class struggle we witness the emergence of all the hidden forces that usually lie concealed behind the façade of economic life, at which the capitalists and their apologists gaze as though transfixed. These forces appear in such a way that they cannot possibly be ignored. So much so that even when capitalism was in the ascendant and the proletariat could only give vent to its protests in the form of vehement spontaneous explosions, even the ideological exponents of the rising bourgeoisie acknowledged the class struggle as a basic fact of history. (For example, Marat and later historians such as Mignet.) But in proportion as the theory and practice of the proletariat made society conscious of this unconscious, revolutionary principle inherent in capitalism, the bourgeoisie was thrown back increasingly onto a conscious defensive. The dialectical contradiction in the "false" consciousness of the bourgeoisie became more and more acute: the "false" consciousness was converted into a mendacious consciousness. What had been at first an objective contradiction now became subjective also: the theoretical problem turned into a moral posture which decisively influenced every practical class attitude in every situation and on every issue.

Thus the situation in which the bourgeoisie finds itself determines the function of its class consciousness in its struggle to achieve control of society. The hegemony of the bourgeoisie really does embrace the whole of society; it really does attempt to organize the whole of society in its own interests (and in this it has had some success). To achieve this it was forced both to develop a coherent theory of economics, politics and society (which in itself presupposes and amounts to a "Weltanschauung"), and also to make conscious and sustain its faith in its own *mission* to control and organize society. The tragic dialectics of the bourgeoisie can be seen in the fact that it is not only desirable but essential for it to clarify its own class interests on *every particular issue,* while at the same time such a clear awareness becomes fatal when it is extended to *the question of the totality*. The chief reason for this is that the rule of the bourgeoisie can only be the rule of a minority. Its hegemony is exercised not merely *by* a minority but *in the interest* of that minority, so the need to deceive the other classes and to ensure that their class consciousness remains amorphous is inescapable for a bourgeois regime. (Consider here the theory of the state that stands "above" class antagonisms, or the notion of an "impartial" system of justice.)

But the veil drawn over the nature of bourgeois society is indispensable to the bourgeoisie itself. For the insoluble internal contradictions of the system become revealed with increasing starkness and so confront its supporters with a choice. Either they must consciously ignore insights which become increasingly urgent or else they must suppress their own moral instincts in order to be able to support with a good conscience an economic system that serves only their own interests.

Without overestimating the efficacy of such ideological factors it must be agreed that the fighting power of a class grows with its ability to carry out its own mission with a good conscience and to adapt all phenomena to its own interests with unbroken confidence in itself. If we consider Sismondi's criticism of classical economics, German criticisms of natural law and the youthful critiques of Carlyle it becomes evident that from a very early stage the ideological history of the bourgeoisie was *nothing but a desperate resistance to every insight into the true nature of the society it had created and thus to a real understanding of its class situation*. When the *Communist Manifesto* makes the point that the bourgeoisie produces its own gravediggers this is valid ideologically as well as economically. The whole of bourgeois thought in the nineteenth century made the most strenuous efforts to mask the real foundations of bourgeois society; everything was tried: from the greatest falsifications of fact to the "sublime" theories about the "essence" of history and the state. But in vain: with the end of the century the issue was resolved by the advances of science and their corresponding effects on the consciousness of the capitalist elite.

This can be seen very clearly in the bourgeoisie's greater readiness to accept the idea of conscious organization. A greater measure of concentration was achieved first in the stock companies and in the cartels and trusts. This process revealed the social character of capital more and more clearly without affecting the general anarchy in production. What it did was to confer near-monopoly status on a number of giant individual capitalists. Objectively, then, the social character of capital was brought into play with great energy but in such a manner as to keep its nature concealed from the capitalist class. Indeed this illusory elimination of economic anarchy successfully diverted their attention from the true situation. With the crises of the war and the postwar period this tendency has advanced still further: the idea of a "planned" economy has gained ground at least among the more progressive elements of the bourgeoisie. Admittedly this applies only within quite narrow strata of the bourgeoisie and even there it is thought of more as a theoretical experiment than as a practical way out of the impasse brought about by the crises.

When capitalism was still expanding it rejected every sort of social organization on the grounds that it was "an inroad upon such sacred things as the rights of property, freedom and unrestricted play for the initiative of the individual capitalist." If we compare that with current attempts to harmonize a "planned" economy with the class interests of the bourgeoisie, we are forced to admit that what we are witnessing is *the capitulation of the class consciousness of the bourgeoisie before that of the proletariat*. Of course, the section of the bourgeoisie that accepts the notion of a "planned" economy does not mean by it the same as does the proletariat: it regards it as a last attempt to save capitalism by driving its internal contradictions to breaking point. Nevertheless this means jettisoning the last theoretical line of defense. (As a strange counterpart to this we may note that *at just this point in time* certain sectors of the proletariat *capitulate before the bourgeoisie* and adopt this, the most problematic form of bourgeois organization.)

With this the whole existence of the bourgeoisie and its culture is plunged into the most terrible crisis. On the one hand, we find the utter sterility of an ideology divorced from life, of a more or less conscious attempt at forgery. On the other hand, a cynicism no less terribly jejune lives on in the world-historical irrelevances and nullities of its own existence and concerns itself only with the defense of that existence and with its own naked self-interest. This ideological crisis is an unfailing sign of decay. The bourgeoisie has already been thrown on the defensive; however aggressive its *weapons* may be, it is fighting for self-preservation. *Its power to dominate has vanished beyond recall.*

4

In this struggle for consciousness historical materialism plays a crucial role. Ideologically no less than economically, the bourgeoisie and the proletariat are mutually interdependent. The same process that the bourgeoisie experiences as a permanent crisis and gradual dissolution appears to the proletariat, likewise in crisis-form, as the gathering of strength and the springboard to victory. Ideologically this means that the same growth of insight into the nature of society, which reflects the protracted death struggle of the bourgeoisie, entails a steady growth in the strength of the proletariat. For the proletariat the truth is a weapon that brings victory; and the more ruthless, the greater the victory. This makes more comprehensible the desperate fury with which bourgeois science assails historical materialism: for as soon as the bourgeoisie is forced to take up its stand on this terrain, it is lost. And, at the same time, this explains why the proletariat and *only* the proletariat can discern in the correct understanding of *the nature of society* a power-factor of the first, and perhaps decisive importance.

The unique function of consciousness in the class struggle of the proletariat has consistently been overlooked by the vulgar-marxists who have substituted a petty "Realpolitik" for the great battle of principle which reaches back to the ultimate problems of the objective economic process. Naturally we do not wish to deny that the proletariat must proceed from the facts of a given situation. But it is to be distinguished from other classes by the fact that it goes beyond the contingencies of history; far from being driven forward by them, it is itself their driving force and impinges centrally upon the process of social change. When the vulgar-marxists detach themselves from this central point of view, i.e., from the point where a proletarian class consciousness arises, *they thereby place themselves on the level of consciousness of the bourgeoisie*. And that the bourgeoisie fighting on its own ground will prove superior to the proletariat both economically and ideologically can come as a surprise only to a vulgar-marxist. Moreover only a vulgar-marxist would infer from this fact, which after all derives exclusively from his own attitude, that the bourgeoisie *generally* occupies the stronger position. For quite apart from the very real force at its disposal, it is self-evident that the bourgeoisie *fighting on its own ground* will be both more experienced and more expert. Nor will it come as a surprise if the bourgeoisie automatically obtains the upper hand when its opponents abandon their own position for that of the bourgeoisie.

As the bourgeoisie has the intellectual, organizational and every other advantage, the superiority of the proletariat must lie exclusively in its ability to see society from the center, as a coherent whole. This means that it is able to act in such a way as to change reality; in the class consciousness of the proletariat theory and practice coincide and so it can consciously throw the weight of its actions onto the scales of history—and this is the deciding factor. When the vulgar-marxists destroy this unity they cut the nerve that binds proletarian theory to proletarian action. They reduce theory to the "scientific" treatment of the symptoms of social change and as for practice they are themselves reduced to being buffeted about aimlessly and uncontrollably by the various elements of the process they had hoped to master.

The class consciousness that springs from this position must exhibit the same internal structure as that of the bourgeoisie. But when the logic of events drives the same dialectical contradictions to the surface of consciousness the consequences for the proletariat are even more disastrous than for the bourgeoisie. For despite all the dialectical contradictions, despite all its objective falseness, the self-deceiving "false" consciousness that we find in the bourgeoisie is at least in accord with its class situation. It cannot save the bourgeoisie from the constant exacerbation of these contradictions and so from destruction, but it can enable it to continue the struggle and even engineer victories, albeit of short duration.

But in the case of the proletariat such a consciousness not only has to overcome these internal (bourgeois) contradictions, but it also conflicts with the course of action to which the economic situation necessarily commits the proletariat (regardless of its own thoughts on the subject). The proletariat must act in a proletarian manner, but its own vulgar-marxist theory blocks its vision of the right course to adopt. The dialectical contradiction between necessary proletarian action and vulgar-marxist (bourgeois) theory becomes more and more acute. As the decisive battle in the class struggle approaches, the power of a true or false theory to accelerate or retard progress grows in proportion. The "realm of freedom," the end of the "prehistory of mankind" means precisely that the power of the objectified, reified relations between men begins to revert to *man*. The closer this process comes to its goal, the more urgent it becomes for the proletariat to understand its own historical mission and the more vigorously and directly proletarian class consciousness will determine each of its actions. For the blind power of the forces at work will only advance "automatically" to their goal of self-annihilation as long as that goal is not within reach. When the moment of transition to the "realm of freedom" arrives this will become apparent just because the blind forces really will hurtle blindly toward the abyss, and only the conscious will of the proletariat will be able to save mankind from the impending catastrophe. In other words, when the final economic crisis of capitalism develops, *the fate of the revolution (and with it the fate of mankind) will depend on the ideological maturity of the proletariat, i.e., on its class consciousness.*

• • • • •

Notes

1. *Feurbach and the End of Classical German Philosophy,* S.W. II, pp. 354ff.

2. *Capital* 1, p. 75.

3. And also of the "pessimism" which *perpetuates* the present state of affairs and represents it as the uttermost limit of human development just as much as does "optimism." In this respect (and in this respect alone) Hegel and Schopenhauer are on a par with each other.

4. *The Poverty of Philosophy,* p. 135.

5. Ibid., p. 117.

6. Ibid., p. 122.

7. *Capital* I, p. 75 (my italics). Cf. also Engels, *The Origin of the Family, Private Property and the State,* S.W. II, pp. 292–93.

8. *Capital* I, p. 766. Cf. also *Wage Labour and Capital,* S.W. II, p. 83; on machines see *The Poverty of Philosophy,* p. 149; on money, ibid., p. 89, etc.

9. *Dokumente des Sozialismus* II, p. 76.

10. *The Poverty of Philosophy,* p. 112.

11. In this context it is unfortunately not possible to discuss in greater detail some of the ramifications of these ideas in Marxism, e.g., the very important category of the "economic persona." Even less can we pause to glance at the relation of historical materialism to comparable trends in bourgeois thought (such as Max Weber's ideal types).

12. This is the point from which to gain an historical understanding of the great utopians such as Plato or Sir Thomas More. Cf. also Marx on Aristotle, *Capital* I, pp. 59–60.

13. "But although ignorant of this, yet he says it," Marx says of Franklin, *Capital* I, p. 51. And similarly: "They know not what they do, but they do it," Ibid., p. 74.

14. *Wages, Price and Profit,* S.W. I, pp. 388–89.

15. Engels, *Umriss zu einer Kritik der Nationalkökonomie,* Nachlass I, p. 449.

16. *The Eighteenth Brumaire of Louis Bonaparte*, S.W. I. p. 252.
17. Ibid., p. 249.
18. Ibid., pp. 302–3.
19. But no more than the tendency. It is Rosa Luxemburg's great achievement to have shown that this is not just a passing phase but that capitalism can only survive—economically—while it moves society in the direction of capitalism but has not yet fully penetrated it. This economic self-contradiction of any purely capitalist society is undoubtedly one of the reasons for the contradictions in the class consciousness of the bourgeoisie.
20. *A Contribution to the Critique of Political Economy*, p. 285.
21. *Capital* III, pp. 136, 307–8, 318, etc. It is self-evident that the different groups of capitalists, such as industrialists and merchants, etc., are differently placed; but the distinctions are not relevant in this context.
22. Ibid., p. 428.
23. On this point cf. the essay "The Marxism of Rosa Luxemburg."
24. *A Contribution to the Critique of Political Economy*, p. 198.
25. *Capital* III, pp. 245 and also 252.

REIFICATION AND THE CONSCIOUSNESS OF THE PROLETARIAT

> To be radical is to go to the root of the matter. For man, however, the root is man himself.
>
> Marx, *Critique of Hegel's Philosophy of Right*

It is no accident that Marx should have begun with an analysis of commodities when, in the two great works of his mature period, he set out to portray capitalist society in its totality and to lay bare its fundamental nature. For at this stage in the history of mankind there is no problem that does not ultimately lead back to that question and there is no solution that could not be found in the solution to the riddle of commodity-*structure*. Of course the problem can only be discussed with this degree of generality if it achieves the depth and breadth to be found in Marx's own analyses. That is to say, the problem of commodities must not be considered in isolation or even regarded as the central problem in economics, but as the central, structural problem of capitalist society in all its aspects. Only in this case can the structure of commodity-relations be made to yield a model of all the objective forms of bourgeois society together with all the subjective forms corresponding to them.

I. The Phenomenon of Reification

1

The essence of commodity-structure has often been pointed out. Its basis is that a relation between people takes on the character of a thing and thus acquires a "phantom objectivity," an autonomy that seems so strictly rational and all-embracing as to conceal every trace of its fundamental nature: the relation between people. It is beyond the scope of this essay to discuss the central importance of this problem for economics itself. Nor shall we consider its implications for the economic doctrines of the vulgar-marxists which follow from their abandonment of this starting-point.

Our intention here is to *base* ourselves on Marx's economic analyses and to proceed from there to a discussion of the problems growing out of the fetish character of commodities, both as an objective form and also as a subjective stance corresponding to it. Only by understanding this can we obtain a clear insight into the ideological problems of capitalism and its downfall.

Before tackling the problem itself we must be quite clear in our minds that commodity fetishism is a *specific* problem of our age, the age of modern capitalism. Commodity exchange and the corresponding subjective and objective commodity relations existed, as we know, when society was still very primitive. What is at issue *here,* however, is the question: how far is commodity exchange together with its structural consequences able to influence the *total* outer and inner life of society? Thus the extent to which such exchange is the dominant form of metabolic change in a society cannot simply be treated in quantitative terms—as would harmonize with the modern modes of thought already eroded by the reifying effects of the dominant commodity form. The distinction between a society where this form is dominant, permeating every expression of life, and a society where it only makes an episodic appearance is essentially one of quality. For depending on which is the case, all the subjective and objective phenomena in the societies concerned are objectified in qualitatively different ways.

Marx lays great stress on the essentially episodic appearance of the commodity form in primitive societies:

> Direct barter, the original natural form of exchange, represents rather the beginning of the transformation of use-values into commodities, than that

> of commodities into money. Exchange value has as yet no form of its own, but is still directly bound up with use-value. This is manifested in two ways. Production, in its entire organisation, aims at the creation of use-values and not of exchange values, and it is only when their supply exceeds the measure of consumption that use-values cease to be use-values, and become means of exchange, i.e. commodities. At the same time, they become commodities only within the limits of being direct use-values distributed at opposite poles, so that the commodities to be exchanged by their possessors must be use-values to both—each commodity to its non-possessor. As a matter of fact, the exchange of commodities originates not within the primitive communities, but where they end, on their borders at the few points where they come in contact with other communities. That is where barter begins, and from here it strikes back into the interior of the community, decomposing it.[1]

We note that the observation about the disintegrating effect of a commodity exchange directed in upon itself clearly shows the qualitative change engendered by the dominance of commodities.

However, even when commodities have this impact on the internal structure of a society, this does not suffice to make them constitutive of that society. To achieve that it would be necessary—as we emphasized above—for the commodity structure to penetrate society in all its aspects and to remold it in its own image. It is not enough merely to establish an external link with independent processes concerned with the production of exchange values. The qualitative difference between the commodity as one form among many regulating the metabolism of human society and the commodity as the universal structuring principle has effects over and above the fact that the commodity relation as an isolated phenomenon exerts a negative influence at best on the structure and organization of society. The distinction also has repercussions upon the nature and validity of the category itself. Where the commodity is universal it manifests itself differently from the commodity as a particular, isolated, nondominant phenomenon.

The fact that the boundaries lack sharp definition must not be allowed to blur the qualitative nature of the decisive distinction. The situation where commodity exchange is not dominant has been defined by Marx as follows:

> The quantitative ratio in which products are exchanged is at first quite arbitrary. They assume the form of commodities inasmuch as they are exchangeables, i.e. expressions of one and the same third. Continued exchange and more regular reproduction for exchange reduces this arbitrari-

> ness more and more. But at first not for the producer and consumer, but for their go-between, the merchant, who compares money-prices and pockets the difference. It is through his own movements that he establishes equivalence. Merchant's capital is originally merely the intervening movement between extremes which it does not control and between premises which it does not create.[2]

And *this* development of the commodity to the point where it becomes the dominant form in society did not take place until the advent of modern capitalism. Hence it is not to be wondered at that the personal nature of economic relations was still understood clearly on occasion at the start of capitalist development, but that as the process advanced and forms became more complex and less direct, it became increasingly difficult and rare to find anyone penetrating the veil of reification. Marx sees the matter in this way.

> In preceding forms of society this economic mystification arose principally with respect to money and interest-bearing capital. In the nature of things it is excluded, in the first place, where production for the use-value, for immediate personal requirements, predominates; and secondly, where slavery or serfdom form the broad foundation of social production, as in antiquity and during the Middle Ages. Here, the domination of the producers by the conditions of production is concealed by the relations of dominion and servitude which appear and are evident as the direct motive power of the process of production.[3]

The commodity can only be understood in its undistorted essence when it becomes the universal category of society as a whole. Only in this context does the reification produced by commodity relations assume decisive importance both for the objective evolution of society and for the stance adopted by men toward it. Only then does the commodity become crucial for the subjugation of men's consciousness to the forms in which this reification finds expression and for their attempts to comprehend the process or to rebel against its disastrous effects and liberate themselves from servitude to the "second nature" so created.

Marx describes the basic phenomenon of reification as follows:

> A commodity is therefore a mysterious thing, simply because in it the social character of men's labour appears to them as an objective character stamped upon the product of that labour; because the relation of the producers to the sum total of their own labour is presented to them as a social relation, existing not between themselves, but between the products of their labour. This is the reason why the products of labour become commodities,

> social things whose qualities are at the same time perceptible and imperceptible by the senses. . . . It is only a definite social relation between men that assumes, in their eyes, the fantastic form of a relation between things.[4]

What is of central importance here is that because of this situation a man's own activity, his own labour becomes something objective and independent of him, something that controls him by virtue of an autonomy alien to man. There is both an objective and a subjective side to this phenomenon. *Objectively* a world of objects and relations between things springs into being (the world of commodities and their movements on the market). The laws governing these objects are indeed gradually discovered by man, but even so they confront him as invisible forces that generate their own power. The individual can use his knowledge of these laws to his own advantage, but he is not able to modify the process by his own activity. *Subjectively*—where the market economy has been fully developed—a man's activity becomes estranged from himself, it turns into a commodity which, subject to the nonhuman objectivity of the natural laws of society, must go its own way independently of man just like any consumer article. "What is characteristic of the capitalist age," says Marx, "is that in the eyes of the labourer himself labour-power assumes the form of a commodity belonging to him. On the other hand it is only at this moment that the commodity form of the products of labour becomes general."[5]

Thus the universality of the commodity form is responsible both objectively and subjectively for the abstraction of the human labor incorporated in commodities. (On the other hand, this universality becomes historically possible because this process of abstraction has been completed.) *Objectively,* in so far as the commodity form facilitates the equal exchange of qualitatively different objects, it can only exist if that formal equality is in fact recognized—at any rate in *this* relation, which indeed confers upon them their commodity nature. *Subjectively,* this formal equality of human labor in the abstract is not only the common factor to which the various commodities are reduced; it also becomes the real principle governing the actual production of commodities.

Clearly, it cannot be our aim here to describe even in outline the growth of the modern process of labor, of the isolated, "free" laborer and of the division of labor. Here we need only establish that labor, abstract, equal, comparable labor, measurable with increasing precision according to the time socially necessary for its accomplishment, the labor of the capitalist division of labor existing both as the presupposition and the product of capitalist production, is born only in the course of the development of the capitalist system. Only then does it become a category of society influencing decisively the objective form of things and people in the society thus emerging, their relation to nature and the possible relations of men to each other.[6]

If we follow the path taken by labor in its development from the handicraft via cooperation and manufacture to machine industry we can see a continuous trend toward greater rationalization, the progressive elimination of the qualitative, human and individual attributes of the worker. On the one hand, the process of labor is progressively broken down into abstract, rational, specialized operations so that the worker loses contact with the finished product and his work is reduced to the mechanical repetition of a specialized set of actions. On the other hand, the period of time necessary for work to be accomplished (which forms the basis of rational calculation) is converted, as mechanization and rationalization are intensified, from a merely empirical average figure to an objectively calculable work-stint that confronts the worker as a fixed and established reality. With the modern "psychological" analysis of the work-process (in Taylorism) this rational mechanization extends right into the worker's "soul": even his psychological attributes are separated from his total personality and placed in opposition to it so as to facilitate their integration into specialized rational systems and their reduction to statistically viable concepts.[7]

We are concerned above all with the *principle* at work here: the principle of rationalization based on what is and *can be calculated*. The chief changes undergone by the subject and object of the economic process are as follows: (1) In the first place, the mathematical analysis of work-processes denotes a break with the organic, irrational and qualitatively determined unity of the product. Rationalization in the sense of being able to predict with ever greater precision all the results to be achieved is only to be acquired by the exact breakdown of every complex into its elements and by the study of the special laws governing production. Accordingly it must declare war on the organic manufacture of whole products based on the *traditional amalgam of empirical experiences of work*: rationalization is unthinkable without specialization.[8]

The finished article ceases to be the object of the work-process. The latter turns into the objective synthesis of rationalized special systems whose unity is determined by pure calculation and which must therefore seem to be arbitrarily connected with each other. This destroys the organic necessity with which interrelated special operations are unified in the end-product. The unity of a product as a *commodity* no longer coincides with its unity as a use-value: as society becomes more radically capitalistic the increasing technical autonomy of the special operations involved in production is expressed also, as an economic autonomy, as the growing relativization of the commodity character of a product at the various stages of production.[9] It is thus possible to separate forcibly the production of a use-value in time and space. This goes hand in hand with the union in time and space of special operations that are related to a set of heterogeneous use-values.

(2) In the second place, this fragmentation of the object of production necessarily entails the fragmentation of its subject. In consequence of the rationalization of the work-process the human qualities and idiosyncrasies of the worker appear increasingly as *mere sources of error* when contrasted with these abstract special laws functioning according to rational predictions. Neither objectively nor in his relation to his work does man appear as the authentic master of the process; on the contrary, he is a mechanical part incorporated into a mechanical system. He finds it already preexisting and self-sufficient, it functions independently of him and he has to conform to its laws whether he likes it or not.[10] As labor is progressively rationalized and mechanized his lack of will is reinforced by the way in which his activity becomes less and less active and more and more *contemplative*.[11] The contemplative stance adopted toward a process mechanically conforming to fixed laws and enacted independently of man's consciousness and impervious to human intervention, i.e., a perfectly closed system, must likewise transform the basic categories of man's immediate attitude to the world: it reduces space and time to a common denominator and degrades time to the dimension of space.

Marx puts it thus:

> Through the subordination of man to the machine the situation arises in which men are effaced by their labour; in which the pendulum of the clock has become as accurate a measure of the relative activity of two workers as it is of the speed of two locomotives. Therefore, we should not say that one man's hour is worth another man's hour, but rather that one man during an hour is worth just as much as another man during an hour. Time is everything, man is nothing; he is at the most the incarnation of time. Quality no longer matters. Quantity alone decides everything: hour for hour, day for day. . . .[12]

Thus time sheds its qualitative, variable, flowing nature; it freezes into an exactly delimited, quantifiable continuum filled with quantifiable "things" (the reified, mechanically objectified "performance" of the worker, wholly separated from his total human personality): in short, it becomes space.[13] In this environment where time is transformed into abstract, exactly measurable, physical space, an environment at once the cause and effect of the scientifically and mechanically fragmented and specialized production of the object of labor, the subjects of labor must likewise be rationally fragmented. On the one hand, the objectification of their labor-power into something opposed to their total pesonality (a process already accomplished with the sale of that labor-power as a commodity) is now made into the permanent ineluctable reality of their daily life. Here, too, the personality can do no more than look on helplessly while its own existence is reduced to an isolated particle and fed into an alien system. On the other hand, the mechanical disintegration of the process of production into its components also destroys those bonds that had bound individuals to a community in the days when production was still "organic." In this respect, too, mechanization makes of them isolated abstract atoms whose work no longer brings them together directly and organically; it becomes mediated to an increasing extent exclusively by the abstract laws of the mechanism which imprisons them.

The internal organization of a factory could not possibly have such an effect—even within the factory itself—were it not for the fact that it contained in concentrated form the whole structure of capitalist society. Oppression and an exploitation that knows no bounds and scorns every human dignity were known even to precapitalist ages. So too was mass production with mechanical, standardized labor, as we can see, for instance, with canal construction in Egypt and Asia Minor and the mines in Rome.[14] But mass projects of this type could never be *rationally mechanized;* they remained isolated phenomena within a community that organized its production on a different ("natural") basis and which therefore lived a different life. The slaves subjected to this exploitation, therefore, stood outside what was thought of as "human" society and even the greatest and noblest thinkers of the time were unable to consider their fate as that of human beings.

As the commodity becomes universally dominant, this situation changes radically and qualitatively. The fate of the worker becomes the fate of society as a whole; indeed, this fate must become universal as otherwise industrialization could not develop in this direction. For it depends on the emergence of the "free" worker who is freely able to take his labor-power to market and offer it for sale as a commodity "belonging" to him, a thing that he "possesses."

While this process is still incomplete the methods used to extract surplus labor are, it is true, more obviously brutal than in the later, more highly developed phase, but the process of reification of work and hence also of the consciousness of the worker is much less advanced. Reification requires that a society should learn to satisfy all its needs in terms of commodity exchange. The separation of the producer from his means of production, the dissolution and destruction of all "natural" production units, etc., and all the social and economic conditions necessary for the emergence of modern capitalism tend to replace "natural" relations which exhibit human relations more plainly by rationally reified relations. "The social relations between individuals in the performance of their labour," Marx observes with reference to precapitalist societies, "appear at all events as their own personal relations, and are not disguised under the shape of social relations between the products of labour."[15]

But this implies that the principle of rational mechanization and calculability must embrace every aspect of life. Consumer articles no longer appear as the products of an organic process within a community (as for example in a village community). They now appear, on the one hand, as abstract members of a species identical by definition with its other members and, on the other hand, as isolated objects the possession or non-possession of which depends on rational calculations. Only when the whole life of society is thus fragmented into the isolated acts of commodity exchange can the "free" worker come into being; at the same time his fate becomes the typical fate of the whole society.

Of course, this isolation and fragmentation is only apparent. The movement of commodities on the market, the birth of their value, in a word, the real framework of every rational calculation is not merely subject to strict laws but also presupposes the strict ordering of all that happens. The atomization of the individual is, then, only the reflex in consciousness of the fact that the "natural laws" of capitalist production have been extended to cover every manifestation of life in society; that—for the first time in history—the whole of society is subjected, or tends to be subjected, to a unified economic process, and that the fate of every member of society is determined by unified laws. (By contrast, the organic unities of precapitalist societies organized their metabolism largely in independence of each other).

However, if this atomization is only an illusion it is a necessary one. That is to say, the immediate, practical as well as intellectual confrontation of the individual with society, the immediate production and reproduction of life—in which for the individual the commodity structure of all "things" and their obedience to "natural laws" is found to exist already in a finished form, as something immutably given—could only take place in the form of rational and isolated acts of exchange between isolated commodity owners. As emphasized above, the worker, too, must present himself as the "owner" of his labor-power, as if it were a commodity. His specific situation is defined by the fact that his labor-power is his only possession. His fate is typical of society as a whole in that this self-objectification, this transformation of a human function into a commodity reveals in all its starkness the dehumanized and dehumanizing function of the commodity relation.

2

This rational objectification conceals above all the immediate—qualitative and material—character of things as things. When use-values appear universally as commodities they acquire a new objectivity, a new substantiality which they did not possess in an age of episodic exchange and which destroys their original and authentic substantiality. As Marx observes:

> Private property *alienates* not only the individuality of men, but also of things. The ground and the earth have nothing to do with ground-rent, machines have nothing to do with profit. For the landowner ground and earth mean nothing but ground-rent; he lets his land to tenants and receives the rent—a quality which the ground can lose without losing any of its inherent qualities such as its fertility; it is a quality whose magnitude and indeed existence depends on social relations that are created and abolished without any intervention by the landowner. Likewise with the machine.[16]

Thus even the individual object which man confronts directly, either as producer or consumer, is distorted in its objectivity by its commodity character. If that can happen then it is evident that this process will be intensified in proportion as the relations which man establishes with objects as objects of the life process are mediated in the course of his social activity. It is obviously not possible here to give an analysis of the whole economic structure of capitalism. It must suffice to point out that modern capitalism does not content itself with transforming the relations of production in accordance with its own needs. It also integrates into its own system those forms of primitive capitalism that led an isolated existence in precapitalist times, divorced from production; it converts them into members of the henceforth unified process of radical capitalism. (Cf. merchant capital, the role of money as a hoard or as finance capital, etc.)

These forms of capital are objectively subordinated, it is true, to the real life-process of capitalism, the extraction of surplus value in the course of production. They are, therefore, only to be explained in terms of the nature of industrial capitalism itself. But in the minds of people in bourgeois society they constitute the pure, authentic, unadulterated forms of capital. In them the relations between men that lie hidden in the immediate commodity relation, as well as the relations between men and the objects that should really gratify their needs, have faded to the point where they can be neither recognized nor even perceived.

For that very reason the reified mind has come to regard them as the true representatives of his societal existence. The commodity character of the commodity, the abstract, quantitative mode of calculability shows itself here in its purest form: the reified mind necessarily sees it as the form in which its own authentic immediacy becomes manifest and—as reified consciousness—does not even attempt to transcend it. On the contrary, it is concerned to make it permanent by "scientifically deepening" the laws at work. Just as the capitalist system continuously produces and reproduces itself economically on higher and higher levels, the structure of reification progressively sinks more deeply, more fatefully and more definitively into the consciousness of man. Marx often describes this potentiation of reification in incisive fashion. One example must suffice here:

> In interest-bearing capital, therefore, this automatic fetish, self-expanding value, money generating money, is brought out in its pure state and in this form it no longer bears the birth-marks of its origin. The social relation is consummated in the relation of a thing, of money, to itself. Instead of the actual transformation of money into capital, we see here only form without content. . . . It becomes a property of money to generate value and yield interest, much as it is an attribute of pear trees to bear pears. And the money-lender sells his money as just such an interest-bearing thing. But that is not all. The actually functioning capital, as we have seen, presents itself in such a light that it seems to yield interest not as functioning capital, but as capital in itself, as money-capital. This, too, becomes distorted. While interest is only a portion of the profit, i.e. of the surplus value, which the functioning capitalist squeezes out of the labourer, it appears now, on the contrary, as though interest were the typical product of capital, the primary matter, and profit, in the shape of profit of enterprise, were a mere accessory and by-product of the process of reproduction. Thus we get a fetish form of capital, and the conception of fetish capital. In M-M′ we have the meaningless form of capital, the perversion and objectification of production relations in their highest degree, the interest-bearing form, the simple form of capital, in which it antecedes its own process of reproduction. It is the capacity of money, or of a commodity, to expand its own value independently of reproduction—which is a mystification of capital in its most flagrant form. For vulgar political economy, which seeks to represent capital as an independent source of value, of value creation, this

> form is naturally a veritable find, a form in which the source of profit is no longer discernible, and in which the result of the capitalist process of production—divorced from the process—acquires an independent existence.[17]

Just as the economic theory of capitalism remains stuck fast in its self-created immediacy, the same thing happens to bourgeois attempts to comprehend the ideological phenomenon of reification. Even thinkers who have no desire to deny or obscure its existence and who are more or less clear in their own minds about its humanly destructive consequences remain on the surface and make no attempt to advance beyond its objectively most derivative forms, the forms furthest from the real life-process of capitalism, i.e., the most external and vacuous forms, to the basic phenomenon of reification itself.

Indeed, they divorce these empty manifestations from their real capitalist foundation and make them independent and permanent by regarding them as the timeless model of human relations in general. (This can be seen most clearly in Simmel's book, *The Philosophy of Money,* a very interesting and perceptive work in matters of detail.) They offer no more than a description of this "enchanted, perverted, topsy-turvy world, in which Monsieur Le Capital and Madame La Terre do their ghost-walking as social characters and at the same time as mere things."[18] But they do not go further than a description and their "deepening" of the problem runs in circles around the eternal manifestations of reification.

The divorce of the phenomena of reification from their economic bases and from the vantage point from which alone they can be understood is facilitated by the fact that the [capitalist] process of transformation must embrace every manifestation of the life of society if the preconditions for the complete self-realization of capitalist production are to be fulfilled.

Thus capitalism has created a form for the state and a system of law corresponding to its needs and harmonizing with its own structure. The structural similarity is so great that no truly perceptive historian of modern capitalism could fail to notice it. Max Weber, for instance, gives this description of the basic lines of this development:

> Both are, rather, quite similar in their fundamental nature. Viewed sociologically, a "business-concern" is the modern state; the same holds good for a factory: and this, precisely, is what is specific to it historically. And, likewise, the power relations in a business are also of the same kind. The relative independence of the artisan (or cottage craftsman), of the land-owning peasant, the owner of a benefice, the knight and vassal was based on the fact that he himself owned the tools, supplies, financial resources

> or weapons with the aid of which he fulfilled his economic, political or military function and from which he lived while this duty was being discharged. Similarly, the hierarchic dependence of the worker, the clerk, the technical assistant, the assistant in an academic institute *and* the civil servant and soldier has a comparable basis: namely that the tools, supplies and financial resources essential both for the business-concern and for economic survival are in the hands, in the one case, of the entrepreneur and, in the other case, of the political master.[19]

He rounds off this account—very pertinently—with an analysis of the cause and the social implications of this phenomenon:

> The modern capitalist concern is based inwardly above all on *calculation*. It requires for its survival a system of justice and an administration whose workings can be *rationally calculated,* at least in principle, according to fixed general laws, just as the probable performance of *a machine* can be calculated. It is as little able to tolerate the dispensing of justice according to the judge's sense of fair play *in individual cases* or any other irrational means or principles of administering the law . . . as it is able to endure a patriarchal administration that obeys the dictates of its own caprice, or sense of mercy and, for the rest, proceeds in accordance with an inviolable and sacrosanct, but irrational tradition. . . . What is specific to modern capitalism as distinct from the age-old capitalist forms of acquisition is that the strictly rational *organisation of work* on the basis of *rational technology* did not come into being *anywhere* within such irrationally constituted political systems nor could it have done so. For these modern businesses with their fixed capital and their exact calculations are much too sensitive to legal and administrative irrationalities. They could only come into being in the bureaucratic state with its rational laws where . . . the judge is more or less an automatic statute-dispensing machine in which you insert the files together with the necessary costs and dues at the top, whereupon he will eject the judgment together with the more or less cogent reasons for it at the bottom: that is to say, where the judge's behaviour is on the whole *predictable*.

The process we see here is closely related both in its motivation and in its effects to the economic process outlined above. Here, too, there is a breach with the empirical and irrational methods of administration and dispensing justice based on traditions tailored, subjectively, to the requirements of men in action, and, objectively, to those of the concrete matter in hand. There arises a rational systematization of all statutes regulating life, which represents, or at least tends toward a closed system applicable to all possible and imaginable cases. Whether this system is arrived at in a purely logical manner, as an exercise in pure legal dogma or interpretation of the law, or whether the judge is given the task of filling the "gaps" left in the laws, is immaterial for our attempt to understand the *structure* of modern legal reality. In either case the legal system is formally capable of being generalized so as to relate to every possible situation in life and it is susceptible to prediction and calculation. Even Roman law, which comes closest to these developments while remaining, in modern terms, within the framework of precapitalist legal patterns, does not in this respect go beyond the empirical, the concrete and the traditional. The purely systematic categories which were necessary before a judicial system could become universally applicable arose only in modern times.[20]

It requires no further explanation to realize that the need to systematize and to abandon empiricism, tradition and material dependence was the need for exact calculation.[21] However, this same need requires that the legal system should confront the individual events of social existence as something permanently established and exactly defined, i.e., as a rigid system. Of course, this produces an uninterrupted series of conflicts between the unceasingly revolutionary forces of the capitalist economy and the rigid legal system. But this only results in new codifications; and despite these the new system is forced to preserve the fixed, change-resistant structure of the old system.

This is the source of the—apparently—paradoxical situation whereby the "law" of primitive societies, which has scarcely altered in hundreds or sometimes even thousands of years, can be flexible and irrational in character, renewing itself with every new legal decision, while modern law, caught up in the continuous turmoil of change, should appear rigid, static and fixed. But the paradox dissolves when we realize that it arises only because the same situation has been regarded from two different points of view: on the one hand, from that of the historian (who stands "outside" the actual process) and, on the other hand, from that of someone who experiences the effects of the social order in question upon his consciousness.

With the aid of this insight we can see clearly how the antagonism between the traditional and empirical craftsmanship and the scientific and rational factory is repeated in another sphere of activity. At every single stage of its development, the ceaselessly revolutionary techniques of modern production turn a rigid and immobile face toward the individual producer. Whereas the objectively relatively stable, traditional craft production preserves in the minds of its individual practitioners the appearance of something flexible, something constantly renewing itself, something produced by the producers.

In the process we witness, illuminatingly, how here, too, the *contemplative* nature of man under capitalism makes its appearance. For the essence of rational calculation is based ultimately upon the recognition and the inclusion in one's calculations of the inevitable chain of cause and effect in certain events—independently of individual "caprice." In consequence, man's activity does not go beyond the correct calculation of the possible outcome of the sequence of events (the "laws" of which he finds "ready-made"), and beyond the adroit evasion of disruptive "accidents" by means of protective devices and preventive measures (which are based in their turn on the recognition and application of similar laws). Very often it will confine itself to working out the probable effects of such "laws" without making the attempt to intervene in the process by bringing other "laws" to bear (as in insurance schemes, etc.).

The more closely we scrutinize this situation and the better we are able to close our minds to the bourgeois legends of the "creativity" of the exponents of the capitalist age, the more obvious it becomes that we are witnessing in all behavior of this sort the structural analogue to the behavior of the worker vis-à-vis the machine he serves and observes, and whose functions he controls while he contemplates it. The "creative" element can be seen to depend at best on whether these "laws" are applied in a—relatively—independent way or in a wholly subservient one. That is to say, it depends on the degree to which the contemplative stance is repudiated. The distinction between a worker faced with a particular machine, the entrepreneur faced with a given type of mechanical development, the technologist faced with the state of science and the profitability of its application to the state of science and the profitability of its application to technology, is purely quantitative; it does not directly entail *any qualitative difference in the structure of consciousness*.

Only in this context can the problem of modern bureaucracy be properly understood. Bureaucracy implies the adjustment of one's way of life, mode of work and hence of consciousness, to the general socioeconomic premises of the capitalist economy, similar to that which we have observed in the case of the worker in particular business concerns. The formal standardization of justice, the state, the civil service, etc., signifies objectively and factually a comparable reduction of all social functions to their elements, a comparable search for the rational formal laws of these carefully segregated partial systems. Subjectively, the divorce between work and the individual capacities and needs of the worker produces comparable effects upon consciousness. This results in an inhuman, standardized division of labor analogous to that which we have found in industry on the technological and mechanical plane.[22]

It is not only a question of the completely mechanical, "mindless" work of the lower echelons of the bureaucracy which bears such an extraordinarily close resemblance to operating a machine and which indeed often surpasses it in sterility and uniformity. It is also a question, on the one hand, of the way in which objectively all issues are subjected to an increasingly *formal* and standardized treatment and in which there is an ever-increasing remoteness from the qualitative and material essence of the "things" to which bureaucratic activity pertains. On the other hand, there is an even more monstrous intensification of the one-sided specialization which represents such a violation of man's humanity. Marx's comment on factory work that "the individual, himself divided, is transformed into the automatic mechanism of a partial labour" and is thus "crippled to the point of abnormality" is relevant here too. And it becomes all the more clear, the more elevated, advanced and "intellectual" is the attainment exacted by the division of labor.

The split between the worker's labor-power and his personality, its metamorphosis into a thing, an object that he sells on the market is repeated here too. But with the difference that not every mental faculty is suppressed by mechanization; only one faculty (or complex of faculties) is detached from the whole personality and placed in opposition to it, becoming a thing, a commodity. But the basic phenomenon remains the same even though both the means by which society instills such abilities and their material and "moral" exchange value are fundamentally different from labor-power (not forgetting, of course, the many connecting links and nuances).

The specific type of bureaucratic "conscientiousness" and impartiality, the individual bureaucrat's inevitable total subjection to a system of relations between the things to which he is exposed, the idea that it is precisely his "honor" and his "sense of responsibility" that exact this total submission,[23] all this points to the fact that the division of labor which in the case of Taylorism invaded the psyche, here invades the realm of ethics. Far from weakening the reified structure of consciousness, this actually strengthens it. For as long as the fate of the worker still appears to be an individual fate (as in the case of the slave in antiquity), the life of the ruling classes is still free to assume quite different forms. Not until the rise of capitalism was a unified economic structure, and hence a—formally—unified structure of consciousness that embraced the whole society, brought into being. This unity expressed itself in the fact that the problems of consciousness arising from wage-labor were repeated in the ruling class in a refined and spiritualized, but, for that very reason, more intensified form. The specialized "virtuoso," the vendor of his objectified and reified faculties does not just become the [passive] observer of society; he also lapses into a contemplative attitude vis-à-vis the workings of his own objectified and reified faculties. (It is not possible here even to outline the way in which modern administration and law assume the characteristics of the factory as we noted above rather than those of the handicrafts.) This phenomenon can be seen at its most grotesque in journalism. Here it is precisely subjectivity itself, knowledge, temperament and powers of expression that are reduced both from the personality of their "owner" and from the material and concrete nature of the subject matter in hand. The journalist's "lack of convictions," the prostitution of his experiences and beliefs is comprehensible only as the apogee of capitalist reification.[24]

The transformation of the commodity relation into a thing of "ghostly objectivity" cannot therefore content itself with the reduction of all objects for the gratification of human needs to commodities. It stamps its imprint upon the whole consciousness of man; his qualities and abilities are no longer an organic part of his personality, they are things which he can "own" or "dispose of" like the various objects of the external world. And there is no natural form in which human relations can be cast, no way in which man can bring his physical and psychic "qualities" into play without their being subjected increasingly to this reifying process. We need only think of marriage, and without troubling to point to the developments of the nineteenth century we can remind ourselves of the way in which Kant, for example, described the situation with the naïvely cynical frankness peculiar to great thinkers.

"Sexual community," he says, "is the reciprocal use made by one person of the sexual organs and faculties of another . . . marriage . . . is the union of two people of different sexes with a view to the mutual possession of each other's sexual attributes for the duration of their lives."[25]

This rationalization of the world appears to be complete, it seems to penetrate the very depths of man's physical and psychic nature. It is limited, however, by its own formalism. That is to say, the rationalization of isolated aspects of life results in the creation of—formal—laws. All these things do join together into what seems to the superficial observer to constitute a unified system of general "laws." But the disregard of the concrete aspects of the subject matter of these laws, upon which disregard their authority as laws is based, makes itself felt in the incoherence of the system in fact. This incoherence becomes particularly egregious in periods of crisis. At such times we can see how the immediate continuity between two partial systems is disrupted and their independence from and adventitious connection with each other is suddenly forced into the consciousness of everyone. It is for this reason that Engels is able to define the "natural laws" of capitalist society as the laws of chance.[26]

On closer examination the structure of a crisis is seen to be no more than a heightening of the degree and intensity of the daily life of bourgeois society. In its unthinking, mundane reality *that* life seems firmly held together by "natural laws"; yet it can experience a sudden dislocation because the bonds uniting its various elements and partial systems are a chance affair even at their most normal. So that the pretence that society is regulated by "eternal, iron" laws which branch off into the different special laws applying to particular areas is finally revealed for what it is: a pretence. The true structure of society appears rather in the independent, rationalized and formal partial laws whose links with each other are of necessity purely formal (i.e., their formal interdependence can be formally systematized), while as far as concrete realities are concerned they can only establish fortuitous connections.

On closer inspection this kind of connection can be discovered even in purely economic phenomena. Thus Marx points out—and the cases referred to here are intended only as an indication of the methodological factors involved, not as a substantive treatment of the problems themselves—that "the conditions of direct exploitation [of the laborer], and those of realizing surplus-value, are not identical. They diverge not only in place and time, but also logically."[27] Thus there exists "an accidental rather than a necessary connection between the total amount of social labour applied to a social article" and "the volume whereby society seeks to satisfy the want gratified by the article in question."[28] These are no more than random instances. It is evident that the whole structure of capitalist production rests on the interaction between a necessity subject to strict laws in all isolated phenomena and the relative irrationality of the total process. "Division of labour within the workshop implies the undisputed authority of the capitalist over men, who are but parts of a mechanism that belongs to him. The division of labour within society brings into contact independent commodity-producers who acknowledge no other authority than that of competition, of the coercion exerted by the pressure of their mutual interests."[29]

The capitalist process of rationalization based on private economic calculation requires that every manifestation of life shall exhibit this very interaction between details which are subject to laws and a totality ruled by chance. It presupposes a society so structured. It produces and reproduces this structure in so far as it takes possession of society. This has its foundation already in the nature of speculative calculation, i.e., the economic practice of commodity owners at the stage where the exchange of commodities has become universal. Competition between the different owners of commodities would not be feasible if there were an exact, rational, systematic mode of functioning for the whole of society to correspond to the rationality of isolated phenomena. If a rational calculation is to be possible the commodity owner must be in possession of the laws regulating every detail of his production. The chances of exploitation, the laws of the "market" must likewise be rational in the sense that they must be calculable according to the laws of probability. But they must not be governed by a law in the sense in which "laws" govern individual phenomena; they must not under any circumstances be rationally organized through and through. This does not mean, of course, that there can be no "law" governing the whole. But such a "law" would have to be the "unconscious" product of the activity of the different commodity owners acting independently of one another, i.e., a law of mutually interacting "coincidences" rather than one of truly rational organization. Furthermore, such a law must not merely impose itself despite the wishes of individuals, it may *not even be fully and adequately knowable*. For the complete knowledge of the whole would vouchsafe the knower a monopoly that would amount to the virtual abolition of the capitalist economy.

This irrationality, this—highly problematic—"systematization" of the whole which diverges *qualitatively and in principle* from the laws regulating the parts, is more than just a postulate, a presupposition essential to the workings of a capitalist economy. It is at the same time the product of the capitalist division of labor. It has already been pointed out that the division of labor disrupts every organically unified process of work and life and breaks it down into its components. This enables the artificially isolated partial functions to be performed in the most rational manner by "specialists" who are specially adapted mentally and physically for the purpose. This has the effect of making these partial functions autonomous and so they tend to develop through their own momentum and in accordance with their own special laws independently of the other partial functions of society (or that part of the society to which they belong).

As the division of labor becomes more pronounced and more rational, this tendency naturally increases in proportion. For the more highly developed it is, the more powerful become the claims to status and the professional interests of the "specialists" who are the living embodiments of such tendencies. And this centrifugal movement is not confined to aspects of a particular sector. It is even more in evidence when we consider the great spheres of activity created by the division of labor. Engels describes this process with regard to the relation between economics and laws: "Similarly with law. As soon as the new division of labour which creates *professional lawyers* becomes necessary, another new and independent sphere is opened up which, for all its essential dependence on production and trade, still has also a special capacity for reacting upon these spheres. In a modern state, law must not only correspond to the general economic condition and be its expression, but must also be an *internally coherent expression* which does not, owing to inner contradictions, reduce itself to nought. And in order to achieve this, the faithful reflection of economic conditions suffers increasingly. . . ."[30] It is hardly necessary to supplement this with examples of the inbreeding and the interdepartmental conflicts of the civil service (consider the independence of the military apparatus from the civil administration), or of the academic faculties, etc.

3

The specialization of skills leads to the destruction of every image of the whole. And as, despite this, the need to grasp the whole—at least cognitively—cannot die out, we find that science, which is likewise based on specialization and thus caught up in the same immediacy, is criticized for having torn the real world into shreds and having lost its vision of the whole. In reply to allegations that "the various factors are not treated as a whole" Marx retorts that this criticism is leveled "as though it were text-books that impress this separation upon life and not life upon the text-books."[31] Even though this criticism deserves refutation in its naïve form it becomes comprehensible when we look for a moment from the outside, i.e., from a vantage point other than that of a reified consciousness, at the activity of modern science which is both sociologically and methodologically necessary and for that reason "comprehensible." Such a look will reveal (without constituting a "criticism") that the more intricate a modern science becomes and the better it understands itself methodologically, the more resolutely it will turn its back on the ontological problems of its own sphere of influence and eliminate them from the realm where it has achieved some insight. The more highly developed it becomes and the more scientific, the more it will become a formally closed system of partial laws. It will then find that the world lying beyond its confines, and in particular the material base which it is its task to understand, *its own concrete underlying reality* lies, methodologically and in principle, *beyond its grasp*.

Marx acutely summed up this situation with reference to economics when he declared that "use-value as such lies outside the sphere of investigation of political economy."[32] It would be a mistake to suppose that certain analytical devices—such as we find in the "Theory of Marginal Utility"—might show the way out of this impasse. It is possible to set aside objective laws governing the production and movement of commodities which regulate the market and "subjective" modes of behavior on it and to make the attempt to start from "subjective" behavior on the market. But this simply shifts the question from the main issue to more and more derivative and reified stages without negating the formalism of the method and the elimination from the outset of the concrete material underlying it. The formal act of exchange which constitutes the basic fact for the theory of marginal utility likewise suppresses use-value as use-value and establishes a relation of concrete equality between concretely unequal and indeed incomparable objects. It is this that creates the impasse.

Thus the subject of the exchange is just as abstract, formal and reified as its object. The limits of this abstract and formal method are revealed in the fact that its chosen goal is an abstract system of "laws" that focuses on the theory of marginal utility just as much as classical economics had done. But the formal abstraction of these "laws" transform economics into a closed partial system. And this in turn is unable to penetrate its own material substratum, nor can it advance from there to an understanding of society in its entirety and so it is compelled to view that substratum as an immutable, eternal "datum." Science is thereby debarred from comprehending the development and the demise, the social character of its own material base, no less than the range of possible attitudes toward it and the nature of its own formal system.

Here, once again, we can clearly observe the close interaction between a class and the scientific method that arises from the attempt to conceptualize the social character of that class together with its laws and needs. It has often been pointed out—in these pages and elsewhere—that the problem that forms the ultimate barrier to the economic thought of the bourgeoisie is the crisis. If we now—in the full awareness of our own one-sidedness—consider this question from a purely methodological point of view, we see that it is the very success with which the economy is totally rationalized and transformed into an abstract and mathematically orientated system of formal "laws" that creates the methodological barrier to understanding the phenomenon of crisis. In moments of crisis the qualitative existence of the "things" that lead their lives beyond the purview of economics as misunderstood and neglected things-in-themselves, as use-values, suddenly becomes the decisive factor. (Suddenly, that is, for reified, rational thought.) Or rather: these "laws" fail to function and the reified mind is unable to perceive a pattern in this "chaos."

This failure is characteristic not merely of classical economics (which regarded crises as "passing," "accidental" disturbances), but of bourgeois economics in toto. The incomprehensibility and irrationality of crises is indeed a consequence of the class situation and interests of the bourgeoisie but it follows equally from their approach to economics. (There is no need to spell out the fact that for us these are both merely aspects of the same dialectical unity.) This consequence follows with such inevitability that Tugan-Baranovsky, for example, attempts in his theory to draw the necessary conclusions from a century of crises by excluding consumption from economics entirely and founding a "pure" economics based only on production. The source of crises (whose existence cannot be denied) is then found to lie in incongruities between the various elements of production, i.e., in purely quantitative factors. Hilferding puts his finger on the fallacy underlying all such explanations:

> They operate only with economic concepts such as capital, profit, accumulation, etc., and believe that they possess the solution to the problem when they have discovered the quantitative relations on the basis of which either simple and expanded reproduction is possible, or else there are disturbances. They overlook the fact that there are qualitative conditions attached to these quantitative relations, that it is not merely a question of units of value which can easily be compared with each other but also use-values of a definite kind which must fulfil a definite function in production and consumption. Further, they are oblivious of the fact that in the analysis of the process of reproduction more is involved than just aspects of capital in general, so that it is not enough to say that an excess or a deficit of industrial capital can be "balanced" by an appropriate amount of money-capital. Nor is it a matter of fixed or circulating capital, but rather of machines, raw materials, labour-power of a quite definite (technically defined) sort, if disruptions are to be avoided.[33]

Marx has often demonstrated convincingly how inadequate the "laws" of bourgeois economics are to the task of explaining the true movement of economic activity in toto. He has made it clear that this limitation lies in the—methodologically inevitable—failure to comprehend use-value and real consumption.

> Within certain limits, the process of reproduction may take place on the same or on an increased scale even when the commodities expelled from it have not really entered individual or productive consumption. The consumption of commodities is not included in the cycle of the capital from which they originated. For instance, as soon as the yarn is sold the cycle of the capital-value represented by the yarn may begin anew, regardless of

> what may next become of the sold yarn. So long as the product is sold, everything is taking its regular course from the standpoint of the capitalist producer. The cycle of the capital-value he is identified with is not interrupted. And if this process is expanded—which includes increased productive consumption of the means of production—this reproduction of capital may be accompanied by increased individual consumption (hence demand) on the part of the labourers, since this process is initiated and effected by productive consumption. Thus the production of surplus-value, and with it the individual consumption of the capitalist, may increase, the entire process of reproduction may be in a flourishing condition, and yet a large part of the commodities may have entered into consumption only in appearance, while in reality they may still remain unsold in the hands of dealers, may in fact still be lying in the market.[34]

It must be emphasized that this inability to penetrate to the real material substratum of science is not the fault of individuals. It is rather something that becomes all the more apparent the more science has advanced and the more consistently it functions—from the point of view of its own premises. It is therefore no accident, as Rosa Luxemburg has convincingly shown,[35] that the great, if also often primitive, faulty and inexact synoptic view of economic life to be found in Quesnay's "Tableau Economique," disappears progressively as the—formal—process of conceptualization becomes increasingly exact in the course of its development from Adam Smith to Ricardo. For Ricardo the process of the total reproduction of capital (where this problem cannot be avoided) is no longer a central issue.

In jurisprudence this situation emerges with even greater clarity and simplicity—because there is a more conscious reification at work. If only because the question of whether the qualitative content can be understood by means of a rational, calculating approach is no longer seen in terms of a rivalry between two principles within the same sphere (as was the case with use-value and exchange value in economics), but rather, right from the start, as a question of form versus content. The conflict revolving around natural law, and the whole revolutionary period of the bourgeoisie was based on the assumption that the formal equality and universality of the law (and hence its rationality) was able at the same time to determine its content. This was expressed in the assault on the varied and picturesque medley of privileges dating back to the Middle Ages and also in the attack on the Divine Right of Kings. The revolutionary bourgeois class refused to admit that a legal relationship had a *valid* foundation merely because it existed *in fact*. "Burn your laws and make new ones!" Voltaire counseled; "Whence can new laws be obtained? From Reason!"[36]

The war waged against the revolutionary bourgeoisie, say, at the time of the French Revolution, was dominated to such an extent by this idea that it was inevitable that the natural law of the bourgeoisie could only be opposed by yet another natural law (see Burke and also Stahl). Only after the bourgeoisie had gained at least a partial victory did a "critical" and a "historical" view begin to emerge in both camps. Its essence can be summarized as the belief that the content of law is something purely factual and hence not to be comprehended by the formal categories of jurisprudence. Of the tenets of natural law the only one to survive was the idea of the unbroken continuity of the formal system of law; significantly, Bergbohm uses an image borrowed from physics, that of a "juridical vacuum," to describe everything not regulated by law.[37]

Nevertheless, the cohesion of these laws is purely formal: *what* they express, "the content of legal institutions is never of a legal character, but always political and economic."[38] With this the primitive, cynically skeptical campaign against natural law that was launched by the "Kantian" Hugo at the end of the eighteenth century, acquired "scientific" status. Hugo established the juridical basis of slavery, among other things, by arguing that it "had been the law of the land for thousands of years and was acknowledged by millions of cultivated people."[39] In this naïvely cynical frankness the pattern which is to become increasingly characteristic of law in bourgeois society stands clearly revealed. When Jellinek describes the contents of law as metajuristic, when "critical" jurists locate the study of the contents of law in history, sociology and politics what they are doing is, in the last analysis, just what Hugo had demanded: they are systematically abandoning the attempt to ground law in reason and to give it a rational content; law is henceforth to be regarded as a formal calculus with the aid of which the legal consequences of particular actions (*rebus sic stantibus*) can be determined as exactly as possible.

However, this view transforms the process by which law comes into being and passes away into something as incomprehensible to the jurist as crises had been to the political economist. With regard to the origins of law the perceptive "critical" jurist Kelsen observes: "It is the great *mystery* of law and of the state that is consummated with the enactment of laws and for this reason it may be permissible to employ inadequate images in elucidating its nature."[40] Or in other words: "It is symptomatic of the nature of law that a norm may be legitimate even if its origins are iniquitous. That is another way of saying that the legitimate origin of a law cannot be written into the concept of law as one of its conditions."[41] This epistemological clarification could also be a factual one and could thereby lead to an advance in knowledge. To achieve this, however, the other disciplines into which the problem of the origins of law had been diverted would really have to propose a genuine solution to it. But also it would be essential really to penetrate the nature of a legal system which serves purely as a means of calculating the effects of actions and of rationally imposing modes of action relevant to a particular class. In that event the real, material substratum of the law would at one stroke become visible and comprehensible. But neither condition can be fulfilled. The law maintains its close relationship with the "eternal values." This gives birth, in the shape of a philosophy of law to an impoverished and formalistic reedition of natural law (Stammler). Meanwhile, the real basis for the development of law, a change in the power relations between the classes, becomes hazy and vanishes into the sciences that study it, sciences which—in conformity with the modes of thought current in bourgeois society—generate the same problems of transcending their material substratum as we have seen in jurisprudence and economics.

The manner in which this transcendence is conceived shows how vain was the hope that a comprehensive discipline, like philosophy, might yet achieve that overall knowledge which the particular sciences have so conspicuously renounced by turning away from the material substratum of their conceptual apparatus. Such a synthesis would only be possible if philosophy were able to change its approach radically and concentrate on the concrete material totality of what can and should be known. Only then would it be able to break through the barriers erected by a formalism that has degenerated into a state of complete fragmentation. But this would presuppose an awareness of the causes, the genesis and the necessity of this formalism; moreover, it would not be enough to unite the special sciences mechanically: they would have to be transformed inwardly by an inwardly synthesizing philosophical method. It is evident that the philosophy of bourgeois society is incapable of this. Not that the desire for synthesis is absent; nor can it be maintained that the best people have welcomed with open arms a mechanical existence hostile to life and a scientific formalism alien to it. *But a radical change in outlook is not feasible on the soil of bourgeois society*. Philosophy can attempt to assemble the whole of knowledge encyclopaedically (see Wundt). Or it may radically question the value of formal knowledge for a "living life" (see irrationalist philosophies from Hamann to Bergson). But these episodic trends lie to one side of the main philosophical tradition. The latter acknowledges as given and necessary the results and achievements of the special sciences and assigns to philosophy the task of exhibiting and justifying the grounds for regarding as valid the concepts so constructed.

Thus philosophy stands in the same relation to the special sciences as they do with respect to empirical reality. The formalistic conceptualization of the special sciences becomes for philosophy an immutably given substratum and this signals the final and despairing renunciation of every attempt to cast light on the reification that lies at the root of this formalism. The reified world appears henceforth quite definitively—and in philosophy, under the spotlight of "criticism" it is potentiated still further—as the only possible world, the only conceptually accessible, comprehensible world vouchsafed to us humans. Whether this gives rise to ecstasy, resignation or despair, whether we search for a path leading to "life" via irrational mystical experience, this will do absolutely nothing to modify the situation as it is in fact.

By confining itself to the study of the "possible conditions" of the validity of the forms in which its underlying existence is manifested, modern bourgeois thought bars its own way to a clear view of the problems bearing on the birth and death of these forms, and on their real essence and substratum. Its perspicacity finds itself increasingly in the situation of that legendary "critic" in India who was confronted with the ancient story according to which the world rests upon an elephant. He unleashed the "critical" question: upon what does the elephant rest? On receiving the answer that the elephant stands on a tortoise "criticism" declared itself satisfied. It is obvious that even if he had continued to press apparently "critical" questions, he could only have elicited a third miraculous animal. He would not have been able to discover the solution to the real question.

. . . . .

III. The Standpoint of the Proletariat

. . . . .

The desire to leave behind the immediacy of empirical reality and its no less immediate rationalist reflections must not be allowed to become an attempt to abandon immanent (social) reality. The price of such a false process of transcendence would be the reinstating and perpetuating of empirical reality with all its insoluble questions, but this time in a philosophically sublimated way. But in fact, to leave empirical reality behind can only mean that the objects of the empirical world are to be understood as aspects of a totality, i.e., as the aspects of a total social situation caught up in the process of historical change. Thus the category of mediation is a lever with which to overcome the mere immediacy of the empirical world and as such it is not something (subjective) foisted on to the objects from outside, it is no value-judgment or "ought" opposed to their "is." *It is rather the manifestation of their authentic objective structure.* This can only become apparent in the visible objects of consciousness when the false attitude of bourgeois thought to objective reality has been abandoned. Mediation would not be possible were it not for the fact that the empirical existence of objects is itself mediated and only appears to be unmediated in so far as the awareness of mediation is lacking so that the objects are torn from the complex of their true determinants and placed in artificial isolation.[42]

Moreover, it must be borne in mind that the process by which the objects are isolated is not the product of chance or caprice. When true knowledge does away with the false separation of objects (and the even falser connections established by unmediated abstractions) it does much more than merely correct a false or inadequate scientific method or substitute a superior hypothesis for a defective one. It is just as characteristic of the social reality of the present that its objective form should be subjected to this kind of intellectual treatment as it is that the objective starting-point of such treatment should have been chosen. If, then, the standpoint of the proletariat is opposed to that of the bourgeoisie, it is nonetheless true that proletarian thought does not require a tabula rasa, a new start to the task of comprehending reality and one without any preconceptions. In this it is unlike the thought of the bourgeoisie with regard to the medieval forms of feudalism—at least in its basic tendencies. Just because its practical goal is the *fundamental* transformation of the whole of society it conceives of bourgeois society together with its intellectual and artistic productions as the *point of departure* for its own method.

The methodological function of the categories of mediation consists in the fact that with their aid those immanent meanings that necessarily inhere in the objects of bourgeois society but which are absent from the immediate manifestation of those objects as well as from their mental reflection in bourgeois thought, now become objectively effective and can therefore enter the consciousness of the proletariat. That is to say, if the bourgeoisie is held fast in the mire of immediacy from which the proletariat is able to extricate itself, this is neither purely accidental nor a purely theoretical scientific problem. The distance between these two theoretical positions is an expression of the differences between the social existence of the two classes.

Of course, the knowledge yielded by the standpoint of the proletariat stands on a higher scientific plane objectively; it does after all apply a method that makes possible the solution of problems which the greatest thinkers of the bourgeois era have vainly struggled to find and in its substance, it provides the adequate historical analysis of capitalism which must remain beyond the grasp of bourgeois thinkers. However, this attempt to grade the methods objectively in terms of their value to knowledge is itself a social and historical problem, an inevitable result of the types of society represented by the two classes and their place in history. It implies that the "falseness" and the "one-sidedness" of the bourgeois view of history must be seen as a necessary factor in the systematic acquisition of knowledge about society.[43]

But also, it appears that every method is necessarily implicated in the existence of the relevant class. For the bourgeoisie, method arises directly from its social existence and this means that mere immediacy adheres to its thought, constituting its outermost barrier, one that cannot be crossed. In contrast to this the proletariat is confronted by the need to break through this barrier, to overcome it inwardly *from the very start* by adopting its own point of view. And as it is the nature of the dialectical method constantly to produce and reproduce its own essential aspects, as its very being constitutes the denial of any smooth, linear development of ideas, the proletariat finds itself *repeatedly* confronted with the problem of its own point of departure both in its efforts to increase its theoretical grasp of reality and to initiate practical historical measures. For the proletariat the barrier imposed by immediacy has become an inward barrier. With this the problem becomes clear; by putting the problem in this way the road to a possible answer is opened up.[44]

But it is no more than a possible answer. The proposition with which we began, viz., that in capitalist society reality is—immediately—the same for both the bourgeoisie and the proletariat, remains unaltered. But we may now add that this same reality employs the motor of class interests to keep the bourgeoisie imprisoned within this immediacy while forcing the proletariat to go beyond it. For the social existence of the proletariat is far more powerfully affected by the dialectical character of the historical process in which the mediated character of every factor receives the imprint of truth and authentic objectivity only in the mediated totality. For the proletariat to become aware of the dialectical nature of its existence is a matter of life and death, whereas the bourgeoisie uses the abstract categories of reflection, such as quantity and infinite progression, to conceal the dialectical structure of the historical process in daily life only to be confronted by unmediated catastrophes when the pattern is reversed. This is based—as we have shown—on the fact that the bourgeoisie always perceives the subject and object of the historical process and of social reality in a double form: in terms of his consciousness the single individual is a perceiving subject confronting the overwhelming objective necessities imposed by society of which only minute fragments can be comprehended. But in reality it is precisely the conscious activity of the individual that is to be found on the object-side of the process, while the subject (the class) cannot be awakened into consciousness and this activity must always remain beyond the consciousness of the—apparent—subject, the individual.

Thus we find the subject and object of the social process coexisting in a state of dialectical interaction. But as they always appear to exist in a rigidly twofold form, each external to the other, the dialectics remain unconscious and the objects retain their twofold and hence rigid character. This rigidity can only be broken by catastrophe and it then makes way for an equally rigid structure. This unconscious dialectic which is for that very reason unmanageable "breaks forth in their confession of naïve surprise, when what they have just thought to have defined with great difficulty as a thing suddenly appears as a social relation and then reappears to tease them again as a thing, before they have barely managed to define it as a social relation."[45]

For the proletariat social reality does not exist in this double form. It appears in the first instance as the pure *object* of societal events. In every aspect of daily life in which the individual worker imagines himself to be the subject of his own life he finds this to be an illusion that is destroyed by the immediacy of his existence. This forces upon him the knowledge that the most elementary gratification of his needs, "his own individual consumption, whether it proceed within the workshop or outside it, whether it be part of the process of reproduction or not, forms therefore an aspect of the production and the reproduction of capital; just as cleaning machinery does, whether it be done while the machinery is working or while it is standing idle."[46] The quantification of objects, their subordination to abstract mental categories makes its appearance in the life of the worker immediately as a process of abstraction of which he is the victim, and which cuts him off from his labor-power, forcing him to sell it on the market as a commodity, belonging to him. And by selling this, his only commodity, he integrates it (and himself: for his commodity is inseparable from his physical existence) into a specialized process that has been rationalized and mechanized, a process that he discovers already existing, complete and able to function without him and in which he is no more than a cipher reduced to an abstract quantity, a mechanized and rationalized tool.

Thus for the worker the reified character of the immediate manifestations of capitalist society receives the most extreme definition possible. It is true: for the capitalist also there is the same doubling of personality, the same splitting up of man into an element of the movement of commodities and an (objective and impotent) observer of that movement.[47] But for his consciousness it necessarily appears as an activity (albeit this activity is objectively an illusion), in which effects emanate from himself. This illusion blinds him to the true state of affairs, whereas the worker, who is denied the scope for such illusory activity, perceives the split in his being preserved in the brutal form of what is in its whole tendency a slavery without limits. He is therefore forced into becoming the object of the process by which he is turned into a commodity and reduced to a mere quantity.

But this very fact forces him to surpass the immediacy of his condition. For as Marx says, "Time is the place of human development."[48] The quantitative differences in exploitation which appear to the capitalist in the form of quantitative determinants of the objects of his calculation, must appear to the worker as the decisive, qualitative categories of his whole physical, mental and moral existence. The transformation of quantity into quality is not only a particular aspect of the dialectical process of development, as Hegel represents it in his philosophy of nature and, following him, Engels in the *Anti-Dühring*. But going beyond that, as we have just shown with the aid of Hegel's *Logic,* it means the emergence of the truly objective form of existence and the destruction of those confusing categories of reflection which had deformed true objectivity into a posture of merely immediate, passive, contemplation.

Above all, as far as labor-time is concerned, it becomes abundantly clear that quantification is a reified and reifying cloak spread over the true essence of the objects and can only be regarded as an objective form of reality inasmuch as the subject is uninterested in the essence of the object to which it stands in a contemplative or (seemingly) practical relationship. When Engels illustrates the transformation of quantity into quality by pointing to the example of water changing into solid or gaseous form[49] he is in the right so far as these points of transition are concerned. But this ignores the fact that when the point of view is changed even the transitions that had seemed to be purely quantitative now become qualitative. (To give an extremely trivial example, consider what happens when water is drunk; there is here a point at which "quantitative" changes take on a qualitative nature.) The position is even clearer when we consider the example Engels gives from *Capital*. The point under discussion is the amount needed at a particular stage of production to transform a given sum into capital; Marx observes that it is at this point that quantity is changed into quality.[50]

Let us now compare these two series (the growth or reduction in the sum of money and the increase or decrease in labor-time) and examine their possible quantitative changes and their transformation into quality. We note that in the first case we are in fact confronted only by what Hegel calls a "knotted line of proportional relations." Whereas in the second case *every* change is one of quality in its innermost nature and although its quantitative appearance is forced on to the worker by his social environment, its essence for him lies in its qualitative implications. This second aspect of the change obviously has its origin in the fact that for the worker labor-time is not merely the objective form of the commodity he has sold, i.e., his labor-power (for in that form the problem for him, too, is one of the exchange of equivalents, i.e., a quantitative matter). But in addition it is the determining form of his existence as subject, as human being.

This does not mean that immediacy together with its consequences for theory, namely the rigid opposition of subject and object, can be regarded as having been wholly overcome. It is true that in the problem of labor-time, just because it shows reification at its zenith, we can see how proletarian thought is necessarily driven to surpass this immediacy. For, on the one hand, in his social existence the worker is immediately placed *wholly* on the side of the object: he appears to himself immediately as an object and not as the active part of the social process of labor. On the other hand, however, the role of object is no longer purely immediate. That is to say, it is true that the worker is objectively transformed into a mere object of the process of production by the methods of capitalist production (in contrast to those of slavery and servitude), i.e., by the fact that the worker is forced to objectify his labor-power over against his total personality and to sell it as a commodity. But because of the split between subjectivity and objectivity induced in man by the compulsion to objectify himself as a commodity, the situation becomes one that can be made conscious. In earlier, more organic forms of society, work is defined "as the direct function of a member of the social organism":[51] in slavery and servitude the ruling powers appear as the "immediate mainsprings of the production process" and this prevents laborers enmeshed in such a situation with their personalities undivided from achieving clarity about their social position. By contrast, "work which is represented as exchange value has for its premise the work of the isolated individual. It becomes social by assuming the form of its immediate antithesis, the form of abstract universality."

We can already see here more clearly and concretely the factors that create a dialectic between the social existence of the worker and the forms of his consciousness and force them out of their pure immediacy. Above all the worker can only become conscious of his existence in society when he becomes aware of himself as a commodity. As we have seen, his immediate existence integrates him as a pure, naked object into the production process. Once this immediacy turns out to be the consequence of a multiplicity of mediations, once it becomes evident how much it presupposes, then the fetishistic forms of the commodity system begin to dissolve: in the commodity the worker recognizes himself and his own relations with capital. Inasmuch as he is incapable in practice of raising himself above the role of object his consciousness is the *self-consciousness of the commodity;* or in other words it is the self-knowledge, the self-revelation of the capitalist society founded upon the production and exchange of commodities.

By adding self-consciousness to the commodity structure a new element is introduced, one that is different in principle and in quality from what is normally described as consciousness "of" an object. Not just because it is a matter of self-consciousness. For, as in the science of psychology, this might very well be consciousness "of" an object, one which without modifying the way in which consciousness and object are related and thus without changing the knowledge so attained, might still "accidentally" choose itself for an object. From this it would follow that knowledge acquired in this way must have the same truth-criteria as in the case of knowledge of "other" objects. Even when in antiquity a slave, an *instrumentum vocale,* becomes conscious of himself as a slave this is not self-knowledge in the sense we mean here: for he can only attain to knowledge of an object which happens "accidentally" to be himself. Between a "thinking" slave and an "unconscious" slave there is no real distinction to be drawn in an objective social sense. No more than there is between the possibility of a slave's becoming conscious of his own social situation and that of a "free" man's achieving an understanding of slavery. The rigid epistemological doubling of subject and object remains unaffected and hence the perceiving subject fails to impinge upon the structure of the object despite his adequate understanding of it.

In contrast with this, when the worker knows himself as a commodity his knowledge is practical. *That is to say, this knowledge brings about an objective structural change in the object of knowledge.* In this consciousness and through it the special objective character of labor as a commodity, its "use-value" (i.e., its ability to yield surplus produce) which like every use-value is submerged without a trace in the quantitative exchange categories of capitalism, now awakens and becomes *social reality*. The special nature of labor as a commodity which in the absence of this consciousness acts as an unacknowledged driving wheel in the economic process now objectifies itself by means of this consciousness. The specific nature of this kind of commodity had consisted in the fact that beneath the cloak of the thing lay a relation between men, that beneath the quantifying crust there was a qualitative, living core. Now that this core is revealed it becomes possible to recognize the fetish character *of every commodity* based on the commodity character of labor power: in every case we find its core, the relation between men, entering into the evolution of society.

Of course, all of this is only contained implicitly in the dialectical antithesis of quantity and quality as we meet it in the question of labor-time. That is to say, this antithesis with all its implications is only the *beginning* of the complex process of mediation whose goal is the knowledge of society as a historical totality. The dialectical method is distinguished from bourgeois thought not only by the fact that it alone can lead to a knowledge of totality; it is also significant that such knowledge is only attainable because the relationship between parts and whole has become fundamentally different from what it is in thought based on the categories of reflection. In brief, from this point of view, the essence of the dialectical method lies in the fact that in every aspect correctly grasped by the dialectic the whole totality is comprehended and that the whole method can be unraveled from every single aspect.[52] It has often been claimed—and not without a certain justification—that the famous chapter in Hegel's *Logic* treating of Being, Non-Being and Becoming contains the whole of his philosophy. It might be claimed with perhaps equal justification that the chapter dealing with the fetish character of the commodity contains within itself the whole of historical materialism and the whole self-knowledge of the proletariat seen as the knowledge of capitalist society (and of the societies that preceded it). [*Capital* I, Chapter 1, Section 4].

Obviously, this should not be taken to mean that the whole of history with its teeming abundance should be thought of as being superfluous. Quite the reverse. Hegel's program: to see the absolute, the goal of philosophy, as a *result* remains valid for Marxism with its very different objects of knowledge, and is even of greater concern to it, as the dialectical process is seen to be identical with the course of history. The theoretical point we are anxious to emphasize here is merely the structural fact that the single aspect is not a segment of a mechanical totality that could be put together out of such segments, for this would lead us to see knowledge as an infinite progression. It must be seen instead as containing the possibility of unraveling the whole abundance of the totality from within itself. But this in turn can only be done if the aspect is seen as aspect, i.e., as a point of transition to the totality; if every movement beyond the immediacy that had made the aspect an aspect of the dialectical process (whereas before it had been nothing more than the evident contradiction of two categories of thought) is not to freeze once more in a new rigidity and a new immediacy.

This reflection leads us back to our concrete point of departure. In the Marxist analysis of labor under capitalism that we have sketched above, we encountered the antithesis between the isolated individual and the abstract generality within which he finds mediated the relation between his work and society. And once again it is important to emphasize that, as in every immediate and abstract form of existence as it is simply given, here, too, we find bourgeoisie and proletariat placed in an immediately similar situation. But, here too, it appears that while the bourgeoisie remains enmeshed in its immediacy by virtue of its class role, the proletariat is driven by the specific dialectics of its class situation to abandon it. The transformation of all objects into commodities, their quantification into fetishistic exchange-values is more than an intensive process affecting the form of every aspect of life in this way (as we were able to establish in the case of labor-time). But also and inseparably bound up with this we find the extensive expansion of these forms to embrace the whole of society. For the capitalist this side of the process means an increase in the quantity of objects for him to deal with in his calculations and speculations. In so far as this process does acquire the semblance of a qualitative character, this goes no further than an aspiration toward the increased rationalization, mechanization and quantification of the world confronting him. (See the distinction between the dominance of merchant's capital and that of industrial capital, the capitalization of agriculture, etc.) Interrupted abruptly now and again by "irrational" catastrophes, the way is opened up for an infinite progression leading to the thorough going capitalist rationalization of society as a whole.

For the proletariat, however, the "same" process means *its own emergence as a class*. In both cases a transformation from quantity to quality is involved. We need only consider the line of development leading from the medieval craft via simple cooperation and manufacture to the modern factory and we shall see the extent to which even for the bourgeoisie the qualitative changes stand out as milestones on the road. The *class meaning* of these changes lies precisely in the fact that the bourgeoisie regularly transforms each new qualitative gain back on to the quantitative level of yet another rational calculation. Whereas for the proletariat the "same" development has a different class meaning: it means the *abolition of the isolated individual,* it means that workers can become conscious of the social character of labor, it means that the abstract, universal form of the societal principle as it is manifested can be increasingly concretized and overcome.

This enables us to understand why it is only in the proletariat that the process by which a man's achievement is split off from his total personality and becomes a commodity leads to a revolutionary consciousness. It is true, as we demonstrated in Section I, that the basic structure of reification can be found in all the social forms of modern capitalism (e.g., bureaucracy). But this structure can only be made fully conscious in the work-situation of the proletarian. For his work as he experiences it directly possesses the naked and abstract form of the commodity, while in other forms of work this is hidden behind the façade of "mental labor," of "responsibility," etc. (and sometimes it even lies concealed behind "patriarchal" forms). The more deeply reification penetrates into the soul of the man who sells his achievement as a commodity the more deceptive appearances are (as in the case of journalism). Corresponding to the objective concealment of the commodity form, there is the subjective element. This is the fact that while the process by which the worker is reified and becomes a commodity dehumanizes him and cripples and atrophies his "soul"—as long as he does not consciously rebel against it—it remains true that precisely his humanity and his soul are not changed into commodities. He is able therefore to objectify himself completely against his existence while the man reified in the bureaucracy, for instance, is turned into a commodity, mechanized and reified in the only faculties that might enable him to rebel against reification. Even his thoughts and feelings become reified. As Hegel says: "It is much harder to bring movement into fixed ideas than into sensuous existence."[53]

In the end this corruption assumes objective forms also. The worker experiences his place in the production process as ultimate but at the same time it has all the characteristics of the commodity (the uncertainties of day-to-day movements of the market). This stands in contrast to other groups which have both the appearance of stability (the routine of duty, pension, etc.) and also the—abstract—possibility of an *individual's* elevating himself into the ruling class. By such means a "status-consciousness" is created that is calculated to inhibit effectively the growth of a class consciousness. Thus the purely abstract negativity in the life of the worker is objectively the most typical manifestation of reification, it is the constitutive type of capitalist socialization. But for this very reason it is also *subjectively* the point at which this structure is raised to consciousness and where it can be breached in practice. As Marx says: "Labour . . . is no longer grown together with the individual into one particular determination;"[54] once the false manifestations of this unmediated existence are abolished, the true existence of the proletariat as a class will begin.

Notes

1. *A Contribution to the Critique of Political Economy,* p. 53.
2. *Capital* III, p. 324.
3. *Capital* III, p. 810.
4. *Capital* I, p. 72. On this antagonism cf. the purely economic distinction between the exchange of goods in terms of their value and the exchange in terms of their cost of production. *Capital* III, p. 174.
5. *Capital* I, p. 170.
6. Cf. *Capital* I, pp. 322, 345.
7. This whole process is described systematically and historically in *Capital* I. The facts themselves can also be found in the writings of bourgeois economists like Bücher, Sombart, A. Weber and Gottl among others—although for the most part they are not seen in connection with the problem of reification.
8. *Capital* I, p. 384.
9. *Capital* I, p. 355.
10. That this should appear so is fully justified from the point of view of the *individual* consciousness. As far as class is concerned we would point out that this subjugation is the product of a lengthy struggle which enters upon a new stage with the organization of the proletariat into a class—but on a higher plane and with different weapons.
11. *Capital* I, pp. 374–76, 423–24, 460, etc. It goes without saying that this "contemplation" can be more demanding and demoralizing than "active" labor. But we cannot discuss this further here.
12. *The Poverty of Philosophy,* pp. 58–59.
13. *Capital* I, p. 344.
14. Cf. Gottl: *Wirtschaft und Technik,* Grundriss der Sozialokonomik II, 234 et seq.
15. *Capital* I, p. 77.
16. This refers above all to capitalist private property. *Der heilige Max. Dokumente des Sozialismus* III, 363. Marx goes on to make a number of very fine observations about the effects of reification upon language. A philological study from the standpoint of historical materialism could profitably begin here.

17. *Capital* III, pp. 384–85.

18. Ibid., p. 809.

19. *Gesammelte politische Schriften,* Munich, 1921, pp. 140–42. Weber's reference to the development of English law has no bearing on our problem. On the gradual ascendancy of the principle of economic calculation, see also A. Weber, *Standort der Industrien,* especially p. 216.

20. Max Weber, *Wirtschaft und Gesellschaft,* p. 491.

21. Ibid., p. 129.

22. If we do not emphasize the class character of the state in *this* context, this is because our aim is to understand reification as a *general* phenomenon constitutive of the *whole* of bourgeois society. But for this the question of class would have to begin with the machine.

23. Cf. Max Weber, *Politische Schriften,* p. 154.

24. Cf. the essay by A. Fogarasi in *Kommunismus,* Jg. II, No. 25/26.

25. *Die Metaphysik der Sitten,* Pt. I, §24.

26. *The Origin of the Family,* in S. W. II, p. 293.

27. *Capital* III, p. 239.

28. Ibid., p. 183.

29. *Capital* I, p. 356.

30. Letter to Conrad Schmidt in S.W. II, pp. 447–48.

31. *A Contribution to the Critique of Political Economy,* p. 276.

32. Ibid., p. 21.

33. *Finanzkapital,* 2nd ed., pp. 378–79.

34. *Capital* II, pp. 75–76.

35. *Die Akkumulation des Kapitals,* 1st ed., pp. 78–79. It would be a fascinating task to work out the links between this process and the development of the great rationalist systems.

36. Quoted by Bergbohm, *Jurisprudenz und Rechtsphilosphie,* p. 170.

37. Ibid., p. 375.

38. Preuss, *Zur Methode der juristischen Begriffsbildung*. In Schmollers Jahrbuch, 1900, p. 370.

39. *Lehrbuch des Naturrechts,* Berlin, 1799, §141. Marx's polemic against Hugo (Nachlass I, pp. 268 et seq.) is still on Hegelian lines.

40. *Hauptprobleme der Staatsrechtslehre,* p. 411 (my italics).

41. F. Somlo, *Juristiche Grundlehre,* p. 117.

42. Second Introduction to the *Wissenschaftslehre,* Werke III, p. 52. Although Fichte's terminology changes from one work to the next, this should not blind us to the fact that he is always concerned with the same *problem*.

43. Cf. *Die Kritik der praktischen Vernunft,* Philisophische Bibliothek, p. 72.

44. "Now nature is in the common view the existence of things subject to laws." Ibid., p. 57.

45. Ibid., pp. 125–26.

46. *Über die wissenschaftliche Behandlungsarten des Naturrechts,* Werke I, pp. 352–33. Cf. ibid., p. 351. "For it is the absolute abstraction from every

subject-matter of the will; every content posits a heteronomy of the free will." Or, with even greater clarity, in the *Phenomenology of Mind:* "For pure duty is . . . absolutely indifferent towards every content and is compatible with every content." Werke II, p. 485.

47. This is quite clear in the case of the Greeks. But the same structure can be seen in the great systems at the beginning of the modern age, above all in Spinoza.

48. *Die Kritik der reinen Vernunft,* pp. 472–73.

49. Hegel, Werke III, pp. 78 et seq.

50. Nachlass I, p. 117. [*Fragments on The Difference between The Democritean and Epicurean philosophies of Nature*].

51. From this ontological situation it becomes possible to understand the point of departure for the belief, so alien to modern thought in "natural" states, e.g., the "credo ut intellegam" of Anselm of Canterbury, or the attitude of Indian thought ("Only by him whom he chooses will he be understood," it has been said of Atman). Descartes' systematic skepticism, which was the starting-point of *exact* thought, is no more than the sharpest formulation of this antagonism that was very consciously felt at the birth of the modern age. It can be seen again in every important thinker from Galileo to Bacon.

52. For the history of this universal mathematics, see Cassirer, op. cit. I, pp. 446, 563; II, 138, 156 et seq. For the connection between this mathematicization of reality and the bourgeois "praxis" of calculating the anticipated results of the "laws," see Lange, *Geschichte des Materialismus* (Reclam) I, pp. 321–32 on Hobbes, Descartes and Bacon.

53. For the Platonic theory of ideas was indissolubly linked—with what right need not be discussed here—both with the totality and the qualitative existence of the given world. Contemplation means at the very least the bursting of the bonds that hold the "soul" imprisoned within the limitations of the empirical. The Stoic ideal of ataraxy is a much better instance of this quite pure contemplation, but it is of course devoid of the paradoxical union with a feverish and uninterrupted "activity."

54. *Die Differenz des Fichteschen und Schellingschen Systems,* Werke I, p. 242. Every such "atomic" theory of society only represents the ideological reflection of the purely bourgeois point of view; this was shown conclusively by Marx in his critique of Bruno Bauer, Nachlass II, p. 227. But this is not to deny the "objectivity" of such views: they are in fact the necessary forms of consciousness that reified man has of his attitude toward society.

3

Antonio Gramsci (1891–1937)

Born in Italy, Gramsci studied at the University of Turin, where he was influenced by the Italian idealist philosopher Benedetto Croce. He joined the Italian Socialist party in 1913, and in 1921 he helped found the Italian Communist party. In the early 1920s he was active in the Factory Council movement around Turin. He became the party leader and a member of the Italian Parliament in 1924. When the fascists came to power in 1926, he was arrested and sentenced to twenty years in prison. The rest of his life was spent behind bars, where he composed (under conditions of ill health and censorship) most of his highly influential writings.

These selections from Gramsci's Prison Notebooks (1926–37) *touch on a number of basic themes of his thought: the role of intellectuals and class consciousness in political struggle; the rootedness of cultural and intellectual life in history; the absence of determining economic laws in history; and the status of Marxism (which he often called the "philosophy of* praxis"*) as a theory of human experience and social change. All of these themes bear on his crucial notion of hegemony, namely, the way class domination is based not just upon physical force but on the cultural and ideological acquiescence of the working class and the peasantry.*

Prison Notebooks

THE INTELLECTUALS

The Formation of the Intellectuals

Are intellectuals an autonomous and independent social group, or does every social group have its own particular specialized category of intellectuals? The problem is a complex one, because of the variety of forms assumed to date by the real historical process of formation of the different categories of intellectuals.

The most important of these forms are two:

1. Every social group, coming into existence on the original terrain of an essential function in the world of economic production, creates together with itself, organically, one or more strata[1] of intellectuals which give it homogeneity and an awareness of its own function not only in the economic but also in the social and political fields. The capitalist entrepreneur creates alongside himself the industrial technician, the specialist in political economy, the organizers of a new culture, of a new legal system, etc. It should be noted that the entrepreneur himself represents a higher level of social elaboration, already characterized by a certain directive [*dirigente*] and technical (i.e., intellectual) capacity: he must have a certain technical capacity, not only in the limited sphere of his activity and initiative but in other spheres as well, at least in those which are closest to economic production. He must be an organizer of masses of men; he must be an organizer of the "confidence" of investors in his business, of the customers for his product, etc.

If not all entrepreneurs, at least an *élite* amongst them must have the capacity to be an organizer of society in general, including all its complex organism of services, right up to the state organism, because of the need to create the conditions most favorable to the expansion of their own class; or at the least they must possess the capacity to choose the deputies (specialized employees) to whom to entrust this activity of organizing the general system of relationships external to the business itself. It can be observed that the "organic" intellectuals which every new class creates alongside itself and elaborates in the course of its development, are for the most part "specializations" of partial aspects of the primitive activity of the new social type which the new class has brought into prominence.

Even feudal lords were possessors of a particular technical capacity, military capacity, and it is precisely from the moment at which the aristocracy loses its monopoly of technicomilitary capacity that the crisis of feudalism begins. But the formation of intellectuals in the feudal world and in the preceding classical world is a question to be examined separately: this formation and elaboration follows ways and means which must be studied concretely. Thus it is to be noted that the mass of the peasantry, although it performs an essential function in the world of production, does not elaborate its own "organic" intellectuals, nor does it "assimilate" any stratum of "traditional" intellectuals, although it is from the peasantry that other social groups draw many of their intellectuals and a high proportion of traditional intellectuals are of peasant origin.

2. However, every "essential" social group which emerges into history out of the preceding economic structure, and as an expression of a development of this structure, has found (at least in all of history up to the present) categories of intellectuals already in existence and which seemed indeed to represent an historical continuity uninterrupted even by the most complicated and radical changes in political and social forms.

The most typical of these categories of intellectuals is that of the ecclesiastics, who for a long time (for a whole phase of history, which is partly characterized by this very monopoly) held a monopoly of a number of important services: religious ideology, that is the philosophy and science of the age, together with schools, education, morality, justice, charity, good works, etc. The category of ecclesiastics can be considered the category of intellectuals organically bound to the landed aristocracy. It had equal status juridically with the aristocracy, with which it shared the exercise of feudal ownership of land, and the use of state privileges connected with property. But the monopoly held by the ecclesiastics in the superstructural field was not exercised without a struggle or without limitations, and hence there took place the birth, in various forms (to be gone into and studied concretely), of other categories, favored and enabled to expand by the growing strength of the central power of the monarch, right up to absolutism. Thus we find the formation of the *noblesse de robe,* with its own privileges, a stratum of administrators, etc., scholars and scientists, theorists, nonecclesiastical philosophers, etc.

Since these various categories of traditional intellectuals experience through an "esprit de corps" their uninterrupted historical continuity and their special qualification, they thus put themselves forward as autonomous and independent of the dominant social group. This self-assessment is not without consequences in the ideological and political field, consequences of wide-ranging import. The whole of idealist philosophy can easily be connected with this position assumed by the social complex of intellectuals and can be defined as the expression of that social utopia by which the intellectuals think of themselves as "independent," autonomous, endowed with a character of their own, etc.

One should note however that if the Pope and the leading hierarchy of the Church consider themselves more linked to Christ and to the apostles than they are to senators Agnelli and Benni,[2] the same does not hold for Gentile and Croce, for example: Croce in particular feels himself closely linked to Aristotle and Plato, but he does not conceal, on the other hand, his links with senators Agnelli and Benni, and it is precisely here that one can discern the most significant character of Croce's philosophy.

What are the "maximum" limits of acceptance of the term "intellectual?" Can one find a unitary criterion to characterize equally all the diverse and disparate activities of intellectuals and to distinguish these at the same time and in an essential way from the activities of other social groupings? The most widespread error of method seems to me that of having looked for this criterion of distinction in the intrinsic nature of intellectual activities, rather than in the ensemble of the system of relations in which these activities (and therefore the intellectual groups who personify them) have their place within the general complex of social relations. Indeed the worker or proletarian, for example, is not specifically characterized by his manual or instrumental work, but by performing this work in specific conditions and in specific social relations (apart from the consideration that purely physical labor does not exist and that even Taylor's phrase of "trained gorilla" is a metaphor to indicate a limit in a certain direction: in any physical work, even the most degraded and mechanical, there exists a minimum of technical qualification, that is, a minimum of creative intellectual activity). And we have already observed that the entrepreneur, by virtue of his very function must have to some degree a certain number of qualifications of an intellectual nature although his part in society is determined not by these, but by the general social relations which specifically characterize the position of the entrepreneur within industry.

All men are intellectuals, one could therefore say: but not all men have in society the function of intellectuals.[3]

When one distinguishes between intellectuals and nonintellectuals, one is referring in reality only to the immediate social function of the professional category of the intellectuals, that is, one has in mind the direction in which their specific professional activity is weighted, whether toward intellectual elaboration or toward muscular-nervous effort. This means that, although one can speak of intellectuals, one cannot speak of nonintellectuals, because nonintellectuals do not exist. But even the relationship between efforts of intellectual-cerebral elaboration and muscular-nervous effort is not always the same, so that there are varying degrees of specific intellectual activity. There is no human activity from which every form of intellectual participation can be excluded: *Homo faber* cannot be separated from *Homo sapiens*. Each man, finally, outside his professional activity, carries on some form of intellectual activity, that is, he is a "philosopher," an artist, a man of taste, he participates in a particular conception of the world, has a conscious line of moral conduct, and therefore contributes to sustain a conception of the world or to modify it, that is, to bring into being new modes of thought.

The problem of creating a new stratum of intellectuals consists therefore in the critical elaboration of the intellectual activity that exists in everyone at a certain degree of development, modifying its relationship with the muscular-nervous effort toward a new equilibrium, and ensuring that the muscular-nervous effort itself, in so far as it is an element of a general practical activity, which is perpetually innovating the physical and social world, becomes the foundation of a new and integral conception of the world. The traditional and vulgarized type of the intellectual is given by the man of letters, the philosopher, the artist. Therefore journalists, who claim to be men of letters, philosophers, artists, also regard themselves as the "true" intellectuals. In the modern world, technical education, closely bound to industrial labor even at the most primitive and unqualified level, must form the basis of the new type of intellectual.

On this basis the weekly *Ordine Nuovo* worked to develop certain forms of new intellectualism and to determine its new concepts, and this was not the least of the reasons for its success, since such a conception corresponded to latent aspirations and conformed to the development of the real forms of life. The mode of being of the new intellectual can no longer consist in eloquence, which is an exterior and momentary mover of feelings and passions, but in active participation in practical life, as constructor, organizer, "permanent persuader" and not just a simple orator (but superior at the same time to the abstract mathematical spirit); from technique-as-work one proceeds to technique-as-science and to the humanistic conception of history, without which one remains "specialized" and does not become "directive" (specialized and political).

Thus there are historically formed specialized categories for the exercise of the intellectual function. They are formed in connection with all social groups, but especially in connection with the more important, and they undergo more extensive and complex elaboration in connection with the dominant social group. One of the most important characteristics of any group that is developing toward dominance is its struggle to assimilate and to conquer "ideologically" the traditional intellectuals, but this assimilation and conquest is made quicker and more efficacious the more the group in question succeeds in simultaneously elaborating its own organic intellectuals.

The enormous development of activity and organization of education in the broad sense in the societies that emerged from the medieval world is an index of the importance assumed in the modern world by intellectual functions and categories. Parallel with the attempt to deepen and to broaden the "intellectuality" of each individual, there has also been an attempt to multiply and narrow the various specializations. This can be seen from educational institutions at all levels, up to and including the organisms that exist to promote so-called high culture in all fields of science and technology.

School is the instrument through which intellectuals of various levels are elaborated. The complexity of the intellectual function in different states can be measured objectively by the number and gradation of specialized schools: the more extensive the "area" covered by education and the more numerous the "vertical" "levels" of schooling, the more complex is the cultural world, the civilization, of a particular state. A point of comparison can be found in the sphere of industrial technology: the industrialization of a country can be measured by how well equipped it is in the production of machines with which to produce machines, and in the manufacture of ever more accurate instruments for making both machines and further instruments for making machines, etc. The country which is best equipped in the construction of instruments for experimental scientific laboratories and in the construction of instruments with which to test the first instruments, can be regarded as the most complex in the technical-industrial field, with the highest level of civilization, etc. The same applies to the preparation of intellectuals and to the schools dedicated to this preparation; schools and institutes of high culture can be assimilated to each other. In this field also, quantity cannot be separated from quality. To the most refined technical-cultural specialization there cannot but correspond the maximum possible diffusion of primary education and the maximum care taken to expand the middle grades numerically as much as possible. Naturally this need to provide the widest base possible for the selection and elaboration of the top intellectual qualifications—i.e., to give a democratic structure to high culture and top-level technology—is not without its disadvantages: it creates the possibility of vast crises of unemployment for the middle intellectual strata, and in all modern societies this actually takes place.

It is worth noting that the elaboration of intellectual strata in concrete reality does not take place on the terrain of abstract democracy but in accordance with very concrete traditional historical processes. Strata have grown up which traditionally "produce" intellectuals and these strata coincide with those which have specialized in "saving," i.e., the petty and middle landed bourgeoisie and certain strata of the petty and middle urban bourgeoisie. The varying distribution of different types of school (classical and professional) over the "economic" territory and the varying aspirations of different categories within these strata determine, or give form to, the production of various branches of intellectual specialization. Thus in Italy the rural bourgeoisie produces in particular state functionaries and professional people, whereas the urban bourgeoisie produces technicians for industry. Consequently it is largely northern Italy which produces technicians and the South which produces functionaries and professional men.

The relationship between the intellectuals and the world of production is not as direct as it is with the fundamental social groups but is, in varying degrees, "mediated" by the whole fabric of society and by the complex of superstructures, of which the intellectuals are, precisely, the "functionaries." It should be possible both to measure the "organic quality" [*organicità*] of the various intellectual strata and their degree of connection with a fundamental social group, and to establish a gradation of their functions and of the superstructures from the bottom to the top (from the structural base upwards). What we can do, for the moment, is to fix two major superstructural "levels": the one that can be called "civil society," that is the ensemble of organisms commonly called "private," and that of "political society" or "the State." These two levels correspond on the one hand to the function of "hegemony" which the dominant group exercises throughout society and on the other hand to that of "direct domination" or command exercised through the State and "juridical" government. The functions in question are precisely organizational and connective. The intellectuals are the dominant group's "deputies" exercising the subaltern functions of social hegemony and political government. These comprise:

1. The "spontaneous" consent given by the great masses of the population to the general direction imposed on social life by the dominant fundamental group; this consent is "historically" caused by the prestige (and consequent confidence) which the dominant group enjoys because of its position and function in the world of production.
2. The apparatus of state coercive power which "legally" enforces discipline on those groups who do not "consent" either actively or passively. This apparatus is, however, constituted for the whole of society in anticipation of moments of crisis of command and direction when spontaneous consent has failed.

This way of posing the problem has as a result a considerable extension of the concept of intellectual, but it is the only way which enables one to reach a concrete approximation of reality. It also clashes with preconceptions of caste. The function of organizing social hegemony and state domination certainly gives rise to a particular division of labor and therefore to a whole hierarchy of qualifications in some of which there is no apparent attribution of directive or organizational functions. For example, in the apparatus of social and state direction there exists a whole series of jobs of a manual and instrumental character (nonexecutive work, agents rather than officials or functionaries). It is obvious that such a distinction has to be made just as it is obvious that other distinctions have to be made as well. Indeed, intellectual activity must also be distinguished in terms of its intrinsic characteristics, according to levels which in moments of extreme opposition represent a real qualitative difference—at the highest level would be the creators of the various sciences, philosophy, art, etc., at the lowest the most humble "administrators" and divulgators of preexisting, traditional, accumulated intellectual wealth.

. . . . .

Notes

1. The Italian word here is "*ceti*" which does not carry quite the same connotations as "strata," but which we have been forced to translate in that way for lack of alternatives. It should be noted that Gramsci tends, for reasons of censorship, to avoid using the word class in contexts where its Marxist overtones would be apparent, preferring (as for example in this sentence) the more neutral "social group." The word "group," however, is not always a euphemism for "class," and to avoid ambiguity Gramsci uses the phrase "fundamental social group" when he wishes to emphasize the fact that he is referring to one or other of the major social classes (bourgeoisie, proletariat) defined in strict Marxist terms by its position in the fundamental relations of production. Class groupings which do not have this fundamental role are often described as "castes" (aristocracy, etc.). The word "category," on the other hand, which also occurs on this page, Gramsci tends to use in the standard Italian sense of members of a trade or profession, though also more generally.

2. Heads of FIAT and Montecatini (Chemicals), respectively.

3. Thus, because it can happen that everyone at some time fries a couple of eggs or sews up a tear in a jacket, we do not necessarily say that everyone is a cook or a tailor.

THE STUDY OF PHILOSOPHY

Some Preliminary Points of Reference

It is essential to destroy the widespread prejudice that philosophy is a strange and difficult thing just because it is the specific intellectual activity of a particular category of specialists or of professional and systematic philosophers. It must first be shown that all men are "philosophers," by defining the limits and characteristics of the "spontaneous philosophy" which is proper to everybody. This philosophy is contained in: (1) language itself, which is a totality of determined notions and concepts and not just of words grammatically devoid of content; (2) "common sense" and "good sense," (3) popular religion and, therefore, also in the entire system of beliefs, superstitions, opinions, ways of seeing things and of acting, which are collectively bundled together under the name of "folklore."

Having first shown that everyone is a philosopher, though in his own way and unconsciously, since even in the slightest manifestation of any intellectual activity whatever, in "language," there is contained a specific conception of the world, one then moves on to the second level, which is that of awareness and criticism. That is to say, one proceeds to the question—is it better to "think," without having a critical awareness, in a disjointed and episodic way? In other words, is it better to take part in a conception of the world mechanically imposed by the external environment, i.e., by one of the many social groups in which everyone is automatically involved from the moment of his entry into the conscious world (and this can be one's village or province; it can have its origins in the parish and the "intellectual activity" of the local priest or aging patriarch whose wisdom is law, or in the little old woman who has inherited the lore of the witches or the minor intellectual soured by his own stupidity and inability to act)? Or, on the other hand, is it better to work out consciously and critically one's own conception of the world and thus, in connection with the labors of one's own brain, choose one's sphere of activity, take an active part in the creation of the history of the world, be one's own guide, refusing to accept passively and supinely from outside the molding of one's personality?

Note I. In acquiring one's conception of the world one always belongs to a particular grouping which is that of all the social elements which share the same mode of thinking and acting. We are all conformists of some conformism or other, always man-in-the-mass or collective man. The question is this: of what historical type is the conformism, the mass humanity to which one belongs? When one's conception of the world is not critical and coherent but disjointed and episodic, one belongs simultaneously to a multiplicity of mass human groups. The personality is strangely composite: it contains Stone Age elements and principles of a more advanced science, prejudices from all past phases of history at the local level and intuitions of a future philosophy which will be that of a human race united the world over. To criticize one's own conception of the world means therefore to make it a coherent unity and to raise it to the level reached by the most advanced thought in the world. It therefore also means criticism of all previous philosophy, in so far as this has left stratified deposits in popular philosophy. The starting-point of critical elaboration is the consciousness of what one really is, and is "knowing thyself" as a product of the historical process to date which has deposited in you an infinity of traces, without leaving an inventory.

Note II. Philosophy cannot be separated from the history of philosophy, nor can culture from the history of culture. In the most immediate and relevant sense, one cannot be a philosopher, by which I mean have a critical and coherent conception of the world, without having a consciousness of its historicity, of the phase of development which it represents and of the fact that it contradicts other conceptions or elements of other conceptions. One's conception of the world is a response to certain specific problems posed by reality, which are quite specific and "original" in their immediate relevance. How is it possible to consider the present, and quite specific present, with a mode of thought elaborated for a past which is often remote and superseded? When someone does this, it means that he is a walking anachronism, a fossil, and not living in the modern world, or at the least that he is strangely composite. And it is in fact the case that social groups which in some ways express the most developed modernity, lag behind in other respects, given their social position, and are therefore incapable of complete historical autonomy.

Note III. If it is true that every language contains the elements of a conception of the world and of a culture, it could also be true that from anyone's language one can assess the greater or lesser complexity of his conception of the world. Someone who only speaks dialect, or understands the standard language incompletely, necessarily has an intuition of the world which is more or less limited and provincial, which is fossilized and anachronistic in relation to the major currents of thought which dominate world history. His interests will be limited, more or less corporate or economistic, not universal. While it is not always possible to learn a number of foreign languages in order to put oneself in contact with other cultural lives, it is at the least necessary to learn the national language properly. A great culture can be translated into the language of another great culture, that is to say a great national language with historic richness and complexity, and it can translate any other great culture and can be a worldwide means of expression. But a dialect cannot do this.

Note IV. Creating a new culture does not only mean one's own individual "original" discoveries. It also, and most particularly, means the diffusion in a critical form of truths already discovered, their "socialization" as it were, and even making them the basis of vital action, an element of coordination and intellectual and moral order. For a mass of people to be led to think coherently and in the same coherent fashion about the real present world, is a "philosophical" event far more important and "original" than the discovery by some philosophical "genius" of a truth which remains the property of small groups of intellectuals.

Connection Between "Common Sense," Religion, and Philosophy

Philosophy is intellectual order, which neither religion nor common sense can be. It is to be observed that religion and common sense do not coincide either, but that religion is an element of fragmented common sense. Moreover common sense is a collective noun, like religion: there is not just one common sense, for that too is a product of history and a part of the historical process. Philosophy is criticism and the superseding of religion and "common sense." In this sense it coincides with "good" as opposed to "common" sense.

Relation Between Science, Religion, and Common Sense

Religion and common sense cannot constitute an intellectual order, because they cannot be reduced to unity and coherence even within an individual consciousness, let alone collective consciousness. Or rather they cannot be so reduced "freely"—for this may be done by "authoritarian" means, and indeed within limits this has been done in the past.

Note the problem of religion taken not in the confessional sense but in the secular sense of a unity of faith between a conception of the world and a corresponding norm of conduct. But why call this unit of faith "religion" and not "ideology," or even frankly "politics"?

Philosophy in general does not in fact exist. Various philosophies or conceptions of the world exist, and one always makes a choice between them. How is this choice made? Is it merely an intellectual event, or is it something more complex? And is it not frequently the case that there is a contradiction between one's intellectual choice and one's mode of conduct? Which therefore would be the real conception of the world: that logically affirmed as an intellectual choice? or that which emerges from the real activity of each man, which is implicit in his mode of action? And since all action is political, can one not say that the real philosophy of each man is contained in its entirety in his political action?

This contrast between thought and action, i.e., the coexistence of two conceptions of the world, one affirmed in words and the other displayed in effective action, is not simply a product of self-deception [*malafede*]. Self-deception can be an adequate explanation for a few individuals taken separately, or even for groups of a certain size, but it is not adequate when the contrast occurs in the life of great masses. In these cases the contrast between thought and action cannot but be the expression of profounder contrasts of a social historical order. It signifies that the social group in question may indeed have its own conception of the world, even if only embryonic; a conception which manifests itself in action, but occasionally and in flashes—when, that is, the group is acting as an organic totality. But this same group has, for reasons of submission and intellectual subordination, adopted a conception which is not its own but is borrowed from another group; and it affirms this conception verbally and believes itself to be following it, because this is the conception which it follows in "normal times"—that is when its conduct is not independent and autonomous, but submissive and subordinate. Hence the reason why philosophy cannot be divorced from politics. And one can show furthermore that the choice and the criticism of a conception of the world is also a political matter.

What must next be explained is how it happens that in all periods there coexist many systems and currents of philosophical thought, how these currents are born, how they are diffused, and why in the process of diffusion they fracture along certain lines and in certain directions. The fact of this process goes to show how necessary it is to order in a systematic, coherent and critical fashion one's own intuitions of life and the world, and to determine exactly what is to be understood by the word "systematic," so that it is not taken in the pedantic and academic sense. But this elaboration must be, and can only be, performed in the context of the history of philosophy, for it is this history which shows how thought has been elaborated over the centuries and what a collective effort has gone into the creation of our present method of thought which has subsumed and absorbed all this past history, including all its follies and mistakes. Nor should these mistakes themselves be neglected, for, although made in the past and since corrected, one cannot be sure that they will not be reproduced in the present and once again require correcting.

What is the popular image of philosophy? It can be reconstructed by looking at expressions in common usage. One of the most usual is "being philosophical about it," which, if you consider it, is not to be entirely rejected as a phrase. It is true that it contains an implicit invitation to resignation and patience, but it seems to me that the most important point is rather the invitation to people to reflect and to realize fully that whatever happens is basically rational and must be confronted as such, and that one should apply one's power of rational concentration and not let oneself be carried away by instinctive and violent impulses. These popular turns of phrase could be compared with similar expressions used by writers of a popular stamp—examples being drawn from a large dictionary—which contain the terms "philosophy" or "philosophically." One can see from these examples that the terms have a quite precise meaning: that of overcoming bestial and elemental passions through a conception of necessity which gives a conscious direction to one's activity. This is the healthy nucleus that exists in "common sense," the part of it which can be called "good sense" and which deserves to be made more unitary and coherent. So it appears that here again it is not possible to separate what is known as "scientific" philosophy from the common and popular philosophy which is only a fragmentary collection of ideas and opinions.

But at this point we reach the fundamental problem facing any conception of the world, any philosophy which has become a cultural movement, a "religion," a "faith," any that has produced a form of practical activity or will in which the philosophy is contained as an implicit theoretical "premiss." One might say "ideology" here, but on condition that the word is used in its highest sense of a conception of the world that is implicitly manifest in art, in law, in economic activity and in all manifestations of individual and collective life. This problem is that of preserving the ideological unity of the entire social bloc which that ideology serves to cement and to unify. The strength of religions, and of the Catholic church in particular, has lain, and still lies, in the fact that they feel very strongly the need for the doctrinal unity of the whole mass of the faithful and strive to ensure that the higher intellectual stratum does not get separated form the lower. The Roman church has always been the most vigorous in the struggle to prevent the "official" formation of two religions, one for the "intellectuals" and the other for the "simple souls." This struggle has not been without serious disadvantages for the Church itself, but these disadvantages are connected with the historical process which is transforming the whole of civil society and which contains overall a corrosive critique of all religion, and they only serve to emphasize the organizational capacity of the clergy in the cultural sphere and the abstractly rational and just relationship which the Church has been able to establish in its own sphere between the intellectuals and the simple. The Jesuits have undoubtedly been the major architects of this equilibrium, and in order to preserve it they have given the Church a progressive forward movement which has tended to allow the demands of science and philosophy to be to a certain extent satisfied. But the rhythm of the movement has been so slow and methodical that the changes have passed unobserved by the mass of the simple, although they appear "revolutionary" and demagogic to the "integralists."

One of the greatest weaknesses of immanentist philosophies in general consists precisely in the fact that they have not been able to create an ideological unity between the bottom and the top, between the "simple" and the intellectuals. In the history of Western civilization the fact is exemplified on a European scale, with the rapid collapse of the Renaissance and to a certain extent also the Reformation faced with the Roman church. Their weakness is demonstrated in the educational field, in that the immanentist philosophies have not even attempted to construct a conception which could take the place of religion in the education of children. Hence the pseudohistoricist sophism whereby nonreligious, nonconfessional, and in reality atheist, educationalists justify allowing the teaching of religion on the grounds that religion is the philosophy of the infancy of mankind renewed in every nonmetaphorical infancy. Idealism has also shown itself opposed to cultural movements which "go out to the people," as happened with the so-called Popular Universities and similar institutions. Nor was the objection solely to the worst aspects of the institutions, because in that case they could simply have tried to improve them. And yet these movements were worthy of attention, and deserved study. They enjoyed a certain success, in the sense that they demonstrated on the part of the "simple" a genuine enthusiasm and a strong determination to attain a higher cultural level and a higher conception of the world. What was lacking, however, was any organic quality either of philosophical thought or of organizational stability and central cultural direction. One got the impression that it was all rather like the first contacts of English merchants and the Negroes of Africa: trashy baubles were handed out in exchange for nuggets of gold. In any case one could only have had cultural stability and an organic quality of thought if there had existed the same unity between the intellectuals and the simple as there should be between theory and practice. That is, if the intellectuals had been organically the intellectuals of those masses, and if they had worked out and made coherent the principles and the problems raised by the masses in their practical activity, thus constituting a cultural and social bloc. The question posed here was the one we have already referred to, namely this: is a philosophical movement properly so called when it is devoted to creating a specialized culture among restricted intellectual groups, or rather when, and only when, in the process of elaborating a form of thought superior to "common sense" and coherent on a scientific plane, it never forgets to remain in contact with the "simple" and indeed finds in this contact the source of the problems it sets out to study and to resolve? Only by this contact does a philosophy become "historical," purify itself of intellectualistic elements of an individual character and become "life."[1]

A philosophy of praxis cannot but present itself at the outset in a polemical and critical guise, as superseding the existing mode of thinking and existing concrete thought (the existing cultural world). First of all, therefore, it must be a criticism of "common sense," basing itself initially, however, on common sense in order to demonstrate that "everyone" is a philosopher and that it is not a question of introducing from scratch a scientific form of thought into everyone's individual life, but of renovating and making "critical" an already existing activity. It must then be a criticism of the philosophy of the intellectuals out of which the history of philosophy developed and which, in so far as it is a phenomenon of individuals (in fact it develops essentially in the activity of single particularly gifted individuals) can be considered as marking the "high points" of the progress made by common sense, or at least the common sense of the more educated strata of society but through them also of the people. Thus an introduction to the study of philosophy must expound in synthetic form the problems that have grown up in the process of the development of culture as a whole and which are only partially reflected in the history of philosophy. (Nevertheless it is the history of philosophy which, in the absence of a history of common sense, impossible to reconstruct for lack of documentary material, must remain the main source of reference.) The purpose of the synthesis must be to criticize the problems, to demonstrate their real value, if any, and the significance they have had as superseded links of an intellectual chain, and to determine what the new contemporary problems are and how the old problems should now be analyzed.

The relation between common sense and the upper level of philosophy is assured by "politics," just as it is politics that assures the relationship between the Catholicism of the intellectuals and that of the simple. There are, however, fundamental differences between the two cases. That the Church has to face up to a problem of the "simple" means precisely that there has been a split in the community of the faithful. This split cannot be healed by raising the simple to the level of the intellectuals (the Church does not even envisage such a task, which is both ideologically and economically beyond its present capacities), but only by imposing an iron discipline on the intellectuals so that they do not exceed certain limits of differentiation and so render the split catastrophic and irreparable. In the past such divisions in the community of the faithful were healed by strong mass movements which led to, or were absorbed in, the creation of new religious orders centered on strong personalities (St. Dominic, St. Francis).[2]

But the Counter-Reformation has rendered sterile this upsurge of popular forces. The Society of Jesus is the last of the great religious orders. Its origins were reactionary and authoritarian, and its character repressive and "diplomatic." Its birth marked the hardening of the Catholic organism. New orders which have grown up since then have very little religious significance but a great "disciplinary" significance for the mass of the faithful. They are, or have become, ramifications and tentacles of the Society of Jesus, instruments of "resistance" to preserve political positions that have been gained, not forces of renovation and development. Catholicism has become "Jesuitism." Modernism has not created "religious orders," but a political party—Christian Democracy.[3]

The position of the philosophy of praxis is the antithesis of the Catholic. The philosophy of praxis does not tend to leave the "simple" in their primitive philosophy of common sense, but rather to lead them to a higher conception of life. If it affirms the need for contact between intellectuals and simple it is not in order to restrict scientific activity and preserve unity at the low level of the masses, but precisely in order to construct an intellectual-moral bloc which can make politically possible the intellectual progress of the mass and not only of small intellectual groups.

The active man-in-the-mass has a practical activity, but has no clear theoretical consciousness of his practical activity, which nonetheless involves understanding the world in so far as it transforms it. His theoretical consciousness can indeed be historically in opposition to his activity. One might almost say that he has two theoretical consciousnesses (or one contradictory consciousness): one which is implicit in his activity and which in reality unites him with all his fellow-workers in the practical transformation of the real world; and one, superficially explicit or verbal, which he has inherited from the past and uncritically absorbed. But this verbal conception is not without consequences. It holds together a specific social group, it influences moral conduct and the direction of will, with varying efficacity but often powerfully enough to produce a situation in which the contradictory state of consciousness does not permit of any action, any decision or any choice, and produces a condition of moral and political passivity. Critical understanding of self takes place therefore through a struggle of political "hegemonies" and of opposing directions, first in the ethical field and then in that of politics proper, in order to arrive at the working out at a higher level of one's own conception of reality. Consciousness of being part of a particular hegemonic force (that is to say, political consciousness) is the first stage toward a further progressive self-consciousness in which theory and practice will finally be one. Thus the unity of theory and practice is not just a matter of mechanical fact, but a part of the historical process, whose elementary and primitive phase is to be found in the sense of being "different" and "apart," in an instinctive feeling of independence, and which progresses to the level of real possession of a single and coherent conception of the world. This is why it must be stressed that the political development of the concept of hegemony represents a great philosophical advance as well as a politicopractical one. For it necessarily supposes an intellectual unity and an ethic in conformity with a conception of reality that has gone beyond common sense and has become, if only within narrow limits, a critical conception.

However, in the most recent developments of the philosophy of praxis the exploration and refinement of the concept of the unity of theory and practice is still only at an early stage. There still remain residues of mechanicism, since people speak about theory as a "complement" or an "accessory" of practice, or as the handmaid of practice. It would seem right for this question too to be considered historically, as an aspect of the political question of the intellectuals. Critical self-consciousness means, historically and politically, the creation of an *élite* of intellectuals. A human mass does not "distinguish" itself, does not become independent in its own right without, in the widest sense, organizing itself; and there is no organization without intellectuals, that is without organizers and leaders, in other words, without the theoretical aspect of the theory-practice nexus being distinguished concretely by the existence of a group of people "specialized" in conceptual and philosophical elaboration of ideas. But the process of creating intellectuals is long, difficult, full of contradictions, advances and retreats, dispersals and regroupings, in which the loyalty of the masses is often sorely tried. (And one must not forget that at this early stage loyalty and discipline are the ways in which the masses participate and collaborate in the development of the cultural movement as a whole.)

The process of development is tied to a dialectic between the intellectuals and the masses. The intellectual stratum develops both quantitatively and qualitatively, but every leap forward toward a new breadth and complexity of the intellectual stratum is tied to an analogous movement on the part of the mass of the "simple," who raise themselves to higher levels of culture and at the same time extend their circle of influence toward the stratum of specialized intellectuals, producing outstanding individuals and groups of greater or less importance. In the process, however, there continually recur moments in which a gap develops between the mass and the intellectuals (at any rate between some of them, or a group of them), a loss of contact, and thus the impression that theory is an "accessory," a "complement" and something subordinate. Insistence on the practical element of the theory-practice nexus, after having not only distinguished but separated and split the two elements (an operation which in itself is merely mechanical and conventional), means that one is going through a relatively primitive historical phase, one which is still economic-corporate, in which the general "structural" framework is being quantitatively transformed and the appropriate quality-superstructure is in the process of emerging, but is not yet organically formed. One should stress the importance and significance which, in the modern world, political parties have in the elaboration and diffusion of conceptions of the world, because essentially what they do is to work out the ethics and the politics corresponding to these conceptions and act as it were as their historical "laboratory." The parties recruit individuals out of the working mass, and the selection is made on practical and theoretical criteria at the same time. The relation between theory and practice becomes even closer the more the conception is vitally and radically innovatory and opposed to old ways of thinking. For this reason one can say that the parties are the elaborators of new integral and totalitarian intelligentsias and the crucibles where the unification of theory and practice, understood as a real historical process, takes place. It is clear from this that the parties should be formed by individual memberships and not on the pattern of the British Labour Party, because, if it is a question of providing an organic leadership for the entire economically active mass, this leadership should not follow old schemas but should innovate. But innovation cannot come from the mass, at least at the beginning, except through the mediation of an *élite* for whom the conception implicit in human activity has already become to a certain degree a coherent and systematic ever-present awareness and a precise and decisive will.

One of these phases can be studied by looking at the recent discussion in which the latest developments of the philosophy of praxis are brought out, and which has been summarized in an article by D. S. Mirsky, a collaborator on *La Cultura*. One can see from this that a change has taken place from a mechanistic and purely external conception to one which is activist and, as has been pointed out, closer to a correct understanding of the unity of theory and practice, although it has not yet attained the full synthetic meaning of the concept. It should be noted how the deterministic, fatalistic and mechanistic element has been a direct ideological "aroma" emanating from the philosophy of praxis, rather like religion or drugs (in their stupefying effect). It has been made necessary and justified historically by the "subaltern" character of certain social strata.

When you don't have the initiative in the struggle and the struggle itself comes eventually to be identified with a series of defeats, mechanical determinism becomes a tremendous force of moral resistance, of cohesion and of patient and obstinate perseverance. "I have been defeated for the moment, but the tide of history is working for me in the long term." Real will takes on the garments of an act of faith in a certain rationality of history and in a primitive and empirical form of impassioned finalism which apears in the role of a substitute for the Predestination or Providence of confessional religions. It should be emphasized, though, that a strong activity of the will is present even here, directly intervening in the "force of circumstance," but only implicitly, and in a veiled and, as it were, shamefaced manner. Consciousness here, therefore, is contradictory and lacking critical unity, etc. But when the "subaltern" becomes directive and responsible for the economic activity of the masses, mechanicism at a certain point becomes an imminent danger and a revision must take place in modes of thinking because a change has taken place in the social mode of existence. The boundaries and the dominion of the "force of circumstance" become restricted. But why? Because, basically, if yesterday the subaltern element was a thing, today it is no longer a thing but an historical person, a protagonist; if yesterday it was not responsible, because "resisting" a will external to itself, now it feels itself to be responsible because it is no longer resisting but an agent, necessarily active and taking the initiative.

But even yesterday was it ever mere "resistance," a mere "thing," mere "nonresponsibility"? Certainly not. Indeed one should emphasize how fatalism is nothing other than the clothing worn by real and active will when in a weak position. This is why it is essential at all times to demonstrate the futility of mechanical determinism: for, although it is explicable as a naïve philosophy of the mass and as such, but only as such, can be an intrinsic element of strength, nevertheless when it is adopted as a thought-out and coherent philosophy on the part of the intellectuals, it becomes a cause of passivity, of idiotic self-sufficiency. This happens when they don't even expect that the subaltern will become directive and responsible. In fact, however, some part of even a subaltern mass is always directive and responsible, and the philosophy of the part always precedes the philosophy of the whole, not only as its theoretical anticipation but as a necessity of real life.

That the mechanist conception has been a religion of the subaltern is shown by an analysis of the development of the Christian religion. Over a certain period of history in certain specific historical conditions religion has been and continues to be a "necessity," a necessary form taken by the will of the popular masses and a specific way of rationalizing the world and real life, which provided the general framework for real practical activity. This quotation from an article in *La Civiltà Cattolica* (*Individualismo pagano e individualismo cristiano:* issue of 5 March 1932) seems to me to express very well this function of Christianity:

> Faith in a secure future, in the immortality of the soul destined to beatitude, in the certainty of arriving at eternal joy, was the force behind the labour for intense interior perfection and spiritual elevation. True Christian individualism found here the impulse that led it to victory. All the strength of the Christian was gathered around this noble end. Free from the flux of speculation which weakens the soul with doubt, and illuminated by immortal principles, man felt his hopes reborn; sure that a superior force was supporting him in the struggle against Evil, he did violence to himself and conquered the world.

But here again it is naïve Christianity that is being referred to, not Jesuitized Christianity, which has become a pure narcotic for the popular masses.

The position of Calvinism, however, with its iron conception of predestination and grace, which produces a vast expansion of the spirit of initiative (or becomes the form of this movement) is even more revealing and significant.[4]

What are the influential factors in the process of diffusion (which is also one of a substitution of the old conception, and, very often, of combining old and new), how do they act, and to what extent? Is it the rational form in which the new conception is expounded and presented? Or is it the authority (in so far as this is recognized and appreciated, of only generically) of the expositor and the thinkers and experts whom the expositor calls in in his support? Or the fact of belonging to the same organization as the man who upholds the new conception (assuming, that is, that one has entered the organization for other reasons than that of already sharing the new conception)?

In reality these elements will vary according to social groups and the cultural level of the groups in question. But the enquiry has a particular interest in relation to the popular masses, who are slower to change their conceptions, or who never change them in the sense of accepting them in their "pure" form, but always and only as a more or less heterogeneous and bizarre combination. The rational and logically coherent form, the exhaustive reasoning which neglects no argument, positive or negative, of any significance, has a certain importance, but is far from being decisive. It can be decisive, but in a secondary way, when the person in question is already in a state of intellectual crisis, wavering between the old and the new, when he has lost his faith in the old and has not yet come down in favor of the new, etc.

One could say this about the authority of thinkers and experts: it is very important among the people, but the fact remains that every conception has its thinkers and experts to put forward, and authority does not belong to one side; further, with every thinker it is possible to make distinctions, to cast doubt on whether he really said such and such a thing, etc.

One can conclude that the process of diffusion of new conceptions takes place for political (that is, in the last analysis, social) reasons; but that the formal element, that of logical coherence, the element of authority and the organizational element have a very important function in this process immediately after the general orientation has been reached, whether by single individuals or groups of a certain size. From this we must conclude, however, that in the masses *as such,* philosophy can only be experienced as a faith.

Imagine the intellectual position of the man of the people: he has formed his own opinions, convictions, criteria of discrimination, standards of conduct. Anyone with a superior intellectual formation with a point of view opposed to his can put forward arguments better than he and really tear him to pieces logically and so on. But should the man of the people change his opinions just because of this? Just because he cannot impose himself in a bout of argument? In that case he might find himself having to change every day, or every time he meets an ideological adversary who is his intellectual superior. On what elements, therefore, can his philosophy be founded? and in particular his philosophy in the form which has the greatest importance for his standards of conduct?

The most important element is undoubtedly one whose character is determined not by reason but by faith. But faith in whom, or in what? In particular in the social group to which he belongs, in so far as in a diffuse way it thinks as he does. The man of the people thinks that so many like-thinking people can't be wrong, not so radically, as the man he is arguing against would like him to believe; he thinks that, while he himself, admittedly, is not able to uphold and develop his arguments as well as the opponent, in his group there is someone who could do this and could certainly argue better than the particular man he has against him; and he remembers, indeed, hearing expounded, discursively, coherently, in a way that left him convinced, the reasons behind his faith. He has no concrete memory of the reasons and could not repeat them, but he knows that reasons exist, because he has heard them expounded, and was convinced by them. The fact of having once suddenly seen the light and been convinced is the permanent reason for his reasons persisting, even if the arguments in its favor cannot be readily produced.

These considerations lead, however, to the conclusion that new conceptions have an extremely unstable position among the popular masses; particularly when they are in contrast with orthodox convictions (which can themselves be new) conforming socially to the general interests of the ruling classes. This can be seen if one considers the fortunes of religions and churches. Religion, or a particular church, maintains its community of faithful (within the limits imposed by the necessities of general historical development) in so far as it nourishes its faith permanently and in an organized fashion, indefatigably repeating its apologetics, struggling at all times and always with the same kind of arguments, and maintaining a hierarchy of intellectuals who give to the faith, in appearance at least, the dignity of thought. Whenever the continuity of relations between the Church and the faithful has been violently interrupted, for political reasons, as happened during the French Revolution, the losses suffered by the Church have been incalculable. If the conditions had persisted for a long time in which it was difficult to carry on practicing one's own religion, it is quite possible that these losses would have been definitive, and a new religion would have emerged, as indeed one did emerge in France in combination with the old Catholicism. Specific necessities can be deduced from this for any cultural movement which aimed to replace common sense and old conceptions of the world in general:

1. Never to tire of repeating its own arguments (though offering literary variation of form): repetition is the best didactic means for working on the popular mentality.

2. To work incessantly to raise the intellectual level of ever-growing strata of the populace, in other words, to give a personality to the amorphous mass element. This means working to produce *élites* of intellectuals of a new type which arise directly out of the masses, but remain in contact with them to become, as it were, the whalebone in the corset.

This second necessity, if satisfied, is what really modifies the "ideological panorama" of the age. But these *élites* cannot be formed or developed without a hierarchy of authority and intellectual competence growing up within them. The culmination of this process can be a great individual philosopher. But he must be capable of reliving concretely the demands of the massive ideological community and of understanding that this cannot have the flexibility of movement proper to an individual brain, and must succeed in giving formal elaboration to the collective doctrine in the most relevant fashion, and the one most suited to the modes of thought of a collective thinker.

It is evident that this kind of mass creation cannot just happen "arbitrarily," around any ideology, simply because of the formally constructive will of a personality or a group which puts it forward solely on the basis of its own fanatical philosophical or religious convictions. Mass adhesion or nonadhesion to an ideology is the real critical test of the rationality and historicity of modes of thinking. Any arbitrary constructions are pretty rapidly eliminated by historical competition, even if sometimes, through a combination of immediately favorable circumstances, they manage to enjoy popularity of a kind; whereas constructions which respond to the demands of a complex organic period of history always impose themselves and prevail in the end, even though they may pass through several intermediary phases during which they manage to affirm themselves only in more or less bizarre and heterogeneous combinations.

These developments pose many problems, the most important of which can be subsumed in the form and the quality of the relations between the various intellectually qualified strata; that is, the importance and the function which the creative contribution of superior groups must and can have in connection with the organic capacity of the intellectually subordinate strata to discuss and develop new critical concepts. It is a question, in other words, of fixing the limits of freedom of discussion and propaganda, a freedom which should not be conceived of in the administrative and police sense, but in the sense of a self-limitation which the leaders impose on their own activity, or, more strictly, in the sense of fixing the direction of cultural policy. In other words—who is to fix the "rights of knowledge" and the limits of the pursuit of knowledge? And can these rights and limits indeed be fixed? It seems necessary to leave the task of researching after new truths and better, more coherent, clearer formulations of the truths themselves to the free initiative of individual specialists, even though they may continually question the very principles that seem most essential. And it will in any case not be difficult to expose the fact whenever such proposals for discussion arise because of interested and not scientific motives. Nor is it inconceivable that individual initiatives should be disciplined and subject to an ordered procedure, so that they have to pass through the sieve of academies or cultural institutes of various kinds and only become public after undergoing a process of selection.

How the concept of Ideology passed from meaning "science of ideas" and "analysis of the origin of ideas" to meaning a specific "system of ideas" needs to be examined historically. In purely logical terms the process is easy to grasp and understand.

It could be asserted that Freud is the last of the Ideologues, and that De Man is also an "ideologue." This makes the "enthusiasm" of Croce and the Croceans for De Man even more curious—or would if there wasn't a "practical" justification for their enthusiasm. One should examine the way in which the author of the *Popular Manual* [Bukharin] has remained trapped in Ideology; whereas the philosophy of praxis represents a distinct advance and historically is precisely in opposition to Ideology. Indeed the meaning which the term "ideology" has assumed in Marxist philosophy implicitly contains a negative value judgment and excludes the possibility that for its founders the origin of ideas should be sought for in sensations, and therefore, in the last analysis, in physiology. "Ideology" itself must be analyzed historically, in the terms of the philosophy of praxis, as a superstructure.

It seems to me that there is a potential element of error in assessing the value of ideologies, due to the fact (by no means casual) that the name ideology is given both to the necessary superstructure of a particular structure and to the arbitrary elucubrations of particular individuals. The bad sense of the word has become widespread, with the effect that the theoretical analysis of the concept of ideology has been modified and denatured. The process leading up to this error can be easily reconstructed:

1. ideology is identified as distinct from the structure, and it is asserted that it is not ideology that changes the structures but vice versa;

2. it is asserted that a given political solution is "ideological"—i.e., that it is not sufficient to change the structure, although it thinks that it can do so; it is asserted that it is useless, stupid, etc.;

3. one then passes to the assertion that every ideology is "pure" appearance, useless, stupid, etc.

One must therefore distinguish between historically organic ideologies, those, that is, which are necessary to a given structure, and ideologies that are arbitrary, rationalistic, or "willed." To the extent that ideologies are historically necessary they have a validity which is "psychological"; they "organize" human masses, and create the terrain on which men move, acquire consciousness of their position, struggle, etc. To the extent that they are arbitrary they only create individual "movements," polemics and so on (though even these are not completely useless, since they function like an error which by contrasting with truth, demonstrates it).

It is worth recalling the frequent affirmation made by Marx on the "solidity of popular beliefs" as a necessary element of a specific situation. What he says more or less is "when this way of conceiving things has the force of popular beliefs," etc. Another proposition of Marx is that a popular conviction often has the same energy as a material force or something of the kind, which is extremely significant. The analysis of these propositions tends, I think, to reinforce the conception of *historical bloc* in which precisely material forces are the content and ideologies are the form, though this distinction between form and content has purely didactic value, since the material forces would be inconceivable historically without form and the ideologies would be individual fancies without the material forces.

Notes

1. Perhaps it is useful to make a "practical" distinction between philosophy and common sense in order to indicate more clearly the passage from one moment to the other. In philosophy the features of individual elaboration of thought are the most salient: in common sense on the other hand it is the diffuse, uncoordinated features of a generic form of thought common to a particular period and a particular popular environment. But every philosophy has a tendency to become the common sense of a fairly limited environment (that of all the intellectuals). It is a matter therefore of starting with a philosophy which already enjoys, or could enjoy, a certain diffusion, because it is connected to and implicit in practical life, and elaborating it so that it becomes a renewed common sense pos-

sessing the coherence and the sinew of individual philosophies. But this can only happen if the demands of cultural contact with the "simple" are continually felt.

2. The heretical movements of the Middle Ages were a simultaneous reaction against the politicking of the Church and against the scholastic philosophy which expressed this. They were based on social conflicts determined by the birth of the Communes, and represented a split between masses and intellectuals within the Church. This split was "stitched over" by the birth of popular religious movements subsequently reabsorbed by the Church through the formation of the mendicant orders and a new religious unity.

3. Recall the anecdote, recounted by Steed in his Memoirs, about the Cardinal who explains to the pro-Catholic English Protestant that the miracles of San Gennaro [St. Januarius] are an article of faith for the ordinary people of Naples, but not for the intellectuals, and that even the Gospels contain "exaggerations," and who answers the question "But aren't we Christians?" with the words "We are the 'prelates,' that is the 'politicians,' of the Church of Rome."

4. On this question see: Max Weber, *L'etica protestante e lo spirito del capitalismo;* published in *Nuovi Studi,* volume for 1931 et seq. [*Die protestantische Ethik und der Geist des Capitalismus;* first published in the *Archiv für Sozialwissenschaft und Sozialpolitik,* Vols. XX and XXI, 1904 and 1905. English translation (by Talcott Parsons) *The Protestant Ethic and the Spirit of Capitalism,* London, Allen and Unwin, 1930.] And see Groethuysen's book on the religious origins of the bourgeoisie in France. [*Origines de l'esprit bourgeois en France,* Vol. I. *L'Eglise et la bourgeoisie,* Paris, 1927.]

PROBLEMS OF MARXISM

• • • • •

Philosophy—Politics—Economics

If these three activities are the necessary constituent elements of the same conception of the world, there must necessarily be, in their theoretical principles, a convertibility from one to the others and a reciprocal translation into the specific language proper to each constituent element. Any one is implicit in the others, and the three together form a homogeneous circle.

From these propositions (still in need of elaboration) there derive for the historian of culture and of ideas a number of research criteria and critical canons of great significance. It can be that a great personality expresses the more fecund aspects of his thought not in the section which, or so it would appear from the point of view of external classification, ought to be the most logical, but elsewhere, in a part which apparently could be judged extraneous. A man of politics writes about philosophy: it could be that his "true" philosophy should be looked for rather in his writings on politics. In every personality there is one dominant and predominant activity: it is here that his thought must be looked for, in a form that is more often than not implicit and at times even in contradiction with what is professly expressed. Admittedly such a criterion of historical judgment contains many dangers of dilettantism and it is necessary to be very cautious in applying it, but that does not deprive it of its capacity to generate truth.

In reality the occasional "philosopher" can succeed only with difficulty in making abstractions from the currents dominant in his age and from interpretations of a certain conception of the world that have become dogmatic (etc.). As a scientist of politics on the other hand he feels himself free from these idols of his age and of his group and treats the same conception with more immediacy and with total originality; he penetrates to its heart and develops it in a vital way. Here again the thought expressed by [Rosa] Luxemburg remains useful and suggestive when she writes about the impossibility of treating certain questions of the philosophy of praxis in so far as they have not yet become *actual* for the course of history in general or that of a given social grouping. To the economicocorporate phase, to the phase of struggle for hegemony in civil society and to the phase of State power there correspond specific intellectual activities which cannot be arbitrarily improvised or anticipated. In the phase of struggle for hegemony it is the science of politics which is developed; in the State phase all the superstructures must be developed, if one is not to risk the dissolution of the State.

. . . . .

Economy and Ideology

The claim, presented as an essential postulate of historical materialism, that every fluctuation of politics and ideology can be presented and expounded as an immediate expression of the structure, must be contested in theory as primitive infantilism, and combated in practice with the authentic testimony of Marx, the author of concrete political and historical works. Particularly important from this point of view are *The 18th Brumaire* and the writings on the Eastern Question, but also other writings

(*Revolution and Counter-Revolution in Germany, The Civil War in France* and lesser works). An analysis of these works allows one to establish better the Marxist historical methodology, integrating, illuminating and interpreting the theoretical affirmations scattered throughout his works.

One will be able to see from this the real precautions introduced by Marx into his concrete researches, precautions which could have no place in his general works.[1] Among these precautions the following examples can be enumerated:

1. The difficulty of identifying at any given time, statically (like an instantaneous photographic image) the structure. Politics in fact is at any given time the reflection of the tendencies of development in the structure, but it is not necessarily the case that these tendencies must be realized. A structural phase can be correctly studied and analyzed only after it has gone through its whole process of development, and not during the process itself, except hypothetically and with the explicit proviso that one is dealing with hypotheses.

2. From this it can be deduced that a particular political act may have been an error of calculation on the part of the leaders [*dirigenti*] of the dominant classes, an error which historical development, through the parliamentary and governmental "crises" of the directive [*dirigenti*] classes, then corrects and goes beyond. Mechanical historical materialism does not allow for the possibility of error, but assumes that every political act is determined, immediately, by the structure, and therefore as a real and permanent (in the sense of achieved) modification of the structure. The principle of "error" is a complex one: one may be dealing with an individual impulse based on mistaken calculations or equally it may be a manifestation of the attempts of specific groups or sects to take over hegemony within the directive grouping, attempts which may well be unsuccessful.

3. It is not sufficiently borne in mind that many political acts are due to internal necessities of an organizational character, that is they are tied to the need to give coherence to a party, a group, a society. This is made clear for example in the history of the Catholic Church. If, for every ideological struggle within the Church one wanted to find an immediate primary explanation in the structure one would really be caught napping: all sorts of politicoeconomic romances have been written for this reason. It is evident on the contrary that the majority of these discussions are connected with sectarian and organizational necessities. In the discussion between Rome and Byzantium on the Procession of the Holy Spirit, it would be ridiculous to look in the structure of the European East for the claim that it proceeds only from the Father, and in that of the West for

the claim that it proceeds from the Father and the Son. The two Churches, whose existence and whose conflict is dependent on the structure and on the whole of history, posed questions which are principles of distinction and internal cohesion for each side, but it could have happened that either of the Churches could have argued what in fact was argued by the other. The principle of distinction and conflict would have been upheld all the same, and it is this problem of distinction and conflict that constitutes the historical problem, and not the banner that happened to be hoisted by one side or the other.

Note II. The author of ideological serial stories in *Problemi del Lavoro* (who must be none other than the notorious Franz Weiss), during his farcical fairy tale "Russian dumping and its historical significance," speaking about precisely these controversies in early Christian times, asserts that they are tied to the immediate material conditions of the age, and that if we do not succeed in identifying this immediate link it is because the facts are so distant from us or because of some other intellectual weakness. The position is a convenient one, but scientifically insignificant. In fact every real historical phase leaves traces of itself in succeeding phases, which then become in a sense the best document of its existence. The process of historical development is a unity in time through which the present contains the whole of the past and in the present is realized that part of the past which is "essential"—with no residue of any "unknowable" representing the true "essence." The part which is lost, i.e., not transmitted dialectically in the historical process, was in itself of no import, casual and contingent "dross," chronicle and not history, a superficial and negligible episode in the last analysis.

Passage from Knowing to Understanding and to Feeling and Vice Versa from Feeling to Understanding and to Knowing

The popular element "feels" but does not always know or understand; the intellectual element "knows" but does not always understand and in particular does not always feel. The two extremes are therefore pedantry and philistinism on the one hand and blind passion and sectarianism on the other. Not that the pedant cannot be impassioned; far from it. Impassioned pedantry is every bit as ridiculous and dangerous as the wildest sectarianism and demagogy. The intellectual's error consists in believing that one can know without understanding and even more without feeling and being impassioned (not only for knowledge in itself but also for the object of knowledge): in other words that the intellectual can be an intellectual (and not a pure pedant) if distinct and separate from the people-nation, that is, without feeling the elementary passions of the people, understanding them and therefore explaining and justifying them in the particular historical situation and connecting them dialectically to the laws of history and to a superior conception of the world, scientifically and coherently elaborated—i.e., knowledge. One cannot make politics-history without this passion, without this sentimental connection between intellectuals and people-nation. In the absence of such a nexus the relations between the intellectual and the people-nation are, or are reduced to, relationships of a purely bureaucratic and formal order; the intellectuals become a caste, or a priesthood (so-called organic centralism).

If the relationship between intellectuals and people-nation, between the leaders and the led, the rulers and the ruled, is provided by an organic cohesion in which feeling-passion becomes understanding and thence knowledge (not mechanically but in a way that is alive), then and only then is the relationship one of representation. Only then can there take place an exchange of individual elements between the rulers and ruled, leaders [*dirigenti*] and led, and can the shared life be realized which alone is a social force—with the creation of the "historical bloc."

De Man "studies" popular feelings: he does not feel with them to guide them, and lead them into a catharsis of modern civilization. His position is that of the scholarly student of folklore who is permanently afraid that modernity is going to destroy the object of his study. What one finds in his book is the pedantic reflection of what is, however, a real need: for popular feelings to be known and studied in the way in which they present themselves objectively and for them not to be considered something negligible and inert within the movement of history.

• • • • •

Note

1. They could have a place only in a systematic and methodical exposition such as that of Bernheim, and Bernheim's book can be held up as a "model" for a scholastic or "popular manual" of historical materialism, in which, apart from the philological and scholarly method (which Bernheim holds to as a matter of principle, although in his treatment there is implicit a conception of the world) the Marxist conception of history should be explicitly treated.

II

BETWEEN PARTY AND CLASS: A RESPONSE TO THE FAILURES OF THE EUROPEAN LEFT

4

Wilhelm Reich (1897–1957)

Born in Austria, Wilhelm Reich studied medicine in Vienna and by 1920 had become a practicing psychoanalyst. During the 1920s he was a highly respected member of the Viennese Psychoanalytic Society. At the same time, however, he grew discontented with Freud's neglect of the social origins of neurosis. This discontent led him both to revise Freud's theories and to involve himself in socialist theory and practice. In 1927 he joined the Austrian Social Democratic party, and after moving to Berlin he joined the German Communist party (KPD) in 1930. In both Vienna and Berlin Reich organized groups focusing on a socialist treatment of sexual issues. His group in Germany grew rapidly and numbered some forty thousand members at its height, including a large percentage of workers. In 1933 the KPD expelled Reich for his "un-Marxist" stress on sexuality and his attempt to unify Freud and Marx. A year later the International Psychoanalytic Society expelled him for his communist politics. Reich, bitterly disappointed by communism's degeneration into Stalinism, thereafter ceased to be a socialist and instead sought a physiological basis for human behavior. He emigrated to the United States in 1939 and, having been persecuted for his research, died in prison in 1957.

In this selection from "What Is Class Consciousness?" (1934) Reich is responding to German communism's recent defeat by fascism. That defeat, he argues, partially stems from a too-narrow conception of politics and a refusal to see the political relevance of the experiences of everyday life. He also charges communists with having adopted "bourgeois politics" that ignore the needs, feelings, beliefs and participation of the masses.

From *Sex-Pol: Essays, 1924–1934* by Wilhelm Reich, edited by Lee Baxandall (New York: Vintage Books, 1972).

"What Is Class Consciousness?"

PREFACE

The central idea running through this essay may be described as follows:

Because of the exhausting struggle that revolutionaries the world over have had to wage on many fronts, they tend to see the lives of human beings only from the standpoint of their ideology, or to pay attention only to those facts of social life which are somehow, whether closely or remotely, related to their thinking and struggle. Yet the majority of the world's population, whose liberation from the yoke of capitalism is the object of that struggle, know little or nothing of their efforts, sufferings or intentions. They lead their subjugated existences more and more unconsciously, and in that way, serve as props for the rule of capital. Ask yourself how many of the forty million adult German citizens really care about the executions of the German revolutionaries that they read about in the newspapers, and how many of them remain more or less unmoved, and you will then grasp what this essay is trying to achieve: *a joining of the consciousness of the revolutionary avant-garde with the consciousness of the average citizen*.

We can only indicate a few possible starting points and throw up a few questions, which until now have been ignored by the working-class movement. Some of what we have to say may be incorrectly framed. Some may be actually wrong. Yet it is an undeniable fact that, psychologically speaking, the real life of human beings takes place on a different level from what the champions of the social revolution believe—and yet their mistaken belief is based, precisely, upon their most profound insights into social existence. In this lies one of the reasons for the failure to date of the working-class movement.

This essay should be read as an appeal by average, nonpolitical men to the future leaders of the revolution—an appeal for a better understanding, with a little less insistence on a grasp of the "historical process"; for a more adequate articulation of their real problems and desires; for a less theoretical grasp of the "subjective factor" in history; and for a better practical understanding of what this factor represents in *the life of the masses*.

TWO KINDS OF CLASS CONSCIOUSNESS

• • • • •

Discussions with a variety of political groups have shown that any reply to the question What is class consciousness? must be preceded by a brief definition of the fundamental problems of the political situation as it is at this moment.

The severe defeat of the socialist movement in Germany is already exercising an adverse effect in other countries, and fascism is today rapidly gaining ground on the revolutionary movement everywhere.

Both the Second and Third Internationals have shown their inability to master the situation even theoretically, to say nothing of the practical side: the Second International, by its fundamentally bourgeois politics; the Third by its lack of self-criticism, the incorrigibility of its mistaken attitudes, and above all by its inability—due in part to lack of will—to eradicate bureaucracy in its own camp.

The Socialist Workers' Party and the International Communists want a "new International." Serious differences have arisen regarding the manner in which the new party is to be founded. Trotsky has already called for the founding of the Fourth International. The Socialist Workers' Party agrees in principle, but wants the new International to be the *result* of the workers' rallying together instead of, as Trotsky wants, creating the Fourth International first and rallying the workers around it.

The question we in the Sex-Pol movement are asking is this: Should an organization be founded at once, and should recruitment to it be based upon its declared program? Or should the program and the ideology be allowed time to penetrate the masses, and organizational steps be taken only later on a broader base? We have opted for the second method—believing that a "looser" preparatory organization offers many advantages, in that it avoids any premature setting of limits and the danger of sectarianism, gives better opportunities for permeating other organizations, and much else besides.

Our considered view of the prospects for further political development also supports this choice. The Sex-Pol working community believes that there are three main possibilities. First, there is the possibility of an unpredictable uprising in Germany in the near future. Since none of the existing organizations is even remotely prepared for this eventuality, none of them could control such a movement or lead it consciously to a conclusion. This possibility, however, is the least likely. Should it happen, the situation would be chaotic and the outcome extremely uncertain, but it would nevertheless be the best solution, and we should support and promote it in every way from the very start. Second, the working-class movement may need a few years before it rallies once more in terms of theory and organization. It will then form an *integrated* movement under good, highly trained, purposeful and determined leadership, will struggle for power in Germany, and will seize it within, say, the next *two* decades. This prospect is the most probable, but it requires energetic, unswerving and tireless preparation beginning today. Third, the last major possibility is that the rallying of the working-class movement under new, good and reliable leadership will not occur quickly enough or will fail to occur altogether; that international fascism will establish itself and consolidate its positions everywhere, especially by reason of its immanent skill in attracting children and youth; that it will acquire a permanent mass base, and will be helped by economic conjunctures, however marginal. In such a case the socialist movement must reckon with a long—a very long—period of economic, political and cultural barbarism lasting many decades. Its task then will be to *prove* that it was not mistaken *in principle* and that, in the last analysis, it was right *after all*. This prospect reveals the full extent of the responsibility we bear.

We propose, so far as conditions permit, to allow for the *first* possibility; to make the *second* the real target of our work, because it is the more likely one, and to concentrate all our efforts on bringing it about while doing everything within human power to avoid the *third*.

If, then, our aim is to create unity and striking power in the working class, and to bring about an alliance of all strata of the working population, we must begin by drawing a sharp dividing line between ourselves and those who talk a great deal about "unity" but, in practice, promote nothing but discord even though this may not be their real intention. Why is it that even now, after the German catastrophe, the forming of sectarian cliques continues undeterred? Why do things look so bleak in responsible circles both inside and outside Germany? Why do the old methods of sterile scholastic discussion and useless reciprocal recrimination refuse to disappear, refuse to yield to livelier, more effective methods better adapted to the reality of today?

We believe that this unhappy state of affairs is due to our clinging to old, worn-out, ossified dogmas, words, schemas and methods of discussion, and that this clinging is in turn due to the lack of *new* ways of posing problems, *new* ways of thinking and of seeing things with a completely fresh, uncorrupted eye. We are convinced that just one good new idea, just one effective new slogan would rally everyone except the completely hopeless addicts of debate, and would put an end to sterile talk. Anyone who feels "insulted" can take it that we mean him. The next task is to turn living Marxism into reality—first of all, in the way we see reality and discuss it.

This brings us to the question of the founding of a new international organization. If the congress convened for this purpose produced nothing but the old methods, slogans and ways of thinking and discussion, the organization would be stillborn. The expropriation of capital, the socialization of the means of production, the establishment of workers', peasants', soldiers' and employees' rule over the capitalists—these are old concepts and we know all this; we also know that we want true democracy for the working people and that the power is not seized in the voting booth but with arms. We know all this and much else. To proclaim it all once more and lay it down in a program would be of little value, for it has all been done before. The great question is why the people did not listen to us, why our organization fell victim to arteiosclerosis, why we allowed ourselves to be suffocated by our bureaucracy, why the masses indeed acted against their own interest in carrying Hitler to power. If we had the masses behind us today, we should not have to spend such an infinite amount of energy on the question of strategy and tactics, important as it may be.

Various groups in the movement today are using strategy and tactics *against one another*. What we must do above all, if we mean to achieve success, is to face these fundamental problems with completely new ideas, completely new methods of influencing the masses, with a completely new structure of both ideology and personnel.

We hardly need to supply detailed arguments to prove that we failed to speak the language of the broad masses—the nonpolitical or ideologically oppressed broad masses—who in the end assured the triumph of reaction. The masses did not understand our resolutions, or what we meant by socialism; they did not and still do not trust us. They read our papers out of a sense of duty, or not at all. Those who joined the movement had an inarticulate socialist feeling. But we were incapable of turning this feeling to advantage, and in the end it carried Hitler to power. The fact that we suffered our greatest defeat in getting hold of the broad masses, in inspiring the masses, is the fundamental cause of the many shortcomings, great and small, of the working-class movement: the rigid party loyalty of the Social Democrats, the resentment and sense of injury felt by many proletarian leaders, our addiction to empty debate and of the scholastic Marxism we practiced.

One element in the fundamental cause of the failure of socialism—only an element, but an important one, no longer to be ignored, no longer to be regarded as secondary—is the absence of an effective Marxist doctrine of political psychology. This does not merely mean that such a doctrine still remains to be created: it also means that the working class as a whole is extremely wary of psychological examination, of conscious practical psychology. This shortcoming of ours has become the greatest advantage of the class enemy, the mightiest weapon of fascism.

While we presented the masses with superb historical analyses and economic treatises on the contradictions of imperialism, Hitler stirred the deepest roots of their emotional being. As Marx would have put it, we left the praxis of the subjective factor to the idealists; we acted like mechanistic, economistic materialists. Am I exaggerating? Am I seeing the problem through the perspective of a narrow specialization?

Let us try to answer this question with the help of concrete examples, both important and apparently less important ones. We do not propose a panacea but only a small contribution which may be a start.

An effective policy, whose ultimate goal is the achievement of socialism and the establishment of the rule of labor over capital, must not only be based on a recognition of those movements and changes which occur objectively and independently of our will as a result of the development of the productive forces. This policy must also, simultaneously and on the same level, take account of what happens "in people's heads," i.e., in the psychical structures of the human beings who are subjected to these processes and who actually carry them out—people from different countries and cities, people of different occupations, ages and sexes.

The concept of class consciousness occupies a central place in the socialist movement and its politics. Great stress is placed upon the oppressed strata of the populations of all countries "becoming class-conscious" as the most urgent precondition of the revolutionary overthrow of the present social system. By this we obviously mean that human beings must undergo a certain change under the effect of economic and social processes so as to become capable of performing the social act of revolution. We know, too, that Lenin created the political vanguard and the revolutionary part in order to encourage this transformation in ordinary men and women—to accelerate and concentrate it, and mold it into a political force. In the vanguard, made up of the finest and most conscious fighters for socialism, the consciousness of the social situation—of the means necessary for mastering it, of the way forward to socialism—was to be concentrated at the approximate level to which the working masses would have to be raised if the task of revolution was to be successfully accomplished. This is no more and no less than a definition of the policy summed in the term "united front."

Two examples should in themselves suffice to show that we are far removed from a concrete understanding of what class consciousness actually is.

In a recently published brochure entitled *Neu Beginnen* (Starting Afresh), the demand is very rightly made for a "revolutionary party," for a leadership which is revolutionary in the full sense of the word; yet the existence of class consciousness in the proletariat is denied.

> The basis of all their [the Second and Third Internationals'] insights and actions is the belief in a revolutionary spontaneity immanent within the proletariat. . . . But what if such revolutionary spontaneity exists only in the imagination of the Socialist Party leaders and not in reality? What if the proletariat is not at all driven toward the "final socialist struggle from within itself," that is to say by natural social forces? . . . Incapable of thinking otherwise than in terms of their dogmas and theories, they [the leaders] believe with truly religious fervor in spontaneous revolutionary forces. . . . (p. 6)

The unparalleled heroism shown by the Austrian workers on February 12–16, 1934, proves that revolutionary spontaneity can very well exist without a consciousness of the "final socialist struggle." Revolutionary spontaneity and consciousness of the "final struggle" are two quite separate things.

We are told that the leadership must carry revolutionary consciousness into the masses. Undoubtedly it must. But—it is our turn to ask—what if we do not yet clearly know what we mean by revolutionary consciousness? In Germany there were, at the end, some thirty million *anticapitalist* workers, more than enough *in number* to make a social revolution; yet it was precisely with the help of the staunchest *anticapitalist* mentality that fascism came into power. Does an anticapitalist mentality qualify as class consciousness, or is it just the beginning of class consciousness, just a precondition for the birth of class consciousness? What is class consciousness, anyway?

Lenin created the concept of the vanguard, of the revolutionary party, as well as the organization itself whose purpose was to do what the masses themselves could not spontaneously achieve. "We have already said," wrote Lenin, "that the workers cannot, in fact, have a social-democratic consciousness. Such consciousness can only be brought in from outside. The history of all countries shows that the working class if left to itself is capable only of attaining a trade-unionist consciousness, i.e., of realizing the necessity for banding together in trade unions, waging a struggle against the entrepreneurs, demanding various forms of labor legislation from the government, etc."

In other words, the working class does derive a "consciousness" from its class situation—a consciousness, it it true, which is not sufficient to shake off the rule of capital (a tightly organized party is needed for this); but can it not be said that preliminary forms or elements of what is called class consciousness, or revolutionary consciousness, do, perhaps, exist after all? What is this consciousness? How can we define it? What does it look like in practice?

The denial of what might be called class consciousness or its elements, or of the preconditions for class consciousness, as a *spontaneous* formation within the oppressed class, is based on the fact that in this concrete form *it is not recognized*. This is what puts the leadership into a hopeless position, for however courageous, well trained and otherwise excellent the leaders may be, if the proletariat possesses nothing that might be called class consciousness, why then, no leadership on earth will succeed in giving it one. Anyway, what is this thing that is supposed to be carried into the masses? Highly specialized understanding of the social process and its contradictions? Complete knowledge of the laws of capitalist exploitation? Did the partisans in revolutionary Russia have such knowledge when they fought so splendidly, or did they, perhaps, not need it at all? Were they "class-conscious" workers and peasants or mere rebels? We raise these questions only to show that they lead nowhere.

Let us try to proceed from simple practice and experience.

A short while ago a great deal was being said within a certain political group about class consciousness and the need to "raise class consciousness on a mass scale." The listener was forced to ask himself, perhaps for the first time: What exactly are they talking about? What do they mean by what they call class consciousness? One of the people present, who had kept very quiet the whole time, asked a leading party official who had insisted with particular fervor on the need for developing class consciousness among the German proletariat whether he could name five concrete features of class consciousness and perhaps also five factors which impede its development. If one wanted to develop class consciousness it was surely necessary to know what it was that one wanted to develop and why it did not develop of its own accord under the pressures of material poverty. The question seemed logical. The party official was at first a little surprised, hesitated for an instant, and then declared confidently, "Why, hunger, of course!" "Is a hungry storm trooper class-conscious?" was the prompt counterquestion. Is a hungry thief class-conscious when he steals a sausage? or an unemployed worker who accepts two marks for joining a reactionary demonstration? or an adolescent who throws stones at the police? But if hunger, on which the CP had based its whole mass psychology, is not in itself an element of class consciousness, then what is? What is freedom? What are its concrete features? Wherein does socialist freedom differ from the national freedom which Hitler promises?

The answers until now have been extremely unsatisfactory. Has the left-wing press ever raised or answered questions of this kind? It has not. The notion that the oppressed class can carry a revolution through to a triumphant conclusion without leadership, and out of a spontaneously generated revolutionary will, is certainly false; but it is just as wrong to believe the opposite—that all that matters is the leadership because it has to *create* class consciousness.

No leadership could ever do so unless the beginnings of class consciousness were already present, unless class consciousness were already being formed spontaneously. But if a certain psychical situation in the masses exists, and has to be brought into harmony with the highly developed consciousness of the revolutionary leadership in order to create the subjective preconditions for a social revolution, then it is all the more essential to find an answer to the question: What is class consciousness? Should anyone object that the question is superfluous because our policy has always consisted in satisfying the workers' day-to-day demands, then we shall ask: Are we developing class consciousness if we insist on electric fans being installed on a shop floor? What if the Nazi shop steward does the same, and is perhaps a better speaker than our men? Will he have the workers on his side? Yes, he will. Where is the difference between the socialist and the fascist defense of "day-to-day interests," between our freedom slogans and the Nazi slogan of Strength Through Joy?

Do we mean the same thing when we speak of the class consciousness of a proletarian apprentice and that of a proletarian youth leader? It is said that the consciousness of the masses must be raised to the level of revolutionary class consciousness; if by this we mean the sophisticated understanding of historical processes which a revolutionary leader must possess, then our aim is utopian. Under capitalism it will never be possible, whatever propaganda methods we use, to instill such highly specialized knowledge in the broad masses who have to do the actual work of insurrection and revolution. When, at electoral meetings, we used simply to shout slogans, or if, as often happened at the Sports Palace in Berlin, a party official spent hours spouting learnedly about the finance politics of the bourgeoisie or the contradictions between the United States and Japan, the spontaneous enthusiasm of the masses was killed every time. By assuming that the masses were interested in objective economic analyses and had the intellectual equipment to follow them, we indeed killed what is rightly called the "class feeling" of the thousands-strong audience.

Revolutionary Marxist policy to date has presupposed the existence of a ready-made class consciousness in the proletariat without being about to define it in concrete detail. It has projected its own, often incorrect idea of sociological processes into the consciousness of the oppressed class, thus making itself guilty, as someone recently pointed out, of "subjective idealism." And yet one could unambiguously sense the mass class consciousness at every Communist meeting, and its atmosphere could be clearly distinguished from that of other political meetings. In other words, there must be something like a class consciousness in the broad masses, and this consciousness is fundamentally different from that of the revolutionary leadership. To put it concretely, there are *two kinds* of class consciousness, *that of the leadership and that of the masses*, and the two have to be brought into harmony with one another. The leadership has no task more urgent, besides that of acquiring a precise understanding of the objective historical process, than to understand: (a) what are the progressive desires, ideas and thoughts which are latent in people of different social strata, occupations, age groups and sexes, and (b) what are the desires, fears, thoughts and ideas ("traditional bonds") which prevent the progressive desires, ideas, etc., from developing.

The class consciousness of the masses is neither ready-formed, as the CP leadership believed, nor is it completely absent or structured in a totally different way, as the Socialist Party leadership believed. It is present as a number of concrete elements, which in themselves do not yet constitute class consciousness (e.g., simple hunger), but which, *in conjunction with one another*, could become class consciousness. These elements are not present in pure form, but are permeated, mixed and interwoven with opposing psychical meanings and forces. A Hitler can go on being successful with his formula that the masses can be influenced like little children—that they simply give back to you what you put into them—only so long as the revolutionary party fails to fulfill its most important task, that of developing and distilling mass class consciousness from its present level to a higher one. There was no question of this being done in Germany.

The content of the revolutionary leader's class consciousness is not of a personal kind—when personal interests (ambition, etc.) are present, they inhibit his activity. The class consciousness of the masses, on the other hand (we are not speaking of the negligibly small minority of consciously revolutionary workers), is entirely personal.

The former is filled with the knowledge of the contradictions of the capitalist economic system, the immense possibilities of a socialist planned economy, the need for social revolution to establish a balance between the form of appropriation and the form of production, the progressive and retrograde forces of history, etc. The latter has no such far-reaching perspectives—it is concerned with the trivial problems of everyday life. The former covers the objective historical and socioeconomic process, the outward conditions, both economic and social, to which men are subject in society. This process must be understood, it must be grasped and mastered if one wishes to become its master rather than its slave. For example, a planned economy is necessary in order to abolish the disastrous crises of capitalism and thus create a firm foundation for the lives of all working people. And creating such an economy requires, inter alia, a precise knowledge of U.S.–Japanese contradictions. But the latter type of consciousness lacks *all* interest in the U.S.–Japanese or British–American contradictions, or even in the development of productive forces; it is guided solely by the subjective reflections and effects of these objective facts in and upon an immense variety of trivial everyday matters; its content is an interest in food, clothing, fashion, family relations, the possibility of sexual satisfaction in the narrowest sense, in sexual play and entertainment in a wider sense, such as the cinema, the theater, amusement arcades, parks and dance halls, and also in such questions as the bringing up of children, the arrangement of living space, leisure activities, etc.

Being and the conditions of being are reflected, anchored and reproduced in the psychical structure of men and women at the same time that they form that structure. The objective process and the ways of inhibiting or encouraging and controlling it are accessible to us only through this psychical structure. We make and change the world only through the mind of man, through his will for work, his longing for happiness—in brief, through his psychical existence. The "Marxists" who have degenerated into "Economists" forgot this a long time ago. A global economic and political policy, if it means to create and secure international socialism (not National Socialism!), must find a point of contact with trivial, banal, primitive, simple everyday life, with the desires of the *broadest* masses of all countries and at all levels. *Only in this way can the objective sociological process become one with the subjective consciousness of men and women, abolishing the contradiction and the distance between the two*. The workers, who create wealth and the material basis of culture, must be shown the stage which culture and education have reached "at the top" and be taught to contrast it with the way *they themselves* live; they must be shown how *modest* they are and how they *make a virtue of their modesty*, even if this has sometimes actually been called a revolutionary virtue! Only when we succeed in merging these two kinds of consciousness, and only then, shall we leave behind us the philosophical inner-party debates on tactics, etc.; only then shall we break through to the living tactics of a living mass movement, to a political activity truly linked with life. We are not exaggerating when we assert that the working-class movement could have saved itself an endless succession of sectarian and scholastic struggles, of factions and splinter groups—that it could have shortened the hard road toward the most *self-evident* of things, which is socialism—if it had drawn the material for its propaganda and tactics and policies not only from books, but, in the first place, from the life of the masses. One aspect of the situation today is that young people are, on the average, far ahead of their "leaders" on a number of questions; for example, it is necessary to speak "tactically" or "tactfully" with the leaders about things like sex, which the young understand as a matter of course. It ought to be the other way about: the leader should be the epitome of class consciousness of the first kind and should work toward developing the second kind.

Anyone familiar with the ideological struggles of the working-class movement will perhaps have followed us more or less readily thus far, and will probably have thought: "But this is nothing new—why the long discourse?" He will soon see that when we get down to brass tacks, many of those who are in general agreement with us will nevertheless hesitate, raise objections, have second thoughts, and invoke Marx and Lenin to oppose us. Before anyone so inclined reads any further, we recommend once more, as a test, that he should try to clarify in his own mind just five concrete elements of class consciousness and five obstacles to it.

The following statement will meet with a great deal of resistance on the part of those who regard class consciousness as a matter of ethics. Political reaction, with fascism and the church at its head, demands that the masses should renounce happiness here on earth; it demands chastity, obedience, self-denial, sacrifice for the nation, the people, the fatherland. The problem is not that the reactionaries demand this, but that the masses, by complying with these demands, are supporting the reactionaries and allowing them to enrich themselves and extend their power. The reactionaries take advantage of the guilt feelings of mass individuals, of their ingrained modesty, their tendency to suffer privation silently and willingly, sometimes even happily, and they take advantage of their identification with the glorious *Führer*, whose "love of the people" is for them a substitute for any real satisfaction of their needs. The revolutionary vanguard, through the conditions of their existence and the aims they pursue, are themselves subject to a similar ideology. But what is true of, shall we say, the youth leaders is in no way applicable to the youth they are supposed to lead. If one wants to lead the mass of the population into battle against capital, to develop their class consciousness, to bring them to the point of revolt, then one must recognize the principle of self-denial as harmful, lifeless, stupid and reactionary.

Socialism affirms that the productive forces of society are sufficiently developed to ensure a life corresponding to the average cultural level of society for the broadest masses of all countries. *Against the principle of self-denial preached by political reaction, we must set the principle of happiness and abundance on earth.* We need hardly point out that by this we do not mean bowling tournaments and beer drinking. The modesty of the "man in the street," which is his cardinal virtue in the eyes of fascism and the church, is his greatest fault from the socialist point of view and one of the many factors which impede his class consciousness. Any socialist political economist can prove that sufficient wealth exists in the world to provide a happy life for all workers. But we must prove this more thoroughly, more consistently, in greater detail than we generally do; we must bring all the meticulous care of scientific scholarship to bear upon demonstrating it.

The average worker in Germany or elsewhere was not interested in the Soviet Five-Year Plan as a revolutionary economic achievement in itself but only insofar as it meant increased satisfaction of the needs of workers. His thoughts went more or less like this: If socialism isn't going to mean anything but sacrifice, self-denial, poverty and privation for us, then we don't care whether such misery is called socialism or capitalism. Let socialist economy prove its excellence by satisfying our needs and keeping pace with their growth.

What I mean is that *heroism, which is a virtue in the leadership, is not transferable to the broad masses*. If the masses suffer privations in a period of revolution, they are entitled to demand definite proof that these privations are only a *passing phase* and thus differ from the privations suffered under capitalism.

This is one of the many difficulties which arise from the theory of "socialism in one country." We fully expect that this statement will meet with indignant denials; we shall doubtless be called "petty-bourgeois" and "epicurean." Yet Lenin promised the peasants that the landowners' lands would be distributed among them, although he was very well aware that land distribution encourages a "petty-bourgeois mentality." It was essentially on the strength of this slogan that he carried the revolution through, *with* the peasants and not *against* them. And in doing so he undoubtedly violated a lofty principle of socialist political theory, the principle of collectivism. The Hungarian revolutionaries of 1919, on the other hand, had lofty principles but no understanding of the subjective factor. *They knew the demands of history but not of the peasants.* They socialized the land at once and—they lost the revolution. Let this example suffice to prove, in place of many others, that the ultimate aims of socialism can only be achieved by fulfilling the immediate aims of mass individuals, by ensuring a much greater degree of satisfaction of their needs. Only then can revolutionary heroism occur in the *broad masses*.

Few errors are as far-reaching as the view that "class consciousness" is an ethical concept. The ascetic view of revolution has led only to complications and defeats.

We can easily test whether class consciousness is an ethical or a non-ethical, rational phenomenon by considering a few examples.

If two human beings, A and B, are starving, one of them may accept his fate, refuse to steal, and take to begging or die of hunger, while the other may take the law into his own hands in order to obtain food. A large part of the proletariat, often called *Lumpenproletariat*, live according to the principles of B. We must be clear about this, although we certainly do not share the romantic admiration of the criminal underworld. Which of the two types has more elements of class consciousness in him? Stealing is *not yet* a sign of class consciousness; but a brief moment of reflection shows, despite our inner moral resistance, that the man who refuses to submit to law and steals when he is hungry, that is to say, the man who manifests a will to live, has more energy and fight in him than the one who lies down unprotesting on the butcher's slab. We persist in believing that the fundamental problem of a correct psychological doctrine is not why a hungry man steals but the exact opposite: Why doesn't he steal?

We have said that stealing is *not yet* class consciousness, and we stick to that. A brick is not yet a house; but you use bricks to build houses with—besides planks, mortar, glass and (here I am thinking of the role of the party) engineers, stonemasons, carpenters, etc.

We shall get nowhere if we regard class consciousness as an ethical imperative, and if, in consequence, we try to outdo the spokesmen of the bourgeoisie in condemning the sexuality of youth, the wickedness of prostitutes and criminals and the immorality of thieves. But, you may ask, if we adopt the opposite view, shall we not be harming the interests of the revolution? Couldn't political reaction turn our amoral conception of class consciousness into propaganda against us? Certainly it could and it will, but it does so anyway, however much we try to prove our unimpeachable morality—it does us no good, for it only drives the victims of capitalism into the arms of political reaction because they do not feel we understand them. Yet in the eyes of political reaction we are no better for all our morality. In its eyes we are thieves because we want to abolish private ownership of the means of production. Do we therefore want to abandon or conceal this fundamental intention? And is it not cited against us?

Everything, without exception, which today bears the name of morality and ethics serves the oppressors of working humanity. We can prove both in theory and in practice that our new order of social life, *just because* it will be an amoral one, is capable of replacing the chaos of today by real order. Lenin's attitude to the question of proletarian ethics was unambiguously connected with the interests of the proletarian revolution. Whatever serves the revolution is ethical, whatever harms it is unethical. Let us try to formulate the question in another way. *Everything that contradicts the bourgeois order, everything that contains a germ of rebellion, can be regarded as an element of class consciousness; everything that creates or maintains a bond with the bourgeois order, that supports and reinforces it, is an impediment to class consciousness.*

When, during the November 1919 revolution, the masses were demonstrating in the Tiergarten in Berlin, most of the demonstrators took great care not to walk on the grass. This story, whether it is true or merely well invented, sums up an important aspect of the tragedy of the revolutionary movement: *the bourgeoisification of those who are to make the revolution.*

BOURGEOIS AND REVOLUTIONARY POLITICS

"Politics" as Fetish

The Sex-Pol movement has to fight on many fronts. One of these concerns the tangled web of ideas in people's minds, ideas that are apparently quite meaningless if one asks the simplest questionss about them. For example: "What is politics?"

Here is an occasion when one might ask it. We are trying to explain the fundamental principles of mass psychology as revealed by sexual economy, and somebody makes the following objection: "What you say may be very true and very useful, but aren't politics and the economic factor more important?" The audience, which has been listening to the report or lecture on mass psychology with great interest and approval, suddenly begins to doubt its own opinion, simply because of the curiously mesmerizing effect of the word "politics."

Often it happens that at this word even the speaker, who is meant to be putting the case for mass psychology, will retreat and say something to the effect that the relationship between politics and the practice of mass psychology "still remains to be examined."

The pundits of high politics and of the "economic factor" (who always think that this factor is being neglected, although in the newspapers and reviews you read about nothing else and never a word about mass psychology) are generally at a loss to explain what exactly "politics" is—a word that nevertheless works like a fetish on ordinary mortals. We must always turn the most blinding searchlight on anything that smacks of fetishism. We must bombard such things with the most naïve questions, which, as we all know, are the most embarrassing ones and generally yield the most interesting results.

The political layman understands "politics" to mean, in the first place, diplomatic negotiations between representatives of great or small powers in which destinies of mankind are decided; of these he rightly says he understands nothing. Or else he sees politics as parliamentary deals concluded between friends and enemies alike, reciprocal swindling, spying, bestowing of favors, and decision-making in accordance with "the established rules of procedure." Of this, too, he understands nothing, but he is often repelled by it, and so he decides, with great relief, that "he wants to have nothing to do with politics." He fails to see the contradiction in the fact that the transactions he so rightly despises affect his own life, and that he is, in effect, leaving his life in the hands of people he considers to be a gang of crooks.

Politics may also mean wanting to win the masses of the population over to one's side. Anyone trained as a Marxist will realize at once that bourgeois politics must always be demagogical because it can only make promises which it cannot keep. Not so revolutionary politics, which can fulfill all the promises it makes to the masses and is therefore in principle undemagogical. Whenever it is or appears to be demagogical we may safely conclude that revolutionary principles have been abandoned.

Let us consider a typical passage of "political" writing of the kind which, in our experience, is thought of by the masses as "high politics."

That is to say, it is not understood but regarded with great timidity and awe; if it produces a reaction, it is a passive one.

> If one prefers the legalization of armaments to the armaments race, as England does, one has to admit that, together with such legalization, guarantees against any renewed breach of agreements must be provided. Such guarantees for the carrying out of a convention on disarmament should be discussed at the so-called disarmament conference in Geneva. But Germany does not accept the condition imposed by France. It remains silent on this subject in its official communications and, in the Berlin talks with Eden, the British Lord Privy Seal, it has so far refused to come to Geneva. As a result, the Franco-British negotiations, as already stated, have lost their object. The diplomatic exchange of views outside the Geneva disarmament conference has come to an end without yielding any result. It is now for the disarmament conference to create, without Germany, the required guarantees for peace. In this, France is counting upon the co-operation of Great Britain.
>
> This is the content and meaning of the long French note of April 17, which is a reply to the British note of March 28 and to Sir John Simon's *aide-mémoire* of April 10.

I have deliberately quoted this passage without reference to its source so as not to hurt anyone's feelings. Anyone whom the cap fits should wear it. Isn't that the only way to deal with the tender sensibilities of politicians?

Who is "Germany," who is "France?" What is a "diplomatic exchange of views?" Is that really the content and meaning of the French note? What relation does this "political note" bear to the needs of the masses, their thoughts and feelings, the way they live or merely vegetate? Why, none at all! Compare it with Lenin's politics at the time of Brest-Litovsk. The smallest famine-stricken child could understand the slogan "End the war" but the adherents of "high politics" were against it.

The broad masses, whose wishes and whose future are to be guaranteed by revolutionary politics, think and talk differently. Anyone who goes on speaking of Barthou's travels today without explaining—simply, clearly, intelligibly to everyone—the reactionary swindle which is the real purpose of these trips, becomes an involuntary accomplice.

If we look for the effect of high politics on the broad masses, we shall see that, at the very most, it is aped in the form of beerhall politics by a few individuals. The vast majority tend always to react passively, without interest, playing the role of mere extras in the fairground show of "high politics." We must clearly realize that this fairground show would come to a sudden end—a very disagreeable one for the diplomats—if the extras were to take up a more active attitude, if, in brief, they stopped being nonpolitical.

If we forget even for a moment to ask ourselves the question: "What is happening among the masses?"—a question absolutely fundamental to revolutionary politics—then we are bound, whether we want to be or not, to get enmeshed in the web of bourgeois politics or else to become nonpolitical. The nonpolitical attitude of the broad masses is one of the political reaction's main strengths. Another is the smoke screen with which it surrounds its politics, so that even socialists are often confused.

One of the revolutionary politician's most important tasks is to sense and to discover the effect of backstage politics on the masses. When in the summer of 1932 Hitler approached Hindenburg for the first time with the demand to appoint him Reich chancellor, and when that demand was rejected following a number of backstage intrigues, of which the people knew little or nothing, Hitler appealed to his supporters with a fervent profession of faith in the "will of the people." The occasion for this was provided by the Potempa case. Some storm troopers had brutally murdered a Polish worker and had been sentenced to death. Hitler interceded for them vociferously. The real motive for this gesture was the snub he had received from Hindenburg. In other words, when his feudal connections failed him, he played the trump card of his mass base.

The masses had absolutely no idea of the game that was being played with them. Rather, they felt themselves "understood" by Hitler in an upsurge of nationalistic identification. Hitler's open support of the men who, out of a "sense of national honor," had shot down a "Marxist dog," and his stand against the hated government that had sentenced the murderers to death, outweighted by far the effect of *erroneous* Communist propaganda whose famous policy of "unmasking" consisted only in calling the murderers murderers. An explanation, offered on a mass scale, of the connection between Hindenburg's refusal and Hitler's appeal to mass feeling would have been effective. But the CP merely insisted that all reactionary parties are the same; it failed to grasp the real contradictions within the bourgeoisie; it had never learned to study and interpret the reactions of the masses on their own or the enemy's side. By doing nothing except to say that the murderers were indeed murderers, it placed itself, in the eyes both of the convinced followers of the Nazis and of those who, at that time, were only mildly sympathetic to them, on the side of the government which the masses loathed.

* * *

A Schema of Revolutionary Politics

If the social revolution is right in asserting that it can really solve the social problems of economics and culture in the spirit of social democracy, the following political questions and principles must be posed:

1. What are the tactics used by bourgeois parties to win over the masses or to take them from other parties?
2. What are the motives that lead the masses to follow political groups or parties which can never fulfill their promises?
3. What are the needs of the masses at all levels?
4. Which of these needs are socially practicable and justified? What are vitally essential?
5. Is the state of the world economy such that these needs can be satisfied by the overthrow of capitalist rule and the substitution of a planned economy for economic anarchy?
6. Do the masses know which social institutions impede the satisfaction of their needs, and why these obstructive institutions exist?
7. How can these institutions be removed and what should replace them?
8. What are the economic, social and mass-psychological preconditions necessary for the satisfaction of the needs of the broad masses?

Each of these questions points to the inexorable necessity for social revolution—each, without exception, in every single sphere of human life. In other words, mass-psychological work must not remain in the shadow of economic policy; quite on the contrary, economic policy must enter the service of a mass psychology which understands and guides the masses. The needs of men and women do not exist to serve economic policy—economic policy exists to satisfy these needs.

The Bourgeois Politics of the German Communist Party

The experience of life in the German Communist Party shows that the only possible form of revolutionary politics, as outlined above, was lacking in Germany. When Communist leaders spoke for hours at the Sports Palace about the conflicting interests of the Great Powers and the economic background of the impending war, they were, without wanting to, imitating bourgeois politics. Our revolutionary politicians are too zealous in emulating the Paul Boncours. What makes them do this, and so lose any chance of success, is a question of the psychical structure of our revolutionary leaders. They will again feel sorely insulted when they read this. They will call it "Trotskyite counter revolutionism." Nor is there any hope of convincing them that the politics they conduct are bourgeois in form and, consequently, also in objective reality. To anticipate their protests, we shall quote just one of many concrete examples to show that the German Communist Party has exchanged the revolutionary principle of politics for a bourgeois one.

In December 1932, the Social Democratic Party organized a demonstration in the Lustgarten. Communist organizations, in particular the *Kampfbünde* (Fighting Unions), joined the demonstration. They mingled with the mass of the Social Democratic demonstrators, and without any talk about U.S.–Japanese contradictions, they formed a united front. That was the will and language of the masses. The Communist Party leaders, who wanted a united front "only under Communist leadership," later reprimanded the party members concerned. The party orders had only been to line the streets and to "cheer" the demonstration. At the same time Torgler was secretly negotiating with the Social Democratic leaders about forming a united front. The masses *knew nothing* about these negotiations; the official line was that a united front led by the Social Democrats would be "counterrevolutionary." I personally took part at the time in a secret meeting on the forming of a united front between leading Communist and Social Democrat functionaries. No one in the party cells was supposed to know anything about it. *That is bourgeois politics*. The exact opposite would have been proletarian-revolutionary politics: the party should have instructed the Communists to support the Social Democrat demonstration and should have told the masses in the Lustgarten over loudspeakers that negotiations were in progress with the Social Democrats on the forming of a united front. That is what is properly called developing the ideology of the masses and giving expression to their wishes. Instead of this the party engaged in "high politics," "strategy" and "tactics"—without the masses, sometimes against the masses, keeping out everyone who wanted and practiced revolutionary politics.

The abolition of secret diplomacy is an old revolutionary principle. It is a self-evident one, for, if social revolution is the execution of the people's will against the owners of the means of production under the leadership of the industrial proletariat, there can be nothing left to keep secret. There should be nothing left that the masses ought not to hear: on the contrary, they must be able to know and check everything that happens.

* * *

The Development of a Revolutionary State Policy from the People's Needs

When a representative of Sex-Pol met with Wilhelm Pieck, the representative of the party's Central Committee, for a discussion in 1932, Pieck said that the views expounded in *The Imposition of Sexual Morality* contradicted those of the party and of Marxism.

Asked to explain, he said, "Your starting point is consumption, ours is production; therefore, you are not Marxists." The Sex-Pol spokesman asked whether human needs arose out of production or whether, on the contrary, production was there to satisfy human needs. Pieck failed to understand this question. Only two years later did the distinction become clear: economistic communism developed its entire work and propaganda solely from the objective aspect of social existence, from the progress of the productive forces, from economic contradictions between states, the superiority of the Soviet planned economy over capitalist anarchy, etc., and it then "tied the politics of state into the small daily needs." But this tie-in was an utter fiasco. Sex-Pol, on the other hand, aroused maximum interest, even among the most politically confused people at every level, by developing the necessities of the social revolution out of subjective needs, and by basing all political issues on the "whether" and the "how" of satisfying the needs of the masses. Herein lies not only the fundamental difference between living revolutionary work and dogmatic, scholastic "Marxism," but also the reason why even the best party officials, once they get stuck in "high state politics," fail to understand what Sex-Pol is all about.

Some Comintern officials, of course, are aware that something is missing from their work. Yet they cannot find the concrete point at which state politics and mass needs come together. For example, Manuilsky in his speech entitled "The Revolutionary Crisis Is Maturing" delivered at the Seventeenth Party Congress of the C.P.S.U. (quoted from *Rundschau*, No. 16, p. 586) said:

> Let us take our Communist Youth International. The Communist Youth International has, over a period of years under the guidance of the Comintern, raised a splendid generation of young Bolsheviks who have more than once proved their boundless devotion to the cause of Communism. But it has not proved capable of penetrating deep into the masses of working youth. The Social Democrats haven't got this youth either. The youth in the capitalist countries belong to the millions-strong sports organizations

> created by the bourgeoisie, by its military staffs and by its priests. In Germany, a certain group of unemployed youth has gone into the fascist barracks. But the members of the Young Communist League have not quite understood this lesson. In Germany they fought the fascists courageously. In a number of countries they are doing quite good work in the army, and are getting long sentences of imprisonment for it, yet it no more occurs to them to join, say, a Catholic sports organization, where tens of thousands of young workers meet, than it would occur to the Pope to join the League of Atheists in hopes of making propaganda for Catholicism. (*Laughter*). But members of the YCL and Communists are not bound by prestige considerations as the Vicar of Christ is. Communist and YCL organizations must be always on the move, they must be present wherever workers are present, they must be in the sports organizations, in such leisure-time organizations as the *Dopolavoro* in Italy, in the labor service camps, but above all they must be in the factories.

All this is perfectly correct, but the most important thing is lacking. When a member of the YCL works inside a Christian youth organization, the economicopolitical analyses of the CP's Central Committee are of absolutely no use to him in attracting the interest of his young Christian colleagues. He has got to know what he should talk about and what solutions Communism has to offer, not so much to problems of political economy as to the special problems of Catholic youth. From this starting point he can go on, very gradually, to show how a planned economy would serve as a basis for solving personal problems. And so we may say that Sex-Pol agrees with Manuilsky in principle, so far as the inner-organizational work of Communists is concerned, but it differs profoundly from him on the concrete questions of the actual interests of average young men and women, Christian or otherwise, and the crucial personal problems that should serve as the starting point for the work of the YCL propagandist.[1] The same applies to every formalistic notion of the Comintern leaders.

They are always saying, quite rightly, that work concerning the masses is necessary, but at the same time they reject the *concrete contents* of such necessary work, especially if these contents are personal and removed from "high politics." They see the personal and the political as opposite poles instead of recognizing the dialectical relationship between them. Not only are some personal problems (such as the question of sexual partners or of separate dwellings for young people) among the most typical social problems, but one could go so far as to say that politics is nothing more than the praxis of the needs and interests of the different strata and age groups of society.

To sum up very briefly: the difference between revolutionary and bourgeois politics is that the former sets out to serve the needs of the masses, whereas the latter is wholly founded on the structural, historically conditioned inability of the masses to formulate their needs.

• • • • •

Conclusions

The class consciousness of the masses is not a knowledge of the historical or economic laws that govern the existence of the human being, but it is

1. knowledge of one's own vital necessities in all spheres;
2. knowledge of ways and possibilities of satisfying them;
3. knowledge of the obstacles that a social system based on private property puts in the way of their satisfaction;
4. knowledge of one's own inhibitions and fears that prevent one from clearly realizing one's needs and the obstacles to their satisfaction ("the enemy within" is a particularly true image of the psychical inhibitions of the oppressed individual);
5. knowledge that mass unity makes an invincible force against the power of oppressors.

The class consciousness of the revolutionary leadership (the revolutionary party) is nothing more than knowledge plus the ability to articulate on behalf of the masses what they cannot express themselves. The revolutionary liberation from capitalism is the final act that will grow spontaneously from the fully developed class consciousness of the masses once the revolutionary leadership has understood the masses in every aspect of their life.

Note

1. See *The Sexual Struggle of Youth*. This book was banned by the German Communist Party, while young people at all levels snatched it up with the utmost eagerness.

III

THE ISOLATED THEORETICIAN: THE FRANKFURT SCHOOL

5

Max Horkheimer (1895–1973)

Born in Germany, Max Horkheimer was trained as a philosopher. Strongly influenced by both the rise of fascism and Marxism's degeneration into Stalinism, Horkheimer was instrumental in the development of the Institute for Social Research, a Frankfurt center for the creation of nondogmatic Marxist theory. From the 1930s on, some of the most important Western Marxist thinkers—Marcuse, Adorno, Habermas, and Erich Fromm—have been part of this circle. In work ranging from socially oriented psychoanalysis to economic theory, members of this "Frankfurt School" established new paradigms of leftist theory opposed both to Stalinist totalitarinism and the "one-dimensionality" of modern bourgeois culture and political life.

In the following selection from his essay "Traditional and Critical Theory" (1937), Horkheimer is seeking a philosophical account of a "critical theory." Such a theory is to be an intellectual structure that transcends the dominant trends of bourgeois positivism and the scientistic tendencies of Marxism. It must also connect the theoretical search for truth to the political commitment to creating a just and humane society.

"Traditional and Critical Theory"

POSTSCRIPT

In the preceding essay I pointed out two ways of knowing: one is based on the *Discourse on Method*, the other on Marx's critique of political economy. Theory in the traditional sense established by Descartes and everywhere practiced in the pursuit of the specialized sciences organizes experience in the light of questions which arise out of life in present-day society. The resultant network of disciplines contains information in a form which makes it useful in any particular circumstances for the greatest possible number of purposes. The social genesis of problems, the real situations in which science is put to use, and the purposes which it is made to serve are all regarded by science as external to itself.

The critical theory of society, on the other hand, has for its object men as producers of their own historical way of life in its totality. The real situations which are the starting-point of science are not regarded simply as data to be verified and to be predicted according to the laws of probability. Every datum depends not on nature alone but also on the power man has over it. Objects, the kind of perception, the questions asked, and the meaning of the answers all bear witness to human activity and the degree of man's power.

In thus relating matter—that is, the apparently irreducible facts which the scientific specialist must respect—to human production, the critical theory of society agrees with German idealism. Ever since Kant, idealism has insisted on the dynamic moment in the relationship and has protested against the adoration of facts and the social conformism this brings with it. "As in mathematics," says Fichte, "so in one's whole view of the world; the only difference is that in interpreting the world one is unconscious that he is interpreting, for the interpretation takes place necessarily, not freely."[1] This thought was a commonplace in German idealism. But the activity exercised on the matter presented to man was regarded as intellectual; it was the activity of a metempirical consciousness-in-itself, an absolute ego, the spirit, and consequently the victory over the dumb, unconscious, irrational side of this activity took place in principle in the person's interior, in the realm of thought.

In the materialist conception, on the contrary, the basic activity involved is work in society, and the class-related form of this work puts its mark on all human patterns of reaction, including theory. The intervention of reason in the processes whereby knowledge and its object are constituted, or the subordination of these processes to conscious control, does not take place therefore in a purely intellectual world, but coincides with the struggle for certain real ways of life.

The elaboration of theories in the traditional sense is regarded in our society as an activity set off from other scientific and nonscientific activities, needing to know nothing of the historical goals and tendencies of which such activity is a part. But the critical theory in its concept formation and in all phases of its development very consciously makes its own that concern for the rational organization of human activity which it is its task to illumine and legitimate. For this theory is not concerned only with goals already imposed by existent ways of life, but with men and all their potentialities.

To that extent the critical theory is the heir not only of German idealism but of philosophy as such. It is not just a research hypothesis which shows its value in the ongoing business of men; it is an essential element in the historical effort to create a world which satisfies the needs and powers of men. However extensive the interaction between the critical theory and the special sciences whose progress the theory must respect and on which it has for decades exercised a liberating and stimulating influence, the theory never aims simply at an increase of knowledge as such. Its goal is man's emancipation from slavery. In this it resembles Greek philosophy, not so much in the Hellenistic age of resignation as in the golden age of Plato and Aristotle. After the fruitless political projects of both these men the Stoics and Epicureans confined themselves to developing a doctrine of individualistic practices. The new dialectical philosophy, however, has held on to the realization that the free development of individuals depends on the rational constitution of society. In radically analyzing present social conditions it became a critique of the economy.

Critique, however, is not identical with its object. Philosophy has not provided a teaching on national economy. The curves of the mathematical political economics of our day are no more able to maintain a link with essentials than are positivist or existential philosophy. Concepts in these disciplines have lost any relation to the fundamental situations of the age. Rigorous investigation has always required the isolating of structures, but today the guidelines for this process are no longer being supplied, as in Adam Smith's time, by conscious, inspiring, historical concerns. Modern analyses have lost all connection with any rounded knowledge that deals with historical reality. It is left to others or to a later generation or to accident to establish a relation of the analyses to reality and specific goals. As long as there is a social demand for and recognition of such acitivity, the sciences are not disturbed by reality or leave the care of it to other disciplines, for example sociology or philosophy, which of course act the same way in turn. The forces which guide the life of society, those rulers of the day, are thereby tacitly accepted by science itself as judges of its meaning and value, and knowledge is declared powerless.

Unlike modern specialized science, however, the critical theory of society has continued to be a philosophical discipline even when it engages in a critique of the economy. For its content is the transformation of the concepts which dominate the economy into their opposites: fair exchange into a deepening of social injustice, a free economy into monopolistic control, productive work into rigid relationships which hinder production, the maintenance of society's life into the pauperization of the peoples. Of central importance here is not so much what remains unchanged as the historical movement of the period which is now approaching its end. *Capital* is no less exact in its analyses than the political economics it criticizes, but in even its most refined estimates of particular, periodically recurring events knowledge of the historical course of society as a whole supplies the dynamic motif. Its distinction from the views of the pure economic specialist is due not to some special philosophical object but to its regard for the tendencies of society as a whole, which regard plays a decisive role even in the most abstract logical and economic discussions.

The philosophical character of the critical theory emerges by comparison not only with political economy but also with economism in practice. The struggle against the illusory harmonies of liberalism and the broadcasting of the contradictions immanent in it and in the abstractness of its concept of freedom have been taken up verbally in very different parts of the world and turned into reactionary slogans. The economy must serve man, not man the economy: this is in the mouths of the very men who have always meant by the economy their own patrons. Society as a whole and the community are being glorified by people who cannot think of them in their simple and proper meaning but only in opposition to the individual. They are identified with the depraved order of things which these people themselves represent. In the concept of "holy egoism" and of the vital concerns of the imaginary "national community," the concern of real men for an uninhibited development and a happy existence is confused with the hunger of influential groups for power.

The popular materialism of practice pure and simple, which dialectical materialism criticizes, is camouflaged by idealist slogans whose very transparency makes them attractive to its most faithful practitioners, and it has become the real religion of the age.[2] Professional scholars, eager to conform, may reject every connection of their disciplines with so-called value judgments and firmly pursue the separation of thought and political attitude. But the real wielders of power in their nihilism take such rejections of illusion with brutal seriousness. Value judgments, they say, belong either in the nation's poetry or in the people's courts but certainly not in the tribunals of thought. The critical theory, on the contrary, having the happiness of all individuals as its goal, does not compromise with continued misery, as do the scientific servants of authoritarian states.

Reason's intuition of itself, regarded by philosophy in former times as the highest degree of happiness, is transformed in modern philosophy into the materialist concept of a free, self-determining society, while retaining from idealism the conviction that men have other possibilities than to lose themselves in the status quo or to accumulate power and profit.

Some elements of the critical theory reappear, with a distorted meaning, in the theory and practice of its opponents. To such an extent, since the setback of all progressive efforts in the developed countries of Europe, has confusion spread even among the enemies of such efforts. The abolition of social relationships which presently hinder development is in fact the next historical goal. But abolition is a dialectical concept. The takeover of what belongs to the individual into the state's keeping, the spread of industry, even in the widespread satisfaction of the masses are facts whose historical significance is determined only by the nature of the totality to which they belong. However important they may be in comparison with realities which are survivals from the past, they can nonetheless be swept up with the latter into a retrogressive movement. The old world is in decline because of an outdated principle of economic organization, and the cultural collapse is bound up with it as well. The economy is the first cause of wretchedness, and critique, theoretical and practical, must address itself primarily to it.

It would be mechanistic, not dialectical thinking, however, to judge the future forms of society solely according to their economy. Historical change does not leave untouched the relations between the spheres of culture, and if in the present state of society economy is the master of man and therefore the lever by which he is to be moved to change, in the future men must themselves determine all their relationships in the face of natural necessities. Economics in isolation will therefore not provide the norm by which the community of men is to be measured. This is also true for the period of transition in which politics will win a new independence from the economy. Only at the end of that period will political problems be reduced to simple problems of administration. Before that point is reached the whole situation can change; thus even the character of the transition remains indeterminate.

Economism, to which the critical theory is often reduced, does not consist in giving too much importance to the economy, but in giving it too narrow a scope. The theory is concerned with society as a whole, but this broad scope is forgotten in economism where limited phenomena are made the final court of appeal. According to critical theory the present economy is essentially determined by the fact that the goods which men produce beyond their needs do not pass directly into the hands of society but are privately acquired and exchanged. The abolition of this state of affairs aims at a higher principle of economic organization and not at all at some philosophical utopia. The old principle drives mankind into a series of catastrophes. But the concept of socialization, which describes the change to a new state of society, contains more than elements from political economy or jurisprudence. If industrial production is under state control, this is a historical fact the significance of which in the critical theory would have to be analyzed for each state. Whether a real socialization is going on, that is, whether a higher principle of economic life is actually being developed, does not depend simply on, for example, a change in certain property relations or on increased productivity in new forms of social collaboration. It depends just as much on the nature and development of the society in which all these particular developments are taking place. The issue, then, is the real nature of the new relations of production.

Even if "natural privileges" which depend on individual talent and efficiency continue to exist for a while, at least no new social privileges are to replace them. In such a provisional situation inequality must not be allowed to become fixed but must be increasingly eliminated. What is to be produced and how, whether relatively fixed social groups with special interests are to exist and social distinctions to be preserved or even deepened, furthermore the active relation of the individual to government, the relation of key administrative acts involving individuals to their own knowledge and will, the dependence of all situations that can be mastered by men upon real agreement—in brief, the degree of development of the essential elements in real democracy and partnership is part of the concept of socialization.

None of these elements is separable from the economic. The critique of economism, however, consists not in turning away from economic analysis but in engaging in it more fully and along the lines indicated by history. The dialectic theory does not practice any criticism based solely on ideas. Even in its idealist form it had rejected the notion of a good-in-itself wholly set over against reality. It does not judge by what is beyond time but by what is within time. When a totalitarian state proceeds to a partial nationalization of property, it justifies itself by appeals to community and collectivist practices. Here the falsehood is obvious. But even where steps are honestly taken, the critical theory has the dialectical function of measuring every historical stage in the light not only of isolated data and concepts but of its primary and total content, and of being concerned that this content be vitally operative. The right philosophy today does not take the form of withdrawing from concrete economic and social analyses in order to work on empty minutiae which are related to nothing and are calculated to hide reality at every point. The critical theory has never been reducible to specialized economic science. The dependence of politics on the economy has been its object, not its program.

Among those who appeal to the critical theory today some with full awareness degrade it to being a pure rationalization of their current enterprises. Others restrict themselves to shallow concepts which even verbally have become odd-sounding and make of it a leveling-down ideology which everyone understands because no thoughts at all pass through anyone's mind. Since its beginning, however, dialectical thought has meant the most advanced state of knowledge, and it is only from this, in the last analysis, that decisive action can come. Its representatives in times of setback have always been relatively few, something it has in common with philosophy. As long as thought has not won a definitive victory, it cannot feel secure in the shadow of power. But if its concepts, which sprang from social movements, today seem empty because no one stands behind them but its pursuing persecutors, yet the truth of them will out. For the thrust toward a rational society, which admittedly seems to exist today only in the realms of fantasy, is really innate in every man.

That is not a claim that should bring a sigh of relief. For the realization of possibilities depends on historical conflicts. The truth about the future does not take the form of a verification of data which differ from others only in having some special importance. Rather, man's own will plays a part in that truth, and he may not take his ease if the prognosis is to come true. And even after the new society shall have come into existence, the happiness of its members will not make up for the wretchedness of those who are being destroyed in our contemporary society. Nor does the theory bring salvation to those who hold it. Inseparable from drive and will, it preaches no psychic condition, as does the Stoa or Christianity. The martyrs of freedom have not sought their own peace of soul. Their philosophy was politics, and if their souls remained calm in the face of terror, this was not their goal. Nor could the dread they experienced bear witness against them.

The apparatus of power has not really gotten less refined since Galileo's penance and recantation; if it took second place to other kinds of machination in the nineteenth century, it has more than made up for its backwardness in the twentieth. Here again the end of the era proves to be a return to its beginnings, but on a higher level. Goethe said that individuality is happiness. Another poet added that its possession is a social achievement and can be lost at any time; Pirandello, who leaned toward fascism, knew his own times better than he realized. Under the totalitarian lordship of evil, men may retain not simply their lives but their very selves only by accident, and recantations mean less today than in the Renaissance. A philosophy that thinks to find peace within itself, in any kind of truth whatsoever, has therefore nothing to do with the critical theory.

Notes

1. Fichte, "Logik und Metaphysik," in *Nachgelassene Schriften*, vol. 2 (Berlin, 1937), p. 47.

2. The form and the content of faith are not indifferent to each other. What is believed influences the act of holding something to be true. The contents of nationalist ideology, which are inconsistent with the level the mind has reached in the industrial world, are not known the way a truth is known. Even the most devoted accept these contents only at the surface of their minds, and all know what the real truth of the matter is. If the listeners realize that the speaker does not believe what he is saying, his power over them is only increased. They bask in the sun of his maliciousness. When circumstances get very much worse such a community, of course, will not survive.

6

Theodor Adorno (1905–1969)
Max Horkheimer (1895–1973)

Born in Switzerland, Theodor Adorno studied both philosophy and music. He taught at the University of Frankfurt until the Nazis came to power, and then emigrated first to England and later to the United States. In 1953 he became the director of the Institute for Social Research, having been associated with it (and having worked closely with Horkheimer) since the 1930s. Adorno's intellectual output was vast, including work in epistemology and metaphysics, ethics, sociology, psychology, music theory, and cultural criticism.

In this selection from Adorno's and Horkheimer's Dialectic of Enlightenment *(1947), these authors introduce a theme that is essential to Western Marxism, namely, the manner in which modern popular culture both reflects and reinforces values and forms of experience endemic to capitalism. This topic is of crucial importance since these writers seek to understand why socialist politics have failed so completely in advanced capitalist societies. Horkheimer and Adorno suggest (in notions later developed by Marcuse) that the culture industry dictates and creates needs, deadens sensibilities, and cripples our capacity to think and feel.*

Dialectic of Enlightenment

THE CULTURE INDUSTRY: ENLIGHTENMENT AS MASS DECEPTION

The sociological theory that the loss of the support of objectively established religion, the dissolution of the last remnants of precapitalism, together with technological and social differentiation or specialization, have led to cultural chaos is disproved every day; for culture now impresses the same stamp on everything. Films, radio and magazines make up a system which is uniform as a whole and in every part. Even the aesthetic activities of political opposites are one in their enthusiastic obedience to the rhythm of the iron system. The decorative industrial management buildings and exhibition centers in authoritarian countries are much the same as anywhere else. The huge gleaming towers that shoot up everywhere are outward signs of the ingenious planning of international concerns, toward which the unleashed entrepreneurial system (whose monuments are a mass of gloomy houses and business premises in grimy, spiritless cities) was already hastening. Even now the older houses just outside the concrete city centers look like slums, and the new bungalows on the outskirts are at one with the flimsy structures of world fairs in their praise of technical progress and their built-in demand to be discarded after a short while like empty food cans. Yet the city housing projects designed to perpetuate the individual as a supposedly independent unit in a small hygienic dwelling make him all the more subservient to his adversary—the absolute power of capitalism. Because the inhabitants, as producers and as consumers, are drawn into the center in search of work and pleasure, all the living units crystallize into well-organized complexes. The striking unity of microcosm and macrocosm presents men with a model of their culture: the false identity of the general and the particular. Under monopoly all mass culture is identical, and the lines of its artificial framework begin to show through. The people at the top are no longer so interested in concealing monopoly: as its violence becomes more open, so its power grows. Movies and radio need no longer pretend to be art. The truth that they are just business is made into an ideology in order to justify the rubbish they deliberately produce. They call themselves industries; and when their directors' incomes are published, any doubt about the social utility of the finished products is removed.

Interested parties explain the culture industry in technological terms. It is alleged that because millions participate in it, certain reproduction processes are necessary that inevitably require identical needs in innumerable places to be satisfied with identical goods. The technical contrast between the few production centers and the large number of widely dispersed consumption points is said to demand organization and planning by management. Furthermore, it is claimed that standards were based in the first place on consumers' needs, and for that reason were accepted with so little resistance. The result is the circle of manipulation and retroactive need in which the unity of the system grows ever stronger. No mention is made of the fact that the basis on which technology acquires power over society is the power of those whose economic hold over society is greatest. A technological rationale is the rationale of domination itself. It is the coercive nature of society alienated from itself. Automobiles, bombs, and movies keep the whole thing together until their leveling element shows its strength in the very wrong which it furthered. It had made the technology of the culture industry no more than the achievement of standardization and mass production, sacrificing whatever involved a distinction between the logic of the work and that of the social system. This is the result not of a law of movement in technology as such but of its function in today's economy. The need which might resist central control has already been suppressed by the control of the individual consciousness. The step from the telephone to the radio has clearly distinguished the roles. The former still allowed the subscriber to play the role of subject, and was liberal. The latter is democratic: it turns all participants into listeners and authoritatively subjects them to broadcast programs which are all exactly the same. No machinery of rejoinder has been devised, and private broadcasters are denied any freedom. They are confined to the apocryphal field of the "amateur," and also have to accept organization from above. But any trace of spontaneity from the public in official broadcasting is controlled and absorbed by talent scouts, studio competitions and official programs of every kind selected by professionals. Talented performers belong to the industry long before it displays them; otherwise they would not be so eager to fit in. The attitude of the public, which ostensibly and actually favors the system of the culture industry, is a part of the system and not an excuse for it. If one branch of art follows the same formula as one with a very different medium and content; if the dramatic intrigue of broadcast soap operas becomes no more than useful material for showing how to master technical problems at both ends of the scale of musical experience—real jazz or a cheap imitation; or if a movement from a Beethoven symphony is crudely "adapted" for a film sound-track in the same way as a Tolstoy novel is garbled in a film script: then the claim that this is done to satisfy the spontaneous wishes of the public is no more than hot air. We are closer to the facts if we explain these phenomena as inherent in the technical and personnel apparatus which, down to its last cog, itself forms part of the economic mechanism of selection. In addition there is the agreement—or at least the determination—of all executive authorities not to produce or sanction anything that in any way differs from their own rules, their own ideas about consumers, or above all themselves.

In our age the objective social tendency is incarnate in the hidden subjective purposes of company directors, the foremost among whom are in the most powerful sectors of industry—steel, petroleum, electricity, and chemicals. Culture monopolies are weak and dependent in comparison. They cannot afford to neglect their appeasement of the real holders of power if their sphere of activity in mass society (a sphere producing a specific type of commodity which anyhow is still too closely bound up with easygoing liberalism and Jewish intellectuals) is not to undergo a series of purges. The dependence of the most powerful broadcasting company on the electrical industry, or of the motion picture industry on the banks, is characteristic of the whole sphere, whose individual branches are themselves economically interwoven. All are in such close contact that the extreme concentration of mental forces allows demarcation lines between different firms and technical branches to be ignored. The ruthless unity in the culture industry is evidence of what will happen in politics. Marked differentiations such as those of A and B films, or of stories in magazines in different price ranges, depend not so much on subject matter as on classifying, organizing, and labeling consumers. Something is provided for all so that none may escape; the distinctions are emphasized and extended. The public is catered for with a hierarchical range of mass-produced products of varying quality, thus advancing the rule of complete quantification. Everybody must behave (as if spontaneously) in accordance with his previously determined and indexed level, and choose the category of mass product turned out for his type. Consumers appear as statistics on research organization charts, and are divided by income groups into red, green, and blue areas; the technique is that used for any type of propaganda.

How formalized the procedure is can be seen when the mechanically differentiated products prove to be all alike in the end. That the difference between the Chrysler range and General Motors products is basically illusory strikes every child with a keen interest in varieties. What connoisseurs discuss as good or bad points serve only to perpetuate the semblance of competition and range of choice. The same applies to the Warner Brothers and Metro Goldwyn Mayer productions. But even the differences between the more expensive and cheaper models put out by the same firm steadily diminish: for automobiles, there are such differences as the number of cylinders, cubic capacity, details of patented gadgets; and for films there are the number of stars, the extravagant use of technology, labor, and equipment, and the introduction of the latest psychological formulas. The universal criterion of merit is the amount of "conspicuous production," of blatant cash investment. The varying budgets in the culture industry do not bear the slightest relation to factual values, to the meaning of the products themselves. Even the technical media are relentlessly forced into uniformity. Television aims at a synthesis of radio and film, and is held up only because the interested parties have not yet reached agreement, but its consequences will be quite enormous and promise to intensify the impoverishment of aesthetic matter so drastically, that by tomorrow the thinly veiled identity of all industrial culture products can come triumphantly out into the open, derisively fulfilling the Wagnerian dream of the *Gesamtkunstwerk*—the fusion of all the arts in one work. The alliance of word, image, and music is all the more perfect than in *Tristan* because the sensuous elements which all approvingly reflect the surface of social reality are in principle embodied in the same technical process, the unity of which becomes its distinctive content. This process integrates all the elements of the production, from the novel (shaped with an eye to the film) to the last sound effect. It is the triumph of invested capital, whose title as absolute master is etched deep into the hearts of the dispossessed in the employment line; it is the meaningful content of every film, whatever plot the production team may have selected.

. . . . .

The stronger the positions of the culture industry become, the more summarily it can deal with consumers' needs, producing them, controlling them, disciplining them, and even withdrawing amusement: no limits are set to cultural progress of this kind. But the tendency is immanent in the principle of amusement itself, which is enlightened in a bourgeois sense. If the need for amusement was in large measure the creation of industry, which used the subject as a means of recommending the work to the masses—the oleograph by the dainty morsel it depicted, or the cake mix by a picture of a cake—amusement always reveals the influence of business, the sales talk, the quack's spiel. But the original affinity of business and amusement is shown in the latter's specific significance: to defend society. To be pleased means to say Yes. It is possible only by insulation from the totality of the social process, by desensitization and, from the first, by senselessly sacrificing the inescapable claim of every work, however inane, within its limits to reflect the whole. Pleasure always means not to think about anything, to forget suffering even where it is shown. Basically it is helplessness. It is flight; not, as is asserted, flight from a wretched reality, but from the last remaining thought of resistance. The liberation which amusement promises is freedom from thought and from negation. The effrontery of the rhetorical question, "What do people want?" lies in the fact that it is addressed—as if to reflective individuals—to those very people who are deliberately to be deprived of this individuality. Even when the public does—exceptionally—rebel against the pleasure industry, all it can muster is that feeble resistance which that very industry has inculcated in it. Nevertheless, it has become increasingly difficult to keep people in this condition. The rate at which they are reduced to stupidity must not fall behind the rate at which their intelligence is increasing. In this age of statistics the masses are too sharp to identify themselves with the millionaire on the screen, and too slow-witted to ignore the law of the largest number. Ideology conceals itself in the calculation of probabilities. Not everyone will be lucky one day—but the person who draws the winning ticket, or rather the one who is marked out to do so by a higher power—usually by the pleasure industry itself, which is represented as unceasingly in search of talent. Those discovered by talent scouts and then publicized on a vast scale by the studio are ideal types of the new dependent average. Of course, the starlet is meant to symbolize the typist in such a way that the splendid evening dress seems meant for the actress as distinct from the real girl. The girls in the audience not only feel that they could be on the screen, but realize the great gulf separating them from it. Only one girl can draw the lucky ticket, only one man can win the prize, and if, mathematically, all have the same chance, yet this is so infinitesimal for each one that he or she will do best to write it off and rejoice in the other's success, which might just as well have been his or hers, and somehow never is. Whenever the culture industry still issues an invitation naïvely to identify, it is immediately withdrawn. No one can escape from himself any more. Once a member of the audience could see his own wedding in the one shown in the film. Now the lucky actors on the screen are copies of the same category as every member of the public, but such equality only demonstrates the insurmountable separation of the human elements. The perfect similarity is the absolute difference. The identity of the category forbids that of the individual cases. Ironically, man as a member of a species has been made a reality by the culture industry. Now any person signifies only those attributes by which he can replace everybody else: he is interchangeable, a copy. As an individual he is completely expendable and utterly insignificant, and this is just what he finds out when time deprives him of this similarity. This changes the inner structure of the religion of success—otherwise strictly maintained. Increasing emphasis is laid not on the path *per aspera ad astra* (which presupposes hardship and effort), but on winning a prize. The element of blind chance in the routine decision about which song deserves to be a hit and which extra a heroine is stressed by the ideology. Movies emphasize chance. By stopping at nothing to ensure that all the characters are essentially alike, with the exception of the villain, and by excluding nonconforming faces (for example, those which, like Garbo's, do not look as if you could say "Hello sister!" to them), life is made easier for movie-goers at first. They are assured that they are all right as they are, that they could do just as well and that nothing beyond their powers will be asked of them. But at the same time they are given a hint that any effort would be useless because even bourgeois luck no longer has any connection with the calculable effect of their own work. They take the hint. Fundamentally they all recognize chance (by which one occasionally makes his fortune) as the other side of planning. Precisely because the forces of society are so deployed in the direction of rationality that anyone might become an engineer or manager, it has ceased entirely to be a rational matter who the one will be in whom society will invest training or confidence for such functions. Chance and planning become one and the same thing, because, given men's equality, individual success and failure—right up to the top—lose any economic meaning. Chance itself is planned, not because it affects any particular individual but precisely because it is believed to play a vital part. It serves the planners as an alibi, and makes it seem that the complex of transactions and measures into which life has been transformed leaves scope for spontaneous and direct relations between man. This freedom is symbolized in the various media of the culture industry by the arbitrary selection of average individuals. In a magazine's detailed accounts of the modestly magnificent pleasure-trips it has arranged for the lucky person, preferably a stenotypist (who has probably won the competition because of her contacts with local bigwigs), the powerlessness of all is reflected. They are mere matter—so much so that those in control can take someone up into their heaven and throw him out again: his rights and his work count for nothing. Industry is interested in people merely as customers and employees, and has in fact reduced mankind as a whole and each of its elements to this all-embracing formula. According to the ruling aspect at the time, ideology emphasizes plan or chance, technology or life, civilization or nature. As employees, men are reminded of the rational organization and urged to fit in like sensible people. As customers, the freedom of choice, the charm of novelty, is demonstrated to them on the screen or in the press by means of the human and personal anecdote. In either case they remain objects.

The less the culture industry has to promise, the less it can offer a meaningful explanation of life, and the emptier is the ideology it disseminates. Even the abstract ideals of the harmony and beneficence of society are too concrete in this age of universal publicity. We have even learned how to identify abstract concepts as sales propaganda. Language based entirely on truth simply arouses impatience to get on with the business deal it is probably advancing. The words that are not means appear senseless; the others seem to be fiction, untrue. Value judgments are taken either as advertising or as empty talk. Accordingly ideology has been made vague and noncommittal, and thus neither clearer nor weaker. Its very vagueness, its almost scientific aversion from committing itself to anything which cannot be verified, acts as an instrument of domination. It becomes a vigorous and prearranged promulgation of the status quo. The culture industry tends to make itself the embodiment of authoritative pronouncements, and thus the irrefutable prophet of the prevailing order. It skillfully steers a winding course between the cliffs of demonstrable misinformation and manifest truth, faithfully reproducing the phenomenon whose opaqueness blocks any insight and installs the ubiquitous and intact phenomenon as ideal. Ideology is split into the photograph of stubborn life and the naked lie about its meaning—which is not expressed but suggested and yet drummed in. To demonstrate its divine nature, reality is always repeated in a purely cynical way. Such a photological proof is of course not stringent, but it is overpowering. Anyone who doubts the power of monotony is a fool. The culture industry refutes the objection made against it just as well as that against the world which it impartially duplicates. The only choice is either to join in or to be left behind: those provincials who have recourse to eternal beauty and the amateur stage in preference to the cinema and the radio are already—politically—at the point to which mass culture drives its supporters. It is sufficiently hardened to deride as ideology, if need be, the old wish-fulfillments, the father-ideal and absolute feeling. The new ideology has as its objects the world as such. It makes use of the worship of facts by no more than elevating a disagreeable existence into the world of facts in representing it meticulously. This transference makes existence itself a substitute for meaning and right. Whatever the camera reproduces is beautiful. The disappointment of the prospect that one might be the typist who wins the world trip is matched by the disappointing appearance of the accurately photographed areas which the voyage might include. Not Italy is offered, but evidence that it exists. A film can even go so far as to show the Paris in which the American girl thinks she will still her desire as a hopelessly desolate place, thus driving her the more inexorably into the arms of the smart American boy she could have met at home anyhow. That this goes on, that, in its most recent phase, the system itself reproduces the life of those of whom it consists instead of immediately doing away with them, is even put down to its credit as giving it meaning and worth. Continuing and continuing to join in are given as justification for the blind persistence of the system and even for its immutability. What repeats itself is healthy, like the natural or industrial cycle. The same babies grin eternally out of the magazines; the jazz machine will pound away for ever. In spite of all the progress in reproduction techniques, in controls and the specialities, and in spite of all the restless industry, the bread which the culture industry offers man is the stone of the stereotype. It draws on the life cycle, on the well-founded amazement that mothers, in spite of everything, still go on bearing children and that the wheels still do not grind to a halt. This serves to confirm the immutability of circumstances.The ears of corn blowing in the wind at the end of Chaplin's *The Great Dictator* give the lie to the anti-Fascist plea for freedom. They are like the blond hair of the German girl whose camp life is photographed by the Nazi film company in the summer breeze. Nature is viewed by the mechanism of social domination as a healthy contrast to society, and is therefore denatured. Pictures showing green trees, a blue sky, and moving clouds make these aspects of nature into so many cryptograms for factory chimneys and service stations. On the other hand, wheels and machine components must seem expressive, having been degraded to the status of agents of the spirit of trees and clouds. Nature and technology are mobilized against all opposition; and we have a falsified memento of liberal society, in which people supposedly wallowed in erotic plush-lined bedrooms instead of taking open-air baths as is the case today, or experiencing breakdowns in prehistoric Benz models instead of shooting off with the speed of a rocket from A (where one is anyhow) to B (where everything is just the same). The triumph of the gigantic concern over the initiative of the entrepreneur is praised by the culture industry as the persistence of entrepreneurial initiative. The enemy who is already defeated, the thinking individual, is the enemy fought. The resurrection in Germany of the anti-bourgeois "Haus Sonnenstösser" and the pleasure felt when watching *Life with Father* have one and the same meaning.

. . . . .

In the culture industry the individual is an illusion not merely because of the standardization of the means of production. He is tolerated only so long as his complete identification with the generality is unquestioned. Pseudoindividuality is rife: from the standardized jazz improvization to the exceptional film star whose hair curls over her eye to demonstrate her originality. What is individual is no more than the generality's power to stamp the accidental detail so firmly that it is accepted as such. The defiant reserve or elegant appearance of the individual on show is mass-produced like Yale locks, whose only difference can be measured in fractions of millimeters. The peculiarity of the self is a monopoly commodity determined by society; it is falsely represented as natural. It is no more than the moustache, the French accent, the deep voice of the woman of the world, the Lubitsch touch: fingerprints on identity cards which are otherwise exactly the same, and into which the lives and faces of every single person are transformed by the power of the generality. Pseudoindividuality is the prerequisite for comprehending tragedy and removing its poison: only because individuals have ceased to be themselves and are now merely centers where the general tendencies meet, is it possible to receive them again, whole and entire, into the generality. In this way mass culture discloses the fictitious character of the "individual" in the bourgeois era, and is merely unjust in boasting on account of this dreary harmony of general and particular. The principle of individuality was always full of contradiction. Individuation has never really been achieved. Self-preservation in the shape of class has kept everyone at the stage of a mere species being. Every bourgeois characteristic, in spite of its deviation and indeed because of it, expressed the same thing: the harshness of the competitive society. The individual who supported society bore its disfiguring mark; seemingly free, he was actually the product of its economic and social apparatus. Power based itself on the prevailing conditions of power when it sought the approval of persons affected by it. As it progressed, bourgeois society did also develop the individual. Against the will of its leaders, technology has changed human beings from children into persons. However, every advance in individuation of this kind took place at the expense of the individuality in whose name it occurred, so that nothing was left but the resolve to pursue one's own particular purpose. The bourgeois whose existence is split into a business and a private life, whose private life is split into keeping up his public image and intimacy, whose intimacy is split into the surly partnership of marriage and the bitter comfort of being quite alone, at odds with himself and everybody else, is already virtually a Nazi, replete both with enthusiasm and abuse; or a modern city-dweller who can now only imagine friendship as a "social contact": that is, as being in social contact with others with whom he has no inward contact. The only reason why the culture industry can deal so successfully with individuality is that the latter has always reproduced the fragility of society. On the faces of private individuals and movie heroes put together according to the patterns on magazine covers vanishes a pretense in which no one now believes; the popularity of the hero models comes partly from a secret satisfaction that the effort to achieve individuation has at last been replaced by the effort to imitate, which is admittedly more breathless. It is idle to hope that this self-contradictory, disintegrating "person" will not last for generations, that the system must collapse because of such a psychological split, or that the deceitful substitution of the stereotype for the individual will of itself become unbearable for mankind. Since Shakespeare's *Hamlet*, the unity of the personality has been seen through as a pretense. Synthetically produced physiognomies show that the people of today have already forgotten that there was ever a notion of what human life was. For centuries society has been preparing for Victor Mature and Mickey Rooney. By destroying they come to fulfill.

The idolization of the cheap involves making the average the heroic. The highest-paid stars resemble pictures advertising unspecified proprietary articles. Not without good purpose are they often selected from the host of commercial models. The prevailing taste takes its ideal from advertising, the beauty in consumption. Hence the Socratic saying that the beautiful is the useful has now been fulfilled—ironically. The cinema makes propaganda for the culture combine as a whole; on radio, goods for whose sake the cultural commodity exists are also recommended individually. For a few coins one can see the film which cost millions, for even less one can buy the chewing gum whose manufacture involved immense riches—a hoard increased still further by sales. In absentia, but by univeral suffrage, the treasure of armies is revealed, but prostitution is not allowed inside the country. The best orchestras in the world—clearly not so—are brought into your living room free of charge. It is all a parody of the never-never land, just as the national society is a parody of the human society. You name it, we supply it. A man up from the country remarked at the old Berlin Metropol theater that it was astonishing what they could do for the money; his comment has long since been adopted by the culture industry and made the very substance of production. This is always coupled with the triumph that it is possible; but this, in large measure, is the very triumph. Putting on a show means showing everybody what there is, and what can be achieved. Even today it is still a fair, but incurably sick with culture. Just as the people who had been attracted by the fairground barkers overcame their disappointment in the booths with a brave smile, because they really knew in advance what would happen, so the movie-goer sticks knowingly to the institution. With the cheapness of mass-produced luxury goods and its complement, the universal swindle, a change in the character of the art commodity itself is coming about. What is new is not that it is a commodity, but that today it deliberately admits it is one; that art renounces its own autonomy and proudly takes its place among consumption goods constitutes the charm of novelty. Art as a separate sphere was always possible only in a bourgeois society. Even as a negation of that social purposiveness which is spreading through the market, its freedom remains essentially bound up with the premise of a commodity economy. Pure works of art which deny the commodity society by the very fact that they obey their own law were always wares all the same. In so far as, until the eighteenth century, the buyer's patronage shielded the artist from the market, they were dependent on the buyer and his objectives. The purposelessness of the great modern work of art depends on the anonymity of the market. Its demands pass through so many intermediaries that the artist is exempt from any definite requirements—though admittedly only to a certain degree, for throughout the whole history of the bourgeoisie his autonomy was only tolerated, and thus contained an element of untruth which ultimately led to the social liquidation of art. When mortally sick, Beethoven hurled away a novel by Sir Walter Scott with the cry: "Why, the fellow writes for money," and yet proved a most experienced and stubborn businessman in disposing of the last quartets, which were a most extreme renunciation of the market; he is the most outstanding example of the unity of those opposites, market and independence, in bourgeois art. Those who succumb to the ideology are precisely those who cover up the contradiction instead of taking it into the consciousness of their own production as Beethoven did: he went on to express in music his anger at losing a few pence, and derived the metaphysical *Es Muss Sein* (which attempts an aesthetic banishment of the pressure of the world by taking it into itself) from the housekeeper's demand for her monthly wages. The principle of idealistic aesthetics—purposefulness without a purpose—reverses the scheme of things to which bourgeois art conforms socially: purposelessness for the purpose declared by the market. At last, in the demand for entertainment and relaxation, purpose has absorbed the realm of purposelessness. But as the insistence that art should be disposable in terms of money becomes absolute, a shift in the internal structure of cultural commodities begins to show itself. The use which men in this antagonistic society promise themselves from the work of art is itself, to a great extent, that very existence of the useless which is abolished by complete inclusion under use. The work of art, by completely assimilating itself to need, deceitfully deprives men of precisely that liberation from the principle of utility which it should inaugurate. What might be called use value in the reception of cultural commodities is replaced by exchange value; in place of enjoyment there are gallery-visiting and factual knowledge: the prestige seeker replaces the connoisseur. The consumer becomes the ideology of the pleasure industry, whose institutions he cannot escape. One simply "has to" have seen *Mrs. Miniver*, just as one "has to" subscribe to *Life* and *Time*. Everything is looked at from only one aspect: that it can be used for something else, however vague the notion of this use may be. No object has an inherent value; it is valuable only to the extent that it can be exchanged. The use value of art, its mode of being, is treated as a fetish; and the fetish, the work's social rating (misinterpreted as its artistic status) becomes its use value—the only quality which is enjoyed. The commodity function of art disappears only to be wholly realized when art becomes a species of commodity instead, marketable and interchangeable like an industrial product. But art as a type of product which existed to be sold and yet to be unsaleable is wholly and hypocritically converted into "unsaleability" as soon as the transaction ceases to be the mere intention and becomes its sole principle. No tickets could be bought when Toscanini conducted over the radio; he was heard without charge, and every sound of the symphony was accompanied, as it were, by the sublime puff that the symphony was not interrupted by any advertising: "This concert is brought to you as a public service." The illusion was made possible by the profits of the united automobile and soap manufacturers, whose payments keep the radio stations going—and, of course, by the increased sales of the electrical industry, which manufactures the radio sets. Radio, the progressive latecomer of mass culture, draws all the consequences at present denied the film by its pseudomarket. The technical structure of the commercial radio system makes it immune from liberal deviations such as those the movie industrialists can still permit themselves in their own sphere. It is a private enterprise which really does represent the sovereign whole and is therefore some distance ahead of the other individual combines. Chesterfield is merely the nation's cigarette, but the radio is the voice of the nation. In bringing cultural products wholly into the sphere of commodities, radio does not try to dispose of its culture goods themselves as commodities straight to the consumer. In America it collects no fees from the public, and so has acquired the illusory form of disinterested, unbiased authority which suits Fascism admirably. The radio becomes the universal mouthpiece of the Führer; his voice rises from street loud-speakers to resemble the howling of sirens announcing panic—from which modern propaganda can scarcely be distinguished anyway. The National Socialists knew that the wireless gave shape to their cause just as the printing press did to the Reformation. The metaphysical charisma of the Führer invented by the sociology of religion has finally turned out to be no more than the omnipresence of his speeches on the radio, which are a demoniacal parody of the omnipresence of the divine spirit. The gigantic fact that the speech penetrates everywhere replaces its content, just as the benefaction of the Toscanini broadcast takes the place of the symphony. No listener can grasp its true meaning any longer, while the Führer's speech is lies anyway. The inherent tendency of radio is to make the speaker's word, the false commandment, absolute. A recommendation becomes an order. The recommendation of the same commodities under different proprietary names, the scientifically based praise of the laxative in the announcer's smooth voice between the overture from *La Traviata* and that from *Rienzi* is the only thing that no longer works, because of its silliness. One day the edict of production, the actual advertisement (whose actuality is at present concealed by the pretense of a choice) can turn into the open command of the Führer. In a society of huge Fascist rackets which agree among themselves what part of the social product should be allotted to the nation's needs, it would eventually seem anachronistic to recommend the use of a particular soap powder. The Führer is more up-to-date in unceremoniously giving direct orders for both the holocaust and the supply of rubbish.

Even today the culture industry dresses works of art like political slogans and forces them upon a resistant public at reduced prices; they are as accessible for public enjoyment as a park. But the disappearance of their genuine commodity character does not mean that they have been abolished in the life of a free society, but that the last defense against their reduction to culture goods has fallen. The abolition of educational privilege by the device of clearance sales does not open for the masses the spheres from which they were formerly excluded, but, given existing social conditions, contributes directly to the decay of education and the progress of barbaric meaninglessness. Those who spent their money in the nineteenth or the early twentieth century to see a play or to go to a concert respected the performance as much as the money they spent. The bourgeois who wanted to get something out of it tried occasionally to establish some rapport with the work. Evidence for this is to be found in the literary "introductions" to works, or in the commentaries on *Faust*. These were the first steps toward the biographical coating and other practices to which a work of art is subjected today. Even in the early, prosperous days of business, exchange-value did carry use-value as a mere appendix but had developed it as a prerequisite for its own existence; this was socially helpful for works of art. Art exercised some restraint on the bourgeois as long as it cost money. That is now a thing of the past. Now that it has lost every restraint and there is no need to pay any money, the proximity of art to those who are exposed to it completes the alienation and assimilates one to the other under the banner of triumphant objectivity. Criticism and respect disappear in the culture industry; the former becomes a mechanical expertise, the latter is succeeded by a shallow cult of leading personalities. Consumers now find nothing expensive. Nevertheless, they suspect that the less anything costs, the less it is being given them. The double mistrust of traditional culture as ideology is combined with mistrust of industrialized culture as a swindle. When thrown in free, the now debased works of art, together with the rubbish to which the medium assimilates them, are secretly rejected by the fortunate recipients, who are supposed to be satisfied by the mere fact that there is so much to be seen and heard. Everything can be obtained. The screenos and vaudevilles in the movie theater, the competitions for guessing music, the free books, rewards and gifts offered on certain radio programs, are not mere accidents but a continuation of the practice obtaining with culture products. The symphony becomes a reward for listening to the radio, and—if technology had its way—the film would be delivered to people's homes as happens with the radio. It is moving toward the commercial system. Television points the way to a development which might easily enough force the Warner Brothers into what would certainly be the unwelcome position of serious musicians and cultural conservatives. But the gift system has already taken hold among consumers. As culture is represented as a bonus with undoubted private and social advantages, they have to seize the chance. They rush in lest they miss something. Exactly what, is not clear, but in any case the only ones with a chance are the participants. Fascism, however, hopes to use the training the culture industry has given these recipients of gifts, in order to organize them into its own forced battalions.

• • • • •

IV

THE NEW MARXISM OF THE NEW LEFT (AND BEYOND)

7

Jean-Paul Sartre (1905–1979)

Born in France, Jean-Paul Sartre began his career as a philosophy instructor and published his first novel in 1938. During World War II he fought in the Resistance and completed Being and Nothingness *(1943), which immediately established him as a leading existentialist thinker. After the war he consistently engaged in left-wing politics (he faced assassination threats, and his apartment was twice bombed as a result of his support of Algerian independence). While he always preserved some distance from the French Communist party, he was consistently sympathetic to workers' and anti-imperialist struggles. After the May 1968 revolt in France, he engaged in increasingly overt political activity, while continuing his literary, philosophical, and polemical output.*

During the 1950s Sartre moved consistently in the direction of Marxism. As he makes clear in the following selections from Search for a Method *(1960), which was originally written as an introduction to his massive theoretical work* Critique of Dialectical Reason, *he sought to create a form of Marxism that would free left-wing thought from its dependence on abstract truisms and correctly assess the role of human action in the creation of social reality. This juxtaposition of existentialism and Marxism is his enduring contribution to Western Marxism.*

Search for a Method

MARXISM AND EXISTENTIALISM

. . . . .

Why then has "existentialism" preserved its autonomy? Why has it not simply dissolved in Marxism?

Lukács believed that he had answered this question in a small book called *Existentialism and Marxism*. According to him, bourgeois intellectuals have been forced "to abandon the method of idealism while safeguarding its results and its foundations; hence the historical necessity of a 'third path' (between materialism and idealism) in actuality and in the bourgeois consciousness during the imperialistic period." I shall show later the havoc which this wish to conceptualize a priori has wrought at the center of Marxism. Here let us simply observe that Lukacs fails absolutely to account for the principal fact: we were convinced *at one and the same time* that historical materialism furnished the only valid interpretation of history and that existentialism remained the only concrete approach to reality. I do not pretend to deny the contradictions in this attitude. I simply assert that Lukacs does not even suspect it. Many intellectuals, many students, have lived and still live with the tension of this double demand. How does this come about? It is due to a circumstance which Lukacs knew perfectly well but which he could not at that time even mention: Marxism, after drawing us to it as the moon draws the tides, after transforming all our ideas, after liquidating the categories of our bourgeois thought, abruptly left us stranded. It did not satisfy our need to understand. In the particular situation in which we were placed, it no longer had anything new to teach us, because it had come to a stop.

Marxism stopped. Precisely because this philosophy wants to change the world, because its aim is "philosophy-becoming-the-world," because it is and wants to be *practical,* there arose within it a veritable schism which rejected theory on one side and praxis on the other. From the moment the U.S.S.R., encircled and alone, undertook its gigantic effort at industrialization, Marxism found itself unable to bear the shock of these new struggles, the practical necessities and the mistakes which are always inseparable from them. At this period of withdrawal (for the U.S.S.R.) and of ebb tide (for the revolutionary proletariats), the ideology itself was subordinated to a double need: security (that is, unity) and the construction of socialism *inside* the U.S.S.R. Concrete thought must be born from praxis and must turn back upon it in order to clarify it, not by chance and without rules, but—as in all sciences and all techniques—in conformity with principles. Now the Party leaders, bent on pushing the integration of the group to the limit, feared that the free process of truth, with all the discussions and all the conflicts which it involves, would break the unity of combat; they reserved for themselves the right to define the line and to interpret the event. In addition, out of fear that the experience might not provide its own clarities, that it might put into question certain of their guiding ideas and might contribute to "weakening the ideological struggle," they put the doctrine out of reach. The separation of theory and practice resulted in transforming the latter into an empiricism without principles; the former into a pure, fixed knowledge. On the other hand, the economic planning imposed by a bureaucracy unwilling to recognize its mistakes became thereby a violence done to reality. And since the future production of a nation was determined in offices, often outside its own territory, this violence had as its counterpart an absolute idealism. Men and things had to yield to ideas—a priori; experience, when it did not verify the predictions, could only be wrong. Budapest's subway was real in Rakosi's head. If Budapest's subsoil did not allow him to construct the subway, this was because the subsoil was counterrevolutionary. Marxism, as a philosophical interpretation of man and of history, necessarily had to reflect the preconceptions of the planned economy.

This fixed image of idealism and of violence did idealistic violence to facts. For years the Marxist intellectual believed that he served his party by violating experience, by overlooking embarrassing details, by grossly simplifying the data, and above all, by conceptualizing the event *before* having studied it. And I do not mean to speak only of Communists, but of all the others—fellow travelers, Trotskyites, and Trotsky sympathizers—for they have been *created* by their sympathy for the Communist Party or by their opposition to it. On November 4, 1956, at the time of the second Soviet intervention in Hungary, each group already had its mind made up before it possessed any information on the situation. It had decided in advance whether it was witnessing an act of aggression on the part of the Russian bureaucracy against the democracy of Workers' Committees, with a revolt of the masses against the bureaucratic system, or with a counterrevolutionary attempt which Soviet moderation had known how to check. Later there was news, a great deal of news; but I have not heard it said that even one Marxist changed his opinion.

Among the interpretations which I have just mentioned, there is one which shows the method in all its nakedness, that which reduces the facts in Hungary to a "Soviet act of aggression against the democracy of Workers' Committees." It is obvious that the Workers' Committees are a democratic institution; one can even maintain that they bear within them the future of the socialist society. But this does not alter the fact that they did not exist in Hungary at the time of the first Soviet intervention; and their appearance during the Insurrection was much too brief and too troubled for us to be able to speak of an organized democracy. No matter. There were Workers' Committees; a Soviet intervention took place. Starting from there, Marxist idealism proceeds to two simultaneous operations: conceptualization and passage to the limit. They push the empirical notion to the perfection of the type, the germ to its total development. At the same time they reject the equivocal givens of experience; these could only lead one astray. We will find ourselves then in the presence of a typical contradiction between two Platonic ideas: on the one side, the wavering policy of the U.S.S.R. gave way to the rigorous and predictable action of that entity, "the Soviet Bureaucracy"; on the other side, the Workers' Committees disappeared before that other entity, "the direct Democracy." I shall call these two objects "general particularities"; they are made to pass for particular, historical realities when we ought not to see in them anything more than the purely formal unity of abstract, universal relations. The process of making them into fetishes will be complete when each one is endowed with real powers: the Democracy of Workers' Committees holds within itself the absolute negation of the Bureaucracy, which reacts by crushing its adversary.

Now there can be no doubt that the fruitfulness of living Marxism stemmed in part from its way of approaching experience. Marx was convinced that facts are never isolated appearances, that if they come into being together, it is always within the higher unity of a whole, that they are bound to each other by internal relations, and that the presence of one profoundly modifies the nature of the other. Consequently, Marx approached the study of the revolution of February 1848 or Louis Napoleon Bonaparte's *coup d'état* with a synthetic intent; he saw in these events totalities produced and at the same time split apart by their internal contradictions. Of course, the physicist's hypothesis, before it has been confirmed by experimentation, is also an interpretation of experience; it rejects empiricism simply because it is mute. But the constitutive schema of this hypothesis is universalizing, not totalizing. It determines a relation, a function, and not a concrete totality. The Marxist approaches the historical process with universalizing and totalizing schemata. Naturally the totalization was not made by chance. The theory had determined the choice of perspective and the order of the conditioning factors; it studied each particular process within the framework of a general system in evolution. But in no case, in Marx's own work, does this putting in perspective claim to prevent or to render useless the appreciation of the process as a *unique* totality. When, for example, he studies the brief and tragic history of the Republic of 1848, he does not limit himself—as would be done today—to stating that the republican petite bourgeoisie betrayed its ally, the Proletariat. On the contrary, he tries to account for this tragedy in its detail and in the aggregate. If he subordinates anecdotal facts to the totality (of a movement, of an attitude), he also seeks to discover the totality by means of the facts. In other words, he gives to each event, in addition to its particular signification, the role of being revealing. Since the ruling principle of the inquiry is the search for the synthetic ensemble, each fact, once established, is questioned and interpreted as part of a whole. It is on the basis of *the fact,* through the study of its lacks and its "over-significations," that one determines, by virtue of a hypothesis, the totality at the heart of which the fact will recover its truth. Thus living Marxism is heuristic; its principles and its prior knowledge appear as regulative in relation to its concrete research. In the work of Marx we never find entities. Totalities (e.g., "the petite bourgeoisie" of the *18 Brumaire*) are living; they furnish their own definitions within the framework of the research. Otherwise we could not understand the importance which Marxists attach (even today) to "the analysis" of a situation. It goes without saying that this analysis is not enough and that it is but the first moment in an effort at synthetic reconstruction. But it is apparent also that the analysis is indispensable to the later reconstruction of the total structures.

Marxist voluntarism, which likes to speak of analysis, has reduced this operation to a simple ceremony. There is no longer any question of studying facts within the general perspective of Marxism so as to enrich our understanding and to clarify action. Analysis consists solely in getting rid of detail, in forcing the signification of certain events, in denaturing facts or even in inventing a nature for them in order to discover it later underneath them, as their substance, as unchangeable, fetishized "synthetic notions." The open concepts of Marxism have closed in. They are no longer *keys,* interpretive schemata; they are posited for themselves as an already totalized knowledge. To use Kantian terms—Marxism makes out of these particularized, fetishized types, constitutive concepts of experience. The real content of these typical concepts is always *past Knowledge;* but today's Marxist makes of it an eternal knowledge. His sole concern, at the moment of analysis, will be to "place" these entities. The more he is convinced that they represent truth a priori, the less fussy he will be about proof. The Kerstein Amendment, the appeals of Radio Free Europe, rumors—these are sufficient for the French Communists to "place" the entity "world imperialism" at the origin of the events in Hungary. The totalizing investigation has given way to a Scholasticism of the totality. The heuristic principle—"to search for the whole in its parts"—has become the terrorist practice[1] of "liquidating the particularity." It is not by chance that Lukács—Lukács who so often violates history—has found in 1956 the best definition of this frozen Marxism. Twenty years of practice give him all the authority necessary to call this pseudo-philosophy *a voluntarist idealism*.

Today social and historical experience falls outside of Knowledge. Bourgeois concepts just manage to revive and quickly break down; those which survive lack any foundation. The real attainments of American Sociology cannot hide its theoretic uncertainty. Psychoanalysis, after a spectacular beginning, has stood still. It knows a great many details, but it lacks any firm foundation. Marxism possesses theoretical bases, it embraces all human activity; but it no longer *knows* anything. Its concepts are *dictates;* its goal is no longer to increase what it knows but to be itself constituted a priori as an absolute Knowledge. In view of this twofold ignorance, existentialism has been able to return and to maintain itself because it reaffirmed the reality of men as Kierkegaard asserted his own reality against Hegel. However, the Dane rejected the Hegelian conception of man and of the real. Existentialism and Marxism, on the contrary, aim at the same object; but Marxism has reabsorbed man into the idea, and existentialism seeks him everywhere *where he is,* at his work, in his home, in the street. We certainly do not claim—as Kierkegaard did—that this real man is unknowable. We say only that he is not known. If for the time being he escapes Knowledge, it is because the only concepts at our disposal for understanding him are borrowed either from the idealism of the Right or from the idealism of the Left. We are careful not to confuse these two idealisms: the former merits its name by the *content* of its concepts, and the latter by the *use* which today it makes of its concepts. It is true also that among the masses Marxist *practice* does not reflect, or only slightly reflects, the sclerosis of its theory. But it is precisely the conflict between revolutionary action and the Scholastic justification of this action which prevents Communist man—in socialist countries as in bourgeois countries—from achieving any clear self-consciousness. One of the most striking characteristics of our time is the fact that history is made without self-awareness. No doubt someone will say this has always been the case; and this was true up until the second half of the last century—that is, until Marx. But what has made the force and richness of Marxism is the fact that it has been the most radical attempt to clarify the historical process in its totality. For the last twenty years, on the contrary, its shadow has obscured history; this is because it has ceased to live *with history* and because it attempts, through a bureaucratic conservatism, to reduce change to identity.

THE PROBLEM OF MEDIATIONS

. . . . .

Today psychoanalysis alone enables us to study the process by which a child, groping in the dark, is going to attempt to play, without understanding it, the social role which adults impose upon him. Only psychoanalysis will show us whether he stifles in his role, whether he seeks to escape it, or is entirely assimilated into it. Psychoanalysis alone allows us to discover the whole man in the adult; that is, not only his present determinations but also the weight of his history. And one would be entirely wrong in supposing that this discipline is opposed to dialectical materialism. To be sure, amateurs in the West have constructed "analytical" theories of society or of History which indeed end up in idealism. How many times has someone attempted the feat of psychoanalyzing Robespierre for us without even understanding that the contradictions in his behavior were conditioned by the objective contradictions of the situation. When one has understood how the bourgeoisie of *Thermidor*, paralyzed by the democratic regime, found itself forced by practical necessity to demand a military dictatorship, then it is most annoying to read from the pen of a psychiatrist that Napoleon is explained by his "will to fail." De Man, the Belgian socialist, went still further when he tried to explain class conflicts by "the Proletariat's inferiority complex." Inversely, Marxism, once it became a universal Knowledge, wanted to integrate psychoanalysis into itself by first twisting its neck. Marxism made of it a dead idea which quite naturally found its place in a desiccated system; it was idealism returning in disguise, an avatar of the fetishism of interiority. In the one case as in the other a method has been transformed into dogmatism: the philosophers of psychoanalysis find their justification in the Marxist "schematizers" and vice versa. The fact is that dialectical materialism cannot deprive itself much longer of the one privileged mediation which permits it to pass from general and abstract determinations to particular traits of the single individual. Psychoanalysis has no principles, it has no theoretical foundation; and this is quite all right if it accompanies—as in the work of Jung and in certain works of Freud—a completely innocuous mythology. In fact, it is a method which is primarily concerned with establishing the way in which the child lives his family relations inside a given society. And this does not mean that it raises any doubts as to the priority of institutions. Quite the contrary, its object itself depends on the structure of a *particular* family, and this is only a certain individual manifestation of the family structure appropriate to such and such a class under such and such conditions. Thus psychoanalytic monographs—if it were always possible to have them—would by themselves throw light upon the evolution of the French family between the eighteenth and the twentieth century, which in its turn would express in its own way the general evolution of the relations of production.

Today's Marxists are concerned only with adults; reading them, one would believe that we are born at the age when we earn our first wages. They have forgotten their own childhoods. As we read them, everything seems to happen as if men experienced their alienation and their reification *first in their own work,* whereas in actuality each one lives it *first,* as a child, *in his parents' work*. Dead set against interpretations too exclusively sexual, Marxists make use of them in order to condemn a method of interpretation which claims only to put History in place of nature in each person. They have not yet understood that sexuality is only one way of living the totality of our condition—at a certain level and within the perspective of a certain individual venture. Existentialism, on the contrary, believes that it can integrate the psychoanalytic method which discovers the point of insertion for man and his class—that is, the particular family—as a mediation between the universal class and the individual. The family in fact is constituted by and in the general movement of History, but is experienced, on the other hand, as an absolute in the depth and opaqueness of childhood.

. . . . .

THE PROGRESSIVE-REGRESSIVE METHOD

I have said that we accept without reservation the thesis set forth by Engels in his letter to Marx: "Men themselves make their history but in a given environment which conditions them." However, this text is not one of the clearest, and it remains open to numerous interpretations. How are we to understand that man makes History if at the same time it is History which makes him? Idealist Marxism seems to have chosen the easiest interpretation: entirely determined by prior circumstances—that is, in the final analysis, by economic conditions—man is a passive product, a sum of conditioned reflexes. Being inserted in the social world amidst other equally conditioned inertias, this inert object, with the nature which it has received, contributes to precipitate or to check the "course of the world." It changes society in the way that a bomb, without ceasing to obey the principle of inertia, can destroy a building. In this case there would be no difference between the human agent and the machine. Marx wrote, in fact: "The invention of a new military weapon, the firearm, of necessity modified the whole inner organization of the army, the relationships inside the cadre on the basis of which individuals form an army and which make of the army an organized whole, and finally, the relations between different armies." In short, the advantage here seems to be on the side of the weapon or the tool; their simple appearance overturns everything.

This conception can be summed up by a statement which appeared in the *Courrier européen* (in Saint Petersburg): "Marx considers social evolution to be a natural process governed by laws which do not depend upon the will, the consciousness, or the intention of men, but which, on the contrary, determine them." Marx quotes this passage in the second preface to *Capital*. Does he really accept it as a fair appraisal of his position? It is difficult to say. He compliments the critic for having excellently described *his* method and points out to him that the real problem concerns *the* dialectical method. But he does not comment on the article in detail, and he concludes by noting that the practical bourgeois *is very clearly conscious* of the contradictions in capitalist society, a remark which seems to be the counterpart of his statement in 1860: "[The workers' movement represents] the conscious participation in the historical process which is overturning society." Now one will observe that the statements in the *Courrier européen* contradict not only the passage quoted earlier from *Herr Vogt* but also the famous third thesis of Feuerbach. "The materialist doctrine according to which men are a product of circumstances and of education . . . does not take into account the fact that circumstances are modified precisely by men and that the educator must be himself educated." Either this is a mere tautology, and we are simply to understand that the educator himself is a product of circumstances and of education—which would render the sentence useless and absurd; or else it is the decisive affirmation of the irreducibility of human praxis. The educator must be educated; this means that education must be an enterprise.

If one wants to grant to Marxist thought its full complexity, one would have to say that man in a period of exploitation is *at once both* the product of his own product and a historical agent who can under no circumstances be taken as a product. This contradiction is not fixed; it must be grasped in the very movement of praxis. Then it will clarify Engels's statement: men make their history on the basis of real, prior conditions (among which we would include acquired characteristics, distortions imposed by the mode of work and of life, alienation, etc.), but it is *the men* who make it and not the prior conditions. Otherwise men would be merely the vehicles of inhuman forces which through them would govern the social world. To be sure, these conditions exist, and it is they, they alone, which can furnish a direction and a material reality to the changes which are in preparation; but the movement of human praxis goes beyond them while conserving them.

. . . . .

The Project

Thus alienation can modify the *results* of an action but not its profound reality. We refuse to confuse the alienated man with a thing or alienation with the physical laws governing external conditions. We affirm the specificity of the human act, which cuts across the social milieu while still holding on to its determinations, and which transforms the world on the basis of given conditions. For us man is characterized above all by his going beyond a situation, and by what he succeeds in making of what he has been made—even if he never recognizes himself in his objectification. This going beyond we find at the very root of the human—in *need*. It is need which, for example, links the scarcity of women in the Marquesas, as a structural fact of the group, and polyandry as a matrimonial institution. For this scarcity is not a simple lack; in its most naked form it expresses a situation in society and contains already an effort to go beyond it. The most rudimentary behavior must be determined both in relation to the real and present factors which condition it and in relation to a certain object, still to come, which it is trying to bring into being. This is what we call *the project*.

Starting with the project, we define a double simultaneous relationship. In relation to the given, the praxis is negativity; but what is always involved is the negation of a negation. In relation to the object aimed at, praxis is positivity, but this positivity opens onto the "nonexistent," to what *has not yet* been. A flight and a leap ahead, at once a refusal and a realization, the project retains and unveils the surpassed reality which is refused by the very movement which surpassed it. Thus knowing is a moment of praxis, even its most fundamental one; but this knowing does not partake of an absolute Knowledge. Defined by the negation of the refused reality in the name of the reality to be produced, it remains the captive of the action which it clarifies, and disappears along with it. Therefore it is perfectly accurate to say that man is the product of his product. The structures of a society which is created by human work define for each man an objective situation as a starting point; the truth of a man is the nature of his work, and it is his wages. But this truth defines him just insofar as he constantly goes beyond it in his practical activity. (In a popular democracy this may be, for example, by working a double shift or by becoming an "activist" or by secretly resisting the raising of work quotas. In a capitalist society it may be by joining a union, by voting to go on strike, etc.) Now this surpassing is conceivable only as a relation of the existent to its possibles. Furthermore, to say what man "is" is also to say what he can be—and vice versa. The material conditions of his existence circumscribe the field of his possibilities (his work is too hard, he is too tired to show any interest in union or political activity). Thus the field of possibles is the goal toward which the agent surpasses his objective situation. And this field in turn depends strictly on the social, historical reality. For example, in a society where everything is bought, the possibilities of culture are practically eliminated for the workers if food absorbs 50 percent or more of their budget. The freedom of the bourgeois, on the contrary, consists in the possibility of his allotting an always increasing part of his income to a great variety of expenditures. Yet the field of possibles, however reduced it may be, always exists, and we must not think of it as a zone of indetermination, but rather as a strongly structured region which depends upon all of History and which includes its own contradictions. It is by transcending the given toward the field of possibles and by realizing one possibility from among all the others that the individual objectifies himself and contributes to making History. The project then takes on a reality which the agent himself may not know, one which, through the conflicts it manifests and engenders, influences the course of events.

Therefore we must conceive of the possibility as doubly determined. On the one side, it is at the very heart of the particular action, the presence of the future as *that which is lacking* and that which, by its very absence, reveals reality. On the other hand, it is the real and permanent future which the collectivity forever maintains and transforms. When common needs bring about the creation of new offices (for example, the multiplication of physicians in a society which is becoming industrialized), these offices, not yet filled—or vacant as the result of retirement or death—constitute for certain people a real, concrete, and *possible* future. These persons *can* go into medicine. This career is not closed to them; at this moment their life lies open before them until death. All things being equal, the professions of army doctor, country doctor, colonial doctor, etc., are characterized by certain advantages and certain obligations which they will quickly know. This future, to be sure, is only partly true; it presupposes a status quo and a minimum of order (barring accidents) which is contradicted precisely by the fact that our societies are in constant process of making history. But neither is it false, since it is this—in other words, the interests of the profession, of class, etc., the ever-increasing division of labor, etc.—which first manifests the present contradictions of society. The future is presented, then, as a schematic, always open possibility and as an immediate action on the present.

Conversely, this future defines the individual in his present reality; the conditions which the medical students must fulfill in a bourgeois society *at the same time* reveal the society, the profession, and the social situation of the one who will meet these conditions. If it is still necessary for parents to be well-off, if the practice of giving scholarships is not widespread, then the future doctor appears in his own eyes as a member of the moneyed classes. In turn, he becomes aware of his class by means of the future which it make possible for him; that is, through his chosen profession. In contrast, for the man who does not meet the required conditions, medicine becomes his *lack,* his *nonhumanity* (all the more so as many other careers are "closed" to him at the same time). It is from this point of view, perhaps, that we ought to approach the problem of relative pauperism. Every man is defined negatively by the sum total of possibles which are impossible for him; that is, by a future more or less blocked off. For the underprivileged classes, each cultural, technical, or material enrichment of society represents a diminution, an impoverishment; the future is almost entirely barred. Thus, both positively and negatively, the social possibles are lived as schematic determinations of the individual future. And the most individual possible is only the internalization and enrichment of a social possible.

. . . . .

Only the project, as a mediation between two moments of objectivity, can account for history; that is, for human *creativity*. It is necessary to choose. In effect: either we reduce everything to identity (which amounts to substituting a mechanistic materialism for dialectical materialism)—or we make of dialectic a celestial law which imposes itself on the Universe, a metaphysical force which by itself engenders the historical process (and this is to fall back into Hegelian idealism)—or we restore to the individual man his power to go beyond his situation by means of work and action. This solution alone enables us to base the movement of totalization *upon the real*. We must look for dialectic in the relation of men with nature, with "the starting conditions," and in the relation of men with one another. There is where it gets its start, *resulting* from the confrontation of projects. The characteristics of the human project alone enable us to understand that this result is a new reality provided with its own signification instead of remaining simply a statistical mean.

. . . . .

Existentialism, then, can only affirm the specificity of the historical *event;* it seeks to restore to the event its function and its multiple dimensions. Of course, Marxists do not ignore the event; in their eyes it expresses the structure of society, the form which the class struggle has assumed, the relations of force, the ascending movement of the rising class, the contradictions which at the center of each class set particular groups with different interests in opposition of each other. But a Marxist aphorism shows how for almost a hundred years now, Marxists have tended not to attach much importance to the event. The outstanding event of the eighteenth century, they say, would not be the French Revolution but the appearance of the steam engine. Marx did not move in this direction, as is demonstrated very well by his excellent article *The Eighteenth Brumaire of Louis Napoleon Bonaparte*. But today the fact—like the person—tends to become more and more symbolic. The duty of the event is to verify the a priori analyses of the situation—or at least not to contradict them. Thus French Communists tend to describe facts in terms of what can-be or must-be. Here is how one of them—and not one of the least important—explains the Soviet intervention in Hungary.

> Certain workers could be deceived, could commit themselves to a path which they did not believe to be that in which the counter-revolution was involving them, but subsequently these workers *could not help reflecting* on the consequences of this policy . . . [they] *could not do otherwise than be uneasy at seeing* [etc.]. . . . [They] could not (without indignation) see the return of the regent, Horthy. . . . It is *entirely natural* that under such circumstances the formation of the present Hungarian government has answered the prayers and expectation of the working class . . . in Hungary.

In this passage—the purpose of which is more political than theoretical—we are not told what the Hungarian workers did but what they *were unable not to do*. And why were they unable? Because they could not contradict their eternal essence as socialist workers. In a curious way, this Stalinized Marxism assumes an air of immobility; a worker is not a real being who changes with the world; he is a Platonic Idea. Indeed, in Plato, the Ideas are the Eternal, the Universal, the True. Motion and the event, as confused reflections of these static forms, are outside of Truth. Plato seeks to approach them through myths. In the Stalinist world the event is an edifying myth. Here we find what we might call the theoretical foundation for those fake confessions. The man who says, I have committed such and such an offense, such an act of treason, is performing a mythical, stereotyped recital, with no concern for verisimilitude, because he is asked to present his so-called crimes as the symbolic expression of an eternal essence. For example, the 1950 confession of abominable acts was for the purpose of unveiling the "true nature" of the Yugoslav regime. For us the most remarkable thing is the fact that the contradictions and errors in date, with which the confessions of Rajk were crammed full, never awakened in the Communists the vaguest suspicion. The materiality of fact is of no interest to these idealists; only its symbolic implications count in their eyes. In other words, Stalinist Marxists are blind to events. When they have reduced the meaning of them to the universal, they are quite willing to recognize that a residue remains, but they make of this residue the simple effect of chance. Fortuitous circumstances have been the occasional cause of what could not be dissolved (date, development, phases, origin and character of agents, ambiguity, misunderstandings, etc.). Thus, like individuals and particular enterprises, the lived falls over to the side of the irrational, the unutilizable, and the theoretician considers it to be *nonsignifying*.

Existentialism reacts by affirming the specificity of the historical event, which it refuses to conceive of as the absurd juxtaposition of a contingent residue and an a priori signification. Its problem is to discover a supple, patient dialectic which espouses movements as they really are and which refuses to consider a priori that all lived conflicts pose contradictories or even contraries. For us, *the interests* which come into play cannot necessarily find a mediation which reconciles them; most of the time they are mutually exclusive, but the fact that they cannot be satisfied at the same time does not necessarily prove that their reality is reduced to a pure contradiction of ideas. The thing stolen is not the contrary of the thief, nor is the exploited the contrary (or the contradictory) of the exploiter. Exploiter and exploited are men in conflict in a system whose principal characteristic is *scarcity*. To be sure, the capitalist owns the instruments of labor, and the worker does not own them: there we have a pure contradiction. But to be precise, the contradiction never succeeds in accounting for each event. It is the framework for the event; it creates a permanent tension in the social environment, a split within the capitalist society; but this fundamental structure of every contemporary event (in our bourgeois societies) does not by any means explain the event in its concrete reality. The day of the tenth of August, of the ninth of *Thermidor,* that day in the month of June 1848, etc., cannot be reduced to concepts. The relation between groups on each of those days is one of armed struggle, to be sure, and violence. But this struggle reflects *in itself* the structure of enemy groups, the immediate insufficiency of their development, the hidden conflicts which, though never clearly declared, result in an internal disequilibrium, the deviations which the present instruments impose on each one's action, the manner in which their needs and claims are manifested to each one.

. . . . .

Man defines himself by his project. This material being perpetually goes beyond the condition which is made for him; he reveals and determines his situation by transcending it in order to objectify himself—by work, action, or gesture. The project must not be confused with the will, which is an abstract entity, although the project can assume a voluntary form under certain circumstances. This immediate relation with the Other than oneself, beyond the given and constituted elements, this perpetual production of oneself by work and praxis, is our peculiar structure. It is neither a will nor a need nor a passion, but our needs—like our passions or like the most abstract of our thoughts—participate in this structure. They are always *outside of themselves toward*. . . . This is what we call existence, and by this we do not mean a stable substance which rests in itself, but rather a perpetual disequilibrium, a wrenching away from itself with all its body. As this impulse toward objectification assumes various forms according to the individual, as it projects us across a field of possibilities, some of which we realize to the exclusion of others, we call it also choice or freedom. But it would be a mistake to accuse us of introducing the irrational here, of inventing a "first beginning" unconnected with the world, or of giving to man a freedom-fetish. This criticism, in fact, could only issue from a mechanist philosophy; those who would direct it at us do so because they would like to *reduce* praxis, creation, invention, to the simple reproduction of the elementary given of our life.

It is because they would like to *explain* the work, the act, or the attitude by the factors which condition it; their desire for explanation is a disguise for the wish to assimilate the complex to the simple, to deny the specificity of structures, and to reduce change to identity. This is to fall back again to the level of scientistic determinism. The dialectical method, on the contrary, refuses to *reduce;* it follows the reverse procedure. It surpasses by conserving, but the terms of the surpassed contradiction cannot account for either the transcending itself or the subsequent synthesis; on the contrary, it is the synthesis which clarifies them and which enables us to understand them. For us the basic contradiction is only one of the factors which delimit and structure the field of possibles; it is the choice which must be interrogated if one wants to explain them in their detail, to reveal their singularity (that is, the particular aspect in which *in this case* generality is presented), and to understand how they have been lived. It is the work or the act of the individual which reveals to us the secret of his conditioning. Flaubert by his choice of writing discloses to us the meaning of his childish fear of death—not the reverse. By misunderstanding these principles, contemporary Marxism has prevented itself from understanding significations and values. For it is as absurd to reduce the signification of an object to the pure inert materiality of that object itself as to want to deduce the law from the fact. The meaning of a conduct and its value can be grasped only in perspective by the movement which realizes the possibles as it reveals the given.

Man is, for himself and for others, a signifying being, since one can never understand the slightest of his gestures without going beyond the pure present and explaining it by the future. Furthermore, he is a creator of signs to the degree that—always ahead of himself—he employs certain objects to designate other absent or future objects. But both operations are reduced to a pure and simple surpassing. To surpass present conditions toward their later change and to surpass the present object toward an absence are one and the same thing. Man constructs signs because in his very reality he is signifying; and he is signifying because he is a dialectical surpassing of all that is simply given. What we call freedom is the irreducibility of the cultural order to the natural order.

To grasp the meaning of any human conduct, it is necesary to have at our disposal what German psychiatrists and historians have called "comprehension." But what is involved here is neither a particular talent nor a special faculty of intuition; this knowing is simply the dialectical movement which explains the act by its terminal signification in terms of its starting conditions. It is originally progressive. If my companion suddenly starts toward the window, I understand his gesture in terms of the material situation in which we both are. It is, for example, because the room is too warm. He is going "to let in some air." This action is not inscribed in the temperature; it is not "set in motion" by the warmth as by a "stimulus" provoking chain reactions. There is present here a synthetic conduct which, by unifying itself, unifies before my eyes the practical field in which we both are. The movements are new, they are adapted to the situation, to particular obstacles. This is because the perceived settings are *abstract* motivating schemata and insufficiently determined; they are determined within the unity of the enterprise. It is necessary to avoid that table; after that the window is of the casement type or a sash window or a sliding one or perhaps—if we are in a strange place—of a style not yet known to us. In every way, if I am to go beyond the succession of gestures and to perceive the unity which they give themselves, I must myself feel the overheated atmosphere as a need for freshness, as a demand for air; that is, I must myself become the lived surpassing of our material situation. Within the room, doors and windows are never entirely passive realities; the work of other people has given to them their meaning, has made out of them instruments, possibilities *for an other* (any other). This means that I *comprehend* them already as instrumental structures and as products of a directed activity. But my companion's movement makes explicit the crystallized indications and designations in these products; his behavior reveals the practical field to me as a "hodological space," and conversely the indications contained in the utensils become the crystallized meaning which allows me to comprehend the enterprise. His conduct *unifies* the room, and the room defines his conduct.

What we have here is so clearly an enriching surpassing *for both of us* that this conduct, instead of being first clarified by the material situation, can reveal the situation to me. Absorbed in the collaborating work of our discussion, I had experienced the warmth as a confused, unnamed discomfort; in my companion's gesture, I see at once both his practical intention and the meaning of my discomfort. The movement of comprehension is simultaneously progressive (toward the objective result) and regressive (I go back toward the original condition). Moreover, it is the act itself which will define the heat as unbearable; if we don't lift a finger, it is because the temperature can be tolerated. Thus the rich, complex unity of the enterprise springs from the poorest condition and turns back upon it to clarify it. Furthermore, at the same time but in another dimension, my companion reveals himself by his conduct. If he gets up deliberately and opens the window a crack before beginning the work or the discussion, this gesture refers to more general objectives (the will to show himself methodical, to play the role of an orderly man, or is real love of order). He will appear very different if he suddenly jumps to his feet and throws the casement window wide open as if he were suffocating. Here also if I am to be able to comprehend him, it is necessary that my own conduct in its projective movement should inform me about my own inner depths—that is, about my wider objectives and the conditions which correspond to the choice of these objectives. Thus *comprehension* is nothing other than my real life; it is the totalizing movement which gathers together my neighbor, myself, and the environment in the synthetic unity of an objectification in process.

Precisely because we are a *pro-ject,* comprehension may be entirely regressive. If neither one of us has been aware of the temperature, a third person coming in will certainly say: "Their discussion is so absorbing that they are about to stifle." This person, from the minute he entered the room, has lived the warmth as a need, as a wish to let in some air, to freshen things up; suddenly the closed window has assumed for him a signification, not because it was going to be opened, but, quite the contrary, because it had not been opened. The close, overheated room reveals to him an act which has not been performed (and which was indicated as a permanent possibility by the work laid down in the present utensils). But this absence, this objectification of non-being, will find a true consistency only if it serves to reveal a positive enterprise. Across the act to be done and not yet done, this witness will discover the passion which we have put into our discussion. And if he laughingly calls us "library rats," he will find still more general significations in our behavior and will illuminate us to the depths of our being.

Because we are men and because we live in the world of men, of work, and of conflicts, all the objects which surround us are signs. By themselves they indicate their use and scarcely mask the real project of those who have made them such *for us* and who address us through them. But their particular ordering, under this or that circumstance, retraces for us an individual action, a project, an event. The cinema has so often used this process that it has become a convention. The director shows us the beginning of a dinner, then he cuts; several hours later in the deserted room, overturned glasses, empty bottles, cigarette stubs littering the floor, indicate by themselves that the guests got drunk. Thus significations come from man and from his project, but they are inscribed everywhere in things and in the order of things. Everything at every instant is always signifying, and significations reveal to us men and relations among men across the structures of our society. But these significations appear to us only insofar as we ourselves are signifying. Our comprehension of the Other is never contemplative; it is only a moment of our praxis, a way of living—in struggle or in complicity—the concrete, human relation which unites us to him.

Among these significations there are some which refer us to a lived situation, to specific behavior, to a collective event. This would be the case, if you like, with those shattered glasses which, on the screen, are charged with retracing for us the story of an evening's orgy. Others are simple indications—such as an arrow on the wall in a subway corridor. Some refer to "collectives." Some are symbols; the reality signified is present in them as the nation is in the flag. Some are statements of utility; certain objects are offered to me as *means*—a pedestrian crossing, a shelter, etc. Still others, which we apprehend especially—but not always—by means of the visible, immediate behavior of real men, are quite simply ends.

We must resolutely reject the so-called positivism which imbues today's Marxist and impels him to deny the existence of these last significations. The supreme mystification of positivism is that it claims to approach social experience without any a priori whereas it has decided at the start to deny one of its fundamental structures and to replace it by its opposite. It was legitimate for the natural sciences to free themselves from the anthropomorphism which consists in bestowing human properties on inanimate objects. But it is perfectly absurd to assume by analogy the same scorn for anthropomorphism where anthropology is concerned. When one is studying man, what can be more exact or more rigorous than to *recognize human properties in him?* The simple inspection of the social field ought to have led to the discovery that the relation to ends is a permanent structure of human enterprises and that it is *on the basis of this relation* that real men evaluate actions, institutions, or economic constructions. It ought to have been established that our comprehension of the other is necessarily attained through ends. A person who from a distance watches a man at work and says: "I don't understand what he is doing," will find that clarification comes when he can unify the disjointed moments of this activity, thanks to the anticipation of the result aimed at. A better example—in order to fight, to outwit the opponent, a person must have at his disposal several systems of ends at once. In boxing, one will grant to a feint its true finality (which is, for example, to force the opponent to lift his guard) if one discovers and rejects at the same time its pretended finality (to land a left hook on the forehead). The double, triple systems of ends which others employ condition our activity as strictly as our own. A positivist who held on to his teleological color blindness in practical life would not live very long.

It is true that in a society which is wholly alienated, in which "capital appears more and more as a social power of which the capitalist is the functionary,"[2] the manifest ends can mask the profound necessity behind an evolution or a mechanism already set. But even then the end as the signification of the lived project of a man or of a group of men remains real, to the extent that, as Hegel said, the appearance possesses a reality as appearance. In this case as well as in the preceding, its role and its practical efficacy must be determined. In *Critique of Dialectical Reason* I shall show how the stabilization of prices in a competitive market *reifies* the relation between seller and buyer. Courtesies, hesitations, bargaining, all that is outmoded and thrust aside, since the chips are already down. And yet each of these *gestures* is lived by its author as an act. Of course, the activity does not belong to the domain of pure representation. But the permanent possibility that an end might be transformed into an illusion characterizes the social field and the modes of alienation; it does not remove from the end its irreducible structure. Still better, the notions of alienation and mystification have meaning only to the precise degree that they steal away the ends and disqualify them. There are therefore two conceptions which we must be careful not to confuse. The first, which is held by numerous American sociologists and by some French Marxists, foolishly substitutes for the givens of experience an abstract causalism or certain metaphysical forms or concepts such as motivation, attitude, or role, which have no meaning except in conjunction with a finality. The second recognizes the existence of ends wherever they are found and limits itself to declaring that certain among them can be neutralized at the heart of the historical process of totalization. This is the position of true Marxism and of existentialism.

. . . . .

Conclusion

These considerations enable us to understand why we can at the same time declare that we are in profound agreement with Marxist philosophy and yet for the present maintain the autonomy of the existential ideology. There is no doubt, indeed, that Marxism appears today to be the only possible anthropology which can be at once historical and structural. It is the only one which at the same time takes man in his totality—that is, in terms of the materiality of his condition. Nobody can propose to it another point of departure, for this would be to offer to it *another man* as the object of its study. It is *inside* the movement of Marxist thought that we discover a flaw of such a sort that despite itself Marxism tends to eliminate the questioner from his investigation and to make of the questioned the object of an absolute Knowledge. The very notions which Marxist research employs to describe our historical society—exploitation, alienation, fetishizing, reification, etc.—are precisely those which most immediately refer to existential structures. The very notion of praxis and that of dialectic—inseparably bound together—are contradictory to the intellectualist idea of a knowledge. And to come to the most important point, *labor,* as man's reproduction of his life, can hold no meaning if its fundamental structure is not to pro-ject. In view of this default—which pertains to the historical development and not to the actual principles of the doctrine—existentialism, at the heart of Marxism and taking the same givens, the same Knowledge, as its point of departure, must attempt in its turn—at least as an experiment—the dialectical interpretation of History. It puts nothing in question except a mechanistic determinism which is not exactly Marxist and which has been introduced from the outside into this total philosophy. Existentialism, too, wants to situate man in his class and in the conflicts which oppose him to other classes, starting with the mode and the relations of production. But it can approach this "situation" in terms of *existence*—that is, of comprehension. It makes itself the questioned and the question as questioner; it does not, as Kierkegaard did apropos of Hegel, set the irrational singularity of the individual in opposition to universal Knowledge. But into this very Knowledge and into the universality of concepts, it wants to reintroduce the unsurpassable singularity of the human adventure.

. . . . .

Notes

1. At one time this intellectual terror corresponded to "the physical liquidation" of particular people.
2. Marx: *Capital,* III, 1, p. 293.

8

Andre Gorz (1924–)

Born in Austria, Andre Gorz was deeply influenced by Sartre's writings. He has been a Paris journalist since the late 1940s and an editor of the theoretical journal Les Temps Modernes. *After his many years of activity on the Left, Gorz's thinking has evolved in the last few decades toward a synthesis of certain traditional Marxist theoretical tools with many of the contributions of the New Left and even more recent political movements. In particular, he has been concerned with the political potential of ecological activism and the various movements of minority groups and women.*

In this excerpt from his essay "Reform and Revolution" (1967), Gorz anticipates some of the political developments of the May 1968 revolt in France. Most critically, he seeks an understanding of an adequate revolutionary strategy in the face of affluent capitalist societies managed by a cooperative and well-organized state apparatus.

"Reform and Revolution"

A Socialist Strategy of Reforms

The working class will not unite politically or man the barricades for the sake of a 10 percent wage increase or an extra 50,000 dwellings. It is unlikely that in the foreseeable future there will be a crisis in capitalism so acute that, in order to protect their vital interests, workers will resort to a revolutionary general strike or armed insurrection.

On the other hand, the bourgeoisie will never relinquish power without a struggle and without being compelled to do so by revolutionary action on the part of the masses.

The main problem confronting socialist strategy is consequently that of *creating the conditions,* both objective and subjective, in which mass revolutionary action becomes possible and in which the bourgeoisie may be engaged and defeated in a trial of strength.

You may not approve of the terms in which I have stated the problem, and you may hold that socialism is not necessary to the liberation and fulfillment of mankind. But if, like most of those who work with their hands or their heads, you consider, or confusedly feel, that capitalism is no more acceptable today than it was yesterday as a form of economic and social development; as a way of life and as a way by which men relate to each other, to their work, to their environment and to peoples in other parts of the world; and also in the use it makes, or fails to make, of the resources of technology and science, and of the actual or potential creative ability of the individual—if, feeling or believing this, you support socialism, then the problem of bringing it about can be stated only in those terms.

Socialism will not be achieved by a gradual reordering of the capitalist system, designed to rationalize its functioning and institutionalize class antagonisms. It will not emerge of its own accord out of the cries and imbalances of which capitalism can eliminate neither the causes nor the effects, but which it now knows how to prevent from becoming explosive, nor will it be born of a spontaneous uprising of the dissatisfied masses or through the anathematizing of social traitors and revisionists. It can be brought about only by deliberate, long-term action of which the *beginning* may be a scaled series of reforms, but which, as it unfolds, must grow into a series of trials of strength, more or less violent, some won and others lost, but of which the outcome will be to mold and organize the socialist resolve and consciousness of the working classes. This is how the struggle will develop provided each battle serves to strengthen, within the capitalist system, the strongpoints, the weapons and the *reasons* which enable the workers to withstand the forces of capitalism and prevent the system from repairing the breaches opened in its own power structure.

There is no, there can be no gradual and imperceptible transition from capitalism to socialism. The economic and political power of the bourgeoisie cannot be slowly nibbled away; nor can it be destroyed by a series of partial reforms, each seemingly harmless and acceptable to capitalism, of which the final effect will be that of the stratagem of the Trojan horse, with the secret army of socialists finally installed in the seats of power.

It cannot be like that. The only thing that can and must be gradual in socialist strategy is the preparatory phase leading to the brink of crisis and the final trial of strength. And this approach, which is incorrectly described as "the nonviolent way to socialism," is not a matter of any a priori decision in favor of gradualism or a priori rejection of violent revolution and armed insurrection. It arises out of the necessity to create favorable conditions, both objective and subjective, and to build social and political positions of strength on the basis of which the conquest of political power by the working class will become possible.

You may object that there can be no genuinely socialist reforms so long as effective power remains in the hands of the bourgeoisie and the capitalist state remains intact. That is true. A socialist strategy of progressive reform does not mean that islands of socialism will emerge in the sea of capitalism. But it does mean the building up of working-class and popular power; it means the creation of centers of social management and of direct democracy, particularly in the major industries and co-operatives of production; it means the conquering of positions of strength in representative bodies; it means free products and services fulfilling collective needs; and this must inevitably result in intensified and deepened antagonism between the social production required by the needs and aspirations of the people, on the one hand, and the requirements of capital accumulation and power on the other.

Moreover it is essential that this antagonism should never become institutionalized, as normally happens under neocapitalist and social democratic regimes, by the integration and subordination of working-class organizations within the state, by concertation and by compulsory arbitration. On the contrary, this antagonism must be able to express itself through the autonomous action of unions and political organizations; it must undermine the capitalist power structure and break down the social and economic equilibrium which tends to be reestablished at a higher level after every act of partial reform. We shall come back to this.

Thus a socialist policy of gradual reform cannot be conceived simply in terms of the winning of an electoral majority or the promulgation of a string of reforms by make-shift coalitions of social democrats and socialists.[1] The electoral struggle, even if it is won, has never led to the forging of the collective will and the genuine political power of the working classes. As Marx and Engels said,[2] suffrage confers the right to govern but not the power to do so. It results in the averaging out of a multiplicity of individual wishes registered in the secrecy of the ballot by men and women who, whatever the convergence of their aspirations, do not have the opportunity to organize and unite in order to fight together.

This is one of the mystifications practiced by bourgeois democracy. Its institutions are so devised as to perpetuate the dispersal and isolation of individuals and deny them all *collective power* over the organization of society; so-called popular power allows them only to delegate power permanently every four or five years to representatives having no direct contact with the masses, and to political parties which are regarded as "acceptable partners" only if they defend the superior interests of the capitalist state against the masses, instead of doing the opposite.

In short, electoral victory does not confer power. Electoral victory based on even a modest program of reform does not confer the power to put the reforms into practice. This is one of the deep-seated reasons for the persistence of conservative majorities, except in times of particularly acute crisis, and for the regular reelection of existing governments, whatever their policy may have been. For this policy always reflects, in its general tendency if not in detail, the balance of power at any given time.

A radically different policy, however eloquently it may be advocated by the opposition, will only convince and appear feasible *if the power to implement it has already been practically demonstrated*—that is to say, if the pattern of social forces has been modified by direct mass action, organized and directed by the working-class parties, leading to a crisis in the policy of the government in office. In other words, the power to implement a policy of genuine reform is not to be achieved through parliament but only by the ability, demonstrated in advance, to mobilize the working classes against the prevailing policy; and this ability can be lasting and fruitful only if the forces of the opposition are capable not only of provoking a crisis in the prevailing policy but of resolving that crisis. They must not merely attack the policy but must be ready with an alternative corresponding to the new pattern of forces, or rather—since no pattern of forces is static—to the new dynamics of struggle made possible by the changed pattern.

In the absence of any change in the pattern of class forces, and of any breakdown in the economic and social equilibrium of the system due to a mass movement of protest, electoral logic will tend inevitably to work in favor of those political leaders for whom the role of the "left" consists essentially in promoting the same policy as the right, but doing it better. For leaders of this kind competition between parties is merely, in the words of Basso,[3] "competition between potential governing teams, each putting forward its claim to run the state more efficiently." But if, on the other hand, mass struggle succeeds in upsetting the equilibrium of the system and plunging it into a state of crisis without (as has happened in recent years in most of the countries of Western Europe) this struggle leading to the definition of a genuinely new economic policy capable of resolving the crisis to the political and material advantage of the workers, then the situation will rapidly degenerate and the working class, despite its tactical victory, will find itself driven back to its original positions. We have seen many examples of this: in France, in 1937, 1947 and 1957; in Belgium in 1961; in Italy in 1962–64; and elsewhere.

The same process, the squandering of an opportunity favorable to the working class, is liable to recur at the present time whenever the government voted into office on a reform program is in fact no more than a makeshift alliance of neocapitalist reformers and socialists. We are now touching upon the genuinely political aspects of a socialist strategy of reform.

Any such strategy, I must repeat, cannot in the circumstances of present-day Europe be aimed at the immediate establishment of socialism. Nor can it look for the immediate achievement of reforms which are directly incompatible with the survival of the capitalist system—for example, the nationalization of all major industries, or of all the enterprises of monopoly or oligopoly-type structure. Reforms of this kind, embodied in a short-term program, cannot serve as a strategy designed to engage a revolutionary process, during which class antagonism would be exacerbated until the final trial of strength: being aimed directly at the destruction of the capitalist system, they require as a precondition that the working class should be sufficiently mature in order for the immediate revolutionary conquest of political power to be feasible. If immediate socialism is not possible, neither is the achievement of reforms directly destructive of capitalism. Those who reject all lesser reforms on the grounds that they are merely reformist are in fact rejecting the whole possibility of a *transitional strategy* and of a process of transition to socialism.

But we need not conclude that because, in the absence of a revolutionary situation, we cannot launch out directly into reforms that would destroy the system, the socialist strategy of reforms must necessarily be confined to the kind of isolated or partial reforms which are termed "democratic" because they lack not only socialist substance but even prospects and revolutionary dynamism. What in practice distinguishes a genuinely socialist policy of reforms from reformism of the neocapitalist or "social democratic" type is less each of the reforms and goals than, first, the presence or absence of organic links between the various reforms, second, the tempo and method of their implementation and, third, the resolve, or absence of resolve, to take advantage of the imbalance created by the initial reforms to promote further disruptive action.

The fact that social democratic leaders and socialist forces are in agreement on the necessity of *certain* reforms should not, therefore, mislead us as to the fundamental difference between their viewpoints and objectives. For a socialist strategy of reforms to become possible, this difference must not be concealed or relegated to second place by tactical agreement at the summit: on the contrary, it must be kept in the forefront of the political debate. Otherwise, by awarding a totally unmerited certificate of socialism to the social democratic leaders, the socialist movement will be paving the way for the defeat, in a welter of ideological and political confusion, of the entire workers' movement and especially its avant-garde.

These remarks apply particularly to the present European situation, in which the precarious economic balance no longer permits, as has happened at other times, the financing of new social benefits and state intervention by means of inflation. The effect of this is that any program of a "social" nature—wage increases at the lower level, housing, development of backward areas, improvements in education and the social services, etc.—must either directly assail the logic and strongholds of capitalist accumulation with a coherent set of reforms, or else it must beat a hasty retreat in face of the shattering response of the forces of capitalism to the threat of injury to their interests.

The fate of a popular front coalition government, coming into power on an agreed *minimum program* of minor reforms, but excluding everything that goes beyond the terms of the agreement, is thus virtually sealed from the start. The essence of any agreed minimum program is that unlike a transitional program or genuine strategy of reforms, it prevents the socialist elements, if they are not to break the agreement, from taking advantage of the impetus created by the initial measures, and even from staging a counteroffensive to the capitalist offensive.

The nature of that offensive is familiar to us all, since it invariably follows the pattern of events in France in 1936. The reaction of the bourgeoisie to the threat to its power and prerogatives takes the form of the flight of capital abroad, the cutting down of investments and massive layoffs of workers, aimed in the first place at militant trade unionists—in short, of an economic crisis in which the working class is the hardest hit. This crisis (which incidentally is not due solely to the deliberate and concerted action of the bourgeoisie, but also to the impossibility of making capitalism work when its essential mechanisms are impaired) enables the bourgeoisie, negotiating from a position of strength, to bring about the revision of the government program and the spreading of its objectives over a longer period of time (in a word, postponing them till the Greek kalends). The bourgeois terms become increasingly harsh as internal rifts appear within the coalition, between the hard-liners and the moderates; and as time passes, and the economic and financial crisis becomes more acute, it is invariably the former who yield ground to the latter. For by now the situation has already been transformed. The original minimum program is already no longer practicable. Its implementation would call for draconian measures not originally contemplated (for example, exchange controls, price freezing, restriction of imports, nationalization of industrial and financial monopolies) and which can only be adopted by a government striking while the iron is hot, with the assurance of massive public support behind it.

The weeks of sterile negotiation, economic crisis and dissension in the ranks of the coalition will inevitably have weakened the militant ardor of the workers. The hard-liners are driven onto the defensive. Confusion spreads; and the forces of capitalism, knowing that time is on their side, harden their own position. The history of the coalition becomes one of steady retreat in which it multiplies concessions in order to win back the confidence of capital. And when eventually it is succeeded by a moderate government, better able to placate the bourgeoisie and "restore the health" of the economy, the popular front coalition has nothing to its credit except the measures of partial reform introduced during its first weeks of power, which will now be emasculated, deprived of all real scope and even turned to profit by the capitalist system.

A repetition of this process, which occurred in France after 1936 and 1945, in Britain after 1950 and 1964 and in Italy after 1947 and 1963, can be prevented only if the coalition is sufficiently homogeneous and conscious of the impending struggle to be able to reply to capitalist reaction with a devastating counteroffensive in the country, among the mass of workers, and by the introduction of governmental measures prepared well in advance of its taking office.

But the reaction of the workers' movement will be effective only if reforms are conceived not as a centralized, governmental course of action, proceeding from the top, for which the coalition will ask the voters for a permanent and disciplined delegation of authority, but as the implementation of an economic policy that from the start goes hand in hand with democratic reforms stimulating the development of structures of popular power and initiatives adapted to the local conditions in the factories, in the cooperatives, at regional and local levels.

At the same time preventive measures against capitalist reaction demand that the coalition should be under no illusions as to the possibility of placating the bourgeoisie and persuading it to cooperate in good faith with the new regime. This has always been the dream of social democratic leaders, even when they are supporting a popular front. They believe that at first an honest attempt should be made to work a policy based on indirect controls and freely accepted managerial disciplines. This line of approach is possible *only* if its advocates realize from the start that it cannot be a *lasting policy* but must inevitably end in a bitter struggle for which they *have to be prepared* in advance. In other words, a policy of indirect governmental control over the machinery of capitalist accumulation and distribution need not necessarily be rejected, provided it is regarded as *transitional,* paving the way for the direct control which is the unavoidable, logical outcome if the system is not to be bogged down by the retaliatory measures of the economic forces.

To suppose that the state can permanently encompass, direct and regulate the economic process without touching the principle of private property is to ignore the political and psychological foundations of capitalism. No doubt it is true that *technically* a policy of selective taxation, price controls and credit may impose a qualitative, geographical and social pattern on the economy by controlling the growth of its different branches, services and regions in accordance with social criteria and global economic considerations. But what is technically possible is not possible politically for any length of time.

Reduction of the cost of growth by eliminating waste (in the form of artificially swollen commercial and administrative costs, representation, advertising, etc.), by preventing the use of company resources for private ends, by preventing investment in new plants and new models which contribute nothing to technological progress or to the improvement of the products but are intended mainly to evade taxation—all this may in theory be achieved by the tightening of controls and the strict regulation of private industry: for example, by reduction of the tax allowance for publicity, by pegging prices and profits in the different branches of industry and even (in the case of the monopolies) by laying down rules for the use to be made of profits, and the nature and purpose of investment, under the threat of heavy fiscal penalties.

But the enforcement of a policy of this kind would rapidly come into conflict with the logic of the capitalist system and would destroy its vitality. It would in fact amount to the destruction of managerial decision-making power, to the de facto socialization of entrepreneurial activity and to the indirect public management of private concerns. It would entail as a sanction the confiscation of excess profits, or at least their very high taxation. Thus it would rob private enterprise of all incentive to develop improved methods and innovations tending to raise profits above the level laid down by the state, and by doing so it would destroy one of the main sources of technological progress. In short, by reducing the employers to the level of civil servants, loading them down with a ponderous bureaucracy and attacking the profit motive, the state would be assailing the very heart of the capitalist system, and would cripple or sclerose it.

To attack the machinery and motivations of capitalism is senseless unless one intends *to abolish it, not to preserve it*. To assail the consequences of the system's logic is of necessity to assail this very logic itself and to plunge the system into crisis. If this crisis is not to rebound against the forces that produced it, it must be resolved by the transfer of all centers of accumulation to public management. Failing more advanced measures of socialization in the wake of the initial reforms, designed to overcome the difficulties created by their reform program itself, the coalition of reformers will fall victim to a war of attrition and the process of decay which we have described.

So in terms of socialist strategy, although we should not reject intermediary reforms (those that do not immediately carry their anticapitalist logic to its conclusion), it is with the strict proviso that they are to be regarded as a means and not an end, as dynamic phases in a progressive struggle, not as stopping places. Their purpose is to educate and unite the actual or potential anticapitalist forces through the campaign for unimpeachable social and economic objectives—above all, the reorientation of economic and social development—by using, in the first place, the methods of peaceful democratic reform. But this approach should be adopted *not because it is viable or intrinsically preferable, but on the contrary because the resistance it will encounter, and the limitations and impossibilities it will bring to light, are alone capable of demonstrating the necessity of a complete changeover to socialism to those segments of the masses which are not yet prepared for such a course*.

Socialists and Reformists—The Program

Clearly a strategy of this kind can never be carried out by an alliance at the top with neocapitalist groups—that is to say, social democratic and center parties whose intention from the outset is to restrict reforms to measures acceptable to the bourgeoisie and who require of their associates a strict acceptance of this limitation. What it calls for, on the part of the political leaders, is full awareness of the nature of the process of transition to socialism, the mechanisms involved, the real aspirations of the masses on which it can be based, and a grasp of the *relatively short span of time* during which the success or failure of the operation will be decided.

In short, a socialist strategy of reforms must aim at disrupting the system and taking advantage of its disruption to embark on the revolutionary process of transition to socialism, which, as we have seen, can only be carried out by striking while the iron is hot. This kind of strategy can be effective only in periods of flux and open conflict and far-reaching social and political upheaval. It cannot be conceived in terms of a long-drawn-out war of attrition, because any temporary stabilization means that the decisive breakthrough, which any socialist strategy must aim at, will have failed. The new balance of forces may well be more favorable to the working class than the old, the contradictions and factors opposed to capitalist logic may be more clearly marked; but these contradictions, once the struggle for reforms begins leveling off, can have only a limited bearing: both sides will attempt to use them in order to weaken the position of the other. Such essentially *tactical* skirmishes are no substitute for a comprehensive *strategy* since, however precarious the balance may be, it rests on the acceptance by both sides of the impossibility of achieving complete victory.

It is therefore unrealistic to regard those tactical engagements, which may be spread over a long period, as part of a "revolutionary process" maturing over one or two decades. However precarious the balance achieved when the struggle for reform begins leveling off, it is nevertheless a balance and therefore opens a period of uneasy truce. The contradictions which the reforms have introduced into the system do not gnaw away its fabric and weaken it like a long-term illness. They cannot retain their power of disruption, but, on the contrary, must lose it. There are no anticapitalist institutions or gains which, in the long term, are not nibbled away, distorted, reabsorbed into the system, completely or partially emptied of their substance, if the imbalance which they originally created is not promptly exploited by further advances. Being compelled to coexist with institutions which at the outset conflict with its own logic and restrict its sphere of sovereignty, capitalism learns to master them by indirect means. Provided it retains control of the key points of accumulation and development, and particularly of those activities which lead to technological progress and growth, it can eventually regain all the ground it has lost.

We cannot therefore think of the transition period, or the period of preparation for transition, as being a long one, something like a decade. If the transition is not promptly set in motion following the rupture caused by the struggle for reforms, it will not happen. The reforms will be dismembered, scattered and absorbed by the system, and the balance will be restored at a higher level. A new period of preparatory struggle, embodying new contradictions, will then be necessary to create the conditions for a new offensive. The discontinuity of socialist strategy is that of history itself.

But we need not assume for this reason that all past democratic reforms have been valueless, which would amount to writing off a century of working-class struggle. Their past gains, even partly or wholly robbed of substance, provide the workers and socialists with a springboard for further advances. This was what Lenin had in mind when he described state monopoly capitalism as the "antechamber of socialism," meaning the farthest stage hitherto reached in the socialization of the capitalist productive process, affording certain levers capable of being employed by the socialist state.

Nevertheless it must be stressed that although past gains may have rendered capitalist predominance, less secure and the equilibrium of the system more fragile, *for this very reason* further piecemeal reforms and shock to the equilibrium *will become politically more difficult*. It is precisely when new anticapitalist measures threaten to jeopardize the system as a whole that bourgeois resistance becomes most ferocious. *The nearer the system is to collapse, or the nearer it has been to collapse in the past, the more difficult it becomes to resume the attack and break down the last defenses*. The bourgeoisie has been alerted. The workers have learned the political and economic penalties of failure. What is now called for is a higher degree of preparation, resolution, and awareness, if the struggle is to be continued.

The idea of "creeping socialism" which will gain ground by a gradual series of reforms until it is ready for the final "qualitative leap" corresponds to no kind of reality except perhaps the very real vigilance on the part of the bourgeoisie which the notion reflects. There can be no *cumulative effect* of a series of gradual reforms if they are introduced over a long period and without a very sharp trial of strength based on a considered strategy. It is particularly in countries where the machinery of capitalist accumulation is already virtually subject to state control, and where (even though the state makes no use of the means at its disposal against the monopolies, and indeed does the opposite) institutional reforms presenting no intrinsic difficulty would suffice to break the power of the bourgeoisie, that capitalism brings to bear its full resources in every field (ideological, political, social) to prevent the awakening of a political will capable of carrying through such reforms.

In a number of Western European countries, notably France, the Scandinavian countries and Italy, the point has now been reached where, because of the vulnerability of the system, the bourgeoisie is defending its power positions to the death and furiously resisting all the workers' claims as well as their agitation for partial reforms. Hence the necessity of raising the struggle to the level of comprehensive strategy, based on an overall vision of society, and of attacking not merely the directly intolerable effects of capitalism but the very nature of the relations of production and the civilization they create.

This comprehensiveness of the struggle is necessary simply because the survival of the system is now imperiled by the achievement of even partial reforms, and the bourgeoisie is aware of the fact. The bourgeoisie meets partial attacks with overall resistance. The workers' movement cannot therefore hope to be victorious in the eventual trial of strength if it is not fully aware from the start of the nature of the stakes it is playing for, and if to this overall resistance it does not oppose an overall political resolve. One cannot win a battle in which the enemy has *everything* to lose if the immediate advantage for which one is fighting does not pave the way for a victory warranting *total* engagement.

There is therefore an element of truth and an element of error in the maximalist tendencies at present developing in face of the degeneration of European social democracy and the increasing difficulty of securing better wages, working conditions and partial reforms. The error consists in postulating that every engagement must now be entered upon with the clearly stated socialist intention that its ultimate aim is the overthrow of the system. This amounts to affirming that the revolutionary intention must *precede* the struggle and supply its impetus. That is a nondialectical position which evades the problem by treating it as though it were already solved. For the fact is that the socialist resolve of the masses never springs out of nothing, nor is it created by political propaganda or scientific demonstration. Socialist resolve is *built* in and by the struggle for feasible objectives corresponding to the experience, needs and aspirations of the workers.

But it is still necessary for these objectives to be interrelated in terms of a strategic whole, so that, as the struggle develops and encounters the structural limits of the system, it will gain not only in breadth but in depth. It is in the vanguard of the workers' movement and among its leaders, not among the masses, that the dialectical development of the struggle presupposes an already existing socialist intention. The intention will not be asserted by speeches and revolutionary propaganda but by ability to grade the objectives, to raise the struggle to a constantly higher plane and to set "intermediary" targets, paving the way for worker power, which must necessarily be surpassed as soon as they have been achieved.

The element of truth in the present maximalist position lies, however, in the fact that the workers' movement will not progress toward socialism if socialism is not the objective meaning of its day-to-day claims and destined eventually to become its conscious (or subjective) intention. No protest or claim put forward in general and therefore abstract terms (for example, overall increase in wages and pensions, development of social services, etc.) can possess this objective meaning, if only because its fulfillment is not within the power of those making the claim and will not be the direct result of their action, even if it is successful. Moreover that kind of claim does not of itself possess an internal anticapitalist logic requiring the immediate target to be surpassed as soon as it has been reached. It involves a graduated implementation which may be met by government action based on technical (or technocratic) reform. The aim of these reforms does not reach beyond their limited and specific goal.

Under present conditions the working class will acquire the maturity and political strength necessary to overcome the increased resistance of the system only if its claims, by their content but also by the *manner* in which they are pressed, represent a living criticism of capitalist civilization, its social structure, productive system and entire *rationale*.

This criticism, deepening the nature of the struggle, is particularly important in the context of neocapitalism, where the socialist movement comes up against the minor reformism of social democrat and center parties. These very often propose the *same* kind of objectives advocated by the radical left (housing, education, collective amenities, "social justice," etc.), but always with the proviso that they are to be gained without causing a breakdown in the capitalist machine—that is to say, without upsetting the economic equilibrium or weakening the position of the bourgeoisie.

The favorite theme of the social democrats is the contention that all problems can be solved or rendered tolerable, all material needs satisfied, within the framework of the existing system, given sufficient time and discipline. No need to "break up the joint" or engage in any trial of strength: we have simply to be patient and realistic, to act responsibly and trust our leaders. Let every man keep his proper place and the neocapitalist state will serve the best interests of all.

For socialists it is no doubt useful to point out that the reformists deny themselves the means of carrying out their own program; that the program will either never be realized or will be subject to such long delays that its remedies will have been rendered out-of-date by changed conditions;

and that in any case it is possible to ask for more and do better by going further in transforming the structure. But however pertinent they may be, arguments of this kind are not enough. They amount simply to countering promises of relative improvement with promises of more rapid or drastic relative improvement. What they do not say, and what the reformists loudly proclaim, is that the more rapid or drastic improvements must entail a major crisis in the system. "You want to smash the machine," the moderates argue. "We want to make it work better."

So long as it adopts a platform of *relative,* general improvement, the socialist movement is ill equipped to meet this position. If it encourages the idea that the difference between its policy and that of the reformists is merely one of *degree,* and that it is basically pursuing the same objectives but with greater energy and intransigence, prepared if need be to bring things to the point of a trial of strength with capitalism, it has very little prospect of winning the support of social democratic voters and constituting itself the dominant force of the working-class movement. A mere difference of degree is not enough to woo the masses away from the slow but "safe" path of minor reforms on to the perilous and arduous road of direct clash with the forces of capital.

People will not be prepared to accept the risks of a serious political and monetary crisis and a head-on battle with the bourgeoisie simply for the sake of 250,000 new houses a year instead of 200,000, a 10 percent wage increase instead of 5 percent and a slightly shorter work week. The game would not be worth the candle, if only because the more ambitious policy of the socialists would start by provoking a savage backlash on the part of the system, a major disturbance of the economy and, in all likelihood, a deterioration in the material circumstances of the workers, for a short time at least.

Moderate social democratic propaganda achieves its greatest effectiveness by asking: "Why be in such a hurry? Why try to force things when, with a little patience and discipline, you can get what you want *within a reasonable time and in a calm and orderly fashion?* Is it worthwhile to risk a major crisis for the sake of doing in five years what can be done in seven or eight without any drastic changes?"

This is the question stated by the European social democrats, and the socialist movement can answer it only by stressing the existence of a *fundamental* difference between its policy and the policy of the reformists. The difference is not merely one of degree, timing and method in achieving the same aims as the social democrats, but better and faster: it is a *total* difference justifying the acceptance of a total risk. Only insofar as it can convincingly demonstrate that its actions and purposes are not those of the reformists, that it is not concerned with relative and partial improvements but with *absolute and global betterment,* can the socialist movement hope to advance and assert itself as the dominant force in the workers' movement.

Absolute and global betterment does not, of course, mean promising an immediate earthly paradise, by the instant creation of a socialist order. It means that every partial improvement, every reform that is campaigned for, shall be related in the context of a comprehensive plan designed to produce an overall change. The import of this change must transcend all the minor gains which in one way or another contribute to it. The absolute betterment it seeks is the emancipation of all those who are exploited by the capitalist system, oppressed, degraded and sterilized in what constitutes their social value and their self-respect as individuals—their work as members of society.

Certainly reformists and socialists want a number of the same things, but they do not want them for the same reasons or in the same way. Reform, to the moderates, means simply "things"—wages, pensions, collective amenities—to be loftily bestowed by the state on the mass of underlings, who are to be kept dispersed and impotent within the system. But what matters to the socialists, as much or more than "things," is the sovereign *power* of the workers to determine for themselves the conditions of their social cooperation and to subject to their collective will the content, goal and division of their labor.

Therein lies the profound difference between reformism and socialism. It is the difference between conceded reforms which perpetuate the subordinate position of the working class in the factories and in society, and reforms dictated, effected and controlled by the masses themselves, based on their capacity for self-management and their own initiative. Finally it is the difference between merely technical, governmental reforms and those which are genuinely democratic, this being understood to mean that they are *of necessity* anticapitalist. As Lelio Basso has written: "To fight for true democracy, for real participation at all levels in the management of collective interests, for all forms of collective control and in particular the control by the workers of all aspects of the production process . . . this is in effect to fight against the capitalists' power of decision. . . . An essential element in the conflict is the struggle of the working class for its own right to self-manage the utilization of its labor power, with all the consequences this entails affecting the organization of work in the factories, the rating of skills, the administration of deferred wages (national insurance), etc."

Thus the difference in intention between neocapitalist and anticapitalist reform must necessarily be paralleled by a difference of method. The liberating value of the reforms can be apparent only if this was already present in the mass action designed to bring them into effect. Where the method is concerned, the difference between technical and democratic reform is the difference between institutional reform coldly applied and reform enforced in hot blood by collective action. In the formal sense any reform, including workers' control, may be robbed of its revolutionary significance and absorbed by capitalism if it is introduced by act of government and operated under bureaucratic control—that is to say, reduced to the status of a "thing."

Certain maximalists conclude from this that all reforms are meaningless while the capitalist state continues to exist. They are right when it is a matter of reforms from above, volunteered and institutionalized in cold blood, but wrong in the case of reforms brought about in hot blood by active struggle from below. It is impossible to separate any reform from the action of which it is the product, and impossible to achieve democratic and anticapitalist reform by action which is neither one nor the other. The emancipation of the working class can become a total objective for the workers, warranting total risk, only if in the course of the struggle they have learned something about self-management, initiative and collective decision—in a word, if they have had a foretaste of what emancipation means.

. . . . .

Notes

1. By socialists I mean all forces actually seeking to achieve socialism, that is to say, the abolition of the capitalist system of production and state, not merely the so-called socialist parties, which are often nothing of the kind.
2. In the 1872 Preface to the *Communist Manifesto*.
3. *International Socialist Journal,* No. 15.

9

Herbert Marcuse (1898–1979)

Born in Germany, Herbert Marcuse was a youthful member of the Social Democratic party (SDP), which he left as a result of its betrayal of the workers' council movement. He studied philosophy and joined the Institute for Social Research in 1933. He fled Germany to escape nazism and subsequently settled in the United States, where he taught in several universities. During the 1960s and 1970s he became world famous for his ideological connections to the American and Western European New Left. His many writings include a critique of Soviet Marxism, an attempt to reconcile Marx and Freud, and critical analyses of industrial capitalism.

In the following excerpt from An Essay on Liberation *(1969), many of Marcuse's basic ideas are woven together. An attempt is made to find a motivation and resource for radical social change beyond Marxism's traditional reliance on an economically exploited proletariat. The dehumanizing culture of affluent capitalist societies is critiqued. Last, a speculative description of "utopian," biologically based impulses toward human liberation is presented.*

An Essay on Liberation

INTRODUCTION

Up to now, it has been one of the principal tenets of the critical theory of society (and particularly Marxian theory) to refrain from what might be reasonably called utopian speculation. Social theory is supposed to analyze existing societies in the light of their own functions and capabilities and to identify demonstrable tendencies (if any) which might lead beyond the existing state of affairs. By logical inference from the prevailing conditions and institutions, critical theory may also be able to determine the basic institutional changes which are the prerequisites for the transition to a higher stage of development: "higher" in the sense of a more rational and equitable use of resources, minimization of destructive conflicts, and enlargement of the realm of freedom. But beyond these limits, critical theory did not venture for fear of losing its scientific character.

I believe that this restrictive conception must be revised, and that the revision is suggested, and even necessitated, by the actual evolution of contemporary societies. The dynamic of their productivity deprives "utopia" of its traditional unreal content: what is denounced as "utopian" is no longer that which has "no place" and cannot have any place in the historical universe, but rather that which is blocked from coming about by the power of the established societies.

Utopian possibilities are inherent in the technical and technological forces of advanced capitalism and socialism: the rational utilization of these forces on a global scale would terminate poverty and scarcity within a very foreseeable future. But we know now that neither their rational use nor—and this is decisive—their collective control by the "immediate producers" (the workers) would by itself eliminate domination and exploitation: a bureaucratic welfare state would still be a state of repression which would continue even into the "second phase of socialism," when each is to receive "according to his needs."

What is now at stake are the needs themselves. At this stage, the question is no longer how can the individual satisfy his own needs without hurting others, but rather how can he satisfy his needs without hurting himself, without reproducing, through his aspirations and satisfactions, his dependence on an exploitative apparatus which, in satisfying his needs, perpetuates his servitude? The advent of a free society would be characterized by the fact that the growth of well-being turns into an essentially new quality of life. This qualitative change must occur in the needs, in the infrastructure of man (itself a dimension of the infrastructure of society): the new direction, the new institutions and relationships of production, must express the ascent of needs and satisfactions very different from and even antagonistic to those prevalent in the exploitative societies. Such a change would constitute the instinctual basis for freedom which the long history of class society has blocked. Freedom would become the environment of an organism which is no longer capable of adapting to the competitive performances required for well-being under domination, no longer capable of tolerating the aggressiveness, brutality, and ugliness of the established way of life. The rebellion would then have taken root in the very nature, the "biology" of the individual; and on these new grounds, the rebels would redefine the objectives and the strategy of the political struggle, in which alone the concrete goals of liberation can be determined.

Is such a change in the "nature" of man conceivable? I believe so, because technical progress has reached a stage in which reality no longer need be defined by the debilitating competition for social survival and advancement. The more these technical capacities outgrow the framework of exploitation within which they continue to be confined and abused, the more they propel the drives and aspirations of men to a point at which the necessities of life cease to demand the aggressive performances of "earning a living," and the "non-necessary" becomes a vital need. This proposition, which is central in Marxian theory, is familiar enough, and the managers and publicists of corporate capitalism are well aware of its meaning; they are prepared to "contain" its dangerous consequences. The radical opposition also is aware of these prospects, but the critical theory which is to guide political practice still lags behind. Marx and Engels refrained from developing concrete concepts of the possible forms of freedom in a socialist society; today, such restraint no longer seems justified. The growth of the productive forces suggests possibilities of human liberty very different from, and beyond those envisaged at the earlier stage. Moreover, these real possibilities suggest that the gap which separates a free society from the existing societies would be wider and deeper precisely to the degree to which the repressive power and productivity of the latter shape man and his environment in their image and interest.

For the world of human freedom cannot be built by the established societies, no matter how much they may streamline and rationalize their dominion. Their class structure, and the perfected controls required to sustain it, generate needs, satisfactions, and values which reproduce the servitude of the human existence. This "voluntary" servitude (voluntary inasmuch as it is introjected into the individuals), which justifies the benevolent masters, can be broken only through a political practice which reaches the roots of containment and contentment in the infrastructure of man, a political practice of methodical disengagement from and refusal of the Establishment, aiming at a radical transvaluation of values. Such a practice involves a break with the familiar, the routine ways of seeing, hearing, feeling, understanding things so that the organism may become receptive to the potential forms of a nonaggressive, nonexploitative world.

No matter how remote from these notions the rebellion may be, no matter how destructive and self-destructive it may appear, no matter how great the distance between the middle-class revolt in the metropoles and the life-and-death struggle of the wretched of the earth—common to them is the depth of the Refusal. It makes them reject the rules of the game that is rigged against them, the ancient strategy of patience and persuasion, the reliance on the Good Will in the Establishment, its false and immoral comforts, its cruel affluence.

A BIOLOGICAL FOUNDATION FOR SOCIALISM?

In the affluent society, capitalism comes into its own. The two mainsprings of its dynamic—the escalation of commodity production and productive exploitation—join and permeate all dimensions of private and public existence. The available material and intellectual resources (the potential of liberation) have so much outgrown the established institutions that only the systematic increase in waste, destruction, and management keeps the system going. The opposition which escapes suppression by the police, the courts, the representatives of the people, and the people themselves, finds expression in the diffused rebellion among the youth and the intelligentsia, and in the daily struggle of the persecuted minorities. The armed class struggle is waged outside: by the wretched of the earth who fight the affluent monster.

The critical analysis of this society calls for new categories: moral, political, aesthetic. I shall try to develop them in the course of the discussion. The category of obscenity will serve as an introduction.

This society is obscene in producing and indecently exposing a stifling abundance of wares while depriving its victims abroad of the necessities of life; obscene in stuffing itself and its garbage cans while poisoning and burning the scarce foodstuffs in the fields of its aggression; obscene in the words and smiles of its politicians and entertainers; in its prayers, in its ignorance, and in the wisdom of its kept intellectuals.

Obscenity is a moral concept in the verbal arsenal of the Establishment, which abuses the term by applying it, not to expressions of its own morality but to those of another. Obscene is not the picture of a naked woman who exposes her pubic hair but that of a fully clad general who exposes his medals rewarded in a war of aggression: obscene is not the ritual of the Hippies but the declaration of a high dignitary of the Church that war is necessary for peace. Linguistic therapy—that is, the effort to free words (and thereby concepts) from the all but total distortion of their meanings by the Establishment—demands the transfer of moral standards (and of their validation) from the Establishment to the revolt against it. Similarly, the sociological and political vocabulary must be radically reshaped: it must be stripped of its false neutrality; it must be methodically and provocatively "moralized" in terms of the Refusal. Morality is not necessarily and not primarily ideological. In the face of an amoral society, it becomes a political weapon, an effective force which drives people to burn their draft cards, to ridicule national leaders, to demonstrate in the streets, and to unfold signs saying "Thou shalt not kill," in the nation's churches.

The reaction to obscenity is shame, usually interpreted as the physiological manifestation of the sense of guilt accompanying the transgression of a taboo. The obscene exposures of the affluent society normally provoke neither shame nor a sense of guilt, although this society violates some of the most fundamental moral taboos of civilization. The term obscenity belongs to the sexual sphere; shame and the sense of guilt arise in the Oedipal situation. If in this respect social morality is rooted in sexual morality, then the shamelessness of the affluent society and its effective repression of the sense of guilt would indicate a decline of shame and guilt feeling in the sexual sphere. And indeed, the exposure of the (for all practical purposes) naked body is permitted and even encouraged, and the taboos on pre- and extramarital intercourse are considerably relaxed. Thus we are faced with the contradiction that the liberalization of sexuality provides an instinctual basis for the repressive and aggressive power of the affluent society.

This contradiction can be resolved if we understand that the liberalization of the Establishment's own morality takes place within the framework of effective controls; kept within this framework, the liberalization strengthens the cohesion of the whole. The relaxation of taboos alleviates the sense of guilt and binds (though with considerable ambivalence) the "free" individuals libidinally to the institutionalized fathers. They are powerful but also tolerant fathers, whose management of the nation and its economy delivers and protects the liberties of the citizens. On the other hand, if the violation of taboos transcends the sexual sphere and leads to refusal and rebellion, the sense of guilt is not alleviated and repressed but rather transferred: not we, but the fathers, are guilty; they are not tolerant but false; they want to redeem their own guilt by making us, the sons, guilty; they have created a world of hypocrisy and violence in which we do not wish to live. Instinctual revolt turns into political rebellion, and against this union, the Establishment mobilizes its full force.

This union provokes such a response because it reveals the prospective scope of social change at this stage of development, the extent to which the radical political practice involves a cultural subversion. The refusal with which the opposition confronts the existing society is affirmative in that it envisages a new culture which fulfills the humanistic promises betrayed by the old culture. Political radicalism thus implies moral radicalism: the emergence of a morality which might precondition man for freedom. This radicalism activates the elementary, organic foundation of morality in the human being. Prior to all ethical behavior in accordance with specific social standards, prior to all ideological expression, morality is a "disposition" of the organism, perhaps rooted in the erotic drive to counter aggressiveness, to create and preserve "ever greater unities" of life. We would then have, this side of all "values," an instinctual foundation for solidarity among human beings—a solidarity which has been effectively repressed in line with the requirements of class society but which now appears as a precondition for liberation.

To the degree to which this foundation is itself historical and the malleability of "human nature" reaches into the depth of man's instinctual structure, changes in morality may "sink down" into the "biological"[1] dimension and modify organic behavior. Once a specific morality is firmly established as a norm of social behavior, it is not only introjected—it also operates as a norm of "organic" behavior: the organism receives and reacts to certain stimuli and "ignores" and repels others in accord with the introjected morality, which is thus promoting or impeding the function of the organism as a living cell in the respective society. In this way, a society constantly recreates, this side of consciousness and ideology, patterns of behavior and aspiration as part of the "nature" of its people, and unless the revolt reaches into this "second" nature, into these ingrown patterns, social change will remain "incomplete," even self-defeating.

The so-called consumer economy and the politics of corporate capitalism have created a second nature of man which ties him libidinally and aggressively to the commodity form. The need for possessing, consuming, handling, and constantly renewing the gadgets, devices, instruments, engines, offered to and imposed upon the people, for using these wares even at the danger of one's own destruction, has become a "biological" need in the sense just defined. The second nature of man thus militates against any change that would disrupt and perhaps even abolish this dependence of man on a market ever more densely filled with merchandise—abolish his existence as a consumer consuming himself in buying and selling. The needs generated by this system are thus eminently stabilizing, conservative needs: the counterrevolution anchored in the instinctual structure.

The market has always been one of exploitation and thereby of domination, insuring the class structure of society. However, the productive process of advanced capitalism has altered the form of domination: the technological veil covers the brute presence and the operation of the class interest in the merchandise. Is it still necessary to state that not technology, not technique, not the machine are the engines of repression, but the presence, in them, of the masters who determine their number, their life span, their power, their place in life, and the need for them? Is it still necessary to repeat that science and technology are the great vehicles of liberation, and that it is only their use and restriction in the repressive society which makes them into vehicles of domination?

Not the automobile is repressive, not the television set is repressive, not the household gadgets are repressive, but the automobile, the television, the gadgets which, produced in accordance with the requirements of profitable exchange, have become part and parcel of the people's own existence, own "actualization." Thus they have to buy part and parcel of their own existence on the market; this existence is the realization of capital. The naked class interest builds the unsafe and obsolescent automobiles, and through them promotes destructive energy; the class interest employs the mass media for the advertising of violence and stupidity, for the creation of captive audiences. In doing so, the masters only obey the demand of the public, of the masses; the famous law of supply and demand establishes the harmony between the rulers and the ruled. This harmony is indeed preestablished to the degree to which the masters have created the public which asks for their wares, and asks for them more insistently if it can release, in and through the wares, its frustration and the aggressiveness resulting from this frustration. Self-determination, the autonomy of the individual, asserts itself in the right to race his automobile, to handle his power tools, to buy a gun, to communicate to mass audiences his opinion, no matter how ignorant, how aggressive, it may be. Organized capitalism has sublimated and turned to socially productive use frustration and primary aggressiveness on an unprecedented scale—unprecedented not in terms of the quantity of violence but rather in terms of its capacity to produce long-range contentment and satisfaction, to reproduce the "voluntary servitude." To be sure, frustration, unhappiness, and sickness remain the basis of this sublimation, but the productivity and the brute power of the system still keep the basis well under control. The achievements justify the system of domination. The established values become the people's own values: adaptation turns into spontaneity, autonomy; and the choice between social necessities appears as freedom. In this sense, the continuing exploitation is not only hidden behind the technological veil, but actually "transfigured." The capitalist production relations are responsible not only for the servitude and toil but also for the greater happiness and fun available to the majority of the population—and they deliver more goods than before.

Neither its vastly increased capacity to produce the commodities of satisfaction nor the peaceful management of class conflicts rendered possible by this capacity cancels the essential features of capitalism, namely, the private appropriation of surplus value (steered but not abolished by government intervention) and its realization in the corporate interest. Capitalism reproduces itself by transforming itself, and this transformation is mainly in the improvement of exploitation. Do exploitation and domination cease to be what they are and what they do to man if they are no longer suffered, if they are "compensated" by previously unknown comforts? Does labor cease to be debilitating if mental energy increasingly replaces physical energy in producing the goods and services which sustain a system that makes hell of large areas of the globe? An affirmative answer would justify any form of oppression which keeps the populace calm and content; while a negative answer would deprive the individual of being the judge of his own happiness.

The notion that happiness is an objective condition which demands more than subjective feelings has been effectively obscured; its validity depends on the real solidarity of the species "man," which a society divided into antagonistic classes and nations cannot achieve. As long as this is the history of mankind, the "state of nature," no matter how refined, prevails: a civilized *bellum omnium contra omnes,* in which the happiness of the ones must coexist with the suffering of the others. The First International was the last attempt to realize the solidarity of the species by grounding it in that social class in which the subjective and objective interest, the particular and the universal, coincided (the International is the late concretization of the abstract philosophical concept of "man as man," human being, "*Gattungswesen,*" which plays such a decisive role in Marx's and Engels's early writings). Then, the Spanish civil war aroused this solidarity, which is the driving power of liberation, in the unforgettable, hopeless fight of a tiny minority against the combined forces of fascist and liberal capitalism. Here, in the international brigades which, with their poor weapons, withstood overwhelming technical superiority, was the union of young intellectuals and workers—the union which has become the desperate goal of today's radical opposition.

Attainment of this goal is thwarted by the integration of the organized (and not only the organized) laboring class into the system of advanced capitalism. Under its impact, the distinction between the real and the immediate interest of the exploited has collapsed. This distinction, far from being an abstract idea, was guiding the strategy of the Marxist movements; it expressed the necessity transcending the economic struggle of the laboring classes, to extend wage demands and demands for the improvements of working conditions to the political arena, to drive the class struggle to the point at which the system itself would be at stake, to make foreign as well as domestic policy, the national as well as the class interest, the target of this struggle. The real interest, the attainment of conditions in which man could shape his own life, was that of no longer subordinating his life to the requirements of profitable production, to an apparatus controlled by forces beyond his control. And the attainment of such conditions meant the abolition of capitalism.

It is not simply the higher standard of living, the illusory bridging of the consumer gap between the rulers and the ruled, which has obscured the distinction between the real and the immediate interest of the ruled. Marxian theory soon recognized that impoverishment does not necessarily provide the soil for revolution, that a highly developed consciousness and imagination may generate a vital need for radical change in advanced material conditions. The power of corporate capitalism has stifled the emergence of such a consciousness and imagination; its mass media have adjusted the rational and emotional faculties to its market and its policies and steered them to defense of its dominion. The narrowing of the consumption gap has rendered possible the mental and instinctual coordination of the laboring classes: the majority of organized labor shares the stabilizing, counterrevolutionary needs of the middle classes, as evidenced by their behavior as consumers of the material and cultural merchandise, by their emotional revulsion against the nonconformist intelligentsia. Conversely, where the consumer gap is still wide, where the capitalist culture has not yet reached into every house or hut, the system of stabilizing needs has its limits; the glaring contrast between the privileged class and the exploited leads to a radicalization of the underprivileged. This is the case of the ghetto population and the unemployed in the United States; this is also the case of the laboring classes in the more backward capitalist countries.

By virtue of its basic position in the production process, by virtue of its numerical weight and the weight of exploitation, the working class is still the historical agent of revolution; by virtue of its sharing the stabilizing needs of the system, it has become a conservative, even counterrevolutionary force. Objectively, "in-itself," labor still is the potentially revolutionary class; subjectively, "for-itself," it is not. This theoretical conception has concrete significance in the prevailing situation, in which the working class may help to circumscribe the scope and the targets of political practice.

In the advanced capitalist countries, the radicalization of the working classes is counteracted by a socially engineered arrest of consciousness, and by the development and satisfaction of needs which perpetuate the servitude of the exploited. A vested interest in the existing system is thus fostered in the instinctual structure of the exploited, and the rupture with the continuum of repression—a necessary precondition of liberation—does not occur. It follows that the radical change which is to transform the existing society into a free society must reach into a dimension of the human existence hardly considered in Marxian theory—the "biological" dimension in which the vital, imperative needs and satisfactions of man assert themselves. Inasmuch as these needs and satisfactions reproduce a life in servitude, liberation presupposes changes in this biological dimension, that is to say, different instinctual needs, different reactions of the body as well as the mind.

The qualitative difference between the existing societies and a free society affects all needs and satisfactions beyond the animal level, that is to say, all those which are essential to the *human* species, man as rational animal. All these needs and satisfactions are permeated with the exigencies of profit and exploitation. The entire realm of competitive performances and standardized fun, all the symbols of status, prestige, power, of advertised virility and charm, of commercialized beauty—this entire realm kills in its citizens the very disposition, the organs, for the alternative: freedom without exploitation.

Triumph and end of introjection: the stage where the people cannot reject the system of domination without rejecting themselves, their own repressive instinctual needs and values. We would have to conclude that liberation would mean subversion against the will and against the prevailing interests of the great majority of the people. In this false identification of social and individual needs, in this deep-rooted, "organic" adaptation of the people to a terrible but profitably functioning society, lie the limits of democratic persuasion and evolution. On the overcoming of these limits depends the establishment of democracy.

It is precisely this excessive adaptability of the human organism which propels the perpetuation and extension of the commodity form and, with it, the perpetuation and extension of the social controls over behavior and satisfaction.

The ever-increasing complexity of the social structure will make some form of regimentation unavoidable, freedom and privacy may come to constitute antisocial luxuries and their attainment to involve real hardships. In consequence, there may emerge by selection a stock of human beings suited genetically to accept as a matter of course a regimented and sheltered way of life in a teeming and polluted world, from which all wilderness and fantasy of nature will have disappeared. The domesticated farm animal and the laboratory rodent on a controlled regimen in a controlled environment will then become true models for the study of man.

Thus, it is apparent that food, natural resources, supplies of power, and other elements involved in the operation of the body machine and of the individual establishment are not the only factors to be considered in determining the optimum number of people that can live on earth. Just as important for maintaining the *human qualities* of life is an environment in which it is possible to satisfy the longing for quiet, privacy, independence, initiative, and some open space. . . .[2]

Capitalist progress thus not only reduces the environment of freedom, the "open space" of the human existence, but also the "longing," the need for such an environment. And in doing so, quantitative progress militates against qualitative change even if the institutional barriers against radical education and action are surmounted. This is the vicious circle: the rupture with the self-propelling conservative continuum of needs must *precede* the revolution which is to usher in a free society, but such rupture itself can be envisaged only in a revolution—a revolution which would be driven by the vital need to be freed from the administered comforts and the destructive productivity of the exploitative society, freed from smooth heteronomy, a revolution which, by virtue of this "biological" foundation, would have the chance of turning quantitative technical progress into qualitatively different ways of life—precisely because it would be a revolution occurring at a high level of material and intellectual development, one which would enable man to conquer scarcity and poverty. If this idea of a radical transformation is to be more than idle speculation, it must have an objective foundation in the production process of advanced industrial society, in its technical capabilities and their use.

For freedom indeed depends largely on technical progress, on the advancement of science. But this fact easily obscures the essential precondition: in order to become vehicles of freedom, science and technology would have to change their present direction and goals; they would have to be reconstructed in accord with a new sensibility—the demands of the life instincts. Then one could speak of a technology of liberation, product of a scientific imagination free to project and design the forms of a human universe without exploitation and toil. But this *gaya scienza* is conceivable only after the historical break in the continuum of domination—as expressive of the needs of a new type of man.[3]

The idea of a new type of man as the member (though not as the builder) of a socialist society appears in Marx and Engels in the concept of the "all-round individual," free to engage in the most varying activities. In the socialist society corresponding to this idea, the free development of individual faculties would replace the subjection of the individual to the division of labor. But no matter what activities the all-round individual would choose, they would be activities which are bound to lose the quality of freedom if exercised "en masse"—and they would be "en masse," for even the most authentic socialist society would inherit the population growth and the mass basis of advanced capitalism. The early Marxian example of the free individuals alternating between hunting, fishing, criticizing, and so on, had a joking-ironical sound from the beginning, indicative of the impossibility [of] anticipating the ways in which liberated human beings would use their freedom. However, the embarrassingly ridiculous sound may also indicate the degree to which this vision has become obsolete and pertains to a stage of the development of the productive forces which has been surpassed. The later Marxian concept implies the continued separation between the realm of necessity and the realm of freedom, between labor and leisure—not only in time, but also in such a manner that the same subject lives a different life in the two realms. According to this Marxian conception, the realm of necessity would continue under socialism to such an extent that real human freedom would prevail only outside the entire sphere of socially necessary labor. Marx rejects the idea that work can ever become play.[4] Alienation would be reduced with the progressive reduction of the working day, but the latter would remain a day of unfreedom, rational but not free. However, the development of the productive forces beyond their capitalist organization suggests the possibility of freedom *within* the realm of necessity. The quantitative reduction of necessary labor could turn into quality (freedom), not in proportion to the reduction but rather to the transformation of the working day, a transformation in which the stupefying, enervating, pseudoautomatic jobs of capitalist progress would be abolished. But the construction of such a society presupposes a type of man with a different sensitivity as well as consciousness: men who would speak a different language, have different gestures, follow different impulses; men who have developed an instinctual barrier against cruelty, brutality, ugliness. Such an instinctual transformation is conceivable as a factor of social change only if it enters the social division of labor, the production relations themselves. They would be shaped by men and women who have the good conscience of being human, tender, sensuous, who are no longer ashamed of themselves—for "the token of freedom attained, that is, no longer being ashamed of ourselves" (Nietzsche, *Die Fröhliche Wissenschaft,* Book III, p. 275). The imagination of such men and women would fashion their reason and tend to make the process of production a process of creation. This is the utopian concept of socialism which envisages the ingression of freedom into the realm of necessity, and the union between causality by necessity and causality by freedom. The first would mean passing from Marx to Fourier; the second from realism to surrealism.

A utopian conception? It has been the great, real, transcending force, the "*idée neuve,*" in the first powerful rebellion against the whole of the existing society, the rebellion for the total transvaluation of values, for qualitatively different ways of life: the May rebellion in France. The graffiti of the "*jeunesse en colère*" joined Karl Marx and André Breton; the slogan "*l'imagination au pouvoir*" went well with "*les comités (soviets) partout*"; the piano with the jazz player stood well between the barricades; the red flag well fitted the statue of the author of *Les Misérables*; and striking students in Toulouse demanded the revival of the language of the Troubadours, the Albigensians. The new sensibility has become a political force. It crosses the frontier between the capitalist and the communist orbit; it is contagious because the atmosphere, the climate of the established societies, carries the virus.

Notes

1. I use the terms "biological" and "biology" not in the sense of the scientific discipline, but in order to designate the process and the dimension in which inclinations, behavior patterns, and aspirations become vital needs which, if not satisfied, would cause dysfunction of the organism. Conversely, socially induced needs and aspirations may result in a more pleasurable organic behavior. If biological needs are defined as those which must be satisfied and for which no adequate substitute can be provided, certain cultural needs can "sink down" into the biology of man. We could then speak, for example, of the biological need of freedom, or of some aesthetic needs as having taken root in the organic structure of man, in his "nature," or rather "second nature." This usage of the term "biological" does not imply or assume anything as to the way in which needs are physiologically expressed and transmitted.

2. René Dubos, *Man Adapting* (New Haven and London: Yale University Press, 1965), pp. 313–14.

3. The critique of the prevailing scientific establishment as ideological, and

the idea of a science which has really come into its own, was expressed in a manifesto issued by the militant students of Paris in May 1968 as follows:

"Refusons aussi la division de la *science* et de *l'idéologie*, la plus pernicieuse de toutes puisqu'elle est sécrétée par nous-mêmes. Nous ne voulons pas plus être gouvernés passivement par les lois de la *science* que par celle de l'économie ou les *impératifs* de la technique. La science est un art dont l'originalité est d'avoir des applications possibles hors d'elle-même.

"Elle ne peut cependant être normative que pour elle-même. Refusons son impérialisme mystifiant, caution de tous les abus et reculs, y compris en son sein, et remplaçons-le par un choix réel parmi les possibles qu'elle nous offre" (*Quelle Université? Quelle Société?* Textes réunis par le centre de regroupement des informations universitaires. Paris: Editions du Seuil, 1968, p. 148).

4. For a far more "utopian" conception see the by now familiar passage in the *Grundrisse der Kritik der Politischen Oekonomie* (Berlin: Dietz, 1953), pp. 596 ff.

10

Jürgen Habermas (1929–)

Born in Germany, Jürgen Habermas was radicalized by the late 1950s. He has taught at different German universities and is widely regarded as both the most important heir of the Frankfurt School tradition begun by Horkheimer, Adorno, and Marcuse and one of Europe's leading contemporary philosophers.

Habermas's attempt to philosophically reformulate the notion of a critical theory of society against positivism, phenomenology, hermeneutics, and vulgar Marxism has led him to utilize a wide variety of theoretical resources, including some aspects of traditional Marxism, Freudian concepts, systems theory, theories of moral development, theories of the state, analytical philosophy of language, and the ideas of earlier Western Marxists. The emphasis on symbolic interaction in his later works—to the exclusion of class struggle or economic structure—has led some critics to suggest that Habermas has now lost any real connection to the Marxist tradition.

In this section from his earlier Toward a Rational Society *(1968), Habermas is stressing what is for him the critical distinction between those forms of theory designed to* control nature *and those geared to* understanding human beings. *He feels that the failure to take this distinction seriously is a hallmark of the use of technology and science as ideologies by both Stalinism and bourgeois culture.*

Toward a Rational Society

TECHNOLOGY AND SCIENCE AS "IDEOLOGY"

. . . . .

By means of the concept of "rationalization" Weber attempted to grasp the repercussions of scientific-technical progress on the institutional framework of societies engaged in "modernization." He shared this interest with the classical sociological tradition in general, whose pairs of polar concepts all revolve about the same problem: how to construct a conceptual model of the institutional change brought about by the extension of subsystems of purposive-rational action. Status and contract, *Gemeinschaft* and *Gesellschaft*, mechanical and organic solidarity, informal and formal groups, primary and secondary groups, culture and civilization, traditional and bureaucratic authority, sacral and secular associations, military and industrial society, status group and class—all of these pairs of concepts represent as many attempts to grasp the structural change of the institutional framework of a traditional society on the way to becoming a modern one. Even Parsons's catalog of possible alternatives of value-orientations belongs in the list of these attempts, although he would not admit it. Parsons claims that his list systematically represents the decisions between alternative value-orientations that must be made by the subject of any action whatsoever, regardless of the particular or historical context. But if one examines the list, one can scarcely overlook the historical situation of the inquiry on which it is based. The four pairs of alternative value-orientations,

affectivity versus *affective neutrality*,
particularism versus *universalism*,
ascription versus *achievement*,
diffuseness versus *specificity*,

which are supposed to take into account *all* possible fundamental decisions, are tailored to an analysis of *one* historical process. In fact they define the relative dimensions of the modification of dominant attitudes in the transition from traditional to modern society. Subsystems of purposive-rational action do indeed demand orientation to the postponement of gratification, universal norms, individual achievement and active mastery, and specific and analytic relationships, rather than to the opposite orientations.

In order to reformulate what Weber called "rationalization," I should like to go beyond the subjective approach that Parsons shares with Weber and propose another categorial framework. I shall take as my starting point the fundamental distinction between *work* and *interaction*.[1]

By "work" or *purposive-rational action* I understand either instrumental action or rational choice or their conjunction. Instrumental action is governed by *technical rules* based on empirical knowledge. In every case they imply conditional predictions about observable events, physical or social. These predictions can prove correct or incorrect. The conduct of rational choice is governed by *strategies* based on analytic knowledge. They imply deductions from preference rules (value systems) and decision procedures; these propositions are either correctly or incorrectly deduced. Purposive-rational action realizes defined goals under given conditions. But while instrumental action organizes means that are appropriate or inappropriate according to criteria of an effective control of reality, strategic action depends only on the correct evaluation of possible alternative choices, which results from calculation supplemented by values and maxims.

By "interaction," on the other hand, I understand *communicative action*, symbolic interaction. It is governed by binding *consensual norms*, which define reciprocal expectations about behavior and which must be understood and recognized by at least two acting subjects. Social norms are enforced through sanctions. Their meaning is objectified in ordinary language communication. While the validity of technical rules and strategies depends on that of empirically true or analytically correct propositions, the validity of social norms is grounded only in the intersubjectivity of the mutual understanding of intentions and secured by the general recognition of obligations. Violation of a rule has a different consequence according to type. *Incompetent* behavior, which violates valid technical rules or strategies, is condemned per se to failure through lack of success; the "punishment" is built, so to speak, into its rebuff by reality. *Deviant* behavior, which violates consensual norms, provokes sanctions that are connected with the rules only externally, that is by convention. Learned rules of purposive-rational action supply us with *skills*, internalized norms with *personality structures*. Skills put us in a position to solve problems; motivations allow us to follow norms. The diagram below summarizes these definitions. They demand a more precise explanation, which I cannot give here. It is above all the bottom column which I am neglecting here, and it refers to the very problem for whose solution I am introducing the distinction between work and interaction.

	Institutional framework: symbolic interaction	*Systems of purposive-rational (instrumental and strategic) action*
action-orienting rules	social norms	technical rules
level of definition	intersubjectively shared ordinary language	context-free language
type of definition	reciprocal expectations about behavior	conditional predictions, conditional imperatives
mechanisms of acquisition	role internalization	learning of skills and qualifications
function of action type	maintenance of institutions (conformity to norms on the basis of reciprocal enforcement)	problem-solving (goal attainment, defined in means-ends relations)
sanctions against violation of rules	punishment on the basis of conventional sanctions: failure against authority	inefficacy: failure in reality
"rationalization"	emancipation, individuation; extension of communication free of domination	growth of productive forces; extension of power of technical control

In terms of the two types of action we can distinguish between social systems according to whether purposive-rational action or interaction predominates. The institutional framework of a society consists of norms that guide symbolic interaction. But there are subsystems such as (to keep to Weber's examples) the economic system or the state apparatus, in which primarily sets of purposive-rational action are institutionalized. These contrast with subsystems such as family and kinship structures, which, although linked to a number of tasks and skills, are primarily based on moral rules of interaction. So I shall distinguish generally at the analytic level between (1) the *institutional framework* of a society or the sociocultural life-world and (2) the *subsystems of purposive-rational action* that are "embedded" in it. Insofar as actions are determined by the institutional framework they are both guided and enforced by norms. Insofar as they are determined by subsystems of purposive-rational action, they conform to patterns of instrumental or strategic action. Of course, only institutionalization can guarantee that such action will in fact follow definite technical rules and expected strategies with adequate probability.

With the help of these distinctions we can reformulate Weber's concept of "rationalization."

The term "traditional society" has come to denote all social systems that generally meet the criteria of civilizations. The latter represent a specific stage in the evolution of the human species. They differ in several traits from more primitive social forms: (1) a centralized ruling power (state organization of political power in contrast to tribal organization); (2) the division of society into socioeconomic classes (distribution to individuals of social obligations and rewards according to class membership and not according to kinship status); (3) the prevalence of a central worldview (myth, complex religion) to the end of legitimating political power (thus converting power into authority). Civilizations are established on the basis of a relatively developed technology and of division of labor in the social process of production, which make possible a surplus product, i.e., a quantity of goods exceeding that needed for the satisfaction of immediate and elementary needs. They owe their existence to the solution of the problem that first arises with the production of a surplus product, namely, how to distribute wealth and labor both unequally and yet legitimately according to criteria other than those generated by a kinship system.[2]

In our context it is relevant that despite considerable differences in their level of development, civilizations, based on an economy dependent on agriculture and craft production, have tolerated technical innovation and organizational improvement only within definite limits. One indicator of the traditional limits to the development of the forces of production is that until about three hundred years ago no major social system had produced more than the equivalent of a maximum of two hundred dollars per capita per annum. The stable pattern of a precapitalist mode of production, preindustrial technology, and premodern science makes possible a typical relation of the institutional framework to subsystems of purposive-rational action. For despite considerable progress, these subsystems, developing out of the system of social labor and its stock of accumulated technically exploitable knowledge, never reached that measure of extension after which their "rationality" would have become an open threat to the authority of the cultural traditions that legitimate political power. The expression "traditional society" refers to the circumstance that the institutional framework is grounded in the unquestionable underpinning of legitimation constituted by mythical, religious or metaphysical interpretations of reality—cosmic as well as social—as a whole. "Traditional" societies exist as long as the development of subsystems of purposive-rational action keep within the limits of the legitimating efficacy of cultural traditions.[3] This is the basis for the "superiority" of the institutional framework, which does not preclude structural changes adapted to a potential surplus generated in the economic system but does preclude critically challenging the traditional form of legitimation. This immunity is a meaningful criterion for the delimitation of traditional societies from those which have crossed the threshold to modernization.

The "superiority criterion," consequently, is applicable to all forms of class society organized as a state in which principles of universally valid rationality (whether of technical or strategic means-ends relations) have not explicitly and successfully called into question the cultural validity of intersubjectively shared traditions, which function as legitimations of the political system. It is only since the capitalist mode of production has equipped the economic system with a self-propelling mechanism that ensures long-term continuous growth (despite crises) in the productivity of labor that the introduction of new technologies and strategies, i.e., innovation as such, has been institutionalized. As Marx and Schumpeter have proposed in their respective theories, the capitalist mode of production can be comprehended as a mechanism that guarantees the *permanent* expansion of subsystems of purposive-rational action and thereby overruns the traditionalist "superiority" of the institutional framework to the forces of production. Capitalism is the first mode of production in world history to institutionalize self-sustaining economic growth. It has generated an industrial system that could be freed from the institutional framework of capitalism and connected to mechanisms other than that of the utilization of capital in private form.

What characterizes the passage from traditional society to society commencing the process of modernization is *not* that structural modification of the institutional framework is necessitated under the pressure of relatively developed productive forces, for that is the mechanism of the evolution of the species from the very beginning. What is new is a level of development of the productive forces that makes permanent the extension of subsystems of purposive-rational action and thereby calls into question the traditional form of the legitimation of power. The older mythic, religious, and metaphysical worldviews obey the logic of interaction contexts. They answer the central questions of men's collective existence and of individual life history. Their themes are justice and freedom, violence and oppression, happiness and gratification, poverty, illness, and death. Their categories are victory and defeat, love and hate, salvation and damnation. Their logic accords with the grammar of systematically distorted communication and with the fateful causality of dissociated symbols and suppressed motives.[4] The rationality of language games, associated with communicative action, is confronted at the threshold of the modern period with the rationality of means-ends relations, associated with instrumental and strategic action. As soon as this confrontation can arise, the end of traditional society is in sight: the traditional form of legitimation breaks down.

Capitalism is defined by a mode of production that not only poses this problem but also solves it. It provides a legitimation of domination which is no longer called down from the lofty heights of cultural tradition but instead summoned up from the base of social labor. The institution of the market, in which private property owners exchange commodities—including the market on which propertyless private individuals exchange their labor power as their only commodity—promises that exchange relations will be and are just owing to equivalence. Even this bourgeois ideology of justice, by adopting the category of reciprocity, still employs a relation of communicative action as the basis of legitimation. But the principle of reciprocity is now the organizing principle of the sphere of production and reproduction itself. Thus on the base of a market economy, political domination can be legitimated henceforth "from below" rather than "from above" (through invocation of cultural tradition).

If we suppose that the division of society into socioeconomic classes derives from the differential distribution among social groups of the relevant means of production, and that this distribution itself is based on the institutionalization of relations of social force, then we may assume that in all civilizations this institutional framework has been identical with the system of political domination: traditional authority was political authority. Only with the emergence of the capitalist mode of production can the legitimation of the institutional framework be linked immediately with the system of social labor. Only then can the property order change from a *political relation* to a *production relation,* because it legitimates itself through the rationality of the market, the ideology of exchange society, and no longer through a legitimate power structure. It is now the political system which is justified in terms of the legitimate relations of production: this is the real meaning and function of rationalist natural law from Locke to Kant.[5] The institutional framework of society is only mediately political and immediately economic (the bourgeois constitutional state as "superstructure").

The superiority of the capitalist mode of production to its predecessors has these two roots: the establishment of an economic mechanism that renders permanent the expansion of subsystems of purposive-rational action, and the creation of an economic legitimation by means of which the political system can be adapted to the new requisites of rationality brought about by these developing subsystems. It is this process of adaptation that Weber comprehends as "rationalization." Within it we can distinguish between two tendencies: rationalization "from below" and rationalization "from above."

A permanent pressure for adaptation arises from below as soon as the new mode of production becomes fully operative through the institutionalization of a domestic market for goods and labor power and of the capitalist enterprise. In the system of social labor this institutionalization ensures cumulative progress in the forces of production and an ensuing horizontal extension of subsystems of purposive-rational action—at the cost of economic crises, to be sure. In this way traditional structures are increasingly subordinated to conditions of instrumental or strategic rationality: the organization of labor and of trade, the network of transportation, information, and communication, the institutions of private law, and, starting with financial administration, the state bureaucracy. Thus arises the substructure of a society under the compulsion of modernization. The latter eventually widens to take in all areas of life: the army, the school system, health services, and even the family. Whether in city or country, it induces an urbanization of the *form* of life. That is, it generates subcultures that train the individual to be able to "switch over" at any moment from an interaction context to purposive-rational action.

This pressure for rationalization coming from below is met by a compulsion to rationalize coming from above. For, measured against the new standards of purposive rationality, the power-legitimating and action-orienting traditions—especially mythological interpretations and religious worldviews—lose their cogency. On this level of generalization, what Weber termed "secularization" has two aspects. First, traditional worldviews and objectivations lose their power and validity *as* myth, *as* public religion, *as* customary ritual, *as* justifying metaphysics, *as* unquestionable tradition. Instead, they are reshaped into subjective belief systems and ethics which ensure the private cogency of modern value-orientations (the "Protestant ethic"). Second, they are transformed into constructions that do both at once: criticize tradition and reorganize the released material of tradition according to the principles of former law and the exchange of equivalents (rationalist natural law). Having become fragile, existing legitimations are replaced by new ones. The latter emerge from the critique of the dogmatism of traditional interpretations of the world and claim a scientific character. Yet they retain legitimating functions, thereby keeping actual power relations inaccessible to analysis and to public consciousness. It is in this way that ideologies in the restricted sense first came into being. They replace traditional legitimations of power by appearing in the mantle of modern science and by deriving their justification from the critique of ideology. Ideologies are coeval with the critique of ideology. In this sense there can be no prebourgeois "ideologies."

In this connection modern science assumes a singular function. In distinction from the philosophical sciences of the older sort, the empirical sciences have developed since Galileo's time within a methodological frame of reference that reflects the transcendental viewpoint of possible technical control. Hence the modern sciences produce knowledge which through its *form* (and not through the subjective intention of scientists) is technically exploitable knowledge, although the possible applications generally are realized afterwards. Science and technology were not interdependent until late into the nineteenth century. Until then modern science did not contribute to the acceleration of technical development nor, consequently, to the pressure toward rationalization from below. Rather, its contribution to the modernization process was indirect. Modern physics gave rise to a philosophical approach that interpreted nature and society according to a model borrowed from the natural sciences and induced, so to speak, the mechanistic worldview of the seventeenth century. The reconstruction of classical natural law was carried out in this framework. This modern natural law was the basis of the bourgeois revolutions of the seventeenth, eighteenth, and nineteenth centuries, through which the old legitimations of the power structure were finally destroyed.[6]

By the middle of the nineteenth century the capitalist mode of production had developed so fully in England and France that Marx was able to identify the locus of the institutional framework of society in the relations of production and at the same time criticize the legitimating basis constituted by the exchange of equivalents. He carried out the critique of bourgeois ideology in the form of *political economy*. His labor theory of value destroyed the semblance of freedom, by means of which the legal institution of the free labor contract had made unrecognizable the relationship of social force that underlay the wage-labor relationship. Marcuse's criticism of Weber is that the latter, disregarding this Marxian insight, upholds an abstract concept of rationalization, which not merely fails to express the specific class content of the adaptation of the institutional framework to the developing systems of purposive-rational action, but conceals it. Marcuse knows that the Marxian analysis can no longer be applied as it stands to advanced capitalist society, with which Weber was already confronted. But he wants to show through the example of Weber that the evolution of modern society in the framework of state-regulated capitalism cannot be conceptualized if liberal capitalism has not been analyzed adequately.

Since the last quarter of the nineteenth century two developmental tendencies have become noticeable in the most advanced capitalist countries: an increase in state intervention in order to secure the system's stability, and a growing interdependence of research and technology, which has turned the sciences into the leading productive force. Both tendencies have destroyed the particular constellation of institutional framework and subsystems of purposive-rational action which characterized liberal capitalism, thereby eliminating the conditions relevant for the application of political economy in the version correctly formulated by Marx for liberal capitalism. I believe that Marcuse's basic thesis, according to which technology and science today also take on the function of legitimating political power, is the key to analyzing the changed constellation.

The permanent regulation of the economic process by means of state intervention arose as a defense mechanism against the dysfunctional tendencies, which threaten the system, that capitalism generates when left to itself. Capitalism's actual development manifestly contradicted the capitalist idea of a bourgeois society, emancipated from domination, in which power is neutralized. The root ideology of just exchange, which Marx unmasked in theory, collapsed in practice. The form of capital utilization through private ownership could only be maintained by the governmental corrective of a social and economic policy that stabilized the business cycle. The institutional framework of society was repoliticized. It no longer coincides immediately with the relations of production, i.e., with an order of private law that secures capitalist economic activity and the corresponding general guarantees of order provided by the bourgeois state. But this means a change in the relation of the economy to the political system: politics is no longer *only* a phenomenon of the superstructure. If society no longer "autonomously" perpetuates itself through self-regulation as a sphere preceding and lying at the basis of the state—and its ability to do so was the really novel feature of the capitalist mode of production—then society and the state are no longer in the relationship that Marxian theory had defined as that of base and superstructure. Then, however, a critical theory of society can no longer be constructed in the exclusive form of a critique of political economy. A point of view that methodically isolates the economic laws of motion of society can claim to grasp the overall structure of social life in its essential categories only as long as politics depends on the economic base. It becomes inapplicable when the "base" has to be comprehended as in itself a function of governmental activity and political conflicts. According to Marx, the critique of political economy was the theory of bourgeois society only as *critique of ideology*. If, however, the ideology of just exchange disintegrates, then the power structure can no longer be criticized *immediately* at the level of the relations of production.

With the collapse of this ideology, political power requires a new legitimation. Now since the power indirectly exercised over the exchange process is itself operating under political control and state regulation, legitimation can no longer be derived from the unpolitical order constituted by the relations of production. To this extent the requirement for direct legitimation, which exists in precapitalist societies, reappears. On the other hand, the resuscitation of immediate political domination (in the traditional form of legitimation on the basis of cosmological worldviews) has become impossible. For traditions have already been disempowered. Moreover, in industrially developed societies the results of bourgeois emancipation from immediate political domination (civil and political rights and the mechanism of general elections) can be fully ignored only in periods of reaction. Formally democratic government in systems of state-regulated capitalism is subject to a need for legitimation which cannot be met by a return to a prebourgeois form. Hence the ideology of free exchange is replaced by a substitute program. The latter is oriented not to the social results of the institution of the market but to those of government action designed to compensate for the dysfunctions of free exchange. This policy combines the element of the bourgeois ideology of achievement (which, however, displaces assignment of status according to the standard of individual achievement from the market to the school system) with a guaranteed minimum level of welfare, which offers secure employment and a stable income. This substitute program obliges the political system to maintain stabilizing conditions for an economy that guards against risks to growth and guarantees social security and the chance for individual upward mobility. What is needed to this end is latitude for manipulation by state interventions that, at the cost of limiting the institutions of private law, secure the private form of capital utilization *and bind the masses' loyalty to this form*.

Insofar as government action is directed toward the economic system's stability and growth, politics now takes on a peculiarly negative character. For it is oriented toward the elimination of dysfunctions and the avoidance of risks that threaten the system: not, in other words, toward the *realization of practical goals* but toward the *solution of technical problems*. Claus Offe pointed this out in his paper at the 1968 Frankfurt Sociological Conference:

> In this structure of the relation of economy and the state, "politics" degenerates into action that follows numerous and continually emerging "avoidance imperatives": the mass of differentiated social-scientific information that flows into the political system allows both the early identification of risk zones and the treatment of actual dangers. What is new about this structure is . . . that the risks to stability built into the mechanism of private capital utilization in highly organized markets, risks that can be manipulated, prescribe preventive actions and measures that *must* be accepted as long as they are to accord with the existing legitimation resources (i.e., substitute program).[7]

Offe perceives that through these preventive action-orientations, government activity is restricted to administratively soluble technical problems, so that practical questions evaporate, so to speak. *Practical substance is eliminated*.

Old-style politics was forced, merely through its traditional form of legitimation, to define itself in relation to practical goals: the "good life" was interpreted in a context defined by interaction relations. The same still held for the ideology of bourgeois society. The substitute program prevailing today, in contrast, is aimed exclusively at the functioning of a manipulated system. It eliminates practical questions and therewith precludes discussion about the adoption of standards; the latter could emerge only from a democratic decision-making process. The solution of technical problems is not dependent on public discussion. Rather, public discussions could render problematic the framework within which the tasks of government action present themselves as technical ones. Therefore the new politics of state interventionism requires a depoliticization of the mass of the population. To the extent that practical questions are eliminated, the public realm also loses its political function. At the same time, the institutional framework of society is still distinct from the systems of purposive-rational action themselves. Its organization continues to be a problem of *practice* linked to communication, not one of *technology,* no matter how scientifically guided. Hence, the bracketing out of practice associated with the new kind of politics is not automatic. The substitute program, which legitimates power today, leaves unfilled a vital need for legitimation: how will the depoliticization of the masses be made plausible to them? Marcuse would be able to answer: by having technology and science *also* take on the role of an ideology.

Since the end of the nineteenth century the other developmental tendency characteristic of advanced capitalism has become increasingly momentous: the scientization of technology. The institutional pressure to augment the productivity of labor through the introduction of new technology has always existed under capitalism. But innovations depended on sporadic inventions, which, while economically motivated, were still fortuitous in character. This changed as technical development entered into a feedback relation with the progress of the modern sciences. With the advent of large-scale industrial research, science, technology, and industrial utilization were fused into a system. Since then, industrial research has been linked up with research under government contract, which primarily promotes scientific and technical progress in the military sector. From there information flows back into the sectors of civilian production. Thus technology and science become a leading productive force, rendering inoperative the conditions for Marx's labor theory of value. It is no longer meaningful to calculate the amount of capital investment in research and development on the basis of the value of unskilled (simple) labor power, when scientific-technical progress has become an independent source of surplus value, in relation to which the only source of surplus value considered by Marx, namely the labor power of the immediate producers, plays an ever smaller role.[8]

As long as the productive forces were visibly linked to the rational decisions and instrumental action of men engaged in social production, they could be understood as the potential for a growing power of technical control and not be confused with the institutional framework in which they are embedded. However, with the institutionalization of scientific-technical progress, the potential of the productive forces has assumed a form owing to which men lose consciousness of the dualism of work and interaction.

It is true that social interests still determine the direction, functions, and pace of technical progress. But these interests define the social system so much as a whole that they coincide with the interest in maintaining the system. *As such* the private form of capital utilization and a distribution mechanism for social rewards that guarantees the loyalty of the masses are removed from discussion. The quasi-autonomous progress of science and technology then appears as an independent variable on which the most important single system variable, namely economic growth, depends. Thus arises a perspective in which the development of the social system *seems* to be determined by the logic of scientific-technical progress. The immanent law of this progress seems to produce objective exigencies, which must be obeyed by any politics oriented toward functional needs. But when this semblance has taken root effectively, then propaganda can refer to the role of technology and science in order to explain and legitimate why in modern societies the process of democratic decision-making about practical problems loses its function and "must" be replaced by plebiscitary decisions about alternative sets of leaders of administrative personnel. This technocracy thesis has been worked out in several versions on the intellectual level.[9] What seems to me more important is that it can also become a background ideology that penetrates into the consciousness of the depoliticized mass of the population, where it can take on legitimating power.[10] It is a singular achievement of this ideology to detach society's self-understanding from the frame of reference of communicative action and from the concepts of symbolic interaction and replace it with a scientific model. Accordingly the culturally defined self-understanding of a social life-world is replaced by the self-reification of men under categories of purposive-rational action and adaptive behavior.

The model according to which the planned reconstruction of society is to proceed is taken from systems analysis. It is possible in principle to comprehend and analyze individual enterprises and organizations, even political or economic subsystems and social systems as a whole, according to the pattern of self-regulated systems. It makes a difference, of course, whether we use a cybernetic frame of reference for analytic purposes or *organize* a given social system in accordance with this pattern as a man-machine system. But the transferral of the analytic model to the level of social organization is implied by the very approach taken by systems analysis. Carrying out this intention of an instinct-like self-stabilization of social systems yields the peculiar perspective that the structure of one of the two types of action, namely the behavioral system of purposive-rational action, not only predominates over the institutional framework but gradually absorbs communicative action as such. If, with Arnold Gehlen, one were to see the inner logic of technical development as the step-by-step disconnection of the behavioral system of purposive-rational action from the human organism and its transferral to machines, then the technocratic intention could be understood as the last stage of this development. For the first time man can not only, as *homo faber*, completely objectify himself and confront the achievements that have taken on independent life in his products; he can in addition, as *homo fabricatus*, be integrated into his technical apparatus if the structure of purposive-rational action can be successfully reproduced on the level of social systems. According to this idea the institutional framework of society—which previously was rooted in a different type of action—would now, in a fundamental reversal, be *absorbed* by the subsystems of purposive-rational action, which were embedded in it.

Of course this technocratic intention has not been realized anywhere even in its beginnings. But it serves as an ideology for the new politics, which is adapted to technical problems and brackets out practical questions. Furthermore it does correspond to certain developmental tendencies that could lead to a creeping erosion of what we have called the institutional framework. The manifest domination of the authoritarian state gives way to the manipulative compulsions of technical-operational administration. The moral realization of a normative order is a function of communicative action oriented to shared cultural meaning and presupposing the internalization of values. It is increasingly supplanted by conditioned behavior, while large organizations as such are increasingly patterned after the structure of purposive-rational action. The industrially most advanced societies seem to approximate the model of behavioral control steered by external stimuli rather than guided by norms. Indirect control through fabricated stimuli has increased, especially in areas of putative subjective freedom (such as electoral, consumer, and leisure behavior). Sociopsychologically, the era is typified less by the authoritarian personality than by the destructuring of the superego. The increase in *adaptive behavior* is, however, only the obverse of the dissolution of the sphere of linguistically mediated interaction by the structure of purposive-rational action. This is paralleled subjectively by the disappearance of the difference between purposive-rational action and interaction from the consciousness not only of the sciences of man, but of men themselves. The concealment of this difference proves the ideological power of the technocratic consciousness.

In consequence of the two tendencies that have been discussed, capitalist society has changed to the point where two key categories of Marxian theory, namely class struggle and ideology, can no longer be employed as they stand.

It was on the basis of the capitalist mode of production that the struggle of social classes as such was first constituted, thereby creating an objective situation from which the class structure of traditional society, with its immediately political constitution, could be *recognized* in retrospect. State-regulated capitalism, which emerged from a reaction against the dangers to the system produced by open class antagonism, suspends class conflict. The system of advanced capitalism is so defined by a policy of securing the loyalty of the wage-earning masses through rewards, that is, by avoiding conflict, that the conflict still built into the structure of society in virtue of the private mode of capital utilization is the very area of conflict which has the greatest probability of remaining latent. It recedes behind others, which, while conditioned by the mode of production, can no longer assume the form of class conflicts. In the paper cited, Claus Offe has analyzed this paradoxical state of affairs, showing that open conflicts about social interests break out with greater probability the less their frustration has dangerous consequences for the system. The needs with the greatest conflict potential are those on the periphery of the area of state intervention. They are far from the central conflict being kept in a state of latency and therefore they are not seen as having priority among dangers to be warded off. Conflicts are set off by these needs to the extent that disproportionately scattered state interventions produce backward areas of development and corresponding disparity tensions:

> The disparity between areas of life grows above all in view of the differential state of development obtaining between the actually institutionalized and the possible level of technical and social progress. The disproportion between the most modern apparatuses for industrial and military purposes and the stagnating organization of the transport, health, and educational systems is just as well known an example of this disparity between areas of life as is the contradiction between rational planning and regulation in taxation and finance policy and the unplanned, haphazard development of cities and regions. Such contradictions can no longer be designated accurately as antagonisms between classes, yet they can still be interpreted as results of the still dominant process of the private utilization of capital and of a specifically capitalist power structure. In this process the prevailing interests are those which, without being clearly localizable, are in a position, on the basis of the established mechanism of the capitalist economy, to react to disturbances of the conditions of their stability by producing risks relevant to the system as a whole.[11]

The interests bearing on the maintenance of the mode of production can no longer be "clearly localized" in the social system as class interests. For the power structure, aimed as it is at avoiding dangers to the system, precisely excludes "domination" (as immediate political or economically mediated social force) exercised in such a manner that one class subject *confronts* another as an identifiable group.

This means not that class antagonisms have been abolished but that they have become *latent*. Class distinctions persist in the form of subcultural traditions and corresponding differences not only in the standard of living and life style but also in political attitude. The social structure also makes it probable that the class of wage earners will be hit harder than other groups by social disparities. And finally, the generalized interest in perpetuating the system is still anchored today, on the level of immediate life chances, in a structure of privilege. The concept of an interest that has become *completely* independent of living subjects would cancel itself out. But with the deflection of dangers to the system in state-regulated capitalism, the political system has incorporated an interest—which transcends latent class boundaries—in preserving the compensatory distribution façade.

Furthermore, the displacement of the conflict zone from the class boundary to the underprivileged regions of life does not mean at all that serious conflict potential has been disposed of. As the extreme example of racial conflict in the United States shows, so many consequences of disparity can accumulate in certain areas and groups that explosions resembling civil war can occur. But unless they are connected with protest potential from other sectors of society no conflicts arising from such underprivilege can really overturn the system—they can only provoke it to sharp reactions incompatible with formal democracy. For underprivileged groups are not social classes, nor do they ever even potentially represent the mass of the population. Their *disfranchisement* and pauperization no longer coincide with *exploitation,* because the system does not live off their labor. They can represent at most a past phase of exploitation. But they cannot through the withdrawal of cooperation attain the demands that they legitimately put forward. That is why these demands retain an appellative character. In the case of long-term nonconsideration of their legitimate demands underprivileged groups can in extreme situations react with desperate destruction and self-destruction. But as long as no coalitions are made with privileged groups, such a civil war lacks the chance of revolutionary success that class struggle possesses.

With a series of restrictions this model seems applicable even to the relations between the industrially advanced nations and the formerly colonial areas of the Third World. Here, too, growing disparity leads to a form of underprivilege that in the future surely will be increasingly less comprehensible through categories of exploitation. Economic interests are replaced on this level, however, with immediately military ones.

Be that as it may, in advanced capitalist society deprived and privileged groups no longer confront each other *as* socioeconomic classes—and to some extent the boundaries of underprivilege are no longer even specific to groups and instead run across population categories. Thus the fundamental relation that existed in all traditional societies and that came to the fore under liberal capitalism is mediatized, namely the class antagonism between partners who stand in an institutionalized relationship of force, economic exploitation, and political oppression to one another, and in which communication is so distorted and restricted that the legitimations serving as an ideological veil cannot be called into question. Hegel's concept of the ethical totality of a living relationship which is sundered because one subject does not reciprocally satisfy the needs of the other is no longer an appropriate model for the mediatized class structure of organized, advanced capitalism. The suspended dialectic of the ethical generates the peculiar semblance of *post-histoire*. The reason is that relative growth of the productive forces no longer represents *eo ipso* a potential that points beyond the existing framework with emancipatory consequences, in view of which legitimations of an existing power structure become enfeebled. For the leading productive force—controlled scientific-technical progress itself—has now become the basis of legitimation. Yet this new form of legitimation has cast off the old shape of *ideology*.

Technocratic consciousness is, on the one hand, "less ideological" than all previous ideologies. For it does not have the opaque force of a delusion that only transfigures the implementation of interests. On the other hand today's dominant, rather glassy background ideology, which makes a fetish of science, is more irresistible and farther-reaching than ideologies of the old type. For with the veiling of practical problems it not only justifies a *particular class's* interest in domination and represses *another class's* partial need for emancipation, but affects the human race's emancipatory interest as such.

Technocratic consciousness is not a rationalized, wish-fulfilling fantasy, not an "illusion" in Freud's sense, in which a system of interaction is either represented or interpreted and grounded. Even bourgeois ideologies could be traced back to a basic pattern of just interactions, free of domination and mutually satisfactory. It was these ideologies which met the criteria of wish-fulfillment and substitute gratification; the communication on which they were based was so limited by repressions that the relation of force once institutionalized as the capital-labor relation could not even be called by name. But the technocratic consciousness is not based in the same way on the causality of dissociated symbols and unconscious motives, which generates both false consciousness and the power of reflection to which the critique of ideology is indebted. It is less vulnerable to reflection, because it is no longer *only* ideology. For it does not, in the manner of ideology, express a projection of the "good life" (which even if not identifiable with a bad reality, can at least be brought into virtually satisfactory accord with it). Of course the new ideology, like the old, serves to impede making the foundations of society the object of thought and reflection. Previously, social force lay at the basis of the relation between capitalist and wage-laborers. Today the basis is provided by structural conditions which predefine the tasks of system maintenance: the private form of capital utilization and a political form of distributing social rewards that guarantees mass loyalty. However, the old and new ideology differ in two ways.

First, the capital-labor relation today, because of its linkage to a loyalty-ensuring political distribution mechanism, no longer engenders uncorrected exploitation and oppression. The process through which the persisting class antagonism has been made virtual presupposes that the repression on which the latter is based first came to consciousness in history and *only then* was stabilized in a modified form as a property of the system. Technocratic consciousness, therefore, cannot rest in the same way on collective repression as did earlier ideologies. Second, mass loyalty today is created only with the aid of rewards for *privatized needs*. The achievements in virtue of which the system justifies itself may not in principle be interpreted politically. The acceptable interpretation is immediately in terms of allocations of money and leisure time (neutral with regard to their use), and mediately in terms of the technocratic justification of the occlusion of practical questions. Hence the new ideology is distinguished from its predecessor in that it severs the criteria for justifying the organization of social life from any normative regulation of interaction, thus depoliticizing them. It anchors them instead in functions of a putative system of purposive-rational action.

Technocratic consciousness reflects not the sundering of an ethical situation but the repression of "ethics" as such as a category of life. The common, positivist way of thinking renders inert the frame of reference of interaction in ordinary language, in which domination and ideology both arise under conditions of distorted communication and can be reflectively detected and broken down. The depoliticization of the mass of the population, which is legitimated through technocratic consciousness, is at the same time men's self-objectification in categories equally of both purposive-rational action and adaptive behavior. The reified models of the sciences migrate into the sociocultural life-world and gain objective power over the latter's self-understanding. The ideological nucleus of this consciousness is *the elimination of the distinction between the practical and the technical*. It reflects, but does not objectively account for, the new constellation of a disempowered institutional framework and systems of purposive-rational action that have taken on a life of their own.

The new ideology consequently violates an interest grounded in one of the two fundamental conditions of our cultural existence: in language, or more precisely, in the form of socialization and individuation determined by communication in ordinary language. This interest extends to the maintenance of intersubjectivity of mutual understanding as well as to the creation of communication without domination. Technocratic consciousness makes this practical interest disappear behind the interest in the expansion of our power of technical control. Thus the reflection that the new ideology calls for must penetrate beyond the level of particular historical class interests to disclose the fundamental interests of mankind as such, engaged in the process of self-constitution.[12]

If the relativization of the field of application of the concept of ideology and the theory of class be confirmed, then the category framework developed by Marx in the basic assumptions of historical materialism requires a new formulation. The model of forces of production and relations of production would have to be replaced by the more abstract one of work and interaction. The relations of production designate a level on which the institutional framework was anchored only during the phase of the development of liberal capitalism, and not either before or after. To be sure, the productive forces, in which the learning processes organized in the subsystems of purposive-rational action accumulate, have been from the very beginning the motive force of social evolution. But, they do not appear, as Marx supposed, *under all circumstances* to be a potential for liberation and to set off emancipatory movements—at least not once the continual growth of the productive forces has become dependent on scientific-technical progress that has *also* taken on functions of *legitimating political power*. I suspect that the frame of reference developed in terms of the analogous, but more general relation of institutional framework (interaction) and subsystems of purposive-rational action ("work" in the broad sense of instrumental and strategic action) is more suited to reconstructing the sociocultural phases of the history of mankind.

There are several indications that during the long initial phase until the end of the Mesolithic period, purposive-rational actions could only be motivated at all through ritual attachment to interactions. A profane realm of subsystems of purposive-rational action seems to have separated out from the institutional framework of symbolic interaction in the first settled cultures, based on the domestication of animals and cultivation of plants. But it was probably only in civilizations, that is under the conditions of a class society organized as a state that the differentiation of work and interaction went far enough for the subsystems to yield technically exploitable knowledge that could be stored and expanded relatively independently of mythical and religious interpretations of the world. At the same time social norms became separated from power-legitimating traditions, so that "culture" attained a certain independence from "institutions." The threshold of the modern period would then be characterized by that process of rationalization which commenced with loss of the "superiority" of the institutional framework to the subsystems of purposive-rational action. Traditional legitimations could now be criticized against the standards of rationality of means-ends relations. Concurrently, information from the area of technically exploitable knowledge infiltrated tradition and compelled a reconstruction of traditional world interpretations along the lines of scientific standards.

We have followed this process of "rationalization from above" up to the point where the technology and science themselves in the form of a common positivistic way of thinking, articulated as technocratic consciousness, began to take the role of a substitute ideology for the demolished bourgeois ideologies. This point was reached with the critique of bourgeois ideologies. It introduced ambiguity into the concept of rationalization. This ambiguity was deciphered by Horkheimer and Adorno as the dialectic of enlightenment, which has been refined by Marcuse as the thesis that technology and science themselves become ideological.

From the very beginning the pattern of human sociocultural development has been determined by a growing power of technical control over the external conditions of existence on the one hand, and a more or less passive adaptation of the institutional framework to the expanded subsystems of purposive-rational action on the other. Purposive-rational action represents the form of *active* adaptation, which distinguishes the collective *self*-preservation of societal subjects from the preservation of the species characteristic of other animals. We know how to bring the relevant conditions of life under control, that is, we know how to adapt the environment to our needs culturally rather than adapting ourselves to external nature. In contrast, changes of the institutional framework, to the extent that they are derived immediately or mediately from new technologies or improved strategies (in the areas of production, transportation, weaponry, etc.) have not taken the same form of active adaptation. In general such modifications follow the pattern of *passive* adaptation. They are not the result of planned purposive-rational action geared to its own consequences, but the product of fortuitous, undirected development. Yet it was impossible to become conscious of this disproportion between active and passive adaptation as long as the dynamics of capitalist development remained concealed by bourgeois ideologies. Only with the critique of bourgeois ideologies did this disproportion enter public consciousness.

The most impressive witness to this experience is still the *Communist Manifesto*. In rapturous words Marx eulogizes the revolutionary role of the bourgeoisie:

> The bourgeoisie cannot exist without constantly revolutionizing the instruments of production, and thereby the relations of production, and with them the whole relations of society.

In another passage he writes:

> The bourgeoisie, during its rule of scarce one hundred years, has created more massive and more colossal productive forces than have all preceding generations together. Subjection of nature's forces to man, machinery, application of chemistry to industry and agriculture, steam navigation, railways, electric telegraphs, clearing of whole continents for cultivation, canalization of rivers, whole populations conjured out of the ground . . ..

Marx also perceives the reaction of this development back upon the institutional framework:

> All fixed, fast-frozen relations, with their train of ancient and venerable prejudices and opinions, are swept away, all new-formed ones become antiquated before they can ossify. All that is solid melts into air, all that is holy is profaned, and man is at last compelled to face with sober senses his real conditions of life and his relations with his kind.

It is with regard to the disproportion between the passive adaptation of the institutional framework and the "active subjection of nature" that the assertion that men make their history, but not with will or consciousness, was formulated. It was the aim of Marx's critique to transform the secondary adaptation of the institutional framework as well into an active one, and to bring under control the structural change of society itself.

This would overcome a fundamental condition of all previous history and complete the self-constitution of mankind: the end of prehistory. But this idea was ambiguous.

Marx, to be sure, viewed the problem of making history with will and consciousness as one of the *practical* mastery of previously ungoverned processes of social development. Others, however, have understood it as a *technical* problem. They want to bring society under control in the same way as nature by reconstructing it according to the pattern of self-regulated systems of purposive-rational action and adaptive behavior. This intention is to be found not only among technocrats of capitalist planning but also among those of bureaucratic socialism. Only the technocratic consciousness obscures the fact that this reconstruction could be achieved at no less a cost than closing off the only dimension that is essential, because it is susceptible to humanization, *as* a structure of interactions mediated by ordinary language. In the future the repertoire of control techniques will be considerably expanded. On Herman Kahn's list of the most probable technical innovations of the next thirty years I observe among the first fifty items a large number of techniques of behavioral and personality change:

> 30. new and possibly pervasive techniques for surveillance, monitoring and control of individuals and organizations;
> 33. new and more reliable "educational" and propaganda techniques affecting human behavior—public and private;
> 34. practical use of direct electronic communication with and stimulation of the brain;
> 37. new and relatively effective counterinsurgency techniques;
> 39. new and more varied drugs for control of fatigue, relaxation, alertness, mood, personality, perceptions, and fantasies;
> 41. improved capability to "change" sex;
> 42. other genetic control or influence over the basic constitution of an individual.[13]

A prediction of this sort is extremely controversial. Nevertheless, it points to an area of future possibilities of detaching human behavior from a normative system linked to the grammar of language-games and integrating it instead into self-regulated subsystems of the man-machine type by means of immediate physical or psychological control. Today the psychotechnic manipulation of behavior can already liquidate the old-fashioned detour through norms that are internalized but capable of reflection. Behavioral control could be instituted at an even deeper level tomorrow through biotechnic intervention in the endocrine regulating system, not to mention the even greater consequences of intervening in the genetic transmission of inherited information. If this occurred, old regions of consciousness developed in ordinary-language communication would of necessity completely dry up. At this stage of human engineering, if the end of psychological manipulation could be spoken of in the same sense as the end of ideology is today, the spontaneous alienation derived from the uncontrolled lag of the institutional framework would be overcome. But the self-objectivation of man would have fulfilled itself in planned alienation—men would make their history with will, but without consciousness.

I am not asserting that this cybernetic dream of the instinct-like self-stabilization of societies is being fulfilled or that it is even realizable. I do think, however, that it follows through certain vague but basic assumptions of technocratic consciousness to their conclusion as a negative utopia and thus denotes an evolutionary trend that is taking shape under the slick domination of technology and science as ideology. Above all, it becomes clear against this background that *two concepts of rationalization* must be distinguished. At the level of subsystems of purposive-rational action, scientific-technical progress has already compelled the reorganization of social institutions and sectors, and necessitates it on an even larger scale than heretofore. But this process of the development of the productive forces can be a potential for liberation if and only if it does not replace rationalization on another level. *Rationalization at the level of the institutional framework* can occur only in the medium of symbolic interaction itself, that is, through *removing restrictions on communication*. Public, unrestricted discussion, free from domination, of the suitability and desirability of action-orienting principles and norms in the light of the sociocultural repercussions of developing subsystems of purposive-rational action—such communication at all levels of political and repoliticized decision-making is the only medium in which anything like "rationalization" is possible.

In such a process of generalized reflection institutions would alter their specific composition, going beyond the limit of a mere change in legitimation. A rationalization of social norms would, in fact, be characterized by a decreasing degree of repressiveness (which at the level of personality structure should increase average tolerance of ambivalence in the face of role conflicts), a decreasing degree of rigidity (which should multiply the changes of an individually stable self-presentation in everyday interactions), and approximation to a type of behavioral control that would allow role distance and the flexible application of norms that, while well-internalized, would be accessible to reflection. Rationalization measured by changes in these three dimensions does not lead, as does the rationalization of purposive-rational subsystems, to an increase in technical control over objectified processes of nature and society. It does not lead per se to the better functioning of social systems, but would furnish the members of society with the opportunity for further emancipation and progressive individuation. The growth of productive forces is not the same as the intention of the "good life." It can at best serve it.

I do not even think that the model of a technologically possible surplus that cannot be used in full measure within a repressively maintained institutional framework (Marx speaks of "fettered" forces of production) is appropriate to state-regulated capitalism. Today, better utilization of an unrealized potential leads to improvement of the economic-industrial apparatus, but no longer *eo ipso* to a transformation of the institutional framework with emancipatory consequences. The question is not whether we completely *utilize* an available or creatable potential, but whether we *choose* what we want for the purpose of the pacification and gratification of existence. But it must be immediately noted that we are only posing this question and cannot answer it in advance. For the solution demands precisely that unrestricted communication about the goals of life activity and conduct against which advanced capitalism, structurally dependent on a depoliticized public realm, puts up a strong resistance.

A new conflict zone, in place of the virtualized class antagonism and apart from the disparity conflicts at the margins of the system, can only emerge where advanced capitalist society has to immunize itself, by depoliticizing the masses of the population, against the questioning of its technocratic background ideology: in the public sphere administered through the mass media. For only here is it possible to buttress the concealment of the difference between progress in systems of purposive-rational action and emancipatory transformations of the institutional framework, between technical and practical problems. And it is necessary for the system to conceal this difference. Publicly administered definitions extend to *what* we want for our lives, but not to *how* we would like to live if we could find out, with regard to attainable potentials, how we *could* live.

Who will activate this conflict zone is hard to predict. Neither the old class antagonism nor the new type of underprivilege contains a protest potential whose origins make it tend toward the repoliticization of the desiccated public sphere. For the present, the only protest potential that gravitates toward the new conflict zone owing to identifiable interests is arising among certain groups of university, college, and high school students. Here we can make three observations:

1. Protesting students are a privileged group, which advances no interests that proceed immediately from its social situation or that could be satisfied in conformity with the system through an augmentation of social rewards. The first American studies of student activists conclude that they are predominantly not from upwardly mobile sections of the student body, but rather from sections with privileged status recruited from economically advantaged social strata.[14]

2. For plausible reasons the legitimations offered by the political system do not seem convincing to this group. The welfare-state substitute program for decrepit bourgeois ideologies presupposes a certain status and achievement orientation. According to the studies cited, student activists are less privatistically oriented to professional careers and future families than other students. Their academic achievements, which tend to be above average, and their social origins do not promote a horizon of expectations determined by anticipated exigencies of the labor market. Active students, who relatively frequently are in the social sciences and humanities, tend to be immune to technocratic consciousness because, although for varying motives, their primary experiences in their own intellectual work in neither case accord with the basic technocratic assumptions.

3. Among this group, conflict cannot break out because of the extent of the discipline and burdens imposed, but only because of their quality. Students are not fighting for a larger share of social rewards in the prevalent categories: income and leisure time. Instead, their protest is directed against the very category of reward itself. The few available data confirm the supposition that the protest of youth from bourgeois homes no longer coincides with the pattern of authority conflict typical of previous generations. Student activists tend to have parents who share their critical attitude. They have been brought up relatively frequently with more psychological understanding and according to more liberal educational principles than comparable inactive groups.[15] Their socialization seems to have been achieved in subcultures freed from immediate economic compulsion, in which the traditions of bourgeois morality and their petit-bourgeois derivatives have lost their function. This means that training for switching over to value-orientations of purposive-rational action no longer includes fetishizing this form of action. These educational techniques make possible experiences and favor orientations that clash with the conserved life form of an economy of poverty. What can take shape on this basis is a lack of understanding in principle for the reproduction of virtues and sacrifices that have become superfluous—a lack of understanding why despite the advanced stage of technological development the life of the

individual is still determined by the dictates of professional careers, the ethics of status competition, and by values of possessive individualism and available substitute gratifications: why the institutionalized struggle for existence, the discipline of alienated labor, and the eradication of sensuality and aesthetic gratification are perpetuated. To this sensibility the structural elimination of practical problems from a depoliticized public realm must become unbearable. However, it will give rise to a political force only if this sensibility comes into contact with a problem that the system cannot solve. For the future I see *one* such problem. The amount of social wealth produced by industrially advanced capitalism and the technical and organizational conditions under which this wealth is produced make it ever more difficult to link status assignment in an even subjectively convincing manner to the mechanism for the evaluation of individual achievement.[16] In the long run therefore, student protest could permanently destroy this crumbling achievement-ideology, and thus bring down the already fragile legitimating basis of advanced capitalism, which rests only on depoliticization.

Notes

1. On the context of these concepts in the history of philosophy, see my contribution to the *Festschrift* for Karl Löwith: "Arbeit und Interaktion: Bemerkungen zu Hegels Jenenser Realphilosophie," in *Natur und Geschichte. Karl Löwith zum 70. Geburtstag,* Hermann Braun and Manfred Riedel, eds. (Stuttgart, 1967). This essay is reprinted in *Technik und Wissenschaft als 'Ideologie'* (Frankfurt am Main, 1968) and in English in *Theory and Practice,* published by Beacon Press.

2. Gerhard E. Lenski, *Power and Privilege: A Theory of Social Stratification* (New York, 1966).

3. See Peter L. Berger, *The Sacred Canopy* (New York, 1967).

4. See my study *Erkenntnis und Interesse* (Frankfurt am Main, 1968), published by Beacon Press as *Cognition and Human Interests.*

5. See Leo Strauss, *Natural Right and History* (Chicago, 1963); C. B. MacPherson, *The Political Theory of Possessive Individualism* (London, 1962); and Jürgen Habermas, "Die klassische Lehre von der Politik in ihrem Verhältnis zur Sozialphilosophie," in *Theorie und Praxis,* 2d ed. (Neuwied, 1967), in *Theory and Practice.*

6. See Jürgen Habermas, "Naturrecht und Revolution," in *Theorie und Praxis.*

7. Claus Offe, "Politische Herrschaft und Klassenstrukturen," in Gisela Kress and Dieter Senghaas, eds., *Politikwissenschaft* (Frankfurt am Main, 1969). The quotation in the text is from the original manuscript, which differs in formulation from the published text.

8. The most recent explication of this is Eugen Löbl, *Geistige Arbeit-die*

wahre Quelle des Reichtums, translated from the Czech by Leopold Grünwald (Vienna, 1968).

9. See Helmut Schelsky, *Der Mensch in der wissenschaftlichen Zivilisation* (Cologne-Opladen, 1961); Jacques Ellul, *The Technological Society* (New York, 1967); and Arnold Gehlen, "Über kulturelle Kristallisationen," in *Studien zur Anthropologie und Soziologie* (Berlin 1963), and "Über kulturelle Evolution," in *Die Philosphie und die Frage nach dem Fortschritt,* M. Hahn and F. Wiedmann, eds. (Munich, 1964).

10. To my knowledge there are no empirical studies concerned specifically with the propagation of this background ideology. We are dependent on extrapolations from the findings of other investigations.

11. Offe, op. cit.

12. See my essay "Erkenntnis und Interess" in *Technik und Wissenschaft als 'Ideologie.'* It will appear in English as an appendix to *Cognition and Human Interests.*

13. Herman Kahn and Anthony J. Wiener, "The Next Thirty-Three Years: A Framework for Speculation," in *Toward the Year 2000: Work in Progress,* Daniel Bell, ed. (Boston, 1969), pp. 80 f.

14. Seymour Martin Lipset and Philip G. Altbach, "Student Politics and Higher Education in the U.S.A.," in *Student Politics,* Seymour Martin Lipset, ed. (New York, 1967); Richard W. Flacks, "The Liberated Generation: An Exploration of the Roots of Student Protest," in *Journal of Social Issues,* 23:3, pp. 52–75; and Kenneth Keniston, "The Sources of Student Dissent," ibid., pp. 108 ff.

15. In Flacks' words, "Activists are more radical than their parents; but activists' parents are decidedly more liberal than others of their status. . . . Activism is related to a complex of values, not ostensibly political, shared by both the students and their parents. . . . Activists' parents are more 'permissive' than parents of non-activists."

16. See Robert L. Heilbroner, *The Limits of American Capitalism.* (New York, 1966).

V

SOCIALIST-FEMINISM: NEW CONSCIOUSNESS, NEW PRACTICE

11

Sheila Rowbotham

Born in England, Rowbotham studied history at Oxford. She has taught at various technical colleges, the Workers' Education Association, and the University of Amsterdam. An active member of the socialist movement since her undergraduate years, Rowbotham was on the editorial board of Black Dwarf, *a New Left newspaper. She participated in the first development of socialist-feminism in England in the late 1960s and early 1970s.*

In this selection from Women's Consciousness, Man's World *(1973), Rowbotham provides an example of socialist-feminism's unique contribution to Western Marxism. Taking the early feminist slogan "the personal is political" to heart, she interweaves accounts of her own personal experience of social life and political activism with theoretical reflections on the same themes. Her major concern here is to show the political necessity for women (and other oppressed groups) to understand their experience in their own terms. She concludes that radicals need a new understanding of political life, one that includes experiences of oppression central to women's lives.*

Women's Consciousness, Man's World

THROUGH THE LOOKING-GLASS

> Life is not determined by consciousness but consciousness by life . . . .. The individuals composing the ruling class possess among other things consciousness, and therefore think.
>
> Karl Marx, *German Ideology*

> Though she felt as a woman [Divine] thought as a "man." . . . And all the woman judgements she made were, in reality, poetical conclusions. . . . She does not wish to become a woman completely since she loathes women. She wants to be a man-woman: a woman when she is passive, a man when she acts. Thus this language relates her to an absence.
>
> J.-P, SARTRE, *Saint Genet*

> I'll be your mirror, reflect what you are . . ..
>
> Velvet Underground, "I'll Be Your Mirror"

Mirrors

When I was a little girl I was fascinated by the kind of dressing-table mirror which was in three parts. You could move the outer folding mirrors inwards and if you pressed your nose to the glass you saw reflections of yourself with a squashed nose repeated over and over again. I used to wonder which bit was really me. Where was I in all these broken bits of reflection? The more I tried to grasp the totality, the more I concentrated on capturing myself in my own image, the less I felt I knew who I was. The mirror held a certain magic. The picture started to assume its own reality. My sense of self-ness came back through the shape of my nose. I defined my own possiblity in relation to the fact I saw in front of me. But impatient with the inability of the image to act independently I used to want to walk through the mirror. I had a nagging and irreconcilable notion that if I could only get through the mirror a separate self would emerge who would confirm the existence of the first self by recognizing it. Without this recognition I felt invisible inside myself although my appearance was clearly visible in the glass. Sometimes in the effort to relate my internal bewilderment to the external phenomena of my self I would even peer round the back to see if anything changed round there. Of course it was always frustratingly the same. Just old brown unpolished wood which slightly grazed the tips of your fingers when you touched it. I thought I had finally found the secret in my mother's hand mirror which had glass on both sides. But that was no good either, just another illusion.

The vast mass of human beings have always been mainly invisible to themselves while a tiny minority have exhausted themselves in the isolation of observing their own reflections. Every mass political movement of the oppressed necessarily brings its own vision of itself into sight. At first this consciousness is fragmented and particular. The prevailing social order stands as a great and resplendent hall of mirrors. It owns and occupies the world as it is and the world as it is seen and heard. But the first glimpse of revolutionary possibility leaves a small but indestructible chink in its magnificent self-confidence. Capitalism now carries not chinks but great slits and gashes. It bears the mark of revolution.

In order to create an alternative an oppressed group must at once shatter the self-reflecting world which encircles it and, at the same time, project its own image onto history. In order to discover its own identity as distinct from that of the oppressor it has to become visible to itself. All revolutionary movements create their own ways of seeing. But this is a result of great labor. People who are without names, who do not know themselves, who have no culture, experience a kind of paralysis of consciousness. The first step is to connect and learn to trust one another.

Consciousness within the revolutionary movement can only become coherent and self-critical when its version of the world becomes clear not simply within itself but when it knows itself in relation to what it has created apart from itself. When we can look back at ourselves through our own cultural creations, our actions, our ideas, our pamphlets, our organization, our history, our theory, we begin to integrate a new reality. As we begin to know ourselves in a new relation to one another we can start to understand our movement in relation to the world outside. We can begin to use our self-consciousness strategically. We can see what we could not see before.

But there are many perils. Historical self-consciousness is a tumultuous and wayward odyssey which for many of us has only just begun. If mass revolutionary action has a relatively brief history, female revolutionary politics is a mere flicker in its midst. A new consciousness is a laborious thing. Now we are like babes thrashing around in darkness and unexplored space. The creation of an alternative world and an alternative culture cannot be the work of a day. But we cannot afford to waste time while reaction consolidates itself. Theoretical consistency is difficult—often it comes out as dogmatism. It is hard to steer any steady course while accepting that we will always aspire beyond what we can realize. It is hard to put out our hands and touch the past, harder still to bring the past into the future. Nor does the same definition necessarily do from one day to the next. Circumstances transform themselves and our relationship to them. Nothing seems fixed in the world. Familiar ideas don't fit the new reality. The mirror dissolves into a light show. When you watch a light show you see one colored pattern created by the slides in a projector disintegrating in the very moment in which it appears distinctly and immediately to be altering its relationship to all the other colors which are themselves going through the same process according to their own unique pattern. Revolutionaries now have to accommodate themselves to organizing in the midst of a gigantic three-dimensional light show.

In all the movement and confusion there is a great darkness. Consciousness which comes from political action takes time to communicate itself. Connection is, at first, spasmodic and uncoordinated. It takes time to relate new and surprising versions of the world. We need to make a new reality through the action we take and through our organization in combination with one another. But we have to discover our own reality too or we will simply be subsumed. Solidarity has to be a collective consciousness which at once comes through individual self-consciousness and transforms it.

Yet there are many things which can prevent us from seeing our common identity. Power in the hands of particular groups and classes serves like a prism to refract reality through their own perspective. Within capitalism the prism of the media creates its own version of revolutionary movements which become incorporated into the revolutionaries' own image of themselves. The outside world invades and distorts revolutionary organizations and consciousness. The hall of mirrors turns itself into a fun palace in which revolutionaries walk continually into bent appearances of themselves. The partial image of a particular oppressed group sometimes even serves to magnify the world of the oppressor by projecting itself at the expense of others who share invisibility. For example, male-dominated black and working-class movements can falsely define their "manhood" at the expense of women, just as some women define femaleness at the expense of men. They thus cheat themselves and lose the possibility of man-womanhood. They are in the same position as the old woman in the fairy story who was given three wishes and the chance of happiness for ever but was only able to conceive of longings which canceled out her real desires.

Silence[1]

The oppressed without hope are mysteriously quiet. When the conception of change is beyond the limits of the possible, there are no words to articulate discontent so it is sometimes held not to exist. This mistaken belief arises because we can only grasp silence in the moment in which it is breaking. The sound of silence breaking makes us understand what we could not hear before. But the fact that we could not hear does not prove that no pain existed. The revolutionary must listen very carefully to the language of silence. This is particularly important for women because we come from such a long silence.

We perceived ourselves through anecdote, through immediate experience. The world simply was and we were in it. We could only touch and act upon its outer shapes while seeing through the lens men made for us. We had no means of relating our inner selves to an outer movement of things. All theory, all connecting language and ideas which could make us see ourselves in relation to a continuum or as part of a whole were external to us. We had no part in their making. We lumbered around ungainlylike in borrowed concepts which did not fit the shape we felt ourselves to be. Clumsily we stumbled over our own toes, lost in boots which were completely the wrong size. We struggled to do our/their flies up for us/them. We clowned, mimicked, aped our own absurdity. Nobody else took us seriously, we did not even believe in ourselves. We were dolly, chick, broad. We were 'the ladies,' 'the girls.' Step forward now dears, let's see you perform. Every time we mounted the steps of their platforms we wanted to run away and hide at home. We had a sense of not belonging. It was evident we were intruders. Those of us who ventured into their territory were most subtly taught our place.

We were allowed to play with their words, their ideas, their culture as long as we pretended we were men. As soon as our cunts bobbed into the light of day, they stiffened, their lips tautened, they seemed to draw themselves into themselves, they cut us down. It was better not to try. One part of ourselves mocked another. We joined in their ridicule of our own aspirations. Either you played their game or you didn't play at all. Part of us leapt over into their world, part of us stayed behind at home. There was a continual temptation to duck out of danger. We were more comfortable doing the washing-up. We retreated, would not be drawn out. We sat silent and accusing when they discussed their theory because it took our men away from us, made them start to impress one another, exposed them to ridicule. We judged them but could never enter the ring ourselves. We made sure we were out of the firing line. We could not bear the responsibility of engagement.

We became bitter and defensive. We disliked ourselves. We were distrustful of other women, particularly those who played their game—the women who did not seem to feel like us. But the distinction was only one of circumstance. Sometimes we were them, sometimes we were playing, performing, acting out our part. Then sometimes we were sunk into ourselves. But always we were split in two, straddling silence, not sure where we would begin to find ourselves or one another. From this division, our material dislocation, came the experience of one part of ourselves as strange, foreign and cut off from the other which we encountered as tongue-tied paralysis about our own identity. We were never all together in one place, we were always in transit, immigrants into alien territory. We felt uncomfortable, watched, ill at ease. The manner in which we knew ourselves was at variance with ourselves as an historical being-woman. Our immediate perceptions of ourselves were locked against our own social potential.

The Nature of Silence

But where was an alternative consciousness of ourselves to come from? We were defined in our paralysis from the first gesture. Simone de Beauvoir makes a beginning. She tries to grasp the process through which the girl-child discovers what it is to be a woman. She explores the learned passivity, the squatting urinating, the discouraged aggression and self-assertion, the energy turned in on itself. The little girl is taught to hold herself in and become "feminine." She forces herself into an alien mold. An understanding of how women's consciousness is formed means searching in our most distant memories of ourselves. We still remain very ignorant about the manner in which small children come to self-consciousness. We need to know much more of the specific manner in which particular little girls perceive themselves in particular families in particular forms of society. Equally the process through which the family serves to communicate and reinforce the prevailing values of capitalist society is still only sketchily understood. The generalizations we make about the "authoritarian" family are manifestly inadequate. The tools we use to perceive consciousness in terms of mass movements are too crude to observe the delicate manner in which human beings stifle and define one another at the point of reproduction. For women at least the location of this consciousness is a matter of some political urgency. It is part of our becoming.

There is also the question of language. As soon as we learn words we find ourselves outside them. To some extent this is a shared exclusion. The word carries a sense of going beyond one's self, theory carries the possibility of connecting and transforming in the realm beyond self. Language conveys a certain power. It is one of the instruments of domination. It is carefully guarded by the superior people because it is one of the means through which they conserve their supremacy.

> In the old days they simply cut off a delinquent's tongue; our society which is more humane lets him keep his organs of phonation on condition that he does not use them. . . . The truth is that what they fear most is that he may defile words: in like manner, the women of certain tribes must express themselves by gestures; only the men have a right to use speech. If he violates the prohibition, one must neither listen to him nor, above all, answer him. . . . Obviously they cannot prevent him from speaking soundlessly, in his throat, they cannot prevent him from writing on the walls of his cell, from exchanging signs behind the guards' backs, with the other prisoners: but these furtive, solemn communications confirm him in the feeling that he is stealing language.[2]

The underground language of people who have no power to define and determine themselves in the world develops its own density and precision. It enables them to sniff the wind, sense the atmosphere, defend themselves in a hostile terrain. But it restricts them by affirming their own dependence upon the words of the powerful. It reflects their inability to break out of the imposed reality through to a reality they can define and control for themselves. It keeps them locked against themselves. On the other hand the language of theory—removed language—only expresses a reality experienced by the oppressors. It speaks only for their world, from their point of view. Ultimately a revolutionary movement has to break the hold of the dominant group over theory, it has to structure its own connections. Language is part of the political and ideological power of the rulers.

There is a long inchoate period during which the struggle between the language of experience and the language of theory becomes a kind of agony. In the making of the working class in Britain the conflict of silence with "their" language, the problem of paralysis and connection has been continuous. Every man who has worked up through the labor movement expressed this in some form. The embarrassment about dialect, the divorce between home talking and educated language, the otherness of "culture"—their culture is intense and painful. The struggle is happening now every time a worker on strike has to justify his position in the alien structures of the television studio before the interrogatory camera of the dominant class, or every time a working-class child encounters a middle-class teacher. The degree of accommodation has varied. It has meant sometimes a stilted borrowing from the culture of the ruling class even at the point of denouncing their political and economic hold most fiercely, or it has resulted in a dismissal of theory as something contaminated by belonging to the rulers. The persistent elevation of understanding through direct experience has become both the strength and the weakness of British male-dominated working-class politics. It provides security in the defense of existing strongholds, and weakness in the creation of an offensive strategy. The black movement in America has encountered a similar dilemma.

Although we share the same paralysis, the same estrangement from the world we do not control, the peculiar difficulties we encounter in making words which can become the instruments of our own theory differ. Our oppression is more internalized—the clumsiness of women penetrates the very psyche of our being. It is not just a question of being outside existing language. We can never hope to enter and change it from inside. We can't just occupy existing words. We have to change the meanings of words even before we take them over. Now "she" represents a woman but "he" is mankind. If "she" enters mankind "she" loses herself in "he." She-he cannot then suddenly become the "she" abandoned or the "she" she wants to become. The present inability of "she" to speak for more than herself is a representation of reality. "A man is in the right in being a man, it is the woman who is in the wrong."[3] It is no good pretending this state of affairs does not exist because we would rather it were not so. The exclusion of women from all existing language demonstrates our profound alienation from any culture which can generalize itself. This is as true of revolutionary consciousness and activity as any other. You can't say to a woman with any conviction and expect her to take herself seriously as a woman, "Stand up and be a man." But you can say it to a working-class man or a black man.

Consequently our version of the world has always been fragile and opaque. A woman is repeatedly forced back upon herself. The origin of our oppression, like the roots of all domination, are lost long ago. We are completely without any memory of any alternative. Even the myths of tribes and races of strong women, the golden age of matriarchy, are the creations of male culture. The only means we have of even fantasizing free women is through the projection of male fears. Such women reach our consciousness masculinized by the male imagination. We have little part even in the immediate recorded past. We are the background to history. Our present situation imposes fragmentation and isolation. Divided inside and against ourselves and one another we lack both physical and class solidarity. "They live dispersed among the males attached through residence, housework, economic conditions and social standing to certain men."[4] The family maintains us in the interior world and the class of our man gives us status in the exterior. We reflect the position they attain. We are social attachments in capitalism.

Moreover, the relationship of man to woman is like no other relationship of oppressor to oppressed. It is far more delicate, far more complex. After all, very often the two love one another. It is a rather gentle tyranny. We are subdued at the very moment of intimacy. Such ecstatic subjugation is thus very different from the relationship between worker and capitalist. The workers can conceive of their own world in the future in which the capitalist no longer figures. We cannot imagine our world in which no men exist. "The division between the sexes is a biological fact not an event in human history . . . she is the other in a totality of which the two components are necessary to one another."[5]

Consequently the political emergence of women has to be at once distinct from and in connection to men. But our consciousness of distinctness cannot come just from the external world of work, or the external encounters of life. Female revolutionary consciousness comes from the darkness of our unremembered childhood. Only here does the extent of our colonization become really evident. Think for example how we learn even our psychology and physiology from our oppressors. We substitute our own experience of our genitals, our menstruation, our orgasm, our menopause, for an experience determined by men. We are continually translating our own immediate fragmented sense of what we feel into a framework which is constructed by men. The particular sensations of women have the quality of the exceptional. It is as if everything that relates only to us comes out in footnotes to the main text, as worthy of the odd reference. We come on the agenda somewhere between "Youth" and "Any other business." We encounter ourselves in men's culture as "by the way" and peripheral. According to all the reflections we are not really there. This puzzles us and means it is harder for us to begin to experience our own identity as a group. This gives female consciousness an elusive and disintegrating feeling. We are the negative to their positive. We are oppressed by an overwhelming sense of not being there.

Every time a woman describes to a man any experience which is specific to her as a woman she confronts his recognition of his own experience as normal. More than this, his experience of how he sees the "norm" is reinforced by the dominant ideology which tells both him and the woman that he is right. This inability to find ourselves in existing culture as we experience ourselves is true of course for other groups besides women. The working class, blacks, national minorities within capitalism all encounter themselves as echoes, they lose themselves in the glitter and gloss of the images capitalism projects to them.

However, the problem for women is particularly internalized. This is partly a matter of history. We have no time or place to look back to. The movement we have created to liberate *all* women is incomparably weaker than the labor movement: historically we have sought "brotherhood"; we are still "Yours fraternally." We have not unraveled what we share and what is specific to us.

Equally this internalization is a matter of anatomy and physiology. The sexual distinction at once binds us closely to our oppressors and distinguishes us more sharply from them. This does not mean that we are not more than our biology but it does mean that our difference is penetrated immediately at a level of sensation and experience which does not relate just to the external world. It means also that the exploration of the internal areas of consciousness is a political necessity for us. However, men—especially revolutionary men—often fail to see this. They have defined politics for themselves as something which belongs to the external realm. It is to do with strikes, mass meetings, demonstrations. Their revolution has a symbolism for the outer shape of things and the inner world goes along on the old tracks. But this is an incomplete picture; we know, not as an abstract idea, but from our experience of our specific material situation, that our consciousness as women is inseparable from our relation to the encounters of our anatomy. This is true of childbirth and of sexuality—after all, a man enters us through our vagina; we perceive his body through our sensations of him on top or underneath, inside or outside. The manner in which we touch each other in bed is part of the way in which we learn about ourselves.

Men often speak with amusement about our preoccupation with the orgasm. They brandish it as a sign of our inability to understand the serious world of their politics, but in so doing they suffer from a failure of imagination common among dominant groups. This is part of the way in which they have been hobbled themselves. Both we and they have to recognize the limitations of their perspective. The exploration of our own sexuality is a crucial factor in the creation of a revolutionary female consciousness. We have to rediscover our whole selves, not simply the selves which slot into the existing male world, and the way to start is by communicating with one another. Without a political movement it is barely possible for women to describe even how they experience their own sexuality. It is only a conscious relationship to other women which will encourage us to trust our own isolated, atomized and fragmented sensations.

Our cultural colonization extends not just to sex, but even to illness, and the whole half-articulated world of gynecological complaints. For example, if a woman goes to a doctor complaining of period pains, cystitis, or depression during her menopause, her experience of them will lose itself in male nonexperience of them. This male nonexperience in the shape of the individual doctor and his science which is the embodiment of the nonexperiences of the past will bear down upon her experience to persuade her that she can't possibly really feel as ill as she says. Behind the male nonexperience of female experience lurks the rationalization that women always exaggerate their complaints. When someone steadfastly refuses to hear you, you respond by turning up the amplification. When workers do this they are dismissed blandly as unreasonable and ignorant. When women do this we are regarded as unreasonable, ignorant *and* hysterical. We step neatly into another male dismissive "nonexperience"—hysteria or the view from the womb. The political implications of this have been exposed by women's liberation in relation to childbirth, contraception and abortion. Our lack of control over our own bodies matches the workers' lack of control over production.

Breaking the Silence

When a man curls his lip, when he uses ridicule, when he grows angry, you have touched a raw nerve in domination. Men will often admit other women are oppressed but not you. Well it was true in the past but not now, well yes they are in Liverpool but not in London or wherever you live. Gradually you will force them nearer home. Then they will stick. They will accuse you of rocking the boat, they will demand loyalty to their particular group or party. They will tell you to be patient. They will say you criticize the behavior of men in a personal rather than in a political way. If you are working-class they'll humiliate you with your sex and class ignorances, if you are middle-class they'll call you a petty bourgeois deviationist. We must not be discouraged by them. We must go our own way but remember we are going to have to take them with us. They learn slowly. They are like creatures who have just crawled out of their shells after millennia of protection. They are sore and tender and afraid.

It is impossible to confront a common condition before you have discovered it. The first stage in this discovery is the recognition by the oppressed of a general situation of domination. You can't begin to find your own power until you have consciously recognized your nonpower. It is evident that the idea of female oppression is not new. Nor is the concept of male hegemony. Karen Horney quotes the philosopher Georg Simmel, for example, in her paper of 1926, "The Flight from Womanhood," as saying that all existing culture is male-defined and that the very notion of objectivity can be equated with masculinity. Simmel stated that the standards of estimating male and female nature were not "neutral" . . .

but essentially masculine." He showed how this was concealed by the naïve identification of the concept "human being" and the concept "man" in some languages and noted that "in the most varying fields, inadequate achievements are contemptuously called "feminine," while distinguished achievements on the part of women are called "masculine" as an expression of praise."[6]

Karen Horney related this realization to her study of psychology. She recognized the elements of domination in all existing male-defined ideology. "At any given time, the more powerful side will create an ideology suitable to help maintain its position and to make this position acceptable to the weaker one. In this ideology the differentness of the weaker one will be interpreted as inferiority, and it will be proven that these differences are unchangeable, basic, or God's will. It is the function of such an ideology to deny or conceal the existence of a struggle,"[7] She added that the unawareness of the existence of conflict between the sexes was a result of its concealment by male-dominated culture and the acceptance by women of such a culture. This concealment should be understood not in terms of a conscious plot but as a way of seeing the world which comes directly from a specific material situation which the rulers seek to maintain. The particularity of this world view is obscured. The dominant group sees itself as indistinguishable from civilization.

Simone de Beauvoir takes up the same theme. "The truth is that man today represents the positive and the neutral—that is to say, the male and the human being—whereas woman is only the negative, the female, whenever she behaves as a human being she is declared to be identifying herself with the male."[8] She shows how it is a completely unnatural procedure for the "female human being to make herself a feminine woman" and adds that her sense of inferiority is not a product of her imagination but of her actual social predicament. "Woman feels inferior because, in fact, the requirements of femininity *do* belittle her. She spontaneously chooses to be a complete person, a subject and a free being with the world and the future open before her. If this choice is confused with virility, it is so to the extent that femininity today means mutilation."[9]

Once grasped at a general level ideas become like a kind of shorthand in our consciousness. But it is one thing to encounter a concept, quite another to understand it. In order to understand a general idea like male hegemony it is necessary first to perceive in a whole series of separate moments how this has affected you. Then those moments have to be communicated. This is part of the total process of female self-recognition. It is the way through which we start to make our own language, and discover our own reflections. The confirmation of our understanding comes through our organization and our action.

My own realization of the depth and extent of my colonization came with the force of an electric shock. It jolted me into perceiving all my glimpses of myself in a different light. I had always dreaded all those aspects of myself which might resemble Mathieu's mistress in Sartre's *The Age of Reason*. I looked with contempt at other women who appeared to be sunk into their bodies as she was. I carried this dread around with me and watched my flesh as I grew older for signs that I was becoming like her. One day it occurred to me that she didn't exist as a woman at all. She was merely the creation of a man's projected fears about the things a woman could do to him. He was just a man like any other: a man who was afraid of being stifled by a woman's body. When I realized this I experienced a kind of joy like that which Bunyan describes when Christian's burden rolls off. I felt incomparably light-spirited. My eyes opened a bit wider. It became easier to see that this was a general state of affairs. We learn ourselves through women made by men. A man is not a male film-maker, or a male writer. He is simply a film-maker or a writer. It is all a clever sleight of hand. Even our fears of what we might become are from them.

But I was still rather complacent about my independence. I felt I did not try to please men. Of course I did really but not in ways which could immediately be seen. I'd never washed shirts and darned socks. I had always shared housework with men. When I went to the film *Bonnie and Clyde* I noticed rather smugly how she did her hair in the way he told her. Her face so pathetically took her cue from him. "I'd never submit so meekly," I thought. "I'd have much more pride than that." The thought was scarcely out of my head when the man who was with me turned to me innocently and said, "She looks just like you often look." I'd always thought I knew when I was acting "feminine." Apparently it was quite out of my control.

I had yet to understand the extent to which I identified with men, used their eyes. I was really sliced in two. Half of me was like a man surveying the passive half of me as a woman-thing. On Boxing Day in 1967 the Beatles' *Magical Mystery Tour* appeared on television. A group of people including the Beatles go on a coach trip. There is the atmosphere of excitement of all being on the bus together and of enjoying a treat. When they get off all kinds of things happen: tugs-of-war which remind you of the desperate tugging you felt you had to do when you were a child; a woman who eats and eats and cries and cries until you can't imagine how a human being could carry so many tears around inside her. Then at one point all the boys in the bus are separated from the girls. You follow the boys in the film, wriggling around in your seat in front of the telly, in mounting excitement. It's like going into the Noah's Ark at Blackpool when you're six or listening to very loud rock music when you're thirteen. I got the same tightening down at the bottom of my spine. Well there I was clenching my cunt and where should they go but into a striptease. I had caught myself going to watch another woman as if I were a man. I was experiencing the situation of another woman stripping through men's eyes. I was being asked to desire myself by a film made by men. Catching myself observing myself desiring one of my selves I remained poised for an instant in two halves. But as soon as she started to sing a song which said she'd make you pay for everything you got, I started to laugh. She was not at all frightening to me. But she was frightening to them—she was outside them. They wanted her. I only half-wanted to be like her. She symbolized an attractive woman but it was the kind of woman I'd very early on decided I wouldn't be like. Because her only weapon was her charade at the fair she had to make them pay for it. This was her way of surviving. I had other ways. I had no need to sell myself directly as a commodity. However, she was also not frightening because I knew the gestures she made to excite them from inside. I knew how to drop into the stereotypes we learn as female sexuality. I was familiar with the woman they feared. I could see through their eyes but I could feel with her body. I was a man-woman. I had thus contributed toward making an object of myself and other women. I was partly responsible for our degradation.

In the absence of a political movement we become accomplices. This is a further complexity in the microcosm of domination. Simone de Beauvoir notes some of the inducements to complicity, the manner in which the delights of passivity are made to seem desirable to the young girl. In isolation the individual woman who passes over into activity is bound to define herself at the expense of other women. This is apparent at the level of class. The freedom of the emancipated upper-class woman is simply the other side of the unfreedom of the working-class woman who supports her. But it exists also in terms of sex. The emancipated educated woman is untouchable; she acquires an asexual protected dignity which is the reverse of the closeness of the traditional woman to her body. Individually either she accepts this situation or she attempts to enter the body of the woman who is still passive. As part of you leaps outside yourself, another part tries to reenter a self you have created in your own imagination. You make for yourself a stereotype of suffering womanhood and let it bleed.

You dwell continually on your female troubles. When you sleep with a man you enjoy him forcing you to submit. You are torn between shame and delight. "She simultaneously longs for and dreads the shameful passivity of the willing prey."[10] We exult in the very moment of mutilation. We are encouraged in our masochism by male stereotypes. A whole flock of patient, bruised, black-eyed Griseldas passes through the pages of history. We mistakenly believe that when we have taken all suffering to ourselves we will no longer feel pain, that we are indestructible because we survive a degradation of our own choice and making. "Woman assumes her most delicious triumphs by first falling into the depths of abjection; whether God or a man is concerned; the little girl learns that she will become all-powerful through deepest resignation; she takes delight in a masochism that promises supreme conquests."[11]

To recognize that we are the victims of our own masochism is our political beginning. We can't begin to find our way without the help of other women and ultimately without help from men. We can only break the hold of masochism when we experience the collective self-assertion of a movement for liberation. But we will only realize our own new collectivity by connecting politically with other groups who are oppressed.

• • • • •

The Politics of the Irrational

There are innumerable areas of experience to which our understanding of political class consciousness does not extend. For instance it is not clear what is the relationship between dreams, fantasy, visions, orgasm, love and the revolution. There is a tendency to dismiss these vital aspects of our lives because they are not easily understood in existing political terms. But as long as we continue to dismiss them we cannot work out what effect they have on our actions. This makes it difficult to predict the consequences of things. It is necessary to understand the relationship between our experience in fantasy, dream and ecstasy and the experience which is intelligible to us in terms of political strategy. This is most evident to women because it is clear to us that our consciousness of our orgasms is part not only of the total relationship with the men we are with, but also of our total situation in relation to our bodies, other women, and the world outside. All these materially affect the nature and scope of orgasm. Not only does the general communicate to the particular, the particular defines the course of the general way things are. An essential part of our political emergence is to discover our own particularity, but we are continually taught to distrust the particular feeling that does not fit. If we are to go on and change things we have to do more than grasp this theoretically. "Knowing the cause of a passion is not enough to overcome it, one must live it, one must oppose other passions to it, one must combat it tenaciously, in short one must work oneself over."[12]

I glimpsed this first through my relationship to mascara. It was so important to me I would not be seen without it. I felt ashamed at my own triviality in men's eyes. I could not explain the nature of my fears in a way which was sensible to them. I recognized this was insoluble in terms of "reason":

> It is not a question of simply rational enlightenment. Intellectual awareness of what is going on does not mean object-consciousness dissolves. When I go without mascara on my eyes I experience myself as I knew myself before puberty. It is inconceivable to me that any man could desire me sexually, my body hangs together quite differently. Rationally I can see the absurdity of myself. But this does not mean I experience myself in a different way.[13]

It was not the mascara that was important. This would be to make a fetish of it. It was my relationship to it. But I was not able to modify my relationship to it until other versions of other women's relationships to their artificially created femininity had served to reinforce and extend my own perception of this particular part of myself. A few years ago I was barely able to describe it on paper. I had to fight all my sense of what was a "serious" political matter. I had been unable to connect the politics I learned from men to the politics of my mother's bedroom, the secret world where I watched her again and again "putting on her face." The existence of a women's political movement makes possible such new distinctions and new connections.

In order for Marxism to prove useful as a revolutionary weapon for women, we have at once to encounter it in its existing form and fashion it to fit our particular oppression. This means extending it into areas in which men have been unable to take it by distilling it through the particularities of our own experience. Our own situation is rich in the most bizarre of complexities and combinations and we must translate these strange phenomena of female life as we now live it into the language of theory. This theoretical consciousness will inevitably be confused when so much of ourselves remains opaque. But discouragement should not goad us into the trap of presenting our reality according to an already existing scheme of abstraction. By such false conceits we would only mislead one another.

Such short cuts will only waste time. We are fortunate to live in a time when new connections and communications are becoming possible, when all manner of people who had previously been "trodden in the dirt, people with no place in society, people with no right to speak have audaciously lifted up their heads [and] taken power into their hands."[14]

Amidst this great movement of the riff-raff we have much to learn. But we must remember to transmit too our story of our own most precious distinctions as we move from passivity and silence through the looking-glass of history into communism.

Notes

1. This section is based on Sheila Rowbotham, *Women's Liberation and the New Politics,* Spokesman Pamphlet No. 17, originally published by May Day Manifesto Group, summer 1969, now included in *The Body Politic,* Michelene Wandor, Stage 1, 1972.
2. J.-P. Sartre, *Saint Genet,* W. H. Allen, 1963, pp. 277–78.
3. S. de Beauvoir, *The Nature of the Second Sex,* Four Square, 1968, p. 7.
4. Ibid., p. 11.
5. Ibid.
6. Georg Simmel, *Philosophische Kultur,* in Karen Horney, *Feminine Psychology,* ed. Harold Kelman, Routledge & Kegan Paul, 1967, p. 56.
7. Horney, op. cit., p. 116.
8. S. de Beauvoir, *The Second Sex,* p. 147.
9. Ibid.
10. Ibid., p. 62.
11. Ibid., p. 33.
12. J.-P. Sartre, *The Problem of Method,* Methuen, 1964, p. 12.
13. Sheila Rowbotham, *Women's Liberation and the New Politics,* Spokesman Pamphlet No. 17, p. 27.
14. Mao Tse-tung, "Investigation of Peasant Movement in Hunan," *Selected Readings,* Collet's, 1968.

12

Juliet Mitchell (1940–)

Born in New Zealand but raised in England, Juliet Mitchell studied literature at Oxford and subsequently lectured at various English and foreign colleges. For a while an editor of New Left Review, *Mitchell was active in the socialist women's movement in England since the mid-1960s. She later underwent formal training in psychoanalysis, which she currently practices.*

In this selection from her groundbreaking work Women's Estate *(1971), Mitchell's argument runs contrary to the traditional Marxist claim that women's situation is a simple product of society's economic and class system. She argues instead that women's total social situation results from their position in four social structures: production, reproduction, sexuality, and the socialization of children. One political implication of this position is that overcoming women's oppression requires overcoming sexism in all four areas and not, as traditional Marxism had it, just in the area of production.*

Women's Estate

THE POSITION OF WOMEN: 1

Radical feminism attempts to solve the problem of analyzing the oppression of women by making it *the* problem. The largest, first and foremost. While such a theory remains descriptive of the experience, it *does* nevertheless stress the magnitude of the problem. What we need is a theory that is at once large enough and yet is capable of being specific. We have to see *why* women have always been oppressed, and *how* they are oppressed now, and how differently elsewhere. As radical feminists demand, we must dedicate ourselves to a theory of the oppression of all women and yet, at the same time, not lose sight of the historical specificity in the general statement. We should ask the feminist questions, but try to come up with some Marxist answers.

The situation of women is different from that of any other oppressed social group: they are half of the human species. In some ways they are exploited and oppressed like, and along with, other exploited classes or oppressed groups—the working-class, Blacks, etc. . . . Until there is a revolution in production, the labor situation will prescribe women's situation within the world of men. But women are offered a universe of their own: the family. Women are exploited at work, and relegated to the home: the two positions compound their oppression. Their subservience in production is obscured by their assumed dominance in their own world—the family. What is the family? And what are the actual functions that a woman fulfills within it? Like woman herself, the family appears as a natural object, but is actually a cultural creation. There is nothing inevitable about the form or role of the family, any more than there is about the character or role of women. It is the function of ideology to present these given social types as aspects of Nature itself. Both can be exalted, paradoxically, as ideals. The "true" woman and the "true" family are images of peace and plenty: in actuality they may both be sites of violence and despair. The apparently natural condition can be made to appear more attractive than the arduous advance of human beings toward culture. But what Marx wrote about the bourgeois myths of the Golden Ancient World describes precisely women's realm:

> . . . in one way the child-like world of the ancients appears to be superior; and this is so, insofar as we seek for closed shape, form and established limitation. The ancients provide a narrow satisfaction, whereas the modern world leaves us unsatisfied, or, where it appears to be satisfied with itself, is *vulgar* and *mean*.[1]

The ideology of "woman" presents her as an undifferentiated whole—"a woman," alike the world over, eternally the same. Likewise the "concept" of the family is of a unit that endures across time and space, there have always been families. . . . Within its supposed permanent structure, eternal woman finds her place. So the notion goes. . . . Any analysis of woman, and of the family, must uncoil this ideological concept of their permanence and of their unification into a monolithic whole, mother and child, a woman's place . . . her natural destiny. Theoretical analysis and revolutionary action must destructure and destroy the inevitability of this combination.

Past socialist theory has failed to differentiate woman's condition into its separate structures, which together form a complex—not a simple—unity. To do this will mean rejecting the idea that woman's condition can be deduced derivatively from the economy (Engels), or equated symbolically with society (early Marx). Rather, it must be seen as a *specific* structure, which is a unity of different elements. The variations of woman's condition throughout history will be the result of different combinations of these elements—we will thus have not a linear narrative of economic development (de Beauvoir) for the elements will be combined in different ways at different times. In a complex totality each independent sector has its own autonomous reality though each is ultimately, but only ultimately, determined by the economic factor. This complex totality means that no contradiction in society is ever simple. As each sector can move at a different pace, the synthesis of the different time-scales in the total structure means that sometimes contradictions cancel each other out, and sometimes they reinforce one another. Because the unity of woman's condition at any time is in this way the product of several structures, moving at different paces, it is always "overdetermined."[2]

The key structures of woman's situation can be listed as follows: Production, Reproduction, Sexuality and the Socialization of Children. The concrete combination of these produce the "complex unity" of her position; but each separate structure may have reached a different "moment" at any given historical time. Each then must be examined separately in order to see what the present unity is, and how it might be changed. The notes that follow do not pretend to give a historical account of each sector. They are only concerned with some general reflections on the different roles of women and some of their interconnections.

1. Production

The biological differentiation of the sexes into male and female and the division of labor that is based on this have *seemed,* throughout history, an interlocked necessity. Anatomically smaller and weaker, woman's physiology and her psychobiological metabolism appear to render her a less useful member of a work-force. It is always stressed how, particularly in the early stages of social development, man's physical superiority gave him the means of conquest over nature which was denied to women. Once woman was accorded the menial tasks involved in maintenance while man undertook conquest and creation, she became an aspect of the things preserved: private property and children. Marx, Engels, Bebel, de Beauvoir—the major socialist writers on the subject—link the confirmation and continuation of woman's oppression after the establishment of her physical inferiority for hard manual work with the advent of private property. But woman's physical weakness has never prevented her from performing work as such (quite apart from bringing up children)—only specific types of work, in specific societies. In Primitive, Ancient, Oriental, Medieval and Capitalist societies, the *volume* of work performed by women has always been considerable (it has usually been much more than this). It is only its form that is in question. Domestic labor, even today, is enormous if quantified in terms of productive labor.[3] It has been calculated in Sweden, that 2,340 million hours a year are spent by women in housework compared with 1,290 million hours in industry. The Chase Manhattan Bank estimated a woman's overall working week averaged 99.6 hours. In any case women's physique alone has never permanently or even predominantly relegated them to menial domestic chores. In many peasant societies, women have worked in the fields as much as, or more than, men.

Physical Weakness and Coercion

The assumption behind most socialist analyses is that the crucial factor starting the whole development of feminine subordination was women's lesser capacity for demanding physical work. But, in fact, this is a major oversimplification. Even in these terms, historically it has been woman's lesser capacity for violence as well as for work, that has determined her subordination. In most societies woman has not only been less able than man to perform arduous kinds of work, she has also been less able to fight. Man not only has the strength to assert himself against nature, but also against his fellows. *Social coercion* has interplayed with the straightforward division of labor, based on biological capacity, to a much greater extent than is generally admitted. Women have been *forced* to do "women's work." Of course, this force may not be actualized as direct aggression. In primitive societies women's lesser physical suitability for the hunt is assumed to be evident. In agricultural societies where women's inferiority is socially instituted, they are given the arduous task of tilling and cultivation. For this coercion is necessary. In developed civilizations, and more complex societies, woman's physical deficiencies again become relevant. Women are thought to be of no use either for war or in the construction of cities. But with early industrialization, coercion once more becomes important. As Marx wrote: "insofar as machinery dispenses with muscular power, it becomes a means of employing labourers of slight muscular strength, and those whose bodily development is incomplete, but whose limbs are all the more supple. The labour of women and children was, therefore, the first thing sought for by capitalists who used machinery."[4]

René Dumont points out that in many zones of tropical Africa today men are often idle, while women are forced to work all day. "The African woman experiences a three-fold servitude: through forced marriage; through her dowry and polygamy, which increases the leisure time of men and simultaneously their social prestige; and finally through the very unequal division of labour."[5] This exploitation has no "natural" source whatever. Women may perform their "heavy" duties in contemporary African peasant societies, not for fear of physical reprisal by their men, but because these duties are "customary" and built into the role structures of the society. A further point is that coercion implies a different relationship from coercer to coerced than does exploitation. It is political rather than economic. In describing coercion Marx said that the master treated the slave or serf as the "inorganic and natural condition of its own reproduction." That is to say, labor itself becomes like other natural things—cattle or soil:

> The original conditions of production appear as natural prerequisites, *natural conditions of the existence of the producer,* just as his living body, however reproduced and developed by him, is not originally established by himself, but appears as his *prerequisite*.[6]

This is preeminently woman's condition. For far from woman's *physical* weakness removing her from productive work, her *social* weakness has in these cases evidently made her the major slave of it.

This truth, elementary though it may seem, has nevertheless been constantly ignored by socialist writers on the subject, with the result that there is an unfounded optimism in their predictions of the future. For, if it is just the biological incapacity for the hardest physical work which has determined the subordination of women, then the prospect of an advanced machine technology, abolishing the need for strenuous physical exertion, would seem to promise, therefore, the liberation of women. For a moment industrialization itself thus seems to herald women's liberation. Engels, for instance, wrote:

> The first premise for the emancipation of women is the reintroduction of the entire female sex into public industry. . . . And this has become possible only as a result of modern large-scale industry, which not only permits of the participation of women in production in large numbers, but actually calls for it and, moreover strives to convert private domestic work also into a public industry.[7]

What Marx said of early industrialism is no less, but also *no more* true of an automated society:

> . . . it is obvious that the fact of the collective working group being composed of individuals of both sexes and all ages, must necessarily, *under suitable conditions,* become a source of human development; although in its spontaneously developed, brutal, capitalist form, where the labourer exists for the process of production, and not the process of production for the labourer, that fact is a pestiferous source of corruption and slavery.[8]

Industrial labor and automated technology both promise the preconditions for women's liberation alongside man's—but no more than the preconditions. It is only too obvious that the advent of industrialization has not so far freed women in this sense, either in the West or in the East. De Beauvoir hoped that automation would make a decisive, qualitative difference by abolishing altogether the physical differential between the sexes. But any reliance on this in itself accords an independent role to technique which history does not justify. Under capitalism, automation could possibly lead to an ever-growing structural unemployment which would expel women (along with immigrants)—the latest and least integrated recruits to the labor force and ideologically the most expendable for a bourgeois society—from production after only a brief interlude in it. Technology is mediated by the total structure, and it is this which will determine woman's future in work relations. It is the relationship between the social forces and technology that Firestone's "ecological" revolution ultimately ignores.

Physical deficiency is not now, any more than in the past, a sufficient explanation of woman's relegation to inferior status. Coercion has been ameliorated to an ideology shared by both sexes. Commenting on the results of her questionnaire of working women, Viola Klein notes: "There is no trace of feminine egalitarianism—militant or otherwise—in any of the women's answers to the questionnaire; nor is it even implicitly assumed that women have a 'Right to Work.'"[9] Denied, or refusing, a role in *production,* woman does not even create the preconditions of her liberation. But even her presence in the work force does not erode her oppression in the family.

2. The Reproduction of Children

Women's absence from the critical sector of production historically, of course, has been caused not just by their assumed physical weakness in a context of coercion—but also by their role in reproduction. Maternity necessitates withdrawals from work, but this is not a decisive phenomenon. It is rather women's role in reproduction which has become, in capitalist society at least, the spiritual "complement" of men's role in production. Bearing children, bringing them up, and maintaining the home—these form the core of woman's natural vocation, in this ideology. This belief has attained great force because of the seeming universality of the family as a human institution. There is little doubt that Marxist analyses have underplayed the fundamental problems posed here. The complete failure to give any operative content to the slogan of "abolition" of the family is striking evidence of this (as well as of the vacuity of the notion).

The biological function of maternity is a universal, atemporal fact, and as such has seemed to escape the categories of Marxist historical analysis. However, from it is made to follow the so-called stability and omnipresence of the family if in very different forms.[10] Once this is accepted, women's social subordination—however emphasized as an honorable, but different role (cf. the equal-but-"separate" ideologies of Southern racists)—can be seen to follow inevitably as an *insurmountable* biohistorical fact. The causal chain then goes: maternity, family, absence from production and public life, sexual inequality.

The linchpin in this line of argument is the idea of the family. The notion that "family" and "society" are virtually coextensive or that an advanced society not founded on the nuclear family is now inconceivable, despite revolutionary posturings to the contrary, is still widespread. It can only be seriously discussed by asking just what the family is—or rather what woman's role in the family is. Once this is done, the problem appears in quite a new light. For it is obvious that woman's role in the family—primitive, feudal or bougeois—partakes of three quite different structures: reproduction, sexuality, and the socialization of children. These are historically, not intrinsically, related to each other in the present modern family. We can easily see that they needn't be. For instance, biological parentage is not necessarily identical with social parentage (adoption). Thus it is essential to discuss not the family as an unanalyzed entity, but the separate *structures* which today compose it but which tomorrow may be decomposed into a new pattern.

As I have said, reproduction is seen as an apparently constant atemporal phenomenon—part of biology rather than history. In fact this is an illusion. What is true is that the "mode of reproduction" does not vary with the "mode of production"; it can remain effectively the same through a number of different modes of production. For it has been defined till now by its uncontrollable, natural character and to this extent has been an unmodified biological fact. As long as reproduction remained a natural phenomenon, of course, women were effectively doomed to social exploitation. In any sense, they were not "masters" of a large part of their lives. They had no choice as to whether or how often they gave birth to children (apart from precarious methods of contraception or repeated dangerous abortions); their existence was essentially subject to biological processes outside their control.

Contraception

Contraception which was finally invented as a rational technique only in the nineteenth century was thus an innovation of world-historic importance. It is only just now beginning to show what immense consequences it could have, in the form of the Pill. For what it means is that at last the mode of reproduction potentially could be transformed. Once childbearing becomes totally voluntary (how much so is it in the West, even today?) its significance is fundamentally different. It need no longer be the sole or ultimate vocation of woman; it becomes one option among others.

History is the development of man's transformation of nature, and thereby of himself—of human nature—in different modes of production. Today there are the technical possibilities for the transformation and "humanization" of the most natural part of human culture. This is what a change in the mode of reproduction could mean.

We are far from this state of affairs yet. In Italy the sale of contraceptives remains illegal. In many countries it is difficult to get reliable means. The oral contraceptive is still the privilege of a moneyed minority in a few Western countries. Even here the progress has been realized in a typically conservative and exploitative form. It is made only for women, who are thus "guinea-pigs" in a venture which involves both sexes.

The fact of overwhelming importance is that easily available contraception threatens to dissociate sexual from reproductive experience—which all contemporary ideology tries to make inseparable, as the raison d'être of the family.

Reproduction and Production

At present, reproduction in our society is often a kind of sad mimicry of production. Work in a capitalist society is an alienation of labor in the making of a social product which is confiscated by capital. But it can still sometimes be a real act of creation, purposive and responsible, even in the conditions of the worst exploitation. Maternity is often a caricature of this. The biological product—the child—is treated as if it were a solid product. Parenthood becomes a kind of substitute for work, an activity in which the child is seen as an object created by the mother, in the same way as a commodity is created by a worker. Naturally, the child does not literally escape, but the mother's alienation can be much worse than that of the worker whose product is appropriated by the boss. The child as an autonomous person, inevitably threatens the activity which claims to create it continually merely as a *possession* of the parent. Possessions are felt as extensions of the self. The child as a possession is supremely this. Anything the child does is therefore a threat to the mother herself, who has renounced her autonomy through this misconception of her reproductive role. There are few more precarious ventures on which to base a life.

Furthermore even if the woman has emotional control over her child, legally and economically both she and it are subject to the father. The social cult of maternity is matched by the real socioeconomic powerlessness of the mother. The psychological and practical benefits men receive from this are obvious. The converse of woman's quest for creation in the child is man's retreat from his work into the family: "When we come home, we lay aside our mask and drop our tools, and are no longer lawyers, sailors, soldiers, statesmen, clergymen, but only men. We fall again into our most human relations, which, after all, are the whole of what belongs to us as we are ourselves."[11]

Unlike her nonproductive status, her capacity for maternity *is* a definition of woman. But it is only a physiological definition. Yet so long as it is allowed to remain a substitute for action and creativity, and the home an area of relaxation for men, woman will remain confined to the species, to her universal and natural condition.

3. Sexuality

Sexuality has traditionally been the most tabooed dimension of women's situation. The meaning of sexual freedom and its connection with women's freedom is a subject which few socialist writers have cared to broach. "Socialist morality" in the Soviet Union for a long time debarred serious discussion of the subject within the world communist movement. Marx himself—in this respect somewhat less liberal than Engels—early in his life expressed traditional views on the matter:

> . . . the sanctification of the sexual instinct through exclusivity, the checking of instinct by laws, the moral beauty which makes nature's commandment ideal in the form of an emotional bond—[this is] the spiritual essence of marriage.[12]

Yet it is obvious that throughout history women have been appropriated as sexual objects, as much as progenitors or producers. Indeed, the sexual relationship can be assimilated to the statute of possession much more easily and completely than the productive or reproductive relationship. Contemporary sexual vocabulary bears eloquent witness to this—it is a comprehensive lexicon of reification—"bird, fruit, chick . . . ." Later Marx was well aware of this: "Marriage . . . is incontestably a form of *exclusive private property*."[13] But neither he nor his successors ever tried seriously to envisage the implications of this for socialism, or even for a structural analysis of women's conditions. Communism, Marx stressed in the same passage, would not mean mere "communalization" of women as common property. Beyond this, he never ventured.

Some historical considerations are in order here. For if socialists have said nothing, the gap has been filled by liberal ideologues. Fairly recently, in his book, *Eros Denied,* Wayland Young argues that Western civilization has been uniquely repressive sexually, and, in a plea for greater sexual freedom today, compares it at some length with Oriental and ancient societies. It is striking, however, that his book makes no reference whatever to women's status in these different societies, or to the different forms of marriage-contract prevalent in them. This makes the whole argument a purely formal exercise—an obverse of socialist discussions of women's position which ignore the problem of sexual freedom and its meanings. For while it is true that certain Oriental or ancient (and indeed primitive) cultures were much less puritanical than Western societies, it is absurd to regard this as a kind of "transposable value" which can be abstracted from its social structure. In effect, in many of these societies sexual openness was accompanied by a form of polygamous exploitation which made it, in practice, an expression simply of masculine domination. Since art was the province of man, too, this freedom finds a natural and often powerful expression in art—which is often quoted as if it were evidence of the total quality of human relationships in the society. Nothing could be more misleading. What is necessary, rather than this naïve, hortatory core of historical example, is some account of the covariation between the degrees of sexual liberty and openness, and the position and dignity of women in different societies.

Sexuality and the Position of Women: Some Historical Examples

Some points are immediately obvious. The actual history is much more dialectical than any liberal account presents it. Unlimited juridical polygamy—whatever the sexualization of the culture which accompanies it—is clearly a total derogation of woman's autonomy, and constitutes an extreme form of oppression. Ancient China is a perfect illustration of this. A sensual culture and a society in which the father as head of the household wielded an extraordinary despotism. The Chinese paterfamilias was "a liturgical (semi-official) policeman of his kin group."[14] In the West, however, the advent of monogamy was in no sense an *absolute* improvement. It certainly did not create a one-to-one equality—far from it. Engels commented accurately:

> Monogamy does not by any means make its appearance in history as the reconciliation of man and woman, still less as the highest form of such a reconciliation. On the contrary, it appears as the subjugation of one sex by the other, as the proclamation of a conflict between the sexes entirely unknown hitherto in prehistoric times.[15]

But in the Christian era, monogamy took on a very specific form in the West. It was allied with an unprecedented regime of general sexual repression. In its Pauline version, this had a markedly antifeminine bias, inherited from Judaism. With time this became diluted—feudal society, despite its subsequent reputation for asceticism, practiced formal monogamy with considerable actual acceptance of polygamous behavior, at least within the ruling class. But here again the extent of sexual freedom was only an index of masculine domination. In England, the truly major change occurred in the sixteenth century with the rise of militant puritanism and the increase of market relations in the economy. Lawrence Stone observes:

> In practice, if not in theory, the early sixteenth century nobility was a polygamous society, and some contrived to live with a succession of women despite the official prohibition on divorce. . . . But impressed by Calvinist criticisms of the double standard, in the late sixteenth century public opinion began to object to the open maintenance of a mistress.[16]

Capitalism and the attendant demands of the newly emergent bourgeoisie accorded woman a new status as wife and mother. Her legal rights improved; there was vigorous controversy over her social position: wife-beating was condemned. "In a woman the bourgeois man is looking for a counterpart, not an equal."[17] At the social periphery woman did occasionally achieve an equality which was more than her feminine function in a market society. In the extreme nonconformist sects women often had completely equal rights: the Quaker leader Fox argued that the Redemption restored Prelapsarian equality and Quaker women thereby gained a real autonomy. But once most of the sects were institutionalized, the need for family discipline was reemphasized and woman's obedience with it. As one historian, Keith Thomas, says, the Puritans "had done something to raise women's status, but not really very much."[18] The patriarchal system was retained and maintained by the new economic mode of production—capitalism. The transition to complete effective monogamy accompanied the transition to modern bourgeois society as we know it today. Like the capitalist market system itself, it represented a historic advance, at great historic cost. The formal, juridical equality of capitalist society and capitalist rationality now applied as much to the marital as to the labor contract. In both cases, nominal parity masks real exploitation and inequality. But in both cases the formal equality is itself a certain progress, which can help to make possible a further advance.

Sexuality and the Position of Women: Today

The situation today is defined by a new contradiction. Once formal conjugal equality (monogamy) is established, sexual freedom as such—which under polygamous conditions was usually a form of exploitation—becomes, conversely, a possible force for liberation. It then means, simply, the freedom of both sexes to transcend the limits of present sexual institutions.

Historically, then, there has been a dialectical movement in which sexual expression was "sacrificed" in an epoch of more-or-less puritan repression, which nevertheless produced a greater parity of sexual roles and in turn creates the precondition for a genuine sexual liberation, in the dual sense of equality *and* freedom—whose unity defines socialism.

Love and Marriage

This movement can be verified within the history of the "sentiments." The cult of *love* only emerges in the twelfth century in opposition to legal marital forms and with a heightened valorization of women (courtly love). It thereafter gradually became diffused, and assimilated to marriage as such, producing that absurdity—a *free* choice for *life*. What is striking here is that monogamy as an institution in the West, anticipated the idea of love by many centuries. The two have subsequently been officially harmonized, but the tension between them has never been abolished. There is a formal contradiction between the voluntary contractual character of "marriage" and the spontaneous uncontrollable character of "love"—the passion that is celebrated precisely for its involuntary force. The notion that it occurs only once in every life and can therefore be integrated into a voluntary contract, becomes decreasingly plausible in the light of everyday experience—once sexual repression as a psychoideological system becomes at all relaxed.

Obviously, the main breach in the traditional value-pattern has, so far, been the increase in premarital sexual experience. This is now virtually legitimized in contemporary society. But its implications are explosive for the ideological conception of marriage that dominates this society: that it is an exclusive and permanent bond. An American anthology, *The Family and the Sexual Revolution,* reveals this very clearly:

> As far as extra-marital relations are concerned, the anti-sexualists are still fighting a strong, if losing, battle. The very heart of the Judaeo-Christian sex ethic is that men and women shall remain virginal until marriage and that they shall be completely faithful after marriage. In regard to premarital chastity, this ethic seems clearly on the way out, and in many segments of the populace is more and more becoming a dead letter.[19]

The current wave of sexual liberalization, in the present context, *could* become conducive to the greater general freedom of women. Equally, it could presage new forms of oppression. The puritan-bourgeois creation of "counterpart" (not equal) has produced the *precondition* for emancipation. But it gave statutory legal equality to the sexes at the cost of greatly intensified repression. Subsequently—like private property itself—it has become a brake on the further development of a free sexuality. Capitalist market relations have historically been a precondition of socialism; bourgeois marital relations (contrary to the denunciation of the *Communist Manifesto*) may equally be a precondition of women's liberation.

* * *

4. Socialization of Children

Woman's biological "destiny" as mother becomes a cultural vocation in her role as socializer of children. In bringing up children, woman achieves her main social definition. Her suitability for socialization springs from her physiological condition: her ability to produce milk and occasional relative inability to undertake strenuous work loads. It should be said at the outset that suitability is not inevitability. Several anthropologists make this clear. Lévi-Strauss writes:

> In every human group, women give birth to children and take care of them, and men rather have as their speciality hunting and warlike activities. Even there, though, we have ambiguous cases: of course, men never give birth to babies, but in many societies . . . they are made to act as if they did.[20]

Evans-Pritchard's description of the Nuer tribe depicts just such a situation. Margaret Mead comments on the element of wish-fulfillment in the assumption of a *natural* correlation of femininity and nurturance:

> We have assumed that because it is convenient for a mother to wish to care for her child, this is a trait with which women have been more generously endowed by a careful teleological process of evolution. We have assumed that because men have hunted, an activity requiring enterprise, bravery and initiative, they have been endowed with these useful attitudes as part of their sex-temperament.[21]

However, the cultural allocation of roles in bringing up children—and the limits of its variability—is not the essential problem for consideration. What is much more important is to analyze the nature of the socialization process itself and its requirements.

The sociologist, Talcott Parsons, in his detailed analysis claims that it is essential for the child to have two "parents," one who plays an "expressive" role, and one who plays an "instrumental" role.[22] The nuclear family revolves around the two axes of generational hierarchy (parents and children), and of the two parental roles (mother-expressive and father-instrumental). The role division derives from the mother's ability and the father's inability to breast-feed. In all groups, Parsons and his colleagues assert, even in those primitive tribes where the father appears to nurture the child (such as those discussed by Evans-Pritchard and Mead), the male plays the instrumental role *in relation* to the wife-mother. At one stage the mother plays an instrumental and expressive role *vis-à-vis* her infant: this is in the very first years when she is the source of approval and disapproval as well as of love and care. However, after this, the father, or male substitute (in matrilineal societies the mother's brother) takes over. In a modern industrial society two types of role are clearly important: the adult role in the family of procreation, and the adult occupational role in outside work. The function of the family as such reflects the function of the women within it; it is primarily expressive. The person playing the integrated-adaptive-expressive role cannot be off all the time on instrumental-occupational errands—hence there is a built-in inhibition of the woman's work outside the home. Parsons's analysis makes clear the exact role of the maternal socializer in contemporary American society.[23] It fails to go on to state that other aspects and modes of socialization are conceivable. What is valuable in Parsons'[s] work is simply his insistence on the central importance of socialization as a process which is constitutive of any society (no Marxist has provided a comparable analysis). His general conclusion is that:

> It seems to be without serious qualification the opinion of competent personality psychologists that, though personalities differ greatly in their degrees of rigidity, certain broad fundamental patterns of "character" are laid down in childhood (so far as they are not genetically inherited) and are not radically changed by adult experience. The exact degree to which this is the case or the exact age levels at which plasticity becomes greatly diminished, are not at issue here. The important thing is the fact of childhood character formation and its relative stability after that.[24]

Infancy

This seems indisputable: one of the great revolutions of modern psychology has been the discovery of the decisive specific weight of infancy in the course of an individual life—a psychic time disproportionately greater than the chronological time. Freud began the revolution with his work on infantile sexuality; Melanie Klein radicalized it with her work on the first year of the infant's life. The result is that today we know far more than ever before how delicate and precarious a process the passage from birth to childhood is for everyone. It would seem that the fate of the adult personality can be largely decided in the initial months of life. The preconditions for the later stability and integration demand an extraordinary degree of care and intelligence on the part of the adult who is socializing the child, as well as a persistence through time of the same person.

These undoubted advances in the scientific understanding of childhood have been widely used as an argument to reassert women's quintessential maternal function, at a time when the traditional family has seemed increasingly eroded. The psychologist, Bowlby, studying evacuee children in the Second World War, declared: "essential for mental health is that the infant and young child should experience a warm, intimate, and continuous relationship with his mother,"[25] setting a trend which has become cumulative since. The emphasis of familial ideology has shifted from a cult of the biological ordeal of maternity (the pain which makes the child precious, etc.) to a celebration of mother-care as a social act. This can reach ludicrous extremes:

> For the mother, breast-feeding becomes a complement to the act of creation. It gives her a heightened sense of fulfilment and allows her to participate in a relationship as close to perfection as any that a woman can hope to achieve. . . . The simple fact of giving birth, however, does not of itself fulfil this need and longing. . . . Motherliness is a way of life. It enables a woman to express her total self with the tender feelings, the protective attitudes, the encompassing love of the motherly woman.[26]

The tautologies, the mystifications, the sheer absurdities point to the gap between reality and ideology.

Family Patterns

This ideology corresponds in dislocated form to a real change in the pattern of the family. As the family has become smaller, each child has become more important; the actual *act* of reproduction occupies less and less time, and the socializing and nurturance process increase commensurately in significance. Contemporary society is obsessed by the physical, moral and sexual problems of childhood and adolescence. Ultimate responsibility for these is placed on the mother. Thus the mother's reproductive role has retreated as her socializing role has increased. In the 1890s in England a mother spent fifteen years in a state of pregnancy and lactation: in the 1960s she spent an average of four years. Compulsory schooling from the age of five, of course, reduces the maternal function very greatly after the initial vulnerable years.

The present situation is then one in which the qualitative importance of socialization during the early years of the child's life has acquired a much greater significance than in the past—while the quantitative amount of a mother's life spent either in gestation or child-rearing has greatly diminished. It follows that socialization cannot simply be elevated to the woman's new maternal vocation. Used as a mystique, it becomes an instrument of oppression. Moreover, there is no inherent reason why the biological and social mother should coincide. The process of socialization is, in itself, invariable—but the person of the socializer can vary. Observers of collective methods of child-rearing in the kibbutzim in Israel note that the child who is reared by a trained nurse (though normally maternally breast-fed) does not suffer the back-wash of typical parental anxieties and thus may positively gain by the system. This possibility should not be fetishized in its turn (Jean Baby, speaking of the post-four-year-old child, goes so far as to say that "complete separation appears indispensable to guarantee the liberty of the child as well as the mother."[27]) But what it does reveal is the viability of plural forms of socialization—neither necessarily tied to the nuclear family, not to the biological parent, or rather to *one* of the biological parents—the mother.

Conclusion

The lesson of these reflections is that the liberation of women can only be achieved if *all four* structures in which they are integrated are transformed—Production, Reproduction, Sexuality and Socialization. A modification of any of them can be offset by a reinforcement of another (as increased socialization has made up for decreased reproduction). This means that a mere permutation of the form of exploitation is achieved. The history of the last sixty years provides ample evidence of this. In the early twentieth century, militant feminism in England and the U.S.A. surpassed the labor movement in its violence. The vote—a political right—was eventually won. Nonetheless, though a simple completion of the formal legal equality of bourgeois society, it left the socioeconomic situation of women virtually unchanged. The wider legacy of the suffrage was practically nil: the suffragettes, by and large, proved unable to move beyond their own initial demands, and many of their leading figures later became extreme reactionaries. The Russian Revolution produced a quite different experience. In the Soviet Union in the 1920s, advanced social legislation aimed at liberating women above all in the field of sexuality; divorce was made free and automatic for either partner, thus effectively liquidating marriage; illegitimacy was abolished, abortion was free, etc. The social and demographic effects of these laws in a backward, semi-literate society bent on rapid industrialization (needing, therefore, a high birthrate) were—predictably—catastrophic.[28] Stalinism soon produced a restoration of traditional iron norms. Inheritance was reinstated, divorce made inaccessible, abortion illegal, etc.

> The State cannot exist without the family. Marriage is a positive value for the Socialist Soviet State only if the partners see in it a lifelong union. So-called free love is a bourgeois invention and has nothing in common with the principles of conduct of a Soviet citizen. Moreover, marriage receives its full value for the State only if there is progeny, and the consorts experience the highest happiness of parenthood.
> From the official journal of the Commissariat of Justice in 1939.[29]

Women still retained the right and obligation to work, but because these gains had not been integrated into the earlier attempts to free sexuality and abolish the family no general liberation has occurred.

In China, today there is still another experience. At this stage of the revolution all the emphasis is being placed on liberating women in *production*. This has produced an impressive social promotion of women. But it seems to have been accompanied by a tremendous repression of sexuality and a rigorous puritanism (rampant in civic life). This corresponds not only to the need to mobilize women massively in economic life, but to a deep cultural reaction against the brutality, corruption and prostitution prevalent in Imperial and Kuo Ming Tang China (a phenomenon unlike anything in Czarist Russia). Because the exploitation of women was so great in the ancien régime women's participation at village level in the Chinese Revolution was uniquely high. As for reproduction, the Russian cult of maternity in the 1930s and 1940s has not been repeated for demographic reasons: indeed, China may be one of the first countries in the world to provide free State authorized contraception on a universal scale to the population. Again, however, given the low level of industrialization and fear produced by imperialist encirclement, no all-round advance could be expected.

Probably it is only in the highly developed societies of the West that an authentic liberation of women can be envisaged today. But for this to occur, there must be a transformation of *all* the structures into which they are integrated, and all the contradictions must coalesce, to explode—a *unité de rupture*. A revolutionary movement must base its analysis on the uneven development of each structure, and attack the weakest link in the combination. This may then become the point of departure for a general transformation. What is the situation of the different structures today? What is the concrete situation of the women in each of the positions in which they are inserted?

Notes

1. Karl Marx: *Pre-Capitalist Economic Formations,* ed. Hobsbawm, Lawrence & Wishart, 1964, p. 85.

2. See Louis Althusser, "Contradiction and Overdetermination," in *For Marx,* Allen Lane, London, 1970. To describe the movement of this complexity, as I have mentioned above, Althusser uses the Freudian term "overdetermination." The phrase "*unité de rupture*" (mentioned below) refers to the moment when the contradictions so reinforce one another as to coalesce into the conditions for a revolutionary change.

3. Apologists who make out that housework, though time-consuming, is light and relatively enjoyable, are refusing to acknowledge the dull and degrading routine it entails. Lenin commented crisply: "You all know that even when women have full rights, they still remain factually downtrodden because all housework is left to them. In most cases housework is the most unproductive, the most barbarous and the most arduous work a woman can do. It is exceptionally petty and does not include anything that would in any way promote the development of the woman." (*Collected Works,* vol. XXX, p. 43.)

4. Karl Marx: Capital, I, p. 394.

5. René Dumont, *L'Afrique Noire est Mal Partie,* 1962, p. 210.

6. Karl Marx, *Precapitalist Economic Formations,* p. 87.

7. Friedrich Engels, op. cit., II, pp. 233, 311.

8. Karl Marx: *Capital,* I, p. 394.

9. Viola Klein, "Working Wives," *Institute of Personnel Management Occasional Papers,* no. 15, 1960, p. 13.

10. Philippe Ariès in *Centuries of Childhood,* 1962, shows that though the family may in some form always have existed it was often submerged under more forceful structures. In fact according to Ariès it has only acquired its present significance with the advent of industrialization.

11. J. A. Froude, *Nemesis of Faith,* 1849, p. 103.

12. Karl Marx, "Chapitre de Mariage," *Oeuvres Complètes,* ed. Molitor *Oeuvres Philosophiques,* I, p. 25.

13. Karl Marx, *Private Property and Communism,* p. 153.

14. Karl Wittfogel, *Oriental Despotism,* 1957, p. 116.

15. Friedrich Engels, op. cit., II, p. 224.

16. Lawrence Stone, *The Crisis of the Aristocracy,* 1965, pp. 663–64.

17. Simone de Beauvoir, *La Marche Longue,* 1957, trans. *The Long March,* 1958, p. 141.

18. Keith Thomas, *Women and the Civil War Sects,* Past and Present, No. 13, 1958, p. 43.

19. Albert Ellis, "The Folklore of Sex," in *The Family and the Sexual Revolution,* ed. E. M. Schur, 1966, p. 35.

20. Claude Lévi-Strauss, "The Family," in *Man, Culture and Society,* ed. H. L. Shapiro, 1956, p. 274.

21. Margaret Mead, "Sex and Temperament," in *The Family and the Sexual Revolution,* pp. 207–8.

22. Talcott Parsons and Robert F. Bales, *Family, Socialization and Interaction Process,* 1956, p. 47. "The area of instrumental function concerns relations of the system to its situation outside the system . . . and "instrumentally" establishing the desired relations to *external* goal-objects. The expressive area concerns the 'internal' affairs of the system, the maintenance of integrative relations between the members, and regulation of the patterns and tension levels of its component units."

23. One of Parsons'[s] main theoretical innovations is his contention that what the child strives to internalize will vary with the content of the reciprocal role relationships in which he is a participant. R. D. Laing, in *Family and Individual Structure,* 1966, contends that a child may internalize an entire system—i.e., "the family."

24. Talcott Parsons, *The Social System,* 1952, p. 227. There is no doubt that the Women's Liberation Movement, with its practical and theoretical stress on the importance of child-care, has accorded the subject the seriousness it needs. See, for instance, "Women's Liberation: Notes on Child-Care" produced by the Women's Center, 36 West 22nd St., New York.

25. John Bowlby, cit. Bruno, Bettelheim: "Does Communal Education Work? The Case of the Kibbutz," in *The Family and the Sexual Revolution,* p. 295. These evacuee war children were probably suffering from more than mother-loss, e.g., bombings and air-raids?

26. Betty Ann Countrywoman, *Redbrook,* June 1960, cit. Betty Friedan: *The Feminine Mystique,* Penguin, 1965, p. 51.

27. Jean Baby, *Un Monde Meilleur,* Maspero, 1964, p. 99.

28. For a fuller account of this see Chapter IVA of Kate Millet's *Sexual Politics*.

29. *Sotsialistichbeskaya Zakonnost,* 1939, no. 2, cit. N. Timasheff: "The Attempt to Abolish the Family in Russia," in *The Family,* ed. N. W. Bell and E. F. Vogel, 1960, p. 59.

13

Heidi Hartmann (1942–)

Born in the United States, Heidi Hartmann is an economist working at the National Research Council/National Academy of Science in the Assembly of Behavioral and Social Sciences. An editor of Feminist Studies, *Hartmann has written widely on a variety of topics, including technology and housework, women and employment, and Marxist-feminist theory.*

In this excerpt from her widely read essay "The Unhappy Marriage of Marxism and Feminism: Towards a More Progressive Union" (1979), Hartmann formulates a materialistic understanding of male domination and applies that understanding to the way patriarchy and capitalism interact in the oppression of women.

"The Unhappy Marriage of Marxism and Feminism: Towards a More Progressive Union"

. . . . .

Radical Feminism and Patriarchy

The great thrust of radical feminist writing has been directed to the documentation of the slogan "the personal is political." Women's discontent, radical feminists argued, is not the neurotic lament of the maladjusted,

From "The Unhappy Marriage of Marxism and Feminism: Towards a More Progressive Union," by Heidi Hartmann, published in *Women and Revolution,* edited by Lydia Sargent, South End Press 1981. Notes have been renumbered.

but a response to a social structure in which women are systematically dominated, exploited, and oppressed. Women's inferior position in the labor market, the male-centered emotional structure of middle class marriage, the use of women in advertising, the so-called understanding of women's psyche as neurotic—popularized by academic and clinical psychology—aspect after aspect of women's lives in advanced capitalist society was researched and analyzed. The radical feminist literature is enormous and defies easy summary. At the same time, its focus on psychology is consistent. The New York Radical Feminists' organizing document was "The Politics of the Ego." "The personal is political" means for radical feminists, that the original and basic class division is between the sexes, and that the motive force of history is the striving of men for power and domination over women, the dialectic of sex.[1]

Accordingly, Firestone rewrote Freud to understand the development of boys and girls into men and women in terms of power.[2] Her characterizations of what are "male" and "female" character traits are typical of radical feminist writing. The male seeks power and domination; he is egocentric and individualistic, competitive and pragmatic; the "technological mode," according to Firestone, is male. The female is nurturant, artistic, and philosophical; the "aesthetic mode" is female.

No doubt, the idea that the aesthetic mode is female would have come as quite a shock to the ancient Greeks. Here lies the error of radical feminist analysis: the dialectic of sex as radical feminists present it projects male and female characteristics as they appear in the present back into all of history. Radical feminist analysis has greatest strength in its insights into the present. Its greatest weakness is a focus on the psychological which blinds it to history.

The reason for this lies not only in radical feminist method, but also in the nature of patriarchy itself, for patriarchy is a strikingly resilient form of social organization. Radical feminists use patriarchy to refer to a social system characterized by male domination over women. Kate Miller's definition is classic:

> our society . . . is a patriarchy. The fact is evident at once if one recalls that the military, industry, technology, universities, science, political offices, finances—in short, every avenue of power within the society, including the coercive force of the police, is entirely in male hands.[3]

This radical feminist definition of patriarchy applies to most societies we know of and cannot distinguish among them. The use of history by radical feminists is typically limited to providing examples of the existence of patriarchy in all times and places.[4] For both Marxist and mainstream social scientists before the women's movement, patriarchy referred to a system of relations between men, which formed the political and economic outlines of feudal and some prefeudal societies, in which hierarchy followed ascribed characteristics. Capitalist societies are understood as meritocratic, bureaucratic, and impersonal by bourgeois social scientists; Marxists see capitalist societies as systems of class domination.[5] For both kinds of social scientists neither the historical patriarchal societies nor today's western capitalist societies are understood as systems of relations between men that enable them to dominate women.

Toward a Definition of Patriarchy

We can usefully define patriarchy as a set of social relations between men, which have a material base, and which, though hierarchical, establish or create interdependence and solidarity among men that enable them to dominate women. Though patriarchy is hierarchical and men of different classes, races, or ethnic groups have different places in the patriarchy, they also are united in their shared relationship of dominance over their women; they are dependent on each other to maintain that domination. Hierarchies "work" at least in part because they create vested interests in the status quo. Those at the higher levels can "buy off" those at the lower levels by offering them power over those still lower. In the hierarchy of patriarchy, all men, whatever their rank in the patriarchy, are bought off by being able to control at least some women. There is some evidence to suggest that when patriarchy was first institutionalized in state societies, the ascending rulers literally made men the heads of their families (enforcing their control over their wives and children) in exchange for the men's ceding some of their tribal resources to the new rulers.[6] Men are dependent on one another (despite their hierarchical ordering) to maintain their control over women.

The material base upon which patriarchy rests lies most fundamentally in men's control over women's labor power. Men maintain this control by excluding women from access to some essential productive resources (in capitalist societies, for example, jobs that pay living wages) and by restricting women's sexuality.[7] Monogamous heterosexual marriage is one relatively recent and efficient form that seems to allow men to control both these areas. Controlling women's access to resources and their sexuality, in turn, allows men to control women's labor power, both for the purpose of serving men in many personal and sexual ways and for the purpose of rearing children. The services women render men, and which exonerate men from having to perform many unpleasant tasks (like cleaning toilets) occur outside as well as inside the family setting. Examples outside the family include the harassment of women workers and students by male bosses and professors as well as the common use of secretaries to run personal errands, make coffee, and provide "sexy" surroundings. Rearing children, whether or not the children's labor power is of immediate benefit to their fathers, is nevertheless a crucial task in perpetuating patriarchy as a system. Just as class society must be reproduced by schools, work places, consumption norms, etc., so must patriarchal social relations. In our society children are generally reared by women at home, women socially defined and recognized as inferior to men, while men appear in the domestic picture only rarely. Children raised in this way generally learn their places in the gender hierarchy well. Central to this process, however, are the areas outside the home where patriarchal behaviors are taught and the inferior position of women enforced and reinforced: churches, schools, sports, clubs, unions, armies, factories, offices, health centers, the media, etc.

The material base of patriarchy, then, does not rest solely on childrearing in the family, but on all the social structures that enable men to control women's labor. The aspects of social structures that perpetuate patriarchy are theoretically identifiable, hence separable from their other aspects. Gayle Rubin has increased our ability to identify the patriarchal element of these social structures enormously by identifying "sex/gender systems":

> a "sex/gender system" is the set of arrangements by which a society transforms biological sexuality into products of human activity, and in which these transformed sexual needs are satisfied.[8]

We are born female and male, biological sexes, but we are created woman and man, socially recognized genders. *How* we are so created is that second aspect of the *mode* of production of which Engels spoke, "the production of human beings themselves, the propagation of the species."

How people propagate the species is socially determined. If, biologically, people are sexually polymorphous, and society were organized in such a way that all forms of sexual expression were equally permissible, reproduction would result only from some sexual encounters, the heterosexual ones. The strict division of labor by sex, a social invention common to all known societies, creates two very separate genders and a need for men and women to get together for economic reasons. It thus helps to direct their sexual needs toward heterosexual fulfillment, and helps to ensure biological reproduction. In more imaginative societies, biological reproduction might be ensured by other techniques, but the division of labor by sex appears to be the universal solution to date. Although it is theoretically possible that a sexual division of labor not imply inequality between the sexes, in most known societies, the socially acceptable division of labor by sex is one which accords lower status to women's work. The sexual division of labor is also the underpinning of sexual subcultures in which men and women experience life differently; it is the material base of male power which is exercised (in our society) not just in doing housework and in securing superior employment, but psychologically as well.

How people meet their sexual needs, how they reproduce, how they inculcate social norms in new generations, how they learn gender, how it feels to be a man or a woman—all occur in the realm Rubin labels the sex/gender system. Rubin emphasizes the influence of kinship (which tells you with whom you can satisfy sexual needs) and the development of gender specific personalities via childrearing and the "oedipal machine." In addition, however, we can use the concept of the sex/gender system to examine all other social institutions for the roles they play in defining and reinforcing gender hierarchies. Rubin notes that theoretically a sex/gender system could be female dominant, male dominant, or egalitarian, but declines to label various known sex/gender systems or to periodize history accordingly. We choose to label our present sex/gender system patriarchy, because it appropriately captures the notion of hierarchy and male dominance which we see as central to the present system.

Economic production (what Marxists are used to referring to as *the* mode of production) and the production of people in the sex/gender sphere both determine "the social organization under which the people of a particular historical epoch and a particular country live," according to Engels. The whole of society, then, can be understood by looking at both these types of production and reproduction, people and things.[9] There is no such thing as "pure capitalism," nor does "pure patriarchy" exist, for they must of necessity coexist. What exists is patriarchal capitalism, or patriarchal feudalism, or egalitarian hunting/gathering societies, or matriarchal horticultural societies, or patriarchal horticultural societies, and so on. There appears to be no necessary connection between *changes* in the one aspect of production and changes in the other. A society would undergo transition from capitalism to socialism, for example, and remain patriarchal.[10] Common sense, history, and our experience tell us, however, that these two aspects of production are so closely intertwined, that change in one ordinarily creates movement, tension, or contradiction in the other.

Racial hierarchies can also be understood in this context. Further elaboration may be possible along the lines of defining color/race systems, arenas of social life that take biological color and turn it into a social category, race. Racial hierarchies, like gender hierarchies, are aspects of social organization, of how people are produced and reproduced. They are not fundamentally ideological; they constitute that second aspect of our mode of production, the production and reproduction of people. It might be most accurate then to refer to our societies not as, for example, simply capitalist, but as patriarchal capitalist white supremacist. In the next part, we illustrate one case of capitalism adapting to and making use of racial orders and several examples of the interrelations between capitalism and patriarchy.

Capitalist development creates the places for a hierarchy of workers, but traditional Marxist categories cannot tell us who will fill which places. Gender and racial hierarchies determine who fills the empty places. *Patriarchy is not simply hierarchical* organization, but hierarchy in which *particular* people fill *particular* places. It is in studying patriarchy that we learn why it is women who are dominated and how. While we believe that most known societies have been patriarchal, we do not view patriarchy as a universal, unchanging phenomenon. Rather patriarchy, the set of interrelations among men that allow men to dominate women, has changed in form and intensity over time. It is crucial that the hierarchy among men, and their differential access to patriarchal benefits, be examined. Surely, class, race, nationality, and even marital status and sexual orientation, as well as the obvious age, come into play here. And women of different class, race, national, marital status, or sexual orientation groups are subjected to different degrees of patriarchal power. Women may themselves exercise class, race, or national power, or even patriarchal power (through their family connections) over men lower in the patriarchal hierarchy than their own male kin.

To recapitulate, we define patriarchy as a set of social relations which has a material base and in which there are hierarchical relations between men and solidarity among them which enable them in turn to dominate women. The material base of patriarchy is men's control over women's labor power. That control is maintained by excluding women from access to necessary economically productive resources and by restricting women's sexuality. Men exercise their control in receiving personal service work from women, in not having to do housework or rear children, in having access to women's bodies for sex, and in feeling powerful and being powerful. The crucial elements of patriarchy as we *currently* experience them are: heterosexual marriage (and consequent homophobia), female childrearing and housework, women's economic dependence on men (enforced by arrangements in the labor market), the state, and numerous institutions based on social relations among men—clubs, sports, unions, professions, universities, churches, corporations, and armies. All of these elements need to be examined if we are to understand patriarchal capitalism.

Both hierarchy and interdependence among men and the subordination of women are *integral* to the functioning of our society; that is, these relationships are *systemic*. We leave aside the question of the creation of these relations and ask, can we recognize patriarchal relations in capitalist societies? Within capitalist societies we must discover those same bonds between men which both bourgeois and Marxist social scientists claim no longer exist or are, at the most, unimportant leftovers. Can we understand how these relations among men are perpetuated in capitalist societies? Can we identify ways in which patriarchy has shaped the course of capitalist development?

The Partnership of Patriarchy and Capital

How are we to recognize patriarchal social relations in capitalist societies? It appears as if each woman is oppressed by her own man alone; her oppression seems a private affair. Relationships among men and among families seem equally fragmented. It is hard to recognize relationships among men, and between men and women, as *systematically* patriarchal. We argue, however, that patriarchy as a system of relations between men and women exists in capitalism, and that in capitalist societies a healthy and strong partnership exists between patriarchy and capital. Yet if one begins with the concept of patriarchy and an understanding of the capitalist mode of production, one recognizes immediately that the partnership of patriarchy and capital was not inevitable; men and capitalists often have conflicting interests, particularly over the use of women's labor power. Here is one way in which this conflict might manifest itself: the vast majority of men might want their women at home to personally service them. A smaller number of men, who are capitalists, might want most women (not their own) to work in the wage labor market. In examining the tensions of this conflict over women's labor power historically, we will be able to identify the material base of patriarchal relations in capitalist societies, as well as the basis for the partnership between capital and patriarchy.

Industrialization and the Development of Family Wages

Marxists made quite logical inferences from a selection of the social phenomena they witnessed in the nineteenth century. But Marxists ultimately underestimated the strength of the preexisting patriarchal social forces with which fledgling capital had to contend and the need for capital to adjust to these forces. The industrial revolution was drawing all people into the labor force, including women and children; in fact the first factories used child and female labor almost exclusively.[11] That women and children could earn wages separately from men both undermined authority relations (as discussed in the preceding part) and kept wages low for everyone. Kautsky, writing in 1892, described the process this way:

> [Then with] the wife and young children of the workingman . . . able to take care of themselves, the wages of the male worker can safely be reduced to the level of his own personal needs without the risk of stopping the fresh supply of labor power.
>
> The labor of women and children, moreover, affords the additional advantage that these are less capable of resistance than men [sic]; and their introduction into the ranks of the workers increases tremendously the quantity of labor that is offered for sale in the market.
>
> Accordingly, the labor of women and children . . . also diminishes [the] capacity [of the male worker] for resistance in that it overstocks the market; owing to both these circumstances it lowers the wages of the workingman.[12]

The terrible effects on working class family life of low wages and of forced participation of all family members in the labor force were recognized by Marxists. Kautsky wrote:

> The capitalist system of production does not in most cases destroy the single household of the working-man, but robs it of all but its unpleasant features. The activity of woman today in industrial pursuits . . . means an increase of her former burden by a new one. *But one cannot serve two masters*. The household of the working-man suffers whenever his wife must help to earn the daily bread.[13]

Working men as well as Kautsky recognized the disadvantages of female wage labor. Not only were women "cheap competition" but working women were their very wives, who could not "serve two masters" well.

Male workers resisted the wholesale entrance of women and children into the labor force, and sought to exclude them from union membership and the labor force as well. In 1846 the *Ten-Hours' Advocate* stated:

> It is needless for us to say, that all attempts to improve the morals and physical condition of female factory workers will be abortive, unless their hours are materially reduced. Indeed we may go so far as to say, that married females would be much better occupied in performing the domestic duties of the household, than following the never-tiring motion of machinery. We therefore hope the day is not distant, when the husband will be able to provide for his wife and family, without sending the former to endure the drudgery of a cotton mill.[14]

In the United States in 1854 the National Typographical Union resolved not to "encourage by its act the employment of female compositors." Male unionists did not want to afford union protection to women workers; they tried to exclude them instead. In 1879 Adolph Strasser, president of the Cigarmakers International Union, said: "We cannot drive the females out of the trade, but we can restrict their daily quota of labor through factory laws."[15]

While the problem of cheap competition could have been solved by organizing the wage earning women and youths, the problem of disrupted family life could not be. Men reserved union protection for men and argued for protective labor laws for women and children.[16] Protective labor laws, while they may have ameliorated some of the worst abuses of female and child labor, also limited the participation of adult women in many "male" jobs.[17] Men sought to keep high wage jobs for themselves and to raise male wages generally. They argued for wages sufficient for their wage labor alone to support their families. This "family wage" system gradually came to be the norm for stable working class families at the end of the nineteenth century and the beginning of the twentieth.[18] Several observers have declared the non-wage-working wife to be part of the standard of living of male workers.[19] Instead of fighting for equal wages for men and women, male workers sought the family wage, wanting to retain their wives' services at home. In the absence of patriarchy a unified working class might have confronted capitalism, but patriarchal social relations divided the working class, allowing one part (men) to be bought off at the expense of the other (women). Both the hierarchy between men and the solidarity among them were crucial in this process of resolution. Family wages may be understood as a resolution of the conflict over women's labor power which was occurring between patriarchal and capitalist interests at that time.

Family wages for most adult men imply men's acceptance, and collusion in, lower wages for others, young people, women and socially defined inferior men as well (Irish, blacks, etc., the lowest groups in the patriarchal hierarchy who are denied many of the patriarchal benefits). Lower wages for women and children and inferior men are enforced by job segregation in the labor market, in turn maintained by unions and management as well as by auxiliary institutions like schools, training programs, and even families. Job segregation by sex, by insuring that women have the lower paid jobs, both assures women's economic dependence on men and reinforces notions of appropriate spheres for women and men. For most men, then, the development of family wages, secured the material base of male domination in two ways. First, men have the better jobs in the labor market and earn higher wages than women. The lower pay women receive in the labor market both perpetuates men's material advantage over women and encourages women to choose wifery as a career. Second, then, women do housework, childcare, and perform other services at home which benefit men directly.[20] Women's home responsibilities in turn reinforce their inferior labor market position.[21]

The resolution that developed in the early twentieth century can be seen to benefit capitalist interests as well as patriarchal interests. Capitalists, it is often argued, recognized that in the extreme conditions which prevailed in the [*sic*] early nineteenth century industrialization, working class families could not adequately reproduce themselves. They realized that housewives produced and maintained healthier workers than wage-working wives and that educated children became better workers than non-educated ones. The bargain, paying family wages to men and keeping women home, suited the capitalists at the time as well as the male workers. Although the terms of the bargain have altered over time, it is still true that the family and women's work in the family serve capital by providing a labor force and serve men as the space in which they exercise their privilege. Women, working to serve men and their families, also serve capital as consumers.[22] The family is also the place where dominance and submission are learned, as Firestone, the Frankfurt School, and many others have explained.[23] Obedient children become obedient workers; girls and boys each learn their proper roles.

While the family wage shows that capitalism adjusts to patriarchy, the changing status of children shows that patriarchy adjusts to capital. Children, like women, came to be excluded from wage labor. As children's ability to earn money declined, their legal relationship to their parents changed. At the beginning of the industrial era in the United States, fulfilling children's need for their fathers was thought to be crucial, even primary, to their happy development; fathers had legal priority in cases of contested custody. As children's ability to contribute to the economic well-being of the family declined, mothers came increasingly to be viewed as crucial to the happy development of their children, and gained legal priority in cases of contested custody.[24] Here patriarchy adapted to the changing economic role of children: when children were productive, men claimed them; as children became unproductive, they were given to women.

The Partnership in the Twentieth Century

The prediction of nineteenth century Marxists that patriarchy would wither away in the face of capitalism's need to proletarianize everyone has not come true. Not only did Marxists underestimate the strength and flexibility of patriarchy, they also overestimated the strength of capital. They envisioned the new social force of capitalism, which had torn feudal relations apart, as virtually all powerful. Contemporary observers are in a better position to see the difference between the tendencies of "pure" capitalism and those of "actual" capitalism as it confronts historical forces in everyday practice. Discussions of the partnership between capital and racial orders and of labor market segmentation provide additional examples of how "pure" capitalist forces meet up with historical reality. Great flexibility has been displayed by capitalism in this process.

Marxists who have studied South Africa argue that although racial orders may not allow the equal proletarianization of everyone, this does not mean that racial barriers prevent capital accumulation.[25] In the abstract, analysts could argue about which arrangements would allow capitalists to extract the most surplus value. Yet in a particular historical situation, capitalists must be concerned with social control, the resistance of groups of workers, and the intervention of the state. The state might intervene in order to reproduce society as a whole; it might be necessary to police some capitalists, to overcome the worst tendencies of capital. Taking these factors into account, capital*ists* maximize greatest *practicable* profits. If for purposes of social control, capitalists organize work in a particular way, nothing about capital itself determines who (that is, which individuals with which ascriptive characteristics) shall occupy the higher, and who the lower rungs of the wage labor force. It helps, of course, that capitalists themselves are likely to be the dominant social group and hence racist (and sexist). Capitalism inherits the ascribed characteristics of the dominant groups as well as of the subordinate ones.

Recent arguments about the tendency of monopoly capital to create labor market segmentation are consistent with this understanding.[26] Where capitalists purposely segment the labor force, using ascriptive characteristics to divide the working class, this clearly derives from the need for social control rather than accumulation needs in the narrow sense.[27] And over time, not all such divisive attempts are either successful (in dividing) or profitable. The ability of capital to shape the workforce depends both on the particular imperatives of accumulation in a narrow sense (for example, is production organized in a way that requires communication among a large number of workers? if so, they had better all speak the same language)[28] and on social forces within a society which may encourage/force capital to adapt (the maintenance of separate washroom facilities in South Africa for whites and blacks can only be understood as an economic cost to capitalists, but one less than the social cost of trying to force South African whites to wash up with blacks).

If the first element of our argument about the course of capitalist development is that capital is not all-powerful, the second is that capital is tremendously flexible. Capital accumulation encounters preexisting social forms, and both destroys them and adapts to them. The adaptation of capital can be seen as a reflection of the *strength* of these preëxisting forms to persevere in new environments. Yet even as they persevere, they are not unchanged. The ideology with which race and sex are understood today, for example, is strongly shaped by the particular ways racial and sexual divisions are reinforced in the accumulation process.

The Family and the Family Wage Today

We argued above, that, with respect to capitalism and patriarchy, the adaptation, or mutual accommodation, took the form of the development of the family wage in the early twentieth century. The family wage cemented the partnership between patriarchy and capital. Despite women's increased labor force participation, particularly rapid since World War II, the family wage is still, we argue, the cornerstone of the present sexual division of labor—in which women are primarily responsible for housework and men primarily for wage work. Women's lower wages in the labor market (combined with the need for children to be reared by someone) assure the continued existence of the family as a necessary income pooling unit. The family, supported by the family wage, thus allows the control of women's labor by men both within and without the family.

Though women's increased wage work may cause stress for the family (similar to the stress Kautsky and Engels noted in the nineteenth century), it would be wrong to think that as a consequence, the concepts and the realities of the family and of the sexual division of labor will soon disappear. The sexual division of labor reappears in the labor market, where women work at women's jobs, often the very jobs they used to do only at home—food preparation and service, cleaning of all kinds, caring for people, and so on. As these jobs are low-status and low-paying patriarchal relations remain intact, though their material base shifts somewhat from the family to the wage differential, from family-based to industrially-based patriarchy.[29]

Industrially based patriarchal relations are enforced in a variety of ways. Union contracts which specify lower wages, lesser benefits, and fewer advancement opportunities for women are not just atavistic hangovers—a case of sexist attitudes or male supremacist ideology—they maintain the material base of the patriarchal system. While some would go so far as to argue that patriarchy is already absent from the family (see, for example, Stewart Ewen, *Captains of Consciousness*),[30] we would not. Although the terms of the compromise between capital and patriarchy are changing as additional tasks formerly located in the family are capitalized, and the location of the deployment of women's labor power shifts,[31] it is nevertheless true, as we have argued above, that the wage differential caused by extreme job segregation in the labor market reinforces the family, and, with it, the domestic division of labor, by encouraging women to marry. The "ideal" of the family wage—that a man can earn enough to support an entire family—may be giving way to a new ideal that both men and women contribute through wage earning to the cash income of the family. The wage differential, then, will become increasingly necessary in perpetuating patriarchy, the male control of women's labor power. The wage differential will aid in *defining* women's work as secondary to men's at the same time it necessitates women's actual continued economic dependence on men. The sexual division of labor in the labor market and elsewhere should be understood as a manifestation of patriarchy which serves to perpetuate it.

Many people have argued that though the partnership between capital and patriarchy exists now, it may *in the long run* prove intolerable to capitalism; capital may eventually destroy both familial relations and patriarchy. The argument proceeds logically that capitalist social relations (of which the family is not an example) tend to become universalized, that women will become increasingly able to earn money and will increasingly refuse to submit to subordination in the family, and that since the family is oppressive particularly to women and children, it will collapse as soon as people can support themselves outside it.

We do not think that the patriarchal relations embodied in the family can be destroyed so easily by capital, and we see little evidence that the family system is presently disintegrating. Although the increasing labor force participation of women has made divorce more feasible, the incentives to divorce are not overwhelming for women. Women's wages allow very few women to support themselves and their children independently and adequately. The evidence for the decay of the traditional family is weak at best. The divorce rate has not so much increased, as it has evened out among classes; moreover, the remarriage rate is also very high. Up until the 1970 census, the first-marriage age was continuing its historic decline. Since 1970 people seem to have been delaying marriage and childbearing, but most recently, the birth rate has begun to increase again. It is true that larger proportions of the population are now living outside traditional families. Young people, especially, are leaving their parents' homes and establishing their own households before they marry and start traditional families. Older people, especially women, are finding themselves alone in their own households, after their children are grown and they experience separation or death of a spouse. Nevertheless, trends indicate that the new generations of young people will form nuclear families at some time in their adult lives in higher proportions than ever before. The cohorts, or groups of people, born since 1930 have much higher rates of eventual marriage and childrearing than previous cohorts. The duration of marriage and childrearing may be shortening, but its incidence is still spreading.[32]

The argument that capital destroys the family also overlooks the social forces which make family life appealing. Despite critiques of nuclear families as psychologically destructive, in a competitive society the family still meets real needs for many people. This is true not only of long-term monogamy, but even more so for raising children. Single parents bear both financial and psychic burdens. For working class women, in particular, these burdens make the "independence" of labor force participation illusory. Single parent families have recently been seen by policy analysts as transitional family formations which become two-parent families upon remarriage.[33]

It could be that the effects of women's increasing labor force participation are found in a declining sexual division of labor within the family, rather than in more frequent divorce, but evidence for this is also lacking. Statistics on who does housework, even in families with wage-earning wives, show little change in recent years; women still do most of it.[34] The double day is a reality for wage-working women. This is hardly surprising since the sexual division of labor outside the family, in the labor market, keeps women financially dependent on men—even when they earn a wage themselves. The future of patriarchy does not, however, rest solely on the future of familial relations. For patriarchy, like capital, can be surprisingly flexible and adaptable.

Whether or not the patriarchal division of labor, inside the family and elsewhere, is "ultimately" intolerable to capital, it is shaping capitalism now. As we illustrate below, patriarchy both legitimates capitalist control and delegitimates certain forms of struggle against capital.

Ideology in the Twentieth Century

Patriarchy, by establishing and legitimating hierarchy among men (by allowing men of all groups to control at least some women), reinforces capitalist control, and capitalist values shape the definition of patriarchal good.

The psychological phenomena Shulamith Firestone identifies are particular examples of what happens in relationships of dependence and domination. They follow from the realities of men's social power—which women are denied—but they are shaped by the fact that they happen in the context of a capitalist society.[35] If we examine the characteristics of men as radical feminists describe them—competitive, rationalistic, dominating—they are much like our description of the dominant values of capitalist society.

This "coincidence" may be explained in two ways. In the first instance, men, as wage laborers, are absorbed in capitalist social relations at work, driven into the competition these relations prescribe, and absorb the corresponding values.[36] The radical feminist description of men was not altogether out of line for capitalist societies. Secondly, even when men and women do not actually behave in the way sexual norms prescribe, men *claim for themselves* those characteristics which are valued in the dominant ideology. So, for example, the authors of *Crestwood Heights* found that while the men, who were professionals, spent their days manipulating subordinates (often using techniques that appeal to fundamentally irrational motives to elicit the preferred behavior), men and women characterized men as "rational and pragmatic." And while the women devoted great energies to studying scientific methods of childrearing and child development, men and women in Crestwood Heights characterized women as "irrational and emotional."[37]

This helps to account not only for "male" and "female" characteristics in capitalist societies, but for the particular form sexist ideology takes in capitalist societies. Just as women's work serves the dual purpose of perpetuating male domination and capitalist production, so sexist ideology serves the dual purpose of glorifying male characteristics/capitalist values, and denigrating female characteristics/social need. If women were degraded or powerless in other societies, the reasons (rationalizations) men had for this were different. Only in a capitalist society does it make sense to look down on women as emotional or irrational. As epithets, they would not have made sense in the renaissance. Only in a capitalist society does it make sense to look down on women as "dependent." "Dependent" as an epithet would not make sense in feudal societies. Since the division of labor ensures that women as wives and mothers in the family are largely concerned with the production of use values, the denigration of these activities obscures capital's inability to meet socially determined need at the same time that it degrades women in the eyes of men, providing a rationale for male dominance. An example of this may be seen in the peculiar ambivalence of television commercials. On one hand, they address themselves to the real obstacles to providing for socially determined needs: detergents that destroy clothes and irritate skin, shoddily made goods of all sorts. On the other hand, concern with these problems must be denigrated; this is accomplished by mocking women, the workers who must deal with these problems.

A parallel argument demonstrating the partnership of patriarchy and capitalism may be made about the sexual division of labor in the work force. The sexual division of labor places women in low-paying jobs, and in tasks thought to be appropriate to women's role. Women are teachers, welfare workers, and the great majority of workers in the health fields. The nurturant roles that women play in these jobs are of low status because capitalism emphasizes personal independence and the ability of private enterprise to meet social needs, emphases contradicted by the need for collectively provided social services. As long as the social importance of nurturant tasks can be denigrated because women perform them, the confrontation of capital's priority on exchange value by a demand for use values can be avoided. In this way, it is not feminism, but sexism that divides and debilitates the working class.

. . . . .

Notes

1. "Politics of Ego: A Manifesto for New York Radical Feminists," can be found in *Rebirth of Feminism*, ed. Judith Hole and Ellen Levine (New York: Quadrangle Books, 1971), pp. 440–43. "Radical feminists" are those feminists who argue that the most fundamental dynamic of history is men's striving to

dominate women. "Radical" in this context does *not* mean anticapitalist, socialist, countercultural, etc., but has the specific meaning of this particular set of feminist beliefs or group of feminists. Additional writings of radical feminists, of whom the New York Radical Feminists are probably the most influential, can be found in *Radical Feminism,* ed. Ann Koedt (New York: Quadrangle Press, 1972).

2. Focusing on power was an important step forward in the feminist critique of Freud. Firestone argues, for example, that if little girls "envied" penises it was because they recognized that little boys grew up to be members of a powerful class and little girls grew up to be dominated by them. Powerlessness, not neurosis, was the heart of women's situation. More recently, feminists have criticized Firestone for rejecting the usefulness of the concept of the unconscious. In seeking to explain the strength and continuation of male dominance, recent feminist writing has emphasized the fundamental nature of gender-based personality differences, their origins in the unconscious, and the consequent difficulty of their eradication. See Dorothy Dinnerstein, *The Mermaid and the Minotaur* (New York: Harper Colophon Books, 1977), Nancy Chodorow, *The Reproduction of Mothering* (Berkeley: University of California Press, 1978), and Jane Flax, "The Conflict Between Nurturance and Autonomy in Mother-Daughter Relationships and Within Feminism," *Feminist Studies,* Vol. 4, no. 2 (June 1978), pp. 141–89.

3. Kate Millett, *Sexual Politics* (New York: Avon Books, 1971), p. 25.

4. One example of this type of radical feminist history is Susan Brownmiller's *Against Our Will, Men, Women, and Rape* (New York: Simon & Shuster, 1975).

5. For the bourgeois social science view of patriarchy, see, for example, Weber's distinction between traditional and legal authority, *Max Weber: The Theories of Social and Economic Organization,* ed. Talcott Parsons (New York: The Free Press, 1964), pp. 328–57. These views are also discussed in Elizabeth Fee, "The Sexual Politics of Victorian Social Anthropology," *Feminist Studies,* Vol. 1, nos. 3–4 (Winter–Spring 1973), pp. 23–29, and in Robert A. Nisbet, *The Sociological Tradition* (New York: Basic Books, 1966), especially Chapter 3, "Community."

6. See Viana Muller, "The Formation of the State and the Oppression of Women: Some Theoretical Considerations and a Case Study in England and Wales," *Review of Radical Political Economics,* Vol. 9, no. 3 (Fall 1977), pp. 7–21.

7. The particular ways in which men control women's access to important economic resources and restrict their sexuality vary enormously, both from society to society, from subgroup to subgroup, and across time. The examples we use to illustrate patriarchy in this section, however, are drawn primarily from the experience of whites in western capitalist countries. The diversity is shown in *Toward an Anthropology of Women,* ed. Rayna Rapp Reiter (New York: Monthly Review Press, 1975), *Woman, Culture and Society,* ed. Michelle Rosaldo and Louise Lamphere (Stanford, California: Stanford University Press, 1974), and *Females, Males, Families: A Biosocial Approach,* by Liba Leibowitz (North

uate, Massachusetts: Duxbury Press, 1978). The control of women's sexuality is tightly linked to the place of children. An understanding of the demand (by men and capitalists) for children is crucial to understanding changes in women's subordination.

Where children are needed for their present or future labor power, women's sexuality will tend to be directed toward reproduction and childrearing. When children are seen as superfluous, women's sexuality for other than reproductive purposes is encouraged, but men will attempt to direct it toward satisfying male needs. The Cosmo girl is a good example of a woman "liberated" from childrearing only to find herself turning all her energies toward attracting and satisfying men. Capitalists can also use female sexuality to their own ends, as the success of Cosmo in advertising consumer products shows.

8. Gayle Rubin, "The Traffic in Women," in *Anthropology of Women,* ed. Reiter, p. 159.

9. Himmelweit and Mohun point out that both aspects of production (people and things) are logically necessary to describe a mode of production because by definition a mode of production must be capable of reproducing itself. Either aspect alone is not self-sufficient. To put it simply the production of things requires people, and the production of people requires things. Marx, though recognizing capitalism's need for people did not concern himself with how they were produced or what the connections between the two aspects of production were. See Himmelweit and Mohun, "Domestic Labour and Capital" (note 10 above).

10. For an excellent discussion of one such transition to socialism, see Batya Weinbaum, "Women in Transition to Socialism: Perspectives on the Chinese Case," *Review of Radical Political Economics,* Vol. 8, no. 1 (Spring 1976), pp. 34–58.

11. It is important to remember that in the preindustrial period, women contributed a large share to their families' subsistence—either by participating in a family craft or by agricultural activities. The initiation of wage work for women both allowed and required this contribution to take place independently from the men in the family. The new departure, then, was not that women earned income, but that they did so beyond their husbands' or fathers' control. Alice Clark, *The Working Life of Women in the Seventeenth Century* (New York: Kelly, 1969) describes women's preindustrial economic roles and the changes that occurred as capitalism progressed. It seems to be the case that Marx, Engels, and Kautsky were not fully aware of women's economic role before capitalism.

12. Karl Kautsky, *The Class Struggle* (New York: Norton, 1971), pp. 25–26.

13. We might add, "outside the household," Kautsky, *Class Struggle,* p. 26, our emphasis.

14. Cited in Neil Smelser, *Social Change and the Industrial Revolution* (Chicago: University of Chicago Press, 1959), p. 301.

15. These examples are from Heidi I. Hartmann, "Capitalism, Patriarchy, and Job Segregation by Sex," *Signs: Journal of Women in Culture and Society,* Vol. 1, no. 3, pt. 2 (Spring 1976), pp. 162–63.

16. Just as the factory laws were enacted for the benefit of all capitalists against the protest of some, so too, protective legislation for women and children may have been enacted by the state with a view toward the reproduction of the working class. Only a completely instrumentalist view of the state would deny that the factory laws and protective legislation legitimate the state by providing concessions and are responses to the demands of the working class itself.

17. For a more complete discussion of protective labor legislation and women, see Ann C. Hill, "Protective Labor Legislation for Women: Its Origin and Effect," mimeographed (New Haven, Conn.: Yale Law School, 1970) parts of which have been published in Barbara A. Babcock, Ann E. Freedman, Eleanor H. Norton, and Susan C. Ross, *Sex Discrimination and the Law: Causes and Remedies* (Boston: Little, Brown & Co., 1975), an excellent law text. Also see Hartmann, "Job Segregation by Sex," pp. 164–66.

18. A reading of Alice Clark, *The Working Life of Women*, and Ivy Pinchbeck, *Women Workers,* suggests that the expropriation of production from the home was followed by a social adjustment process creating the social norm of the family wage. Heidi Hartmann, in *Capitalism and Women's Work in the Home,* 1900–1930 (Ph.D. dissertation, Yale University, 1974; forthcoming Temple University Press) argues, based on qualitative data, that this process occurred in the U.S. in the early 20th century. One should be able to test this hypothesis quantitatively by examining family budget studies for different years and noting the trend of the proportion of the family income for different income groups, provided by the husband. However, this data is not available in comparable form for our period. The family wage resolution has probably been undermined in the post World War II period. Carolyn Shaw Bell, in "Working Women's Contribution to Family Income," *Eastern Economic Journal,* Vol. 1, no. 3 (July 1974), pp. 185–201, presents current data and argues that it is now incorrect to assume that the man is the primary earner of the family. Yet whatever the *actual* situation today or earlier in the century, we would argue that the social norm *was* and *is* that men should earn enough to support their families. To say it has been the norm is not to say it has been universally achieved. In fact, it is precisely the failure to achieve the norm that is noteworthy. Hence the observation that in the absence of sufficiently high wages, "normative" family patterns disappear, as for example, among immigrants in the nineteenth century and third world Americans today. Oscar Handlin, *Boston's Immigrants* (New York: Atheneum, 1968) discusses mid-nineteenth century Boston, where Irish women were employed in textiles; women constituted more than half of all wage laborers and often supported unemployed husbands. The debate about family structure among Black Americans today still rages; see Carol B. Stack, *All Our Kin: Strategies for Survival in a Black Community* (New York: Harper and Row, 1974), esp. Chap. 1. We would also argue (see below) that for most families the norm is upheld by the relative places men and women hold in the labor market.

19. Hartmann, *Women's Work,* argues that the nonworking wife was generally regarded as part of the male standard of living in the early twentieth century (see

p. 136, n. 6) and Gerstein, "Domestic Work," suggests that the norm of the working wife enters into the determination of the value of male labor power (see p. 121).

20. The importance of the fact that women perform labor services for men in the home cannot be overemphasized. As Pat Mainardi said in "The Politics of Housework" "[t]he measure of your oppression is his resistance" (in *Sisterhood Is Powerful,* ed. Robin Morgan [New York: Vintage Books, 1970], p. 451). Her article, perhaps as important for us as Firestone on love, is an analysis of power relations between women and men as exemplified by housework.

21. Libby Zimmerman has explored the relation of membership in the primary and secondary labor markets to family patterns in New England. See her "Women in the Economy: A Case Study of Lynn, Massachusetts, 1760–1974" (Unpublished Ph.D. dissertation, Heller School, Brandeis, 1977). Batya Weinbaum is currently exploring the relationship between family roles and places in the labor market. See her "Redefining the Question of Revolution," *Review of Radical Political Economics,* Vol. 9, no. 3 (Fall 1977), pp. 54, 78, and *The Curious Courtship of Women's Liberation and Socialism* (Boston: South End Press, 1978). Additional studies of the interaction of capitalism and patriarchy can be found in Zillah Eisenstein, ed., *Capitalist Patriarchy and the Case for Socialist Feminism* (New York: Monthly Review Press, 1978).

22. See Batya Weinbaum and Amy Bridges, "The Other Side of the Paycheck: Monopoly Capital and the Structure of Consumption," *Monthly Review,* Vol. 28, no. 3 (July–August 1976), pp. 88–103, for a discussion of women's consumption work.

23. For the view of the Frankfurt School, see Max Horkheimer, "Authority and the Family," in *Critical Theory* (New York: Herder & Herder, 1972) and Frankfurt Institute of Social Research, "The Family," in *Aspects of Sociology* (Boston: Beacon, 1972).

24. Carol Brown, "Patriarchial Capitalism and the Female-Headed Family," *Social Scientist* (India); no. 40–41 (November–December 1975), pp. 28–39.

25. For more on racial orders, see Stanley Greenberg, "Business Enterprise in a Racial Order," *Politics and Society,* Vol. 6, no. 2 (1976), pp. 213–40, and Michael Burroway, *The Color of Class in the Copper Mines: From African Advancement to Zambianization* (Manchester, England: Manchester University Press, Zambia Papers No. 7, 1972).

26. See Michael Reich, David Gordon, and Richard Edwards, "A Theory of Labor Market Segmentation," *American Economic Review,* Vol. 63, no. 2 (May 1973), pp. 359–365, and the book they edited, *Labor Market Segmentation* (Lexington, Mass: D. C. Heath, 1975) for a discussion of labor market segmentation.

27. See David M. Gordon, "Capitalist Efficiency and Socialist Efficiency," *Monthly Review,* Vol. 28, no. 3 (July–August 1976), pp. 19–39, for a discussion of qualitative efficiency (social control needs) and quantitative efficiency (accumulation needs).

28. For example, Milwaukee manufacturers organized workers in production

first according to ethnic groups, but later taught all workers to speak English, as technology and appropriate social control needs changed. See Gerd Korman, *Industrialization, Immigrants, and Americanizers, the View from Milwaukee, 1866–1921* (Madison: The State Historical Society of Wisconsin, 1967).

29. Carol Brown, in "Patriarchal Capitalism," argues, for example, that we are moving from "family-based" to "industrially-based" patriarchy within capitalism.

30. Stewart Ewen, *Captains of Consciousness* (New York: Random House, 1976).

31. Jean Gardiner, in "Women's Domestic Labour" (see n. 10), clarifies the cause for the shift in location of women's labor, from capital's point of view. She examines what capital needs (in terms of the level of real wages, the supply of labor, and the size of markets) at various stages of growth and of the business cycle. She argues that in times of boom or rapid growth it is likely that socializing housework (or more accurately capitalizing it) would be the dominant tendency, and that in times of recession, housework will be maintained in its traditional form. In attempting to assess the likely direction of the British economy, however, Gardiner does not assess the economic needs of patriarchy. We argue in this essay that unless one takes patriarchy as well as capital into account one cannot adequately assess the likely direction of the economic system.

32. For the proportion of people in nuclear families, see Peter Uhlenberg, "Cohort Variations in Family Life Cycle Experiences of U.S. Females," *Journal of Marriage and the Family,* Vol. 36, no. 5 (May 1974), pp. 284–92. For remarriage rates see Paul C. Glick and Arthur J. Norton, "Perspectives on the Recent Upturn in Divorce and Remarriage," *Demography,* Vol. 10 (1974), pp. 301–14. For divorce and income levels see Arthur J. Norton and Paul C. Glick, "Marital Instability: Past, Present, and Future," *Journal of Social Issues,* Vol. 32, no. 1 (1976), pp. 5–20. Also see Mary Jo Bane, *Here to Stay: American Families in the Twentieth Century* (New York: Basic Books, 1976).

33. Heather L. Ross and Isabel B. Sawhill, *Time of Transition: The Growth of Families Headed by Women* (Washington, D.C.: The Urban Institute, 1975).

34. See Kathryn E. Walker and Margaret E. Woods, *Time Use: A Measure of Household Production of Family Goods and Services* (Washington D.C.: American Home Economics Association, 1976); and Heidi I. Hartmann, "The Family as the Locus of Gender, Class, and Political Struggle: The Example of Housework," *Signs: Journal of Women in Culture and Society,* Vol. 6, no. 3 (Spring 1981).

35. Richard Sennett's and Jonathan Cobb's *The Hidden Injuries of Class* (New York: Random House, 1973) examines similar kinds of psychological phenomena within hierarchical relationships between men at work.

36. This should provide some clues to class differences in sexism, which we cannot explore here.

37. See John R. Seeley et al., *Crestwood Heights* (Toronto: University of Toronto Press, 1956), pp. 382–94. While men's place may be characterized as "in

production" this does not mean that women's place is simply "not in production"—her tasks, too, are shaped by capital. Her nonwage work is the resolution, on a day-to-day basis, of production for exchange with socially determined need, the provision of use values in a capitalist society (this is the context of consumption). See Weinbaum and Bridges, "The Other Side of the Paycheck," for a more complete discussion of this argument. The fact that women provide "merely" use values in a society dominated by exchange values can be used to denigrate women.

14

Barbara Ehrenreich (1940–)

Born in the United States, Barbara Ehrenreich was educated at Reed College and Rockefeller University, where she earned her doctorate in biology. Ehrenreich has been active for many years in the women's movement and in other movements for progressive social change. She is a contributing editor of Ms. *magazine and has been a board member of the National Women's Health Network. Since 1983 she has been cochair of the Democratic Socialists of America. She is currently a fellow of the Institute for Policy Studies and the New York Institute for the Humanities. A widely read feminist author, she has published books and articles on gender roles, leftist theory, the history of women's health care, sexuality, and welfare policy.*

The article "Life Without Father: Reconsidering Socialist-Feminist Theory" was written for Socialist Review *in 1984 as part of an effort to assess the development and contributions of, and dilemmas facing, socialist-feminism after nearly a decade of theory and practice.*

Life Without Father: Reconsidering Socialist-Feminist Theory

By the late 1970s, most socialist-feminists accepted as "theory" a certain description of the world: "the system" we confronted was actually composed of two systems or structures, capitalism and patriarchy. These two systems or structures were of roughly equal weight (never mind that capitalism was a mere infant compared to patriarchy, or, on the other hand, that patriarchy had no visible corporate headquarters). And capitalism and patriarchy were remarkably congenial and reinforced each other in thousands of ways (which it was the task of socialist-feminists to enumerate). As Zillah Eisenstein wrote in her 1979 anthology, *Capitalist Patriarchy and the Case for Socialist Feminism,* patriarchy and capitalism meshed so neatly that they had become "an *integral process:* specific elements of each system are necessitated by the other." Capitalism plus patriarchy described the whole world—or nearly: racism usually required extensive addenda—and that world was as orderly and smoothly functioning as the Newtonian universe.

It was a brave idea. Today, just a few years later, few people venture vast theoretical syntheses. In the course of time, many of the socialist-feminist system-builders of the seventies have become struggling academics, constrained to publish in respectable journals and keep their noses to the empirical grindstone. No longer do people meet, as many of us did, intensely and repeatedly, with an agenda of discovering the connections between *everything*—sex and class, housework and factory work, the family and the state, race and gender, sexuality and profits. If "capitalism plus patriarchy" was too easy an answer, at least we (the socialist-feminists of the seventies) asked the hard questions.

In a practical sense, too, it was a good theory, because it served to validate the existence of socialist-feminism. And I do not say this to trivialize the theory as self-serving. In the mid-seventies, in particular, socialist-feminists were an embattled species. On the one hand there was cultural and/or separatist feminism, drifting off toward spirituality, Great Goddess worship, and sociobiological theories of eternal male perfidy. To these "radical" feminists, socialist-feminists were male-identified dupes of the left, which they always described as the "male left." On the other hand, there was the left, which featured at the time a flourishing Marxist-Leninist tendency, bent on self-proletarianization and the "rectification" of everyone else. To it, socialist-feminists were agents of the petite bourgeoisie on assignment to distract working-class women from the main event, the class struggle.[1] The Marxist-Leninists and separatist feminists were extremes in a much wider radical context, but they helped define a political atmosphere in which socialist-feminism was hard put to establish that it was neither an oxymoron nor a form of treason.

The capitalism-plus-patriarchy paradigm was an ingenious defensive stance. If the world were really made up of two systems which were distinct and could not be reduced to each other, it was never enough to be just a socialist or just a feminist. If patriarchy were not only distinct but truly a "system" and not an attitude (like sexism) or a structure of the unconscious (as Juliet Mitchell saw it), those who opposed patriarchy were not just jousting with superstructural windmills: they were doing something real and "material." Finally, if patriarchy and capitalism were mutually reinforcing, it didn't make any sense to take on one without the other. If "the system" were capitalist-patriarchy, the only thoroughgoing oppositional politics was its mirror image, socialist-feminism.

Not all socialist-feminists were perfectly comfortable with the capitalism-plus-patriarchy formulation, however. For one thing, there always seemed to be something a little static and structuralist about it. Deirdre English and I argued, in our book *For Her Own Good,* that "patriarchy" ought to be left where Marx last saw it—in preindustrial European society—and that modern feminists should get on with the task of describing our own "sex-gender system," to use Gayle Rubin's phrase, in all its historic specificity. In addition, we were not convinced that capitalism and patriarchy were on as good terms as socialist-feminist theory demanded. If the theory couldn't account for the clashes as well as the reinforcements, it couldn't account for change—such as the emergence of feminism itself in the late eighteenth-century ferment of bourgeois and *antipatriarchal* liberalism. The world of capitalism plus patriarchy, endlessly abetting each other to form a closed system with just one seam, was a world without change, a world without a subject.

There is another problem. Things *have* changed, and in ways that make capitalist-patriarchy (or, better, "patriarchal capitalism") almost seem like a good deal. Socialist-feminists—not to mention many plain feminists and socialists—went wrong in assuming that "the system," whatever it was called, would, left to itself, reproduce itself.

Woman as Domestic Worker

The linchpin of socialist-feminist theory, the factor that put women, so to speak, on the Marxist map, was domestic work. In theory this work included everything women do in the home, from cooking and cleaning to reading bedtime stories and having sex. Radical feminists were quick to point out how women's efforts, whether serving coffee in a movement office or polishing the coffee table in a suburban home, served the interests of individual men. Socialist-feminists, coming along a few years later, asserted that women's domestic work served not only men, but capital. As Zillah Eisenstein put it:

> All the processes involved in domestic work help in the perpetuation of the existing society: (1) Women stabilize patriarchal structures (the family, housewife, mother, etc.) by fulfilling these roles. (2) Simultaneously, women are reproducing new workers, for both the paid and unpaid labor force . . . (3) They work as well in the labor force for lesser wages. (4) They stabilize the economy through their role as consumers. If the other side of production is consumption, the other side of capitalism is patriarchy.[2]

The discovery of the importance of women's domestic work put some flesh on the abstract union of capitalism and patriarchy. First, it gave patriarchy, which had otherwise had a somewhat ghostly quality (stretched as it was to include everything from rape to domestic slovenliness), a "material base" in "men's control over women's labor power." Second, it revealed a vivid parallel between "the private sphere," where patriarchy was still ensconced, and the "public sphere," where capital called the shots. In the public sphere, men labored at production, and in the private sphere women labored at "reproduction" (not only physical reproduction, but the reproduction of attitudes and capabilities required for all types of work). Finally it showed how essential patriarchy was to capitalism: most capitalist institutions produced only things, but the quintessential patriarchal institution, the family, produced the men who produced things—thanks to the labor of women.

It was not altogether clear where one went with this insight into the centrality of women's domestic work. If what women did in the home was so critical to the reproduction of both capitalism and patriarchy, shouldn't women be advised to stop doing it? Perhaps to sabotage it? The "wages for housework" position, which surfaced in this country in 1974, provided a strategic answer and an unintended caricature of American socialist-feminist theory. American socialist-feminists had argued that women's work was "necessary" to capitalism; the Italian feminists who launched wages for housework insisted, with considerable eloquence, that domestic work actually produced surplus value for the capitalists, just as what we ordinarily thought of as "productive" work in the public sphere did. If you were going to say that women's domestic work reproduced the labor power needed by capital, you might as well go all the way and say it was part of the productive process, just as much as the extraction and preparation of raw materials for manufacturing. Thus the home was an adjunct to the factory; in fact it was part of the great "social factory" (schools and all other sites of social reproduction) that kept the literal factories running. Women's domestic activities were no longer a shadowy contribution, but a potentially quantifiable productive factor with the distinguished Marxist status of "producing surplus value." The only difference between the man laboring for Fiat or Ford, and the woman laboring in her kitchen, was that she was unpaid—a patriarchal oversight that "wages for housework" would correct.

This proposal and the accompanying theory sent shock waves through American and British socialist-feminist networks. There were debates over the practicality of the demand: who would pay the wages for housework, which would, after all, constitute an enormous redistribution of wealth? There were even more debates at the level of high theory: was it scientifically accurate to say that housework produced surplus value? (A debate which, in my opinion, produced almost nothing of value.) Unfortunately there was much less attention to the bizarre, but utterly logical extreme to which wages-for-house-work theory took homegrown socialist-feminist theory. Everything women did in the home was in the service of capital and indispensable to capital. When a mother kissed her children goodnight she was "reproducing labor power." When a childless working woman brushed her teeth she too was reproducing labor power (her own, in this case), as an American wages-for-housework advocate argued in an exchange I participated in. This was commodity fetishism with a vengeance, and even with the modification that kissing, for example, serves the miniature patriarchy of the family more directly than corporate capital, it all boiled down to the same thing, since patriarchy was firmly in league with capital.

The Obsolescence of Capitalism-Plus-Patriarchy

Looking back from the vantage point of 1984, the debates of 1975 have an almost wistful quality. They (men, capitalists) needed us (women) to do all our traditional "womanly" things, and, if theory were to be trusted, they would apparently go to great lengths to keep us at it. Well, they don't seem to need us anymore—at least not that way—and if this weren't completely evident in 1975, it is inescapable today.

No matter how valuable the services of a full-time homemaker may be, fewer and fewer men earn enough to support one. The reasons for the disappearance of the male "family wage" and the associated influx of married women into the workforce have been discussed at length in these pages and elsewhere. The relevant point here is that for all we say about the "double day," employed women do far less housework than those who are full-time homemakers, 26 hours per week as compared to

55 hours per week.[3] Other family members may be compensating in part (though most studies I have seen show little increase in husbands' contributions), but it is hard not to conclude that the net amount of housework done has decreased dramatically. (By as much as 29 million hours per week per year during the peak years of women's influx into the labor market. Of course a certain amount of this work has been taken up by the commercial sector, especially by restaurants and fast-food places.) If women's work were as essential to the status quo as socialist-feminist theory argued, capitalism should have been seriously weakened by this withdrawal of women's labor. Yet no one is arguing, for example, that the decline of American productivity is due to unironed shirts and cold breakfasts. Nor has any sector of capital come forth and offered to restore the male family wage so that women can get back to their housework.

If capital does not seem to need women's domestic work as much as theory predicted, what about individual men? Mid-seventies feminist theory tended to portray men as enthusiastic claimants of women's services and labor, eagerly enlisting us to provide them with clean laundry, home-cooked meals, and heirs. If we have learned anything in the last ten years, it is that men have an unexpected ability to survive on fast food and the emotional solace of short-term relationships. There are, as Marxists say, "material" reasons for this. First, it is physically possible, thanks to laundromats, frozen food, and other conveniences, for even a poor man to live alone and without servants. Second, there have always been alternatives to spending a "family wage" on an actual family, but in the last few decades these alternatives have become more numerous and alluring. Not only are there the classic temptations of drink, gambling, and "loose women" to choose from, but stereos, well-appointed bachelor apartments, Club Med, sports cars, and so forth. For these and other reasons, American men have been abdicating their traditional roles as husbands, breadwinners, and the petty patriarchs of the "capitalism-plus-patriarchy" paradigm.[4]

In a larger sense, events and some belated realizations of the last few years should have undermined any faith we had in capital's willingness to promote the "reproduction of labor power." Capital as well as labor is internationally mobile, making United States corporations relatively independent of a working class born and bred in this or any one country. Furthermore, capitalists are not required to be industrial capitalists; they can disinvest in production and reinvest in real estate, financial speculation, of, if it suits their fancy, antiques, and they have done so despite any number of exhortations and supply-side incentives. In their actual practices and politics, capitalists and their representatives display remarkable indifference to the "reproduction of labor power," or, in less commoditized terms, the perpetuation of human life.

This is not to say that individual companies or industries do not maintain a detailed interest in our lives as consumers. They do, especially if we are lucky enough to be above "the buying point" in personal resources. But it is no longer possible to discern a uniform patriarchal or even pronatalist bias to this concern. Capitalists have figured out that two-paycheck couples buy more than husband-plus-housewife units, and that a society of singles potentially buys more than a society in which households are shared by three or more people. In times of labor insurgency, far-seeing representatives of the capitalist class have taken a minute interest in how ordinary people organize their lives, raise their children, etc. But this is not such a time, and it seems plain to me that the manufacturers of components for missile heads (a mile from where I sit) do not care whether my children are docile or cranky, and that the people who laced our drinking water with toxins (a mile the other way) could not much care whether I scrub the floors.

With hindsight, I am struck by what a *benevolent* system the "capitalism-plus-patriarchy" paradigm implied. In order to put women's hidden and private interests on the economic map, we had to assume that they reflected some much larger, systemic need. Since these efforts of women are in fact efforts to care and nurture, we had to project the functions of caring and nurturing onto the large, impersonal "structures" governing our all-too-functional construct of the world. Capitalism, inscribed with the will to "reproduce," became "patriarchal capitalism." This suggested that, in a sense, our theory was a family metaphor for the world: capitalists were "fathers," male workers were "sons," and all women were wives/daughters, both mediating the relations between fathers and sons[5] and producing more sons (and daughters) to keep the whole system going. The daughters had the worst deal, but at least they were members of the family, and this family, like actual ones, intended to keep on going—a motivation that is no longer so easy to attribute to the men who command our resources and our labor.

I think now that the "capitalism-plus-patriarchy" paradigm overpersonalized (and humanized) capitalism precisely because it depersonalized women. The paradigm granted "the system" an undue benevolence because it had no room for motive or caring on the part of women. Once all the interactions and efforts of childraising have been reduced to "reproducing labor power" (and children have been reduced to units of future labor power), there is no place for human aspiration or resistance. Once it has been determined that "all the processes involved in domestic work help in the perpetuation of the existing society," the women who perform these "processes" have lost all potential autonomy and human subjectivity. And once it is declared that all acts other than production are really "reproduction" (of labor power and the same old system of domination), only one kind of resistance *is* possible. Suicide, or the willful destruction of labor power.

Ironically, the intent of the "capitalism-plus-patriarchy" paradigm was to validate feminism and insert women, as actors, into the Marxist political calculus. The problem was that we were too deferential to Marxism. Socialist-feminists tried to account for large areas of women's experience—actually everyone's experience—in the language of commodities and exchange, as if that were the "scientific" way to proceed. It would have been better perhaps to turn the tables: for example, instead of asking, "How can we account for women's work in the home in Marxist terms?" we should have asked, "How can we account for what *men* do *outside* the home in feminist terms, in women's terms?" Trying to fit all of women's experience into the terms of the market didn't work, and adding on patriarchy, as an additional "structure," didn't help.

So where do we go from here? Is it possible to be a socialist-feminist without a "socialist-feminist theory"? Yes, of course it is. After all, those who are plain socialists or feminists get along—with no evident embarrassment—on just half a theory at best. The socialist-feminist project has always been larger and more daring than that of either of our progenitors, so if we have fumbled, it is in part because we attempted more.

But we do need a better way to understand the world we seek to act in. I hesitate to say we need a new "theory," because that word suggests a new set of structures and laws of mechanics to connect them. If not "capitalism-plus-patriarchy," you are probably thinking, what is it? The point is that "it" is changing, and in a more violent and cataclysmic fashion than we had any reason to expect. The statics of "capitalism-plus-patriarchy" help explain a world that is already receding from view—a world of relative affluence and apparent stability—where categories like "the family," "the state," and "the economy" were fixed and solid anchor-points for theory. Today, there is little we can take as fixed. "The family," so long refined in theory, looks more like an improvisation than an institution. A new technological revolution, on the scale of the one that swept in industrial capitalism (and state socialism) is transforming not only production but perception. Whole industries collapse into obsolescence; entire classes face ruthless dislocation. At the same time, the gap between the races domestically, between the north and the south internationally, widens to obscene proportions. Everywhere, women are being proletarianized, impoverished, becoming migrants, refugees, and inevitably "cheap labor." Meanwhile the great and lesser powers race to omnicide, making a mockery of all our diverse aspirations, struggles, and movements. Truly, "all that is solid melts into air"—that is, if it is not vaporized instantaneously.

I still believe that if there is a vantage point from which to comprehend and change the world, our world today, it will be socialist and feminist. Socialist—or perhaps here I should say Marxist—because a Marxist way of thinking, at its best, helps us understand the cutting edge of change, the blind driving force of capital, the dislocations, innovations, and global reshufflings. Feminist because feminism offers our best insight into that which is most ancient and intractable about our common situation: the gulf that divides the species by gender and, tragically, divides us all from nature and that which is most human in our nature. This is our intellectual heritage, and I do not think we have yet seen its full power—or our own.

Notes

1. Here I am passing over the story of the destruction of organized socialist-feminism by various Marxist-Leninist and Maoist groups in 1975–1977. In that period, sectarian groups joined and harassed or merely attacked from outside more than twenty socialist-feminist women's unions around the country, dragging almost all of them down to their deaths in arcane squabbles over the "correct line." I have never seen an adequate—or even inadequate—account of this nasty phase of left feminist history that addresses why the sects decided to go after socialist-feminist organizations at this time, and why socialist-feminist organizations, including the successful and level-headed Chicago Women's Liberation Union, crumbled in the face of so much bullshit. I would appreciate hearing from anyone with insights or relevant anecdotes to offer.

2. I don't mean to pick on Zillah Eisenstein; many other writers could be quoted, especially if I were doing a thorough review of socialist-feminist theory and its nuances (which I clearly am not). Eisenstein is singled out here because her introduction to and chapter in *Capitalist Patriarchy and the Case for Socialist Feminism* seem to me to provide an excellent state-of-the-art summary of mid-seventies socialist-feminist theory. The passage cited is on page 29.

3. Joann Vanek, "Time Spent in Housework," *Scientific American*, November 1974, p. 116.

4. One poignant indication of this shift in male values and expectations: when I was in my early twenties (in the early sixties), it seemed to require a certain daring and resourcefulness to dodge the traditional female fate of becoming a full-time housewife and mother. Today, I hear over and over from young women

that they would like to have a family or at least a child, but do not expect ever to be in a stable enough relationship to carry this off.

5. Insofar as the capitalists paid their workers enough to support a wife, thus buying off the workers with patriarchal privilege and ensuring labor peace—a crude summary of Heidi Hartmann's much more complex and interesting argument. The family metaphor was developed extensively by Batya Weinbaum in *The Curious Courtship of Women's Liberation and Socialism* (South End Press, 1980).

15

Ann Ferguson (1938–)

Ann Ferguson is a white socialist–feminist philosopher who developed her politics from both personal and theoretical practice. As a civil rights and anti–Vietnam War activist, she developed an interest in Marxism. Involvement in a sexist tenure battle, becoming a stepmother of three boys, adopting a black daughter, and becoming a lesbian led her to feminism. An attempt to synthesize the insights of marxism and feminism yielded a socialist-feminism, which was developed in practice in the seventies through participation in the Pioneer Valley Women's Union (a socialist-feminist community-based organization), and the Marxist Activist Philosophers (MAP), which is now the Socialist Feminist Philosophers Association (SOFPHIA). She has written articles on androgyny, lesbian identity, motherhood and sexuality, and the current sex debates within the women's movement and is currently finishing a book entitled Blood at the Root: Motherhood, Sexuality and Male Dominance *(forthcoming from Unwin Hyman).**

In this previously unpublished essay Ferguson argues that women have a radical political potential based on their joint position in the public world of production and the private world of sex/affective labor.

Sex and Work: Women as a New Revolutionary Class in the United States

Love, sex, and work—these are the areas in which different camps of radical social theorists (radical feminists, neo-Freudians and Marxists, respectively) have sought the creation and perpetuation of male dominance.

*This biographical sketch was written by the author.

The Freudian view is that the Oedipal love of children for their mother, repressed because of the power of the father, creates gender identities and sexual desires which perpetuate male dominance through the masculine desire to possess and dominate women and a feminine desire to be possessed and dominated by men. The standard Marxist position faults Freudianism for its ahistoricism, and argues that sexism is a by-product of class societies that will lose its material base under communism. Radical feminism critiques both Freudianism and Marxism, on the grounds that male power precedes both classism and repressed Oedipal love. Thus, for radical feminists, the primary social contradiction, one that ultimately explains all systems of social domination, is that between men and women.

Contemporary socialist feminists have been uneasy with the three options offered above, and most have argued that there are two interlocking but semiautonomous systems, capitalism and patriarchy, which together reinforce the continued existence of economic classes and male dominance. But there are many different views within the socialist feminist camp of just what patriarchy is, why it continues, and just how it connects with capitalism. What I shall do in this paper is to present one type of socialist feminist analysis which clarifies the base of male dominance, explains its persistence, and draws the conclusion that the changing position of men and women in the family and in the economy creates the possibility of women as a new revolutionary class in the contemporary United States.[1]

Sexuality and History

A basic omission in the classical marxist texts is the lack of a historical theory of the social production of sexuality. My perspective on sexuality is a dialectical materialist one analogous to, yet going beyond, Marx's and Engels's formulation of this position in *The German Ideology*. Marx and Engels waffle on the question of whether sex is a material need that should be considered a part of the material base of social organization. In one place they suggest "the reproduction of daily life" (which could include meeting sexual needs, producing children, and so forth) is coequal in importance to "the production of daily life," while in another they suggest that the family, originally part of the economic base of society (i.e., a primary form of organization to meet material needs) has become part of the superstructure of capitalist society, i.e., no longer a necessary form of organization to meet material needs. In other places,

Marx suggests that sex and procreation, as "natural" needs, do not need to be socially produced.

In short, classical marxism is ambiguous as to whether or not sex is an instinct that requires no social organization, a basic material need whose objects may be plastic but whose fulfillment requires social organization, or a social need created instrumentally to achieve other more basic needs (e.g., to provide for the procreation of the future labor force). Thus, it has no way of posing the question as to whether the different historical organizations of sexuality, the production of children, and social bonding (what I call *modes of sex/affective production*) create systems in which men have a material interest in dominating and exploiting women that does not derive merely from the mechanisms that reproduce class domination (cf. also Rubin, 1975; Flax, 1976; Eisenstein, 1979).

I maintain that the standard marxist idea of an exclusive class position for each individual no longer captures the complicated and contradictory reality of productive relations in racist capitalist public patriarchy. Rather, there are at least *four* different historically developed class relationships that can characterize a person at the same time: *race class, sex class, family class,* and *individual economic class*. Given the appropriate historical conditions, an individual's subordinate class role in any one of these aspects can serve as the material base for their development of revolutionary agency.

A Socialist-Feminist Trisystems Theory

The significance of using the concept of *class* to refer to the social opposition of races, genders, families, and individuals (e.g., race class, sex class, family class, and economic class) in U.S. society today is to insist that referring to an *individual's* relation to production with narrow marxist characterizations of *class* in capitalist society obscures a number of other social oppositions that turn on one's relation to production in other ways than simply whether one is a wage laborer or an owner. Thus, other ways that the material interests of groups may be socially structured in opposition to each other are ignored.

Consider the puzzle of defining an individual's economic class solely by relation to his or her individual relation to capitalist production. On this criterion, someone is a member of the working class if she or he works for wages and a member of the capitalist class if his or her income is gained primarily from returns on private ownership of the means of production. But not all members of society have an individual economic class: for example, full-time housewives are defined by their husband's relation to production, and minors are defined by their parent's relation to production.

Whether or not a person has an individual economic class, they do at least (and in addition) have a family class, that is, a position in a family whose individual "breadwinner(s)" bear(s) (a) certain relation(s) to production. One of the confusions about class identity comes from the situation in which an individual whose family class as defined by the father's work is different than their individual economic class as an adult, or their new family class, if they marry a man with an economic class different position from their father's. This puzzle can be resolved by defining two relations—individual economic and family economic class—and realizing that the historical and cultural self-identity relevant for political organizing will depend as much on the latter as on the former. That is, since one's self-identified class depends to a large degree on education, life-style, social identification and social bonds, we cannot see family class as simply an additive function of the individual economic relations of husband and wife. Thus, a man may own a small grocery store and his wife may work part time in a factory, or she may be a full-time housewife. In either case, because of the cultural implications of the man's position and money, the family class of the couple would likely be petit bourgeois.

Analogously, we can see the sexual and racial divisions of labor in wage labor, family-households, and community living situations as aspects of the productive organization of our society that create an opposition of material interests between men and women, whites and nonwhites. The structural likelihood that women and minorities, no matter what individual or family class they come from, will be in less rewarded types of work than males and whites and that minorities will be in less privileged neighborhoods suggests that racial and gender identities should be seen as economic oppositions in a racist and sexist society that creates gender and race as oppositional classes. Gender- and race-segregated labor and the lower relative income available to minorities and women benefit the white male working class, thus challenging Marx's idea that capitalism homogenizes labor. By conceptualizing racism, sexism, and capitalism as semiautonomous systems of social domination, we see that it is not just the capitalist class who exploits the working class; the white male working class can also be said to exploit women and minorities (Bowles and Gintis, 1977).[2]

Three key overlapping systems of social domination (capitalism, racism, and sexism) define an individual's material interests in our society.

Developing contradictions between these class positions that define individuals (due to changes in the family and the economy) create the potential for women to become a new revolutionary class in the United States. My analysis provides a methodological framework for socialist-feminist intuitions that male control in the family and in wage labor is just as important to understanding the persistence of male domination as is capitalist control of economic production. The historically developing contradictions between race, sex, family, and economic class are instabilities around which it is important to focus our political organizing as feminists.

The Marxist Concept of Class

But are, or can, women be a class? To answer this question we must first define and clarify the concept of class. One of the strengths of the marxist approach to understanding society and revolutionary change is its ability to explain revolutionary change. Marx and Engels justify their theory that class struggle is the moving force of history by using a class analysis to explain the transition from feudalism to capitalism, the French Revolution, the Paris Commune, and so forth. The concept of economic class they develop is not simply an intellectual starting point that must be assumed to accept the rest of their theory; rather, they apply their concept in a way that helps us make sense out of a period of revolutionary change. And their concept not only seems to explain past historical change, it also helps identify those groups who may be key political agents for revolutionary change in present society.

A problem with applying the marxist concept of class to analyze new developments in advanced capitalism is that the cluster of criteria associated with the applications Marx and Engels made of the concept to understand feudalism and early capitalism may no longer identify one unambiguous group in the social relations of production. We need, therefore, to unpack the marxist concept of *economic class* to see which of the traditional criteria still apply.

The common core of the marxist concept of economic class is a group defined in both political and economic terms; that is, a *class* is a group of people who, because of the kind of work they do and the power relations involved in that work in relation to other groups, have a common interest in either maintaining the system or overthrowing it. Class, then, has to be specified in terms of certain relations to production that individuals bear to each other in a given mode of production.

We need to specify more clearly what the relevant relation to production is, and what sort of power relations are involved, in order to make the concept of class concrete. We can isolate at least five criteria of class that have been given or assumed by marxists in their discussions of class differences. The first three criteria are clearly part of the basic conceptual apparatus of the classical marxist theorists: Marx and Engels, Lenin, and Stalin.

Criterion 1: Exploitation Relations. According to this criterion, an exploiting class in a society is one that owns and/or controls the means of production in that society in a way which allows it to expropriate the social surplus of a society. Whether that is defined in terms of surplus labor time or of surplus value depends on what specific mode of production (e.g., feudalism, capitalism) is involved. The other classes of society are then defined in contrast to the exploiting class: that is, producers who are not owners but who have rights to appropriate part of their product (e.g., peasants), producers who sell their labor as a commodity (proletariat). I call this criterion the economic criterion of class.

Criterion 2: Political Relations. Central to the classical marxist conception of history is the idea that class conflict is the moving force for social revolution. Classes thought of as political entities are defined in terms of their potential as a cohesive reactionary or revolutionary force—that is, groups which, because of their economic relation to production as defined in criterion 1, are expected to develop cohesive interests and a common self-consciousness. The four thinkers mentioned earlier all seem to have held an inevitability thesis with respect to the relations between criteria 1 and 2 for certain key classes. That is, certain groups of individuals with objectively similar exploited positions in production, a "class in itself," would come to be a class "for itself," a group that is conscious of its common situation and comes to identify itself as a political group fighting for a common interest.[3] Not all economic classes would become political classes: as we will see, for example, Marx did not think peasants could become a political class. Hence peasants by themselves could not become a revolutionary class. The key to whether or not an economic group will become a political group seems to be the existence of historical and social conditions that give the group *historical cohesiveness*. This is our third criterion of class.

Criterion 3: Historical Cohesiveness. This criterion stresses the point that classes are not simply abstract collections of individuals who fit under certain labels because social scientists find it helpful to so describe them. Rather, they are groups of people who share a common historical background, a common culture, common values, and therefore, in one way or another, some collective self-consciousness of themselves as members of a group with a common identity and common interests.[4] The way I see it, there may be both structural and accidental reasons for an economic class not developing the historical cohesiveness that is a necessary condition for further development into a political class "for itself." Marx appears to be giving some structural arguments why peasants do not form a class, according to criteria 2 and 3, in *The Eighteenth Brumaire:*

> The small-holding peasants form a vast mass, the members of which live in similar conditions but without entering into manifold relations with one another. Their mode of production isolates them from one another instead of bringing them into mutual intercourse. The isolation is increased by France's bad means of communication and by the poverty of the peasants. In so far as there is merely local interconnection among these small-holding peasants, and the identity of their interests begets no community, no national bond and no political organization among them, they do not form a class. They are consequently incapable of enforcing their class interests in their own name, whether through parliament or through a convention. They cannot represent themselves, they must be represented (Marx, 1972 pp. 123–24).

There are plausible historical reasons why the U.S. working class has not developed the class unity necessary to meet criteria 2 and 3, such as ethnic differences resulting from successive waves of immigration from different cultures, racism caused by the historical presence of slavery in the United States, work patterns of noise and isolation, which make it difficult for workers to communicate on the job, suburbanization which fragments workers' sense of common social community with each other, and elitist trade unions which, by dividing skilled from unskilled workers, have defused the trade union movement to the point where fewer than 15 percent of American workers are represented by trade unions.

An implicit appeal to the criterion of historical cohesiveness as a means of categorizing individuals who otherwise have disparate relations to production (hence do not meet criterion 1) seems to underlie Poulantzas's categorization of salaried teachers, entertainers, middle managers, and others as the "new petty bourgeoisie" (Poulantzas, 1975). Though they are not self-employed, as are the traditional petty bourgeoisie, they share the values and ideological outlook of this group, that is, they are individualistic, educated defenders of the values of free enterprise.

The second set of criteria for class has been developed by neo-marxists out of the criteria that may have been implicit in some of the works of the classical writers but were never spelled out. It seems fair to summarize the historical function of these criteria for marxist theory by saying that they all attempt to account for the failure of the working classes in the advanced capitalist countries to become a unified revolutionary class. Either they stress the relations of political *domination and submission* between capitalist and working calsses because of the growth of the state and ideological institutions like the mass media. Or they isolate some new class that has a privileged position in the new social relations of production by virtue of its control and *autonomy* and whose ideological and *social function* perpetuate the status quo (Poulantzas, 1975; Gorz, 1967; Wright, 1978; Ehrenreichs, 1979).

Criterion 4: Domination Relations. This criterion for making distinctions between classes is based on relations of domination and submission, primarily tied to authority and control of the process of work. Those who control the labor power of others are in one class, while those who do not are in another. People who are supervisors, managers, or foremen are obvious examples of those who control other workers. Less obvious examples are doctors' control of nurses, teachers' control over their students, who can be seen as "workers in training," welfare officials' control of recipients' "work" in child-raising, men's control of women's work in the home, and parents' control of children (future workers). Some of these examples would be disputed by those marxists who still hold that exploitation relations are the only means of distinguishing classes. They would deny that work in the home or work in learning at school fits into the category of "productive work," that is, work that produces surplus value. They would conclude that such domination relations cannot be seen to be "exploitative" in the important sense which constitutes a class distinction. Others would call them classes but relegate them to a secondary status in any revolutionary process (e.g., Resnick and Wolff distinguish between "fundamental" and "subsumed" classes: only the former can be dynamic movers and changers of a society whereas the latter serve to reproduce status quo domination relations; see Wolff and Resnick, 1987).

Another aspect of work relations closely related to domination/submission is autonomy, that is, how much autonomy a worker has in producing his or her product and shaping the work process relative to other workers. This suggests a fifth criterion.

Criterion 5: Autonomy. We might want to maintain that those who control their own labor and the product of their labor are in one class while those who are controlled are in another class.[5]

This group overlaps but is not quite coextensive with the dominating, as opposed to the dominated, class covered by criterion 4. Individuals might control their own labor (e.g., a free-lance photographer), yet not control the labor power of others. Conversely, a person might be a dominator (e.g., a foreman or police officer), yet not be autonomous if he or she is, in turn, controlled by bosses.

Sex/Affective Production

If women and men belong to oppositional sex classes, in addition to having different relations to capitalist production as individuals and as members of their specific races and families, what system of production so divides them? My theory holds that sexism is based in a semiautonomous system of social domination that persists throughout different modes of economic production. There are historically various ways of organizing, shaping, and molding the human desires connected to sexuality and love, and consequently parenting and social bonding. These systems, which I call modes of *sex/affective production*, have also been called *desiring production* by Deleuze and Guattari (1977) and *sex/gender systems* by Gayle Rubin (1975). It is in part through these systems, which socially construct and produce the specific forms of the more general human material need for social union and physical sexual satisfaction I call "sex/affective energy," that different forms of male dominance as well as other types of social domination (e.g., racism, ethnicism, capitalism, and other class-divided systems of social domination) are reproduced.

My approach to understanding sexuality, social bonding, and nurturance is that these are all material needs that, since they have no specific biologically given objects, must be socially organized and produced. In this respect sex/affective energy is like the material need of hunger and shelter: though they have a biological base, their specific objects (e.g., particular food and shelter preferences) must be culturally produced. Furthermore, the by-product of heterosexual sexuality, children, not only is functionally connected to the reproduction of the economy of any society, but also generates new sex/affective needs for, and objects of, nurturant energy.

Thus, sex/affective productive systems are both *like* economic modes of production and *functionally part* of such systems in that they are human modes of organizing that both create the social objects of the material needs connected to sex/affective energy and then organize human labor to achieve them. Like economic modes of production, they can also contain dialectical aspects: that is, there may be opposing tendencies in the system that undermine its ability to reproduce itself. Just as Marx thought that the dialectical instabilities in the capitalist system were bound to create a revolutionary movement for social change in the hitherto oppressed working class, the instabilities in our present form of patriarchal sex/affective production present the possibilities for a radical movement for social change in the oppressed sex class of women.

Every society must have one or more historically developed modes of sex/affective production to meet key human needs whose satisfaction is just as basic to the functioning of human society as is the satisfaction of the material needs of hunger and physical security. The satisfaction of these other key human needs—sexuality, nurturance, and children—has been based in the family household in the earlier phases of capitalism. And though our contemporary mode of sex/affective production, racist public patriarchal capitalism, has involved a shift in the *material base* of patriarchy (it is now jointly reproduced by sex/affective relations in the public spheres of wage labor and the welfare state, as well as those in the family), a complete understanding of the power and class relations in capitalism still must include an analysis of the sex/class relations of *family production*.

One way to characterize the interdependence between relations of sex/affective production and the economic system as a whole is to use the concept of a *social formation*. A social formation is a system of production in use in a particular society at a specific time that may contain within it several different historically developed modes of production. A historical example of a social formation is the combined U.S. capitalist/slave modes of production before the Civil War. Our present U.S. economic system can be thought of as a social formation consisting in part of capitalist and patriarchal modes of production. It has a codominant set of relations: (1) those between capital and wage labor and (2) those between men and women in patriarchal sex/affective production. It also has a subordinate set of class relations characteristic of welfare state capitalism—the existence of a class of institutionalized poor, that is, those subsidized by the state on welfare or unemployment. Its racial divisions of wage labor and its general separation of races into different living communities create a set of economic and sex/affective domination relations between the white dominant race and subordinate nonwhite races. Finally, the dominant mode of capitalist production is that controlled by multinational corporations, while a small subordinate sector of capitalist production involves small family businesses (the traditional petite bourgeoisie).

"Patriarchy" I define as a system of social relations in a society such that those who perform what is regarded as the "male" role (e.g., do "male" work) have more social power than, *exploit*, and *control* those who perform what is regarded as the "female" role (i.e., do women's work).[6] This use of the concept of patriarchy is somewhat broader than its original use, to mean "control by the father." I use the term *patriarchy* rather than the vaguer concept of *male dominance* as my technical term because in my view the origin, persistence, and potential undermining of male power and domination of women in all the institutions of society stems from the relative strength or weakness of male dominance and exploitation of women in the family and/or associated kin networks.

An argument for the claim that male/female social relations are co-dominant with other social relations of production is the universal presence in all societies of what Gayle Rubin calls "sex/gender" systems (Rubin, 1975), that is, culturally defined male and female roles children learn as part of their social identity.[7] The sex/gender system organizes material work and services, by defining what is culturally acceptable as man's and woman's work. It also organizes nurturance, sexuality, and procreation by directing sexual urges (in most societies toward heterosexual relations and nonincestuous ties), by indicating possible friendships, and by defining parenthood roles and/or kinship ties and responsibilities.[8]

Patriarchal relations have persisted through many different modes of economic production, including socialist modes of production such as those in Russia, China, and Cuba. The articulation of different modes of patriarchal sex/affective production with different economic modes of production has meant that the *content* of the sexual division of labor varies (e.g., in some modes of sex/affective production and some social formations men work for wage labor and women do not, while in others, e.g., feudal production, neither men nor women work for wages). Other relations of exploitation vary as well (e.g., whether it is a feudal lord, the male head of the family, or a capitalist who benefits from the reproduction of labor power in a family).

Patriarchal family production involves unequal and exploitative relations between men and women in domestic maintenance and sex/affective work. However, the *amount* of power the man has in relation to the woman in the family varies with their relation to the dominant mode of production. So, if the woman has an individual economic class (e.g., if she is working for wage labor, or has an independent income) and if she is making equal wages it will be harder for the man to appropriate the surplus in wages after basic family needs are met. In general the typical nuclear family in the United States is less patriarchal than those in earlier periods, and a substantial minority of households are woman-headed. Nonetheless, the historical prevalence of the patriarchal family and a sexual division of labor has created a male-dominated sexual division of wage labor in which women's work is paid less, is usually part time, and has less job security than men's (Davies, 1979; Hartmann, 1981). Those women-headed households cannot be said to be matriarchal: the fact that the majority live below the poverty line and that more than a third must depend on the federal government for welfare payments (whose size and availability depend on the changing largesse of a male-dominated government) suggests that the *fact* of male domination has not changed as much as the mechanisms by which it is reinforced.

Women as Sex Class in the Patriarchal Nuclear Family

Men and women are in *sex classes* in capitalist society today, classes defined by the sexual division of labor in the family (in both the male-headed nuclear family and the mother-headed family) and reinforced by the sexual division of wage labor. In this section I present my arguments to show that women are exploited relative to men in most contemporary forms of the family, that they are dominated and have little autonomy. They thus meet criteria 1, 4, and 5 for class identity discussed earlier. In the following section I discuss the historical cohesiveness of the class (criterion 3) and the implications of whether women can become a "class for itself" (criterion 2).

By the capitalist patriarchal nuclear family (CPNF) I mean an economic unit of man, woman, and possibly children, in which the man works full time in wage labor (is thus the main breadwinner), while the woman works as the primary domestic and child-care worker in the home.[9] If she is employed in wage labor, she is not employed more than part time.

How then do men exploit women in the CPNF? Four goods are produced in sex/affective production in the family: domestic maintenance, children, nurturance, and sexuality. Since a sex/affective productive system is a system of exchange of goods and labor, we can classify it in terms of the power relations involved; that is, is there an equal exchange between producers? If not, who controls the exchange? Patriarchal sex/affective production is characterized by unequal exchange between men and women: women receive less of the goods produced than men, and typically work harder, that is, spend more time producing them. The relations between men and women can be considered *exploitative* because the man is able to appropriate more of the woman's labor time for his own use than she is of his, and he also gets more of the goods produced (see also Delphy, 1984; Folbre, 1982, 1983).[10] It is *oppressive* because the sex/gender roles taught to boys and girls to perpetuate the sexual division of labor develop a female personality structure that internalizes the goal to produce more for men and to accept less for herself (see also Barrett, 1980).

The points made here about the exploitation and control by men of women in the CPNF apply as well to most other types of family household in the United States today. Although many families are not of the CPNF structure (e.g., female-headed households, or families in which both husband and wife work full time), most other families with children involve exploitation of the mother's work by the father. This result is partly structural and partly due to social pressure on the mother to accept an unequal sexual division of labor. After all the CPNF is the legitimized arrangement to which schools, wage labor jobs, and many social services (e.g., welfare, social security) are coordinated (Barrett and McIntosh, 1982). Those who do not live in a patriarchal nuclear family are not only inconvenienced but suffer a loss of status. Schools and older kin make full-time wage-earning mothers feel guilty for time not spent with their children. The absence of affordable child care and the relatively better pay of husbands makes it reasonable for mothers rather than fathers to work low-pay jobs whose flexible hours allow mothers to do child care. Thus mothers, not fathers, tend to suffer the "second shift" problem of a full shift of wage work added to another shift of child care and housework at home.

Many female-headed households suffer a loss of family class: their new individual economic class is lower than their family class was (when this is defined by their father or former husband's relations to production) (Sidel, 1986). As Delphy (1984) has pointed out, women in such families continue to be exploited by the absent fathers: for women now must perform two full-time jobs without much help: being the breadwinner and doing the housework and child care.

Let me sum up the points presented about the inequalities between men and women in patriarchal capitalism in relation to the criteria for class identity to show why I maintain that women and men form sex classes.

Use of the first criterion, exploitation relations, usually assumes that exploitation involves ownership and/or control of production. I have argued here that men in capitalist patriarchies (whether or not they are actually present in the family household) own the wage and thus control sex/affective production in such a way as to be able to expropriate the surplus: surplus wages, surplus nurturance, and sexuality. Though the CPNF is no longer the dominant union of domestic maintenance and sex/affective production, its historical impact on the sexual division of wage labor, welfare state provisions, and the legal structures of child support continues to create a situation of exploitative sex/affective exchange between men and women, whether in other family households, in wage labor, in politics, or in the courts.

The fourth and fifth criteria, domination and autonomy relations, can be shown to apply to men and women as sex classes, both in the family and in other spheres of social life. If we remember that we are comparing power relations not only in the spheres of housework versus wage work but also the sex/affective work of sexuality and nurturance, it becomes clearer how the analogy holds. After all, the type of work women do in wage labor is primarily gendered sex/affective labor, that is, it involves women doing physical maintenance (nursing, health care), providing nurturance and sexuality (waitressing and other service work with sexual overtones) in which men as clients, bosses, and customers control the exchange.

Men dominate and control women in sexual activity and in nurturance (see Deming, 1973; Tax, 1970). It can be argued further that men are more autonomous in their sexual activities because they do them as consumers and not as part of their gender-defined work in the family. Here is a quote from a worker at Fisher Body Plant about the connections between his sexuality and his wife's:

> Because my need to be sexually re-vitalized each day is so great, it becomes the first and most basic part of a contract I need to make in order to ensure it.
>
> The goal of this contract is stability, and it includes whatever I need to consume: sex, food, clothes, a house, perhaps children. My partner in this contract is in most cases a woman; by now she is as much a slave to my need to consume as I am a slave to Fisher Body's need to consume me. What does she produce? Again, sex, food, clothes, a house, babies. What does she consume for all this effort?—all the material wealth I can offer plus a life outside of a brutal and uncompromising labor market. Within this picture, it's easy to see why many women get bored with sex. They get bored for the same reason I get bored with stacking bucket seats in cars. (Lippert, 1977)

If sex is work for women and play for men, nurturance is as well. This is why those men who have picked up some nurturance skills tend to be more autonomous in their use. That is, since men's sense of gender success is not bound up with being a good nurturer, they are freer not to use nurturance skills in ways that may be self-destructive of their other needs (as in the self-sacrifice women often engage in).

In this section I have argued that three out of the five criteria marxists have put forward to pick out class identity apply to men and women as sex classes. In the next section we consider whether women as a group have the sort of political potential Marx and Engels originally foresaw for the working class in capitalism. Are women a revolutionary class? Do we have historical cohesiveness (criterion 3)? And can we become a "class for itself" (criterion 2)?

Women as a Revolutionary Class

The theoretical framework I have advanced here allows individuals to be members of overlapping classes: *family class, sex class, race class*,[11] and *individual economic class*. We need to know what class an individual will be likely to identify with if she or he is a member of several classes whose interests contradict each other. Are there laws of motion of advanced capitalist patriarchal social formations that can indicate where key contradictions will develop that allow the political importance of membership in one class to supersede that of membership in another class?

The task is to show that women are unlike Marx's characterization of peasants and like his characterization of the working class. Women have to be able to identify with sex class over family class, to be aware of ourselves as a historically cohesive group, with a common culture and common interests by virtue of our position in the sexual division of labor in the family and in society. We need evidence of the existence of different men's and women's cultures, as well as some understanding of how growing contradictions between *sex class* and *family class* identification for women tend to push women to identify with the first.

There is certainly evidence of separate men's and women's cultures that are more distinctive the more patriarchal the society.[12] Historically, however, there are few occasions in which sex class bonding has taken precedence to family class bonding, and these exceptions have often occurred, as in the first wave women's movement in the nineteenth-century United States, when family class positions as well as gender roles were in a state of transition because of changes in the mode of material economic production (Rossi, 1974). That movement failed to sustain the connection between middle-class and working-class women, or between northern white and southern black women because the family class identification of the middle-class women (primarily petit bourgeois and wealthy farmers) prevented them from challenging either the economic or the racial class structure of American racist capitalism (Davis, 1981; Kraditor, 1965).

The situation is changing, however, in advanced capitalist societies. There are increasing contradictions between the social relations of capitalistic production and the social relations of patriarchal sex/affective production in the family. The economic material conditions for these developments include: (1) the existence of wage-labor jobs for women that pay a subsistence wage, (2) the existence of state welfare that will support women and children without a husband, coupled with (3) the availability of mass-produced contraceptives that allow women more control over their fertility, and (4) inflationary pressures on family income, which cause women to seek part- or full-time wage work to supplement their husband's income.

What results from these conditions is an increasingly high rate of instability in patriarchal nuclear families: more divorce, less communal moral sanctions about "keeping the family together for the children," and more of an emphasis on the individual happiness of each partner. U.S. individualism, which always encouraged men to "do their own thing," is now increasingly an acceptable value system for women unhappy in marriage. This shift in morality parallels the change in material conditions that allow for the possibility that women can support themselves outside of the patriarchal family. Inequalities in capitalist patriarchal sex/affective production have historically been maintained because most women have not had many viable alternatives outside the nuclear family except prostitution. But the increasing number of state sector, clerical, and service jobs defined as "women's work" has now provided women with such options. Even those women who are not seeking to stay single or to break out of unhappy marriages can become caught up in the contradiction between the wage-labor job they take to increase their family's income, and the strain that subsequently occurs in family relations because of the increase in the unequal sexual division of labor this causes. (Is the husband now going to shoulder more housework? Are the kids? How will all of them deal with less attention from wife and mom?)

It is not only the new available options for work outside the family that are relevant to women's changing position. The fact is that with the increased instability of nuclear families, women can no longer count on being maintained in families as non-wage-earning housewifes and thus achieve the old "wife-mother" gender ideal.[13] This makes it more likely that women will relate to sex class rather than family class as their prime source of identity. As wage workers women are thrown into proximity with other women not in their family. Because of sexual segregation of the work force into men's and women's jobs, women can identify with other women and make sex class identification primary.

Another reason that women are forced to rely more on their sex class identity than on their family class identity these days is that many women have to face the likelihood that they will lose their family class. Most wage-labor possibilities for women are working-class jobs. If a woman remains single, she must either take a working-class job or be "poor" (e.g., go on welfare, an option open primarily to single mothers). If a woman marries, she will likely be divorced at least once in her lifetime, in which case she faces the same possibilities. Many single and divorced women whose family class was professional-managerial are not members of the working class, as defined by their individual economic class (Sidel, 1986); and increasing numbers of women whose original family class was working class have moved downward to the poor (on welfare).[14]

Alimony and child support do not cushion women from these hazards of being a woman in U.S. society today. Only 14 percent of divorced women in the United States in 1976 were even awarded alimony by the courts, and only half that number collected it regularly. As for child support, a full half of the men ordered to pay child support are paying "practically nothing," and 90 percent of women receiving child support do not receive it regularly (Women's Agenda, 1976b). "No-fault" divorce legislation has not improved matters, either. A recent study of the effects of the California no-fault legislation discovered that women's incomes dropped 45 percent, while men's increased 73 percent as the result of divorce (Weitzman, 1985). Furthermore, a homemaker is not entitled to social security benefits if divorced, so she has no prospects of a pension to support her in old age. A middle-aged divorcee is often thrown on the streets after years of homemaking with no marketable skills and not the energy or sense of self to start from the beginning to make a new life for herself.

Not only can women not count on wife and motherhood as a life concentration that will allow for a secure economic future, but they cannot count on an easy way to care for their children. There is a contradiction between capitalist production demands and the existing patriarchal sex/affective production system for handling child care. Inflation requires many women to supplement the husband's income by wage labor, yet there is little available child care for children under six. In 1976 wage-working mothers had 27.6 million children under six (public school age), yet there were only one million licensed day care slots for these children (Women's

Agenda, 1976a). Sadly, after eleven years the situation is not improved in 1987. Both single and married working mothers thus can identify around the sex class issue of child care.

I have given reasons to support the belief that women constitute a sex class that is developing historical cohesiveness that cuts across family and race class lines because of contradictions in the social relations of material and sex/affective production. But is this enough to make women a revolutionary class?

Yes! Because women are a pivotal class in terms of the work we perform in reproducing both capitalist and patriarchal relations of production. Women are the "culture-bearers" of family class *and* sex class values. We teach children expectations and goals, train them in rules of obedience to authority (acting as their first and most important role models in this area), and in general, as the major child rearers, do essential work in child socialization necessary to continuing capitalist and patriarchal culture. Second, men depend on women for the reproduction of their labor power by continued women's work in domestic maintenance, nurturance, and sexuality.

Women as a sex class, then, do have potential disruptive power in the interconnected systems of capitalist and patriarchal sex/affective production. If women refuse to do their work as presently organized, neither capitalism nor patriarchy could continue to function.

Though women are a sex class that cuts across family, individual economic, and race classes, most women (all but those in the capitalist class) are a potentially revolutionary class because we have no objective interests as a sex class in maintaining the present system. Thus when women organize with other women in sex class identification, we can use the pivotal power gained by the importance of our social function in reproducing capitalist patriarchy to challenge the continuance of the patriarchal family and to raise the progressive aspects involved in family class identification for members of the professional-managerial class, working class, or poor. The fact that women as a sex class cut across the divisions of professional-managerial, working class, and poor, as well as across race class, can be a key to organizing progressive class alliances between these groups. There are some indications that the increasing consciousness of economic class and race issues[15] have allowed the women's movement to correct some of its earlier middle-class approach; for example, broadening such demands as the right to abortion and birth control to include opposition to forced sterilization and demands for state and federal funds for abortion. Developing working women's unions is another way to connect feminism with working-class women (9 to 5 in Boston, CLUW, WAGE in California).

Conclusion

I have argued that women are a potentially revolutionary class. But we are not the only one. The working class is potentially revolutionary, as are minority races and elements of the professional-managerial class. Indeed, because of the complicated objective contradictions between the professional–managerial and working classes, and between sex class, family class, race class, and individual economic class, a socialist and feminist revolution is not possible in this country without class alliances of progressive people who identify the trisystem social formation of capitalism, patriarchy, *and* racism as the enemy. It stands to reason that different people will take different issues as their primary focus for organizing, some identifying working class, some women's issues, some racism, and some joint professional-managerial and working-class issues. It is unclear at this point what kind of structure—coalitions, a party, grass-root organizations, caucuses—is needed to produce the ideal alliance. The practical implication of this essay is that only an analysis which takes into account objective contradictions between classes in the United States today and the diverse class positions occupied by women and men can provide us with the understanding necessary to engage in the kind of practice that will teach us how and who to organize in the fight against racism, capitalism, and patriarchy.

Notes

1. My theory has developed with the aid of numerous discussions with members of the former Marxist Activist Philosophers group (MAP), now the Socialist-Feminist Philosophers Association (SOFPHIA), as well as Sam Bowles and Nancy Folbre. I wish to thank them all for their substantial help, even when they did not agree with me! For more development of my theory, see Ferguson, 1984, 1986, 1987.

2. According to Bowles and Gintis (1977), different rates of exploitation can be assigned to different types of labor within the wage-labor force. Once we can say that some workers *exploit* others, we can argue either that these sectors of the working class occupy class-contradictory positions (Wright, 1978), different

classes (Ehrenreichs, 1979; Poulantzas, 1975), or more than one class at a time including sex class and race class another. The latter is my position.

3. The failure of working classes in Western capitalist countries to become revolutionary classes seems to undermine this prediction, leading Lukács to develop the concept of "false consciousness" (Lukács, 1968) and Gramsci the notion of the cultural "hegemony" (i.e., pervasiveness and power) of values and ideas defending the status quo and hence the interests of the capitalist class (Gramsci, 1971).

4. The classic emphasis on the importance of class culture in the formation of a class is E. P. Thompson's *History of the English Working Class* (1966).

5. Gorz (1967) argues that technicians and professionals are a key strata of the new working class precisely because their autonomous work conditions create an expectation that they should make all decisions controlling their work process. This expectation is increasingly in conflict with the interests of the capitalist class to control production arbitrarily for profit considerations.

6. This definition has an important caveat: technically it should include the restriction that those who perform the male role have more power than those who perform the female role *only if* all other social factors are equal, viz., provided the "male" actors involved are not from individual economic or family classes (or oppressed race or ethnic groups) that are subordinate to those of the "female" actors.

7. One of the important aspects of gender roles is the fact that they are *socially*, not biologically, defined. Although it is almost always men who occupy the male role and women the female role, this is not always so: there are societies in which a woman can become a husband if she has the bride price, and societies like the Mohave Indians in which homosexuals are accepted as male or female regardless of biological sex, depending only on the gender role they decide to play.

8. The universal sexual division of labor, and societies with communal modes of production in which the sexual division of labor nonetheless gives men more power than women, suggests that Engels's historical theory of the origins of patriarchy (that the oppression of women occurs because of the need of men to control heirs and amass private property) is mistaken (Engels, 1972). A counterhypothesis is offered by Lévi-Strauss, who argues that women are the first property, traded to cement bonds between tribes before the development of other types of private property and economic classes (Lévi-Strauss, 1969). Gerda Lerner (1986) adds to this hypothesis the view that women are the first slaves, more valuable than male slaves because of both their reproductive capacity (see also Meillasoux, 1981) and their closer bonds to their offspring, which make them easier to discipline and retain.

Another origin thesis compatible with Lévi-Strauss, Lerner, and Meillasoux is that societies developed matriarchal, egalitarian, or patriarchal kinship arrangements fairly haphazardly throughout the period of human prehistory when tribes were isolated from each other. When societies began to overlap, however, and to compete for hunting areas and land, those that were organized patriarchally were able to overcome matriarchal and egalitarian societies, and to impose their form of male–female patterns on those conquered.

Patriarchal forms of organizing society have two advantages, in survival terms, when they compete with nonpatriarchal societies: (1) they can create very efficient armies; (2) they can generate a high population rate to replace fallen soldiers and/or to provide laborers for production. We can find a direct correlation between high birth rate and high degree of male control over women in historical societies, which suggests that when women have the power to determine their own pregnanices, they tend to keep the birth rate low. If we extrapolate this information to prehistoric societies, we can surmise that many egalitarian or matriarchal societies were not able to compete with militaristic, high-population-producing patriarchal societies. (I owe this line of thought to Nancy Folbre.)

9. It should be noted that this characterization excludes most capitalist-class families for the male breadwinner is usually not working full time because of his unearned income from capital investments. Indeed, male–female relations are sufficiently different that they have no material base for patriarchy. Neither men nor women have to work: they can hire nannies for the children and maintain separate houses for their lovers, so it seems false that women in the capitalist class should be thought of as part of an exploited sex class. Divorced women from this class never lose their family class status because of alimony and child-support, income from trust funds, and so on. The men, on the other hand, are still members of the exploiter sex class, for their relation to the material means of reproduction allows them the power to exploit women from subordinate family and economic class positions.

10. What evidence is there for the view that men exploit women in sex/affective production? There is clear evidence that women spend more time on housework than men do on wage labor. The figure given by the Chase Manhattan Bank survey is that a full-time housewife puts in an average 99.6 hours of housework a week (Girard, 1968). We also know that the inequality in relation to hours of work a week put in by husband and wife persists even when the wife is working in wage labor as well, for in that situation, studies have shown that the wife still puts in roughly 44 hours of housework a week in addition to her wage work, while the husband only puts in 11 hours of work in addition to his wage work (Ryan, 1975).

Since family production is not commodity production, there is no exact quantitative way to measure and compare the values of goods produced for use. Nor does it make sense to speak of the man "building up capital" with his human goods. Nonetheless we can approximate quantitative measurements of the inequalities involved in the exchange by comparing the market commodity costs of the equivalent amounts of sexuality, child care, maintenance, and nurturance done by men and women. For an economic model of this, see Nancy Folbre (1982).

11. The concept of *race class* needs to be further developed. Though the sex-

ual division of labor in the family tends to ensure that women's sex class identity exists across family and economic class lines, the corresponding social divisions of race are not quite as hard and fast. Though there is a racial division of wage labor, the black and other minority petit bourgeois and professionals have escaped that division. And though the neighborhood segregation of many minority middle-class individuals tends to be similar to that of black and minority working-class ghettos, integrated neighborhoods also break down that cultural identification. Some have taken this diffusion of the racial distinctions in productive relations to indicate the declining significance of race in the United States today (Wilson, 1978). Others have strongly disputed this (Marable, 1981). My own view is that *race class* is still a meaningful concept, in part because the *family class* of most middle- and even upper-class black and minority people was *working class*: hence racial identity resulting from racial labor and community segregation was a part of their childhood identity.

12. By "culture," I mean a very broad concept that includes accepted patterns of acting, ways of treating each other, values, aesthetic and expressive forms, preferences for friendships, and so forth. The evidence presented by conservative writers such as Tiger (1969) about male bonding supports the idea that men act as a sex class, and there is also evidence that women bond (Leis, 1974), although in strongly patriarchal societies this tends to be restricted to female kin and bound up with the family.

The recent discussion in the American women's movement on the problem of differences between women related to racism, classism, heterosexual orientation, and cultural ethnicity has raised a serious theoretical question about the early radical feminist claims of a universal women's culture, which cuts across race, class, and cultural differences (see Barry, 1973, Leghorn and Parker, 1981). Although the universal claims of some feminist theorists should indeed be reigned in (e.g., Young, 1984; Joseph and Lewis, 1981; Hooks, 1984), I would defend the view that women's sex/affective labor in the family in nurturing young children *does* create a minimal common cultural base for women from different cultures (e.g., see Justus, 1981 for an application of Chodorow's hypothesis to West Indian society).

13. For some American subcultures, e.g., black Americans, this has long been true (see Degler, 1980).

14. Kollias (1975) has good distinctions between working class and poor.

15. See Myron and Bunch, 1974; Moraga, Anzaldua, and Bambara, 1981; Bulkin, Pratt, and Smith, 1984.

References

Barrett, Michelle. 1980. *Women's Oppression Today*. London: Verso.

———, and McIntosh, Mary. 1982. *The Anti-Social Family*. London: Verso.

Barry, Kathleen. 1973. "The Fourth World Manifesto," in Anne Koedt, Ellen

Levine, and Anita Rapone, eds. *Radical Feminism*. New York: Quadrangle.

Bowles, Samuel, and Herbert, Gintis. 1977. "Heterogeneous Labor and the Labor Theory of Value," *Cambridge Journal of Economics* 1, no. 2.

Bulkin, Elly, Pratt, Minie Bruce, and Smith, Barbara. 1984. *Yours in Struggle: Feminist Perspectives on Anti-Semitism and Racism*. Brooklyn: Long Haul Press.

Davies, Margery. 1979. "Women's Place is at the Typewriter: The Feminization of the Clerical Labor Force," Aillah Eisenstein, ed. 1979.

Davis, Angela. 1981. *Women, Race and Class*. New York: Random House.

Degler, Carl. 1980. *At Odds: Women and the Family in America from the Revolution to the Present*. New York: Oxford University Press.

Deleuze, Giles, and Guattari, Felix. 1977. *Anti-Oedipus*. New York: Viking.

Delphy, Christine. 1984. *Close to Home: A Materialist Analysis of Women's Oppression*. Amherst: University of Massachusetts Press.

Deming, Barbara. 1973. "Love Has Been Exploited Labor," *Liberation* (May 1973).

Ehrenreichs, Barbara and John. 1979. "The Professional-Managerial Class," Pat Walker, ed. *Between Labor and Capital*. Boston: South End Press.

Eisenstein, Zillah, ed. 1979. *Capitalist Patriarchy and the Case for Socialist-Feminism*. New York: Monthly Review Press.

Engels, Frederick. 1972. *Origin of the Family, Private Property and the State*. New York: International Publishers.

Ferguson, Ann. 1984. "On Conceiving Motherhood and Sexuality: A Feminist Materialist Approach," Joyce Trebilcot, ed. 1984: 153–84.

———. 1986. "Pleasure, Power and the Porn Wars," *Women's Review of Books*, III, no. 8 (May 1986): 9–13.

———. 1989. *Blood at the Root: Motherhood, Sexuality and Male Dominance*, London: Unwin Hyman.

Flax, Jane. 1976. "Do Feminists Need Marxism?" *Quest: a Feminist Quarterly*, III, no. 1 (Summer 1976); reprinted in *Quest*, 1981: 174–86.

Folbre, Nancy. 1982. "Exploitation Comes Home: A Critique of the Marxian Theory of Family Labour," *Cambridge Journal of Economics*, 6: 317–29.

———. 1983. "Of Patriarchy Born: The Political Economy of Fertility Decisions," *Feminist Studies*, 9, no. 2 (Summer 1983): 261–84.

Girard, Alain. 1968. "The Time Budget of Married Women in Urban Centers," *Population* (1968).

Gorz, Andre. 1967. *Strategy for Labor*. Boston: Beacon.

Gramsci, Antonio. 1971. *Selections from the Prison Notebooks*, Quinton Hoare and Geoffrey Nowell Smith, eds. New York: International Publishers.

Hartmann, Heidi. 1981. "The Unhappy Marriage of Marxism and Feminism," in Lydia Sargent, ed. *Women and Revolution*. Boston: South End Press.

Hooks, Bell. 1984. *Feminist Theory from Margin to Center*. Boston: South End Press.

Josephs, Gloria and Lewis, Jill. 1981. *Common Differences: Conflicts in Black and White Perspectives,* New York: Doubleday/Anchor.

Justus, Joyce Bennett. 1981. "Women's Role in West Indian Society," in Filomena Steady, ed. *The Black Woman Cross-Culturally*. Cambridge, Mass.: Schenkman.

Kollias, Karen. 1975. "Class Realities: Create a New Power Base," *Quest: A Feminist Quarterly,* 1, no. 3 (Winter, 1975), reprinted in *Quest,* 1981: 125–38.

Kraditor, Aileen. 1965. *The Ideas of the Women's Suffrage Movement 1880–1920*. New York: Columbia University Press.

Leghorn, Lisa, and Parker, Katherine. 1981. *Women's Worth: Sexual Economics and the World of Women*. London: Routledge.

Leis, Nancy. 1974. "Women in Groups: Ijaw Women's Associations," in Michelle Rosaldo and Louise Lamphere, eds. 223–42.

Lerner, Gerda. 1986. *The Creation of Patriarchy*. New York: Oxford University Press.

Lévi-Strauss, Claude. 1969. *The Elementary Structures of Kinship*. Boston: Beacon.

Lippert, J. 1977. "Sexuality as Consumption," in Jon Snodgrass, ed. *For Men Against Sexism*. New York: Times Change Press.

Lukacs, George. 1968. *History and Class Consciousness*. London: Merlin.

Marable, Manning. 1981. "The Third Reconstruction: Black Nationalism and Race in a Revolutionary America," *Social Text* no. 4 (Fall 1981): 3–27; reprinted in Stephen Rosskamm Shalom, eds. 1983. *Socialist Visions*. Boston: South End Press.

Marx, Karl. 1972. *The Eighteenth Brumaire of Louis Bonaparte*. New York: International Publishers.

———, and Engels, Frederick. 1850. *The German Ideology,* David McLellan, ed. 1977. *Karl Marx: Selected Writings*. Oxford: Oxford University Press.

Meillasoux, Claude. 1981. *Maidens, Meal and Money: Capitalism and the Domestic Economy*. New York: Cambridge University Press.

Moraga, Cherri, Anzaldua, Gloria and Bambara, Toni Cade, eds. 1981. *This Bridge Called My Back: Writings by Radical Women of Color*. Watertown, Mass.: Persephone.

Myron, Nancy, and Bunch, Charlotte, eds. 1974. *Class and Feminism*. Baltimore: Diana.

Poulantzas, Nicos. 1975. *Classes in Contemporary Capitalism*. London: New Left Books.

Quest, eds. 1981. *Building Feminist Theory: Essays from Quest*. New York: Longman.

Reiter, Rayna. 1975. *Toward a New Anthropology of Women*. New York: Monthly Review Press.

Rossi, Alice. 1974. "Social Roots of the Women's Movement in America," in Alice Rossi, ed. *Feminist Papers*. New York: Bantam.

Rubin, Gayle. 1975. "The Traffic in Women," in Rayna Reiter, ed. 157–210. *Toward a New Anthropology of Women*. New York: Monthly Review Press.

Ryan, Mary. 1975. *Womanhood in America*. New York: Watts.

Sidel, Ruth. 1986. *Women and Children Last: The Plight of Poor Women in Affluent America*. New York: Viking-Penguin.

Tax, Meredith. 1970. "Woman and Her Mind: The Story of Everyday Life," *New England Free Press Pamphlet*. Boston.

Thompson, E. P. 1966. *The Making of the English Working Class*. New York: Harper & Row.

Tiger, Lionel. 1969. *Men in Groups*. New York: Random House.

Trebilcot, Joyce, ed. 1984. *Mothering: Essays in Feminist Theory*. Totowa, N.J.: Rowman & Allanheld.

Weitzman, Lenore. 1985. *The Divorce Revolution: The Unexpected Social and Economic Consequences for Women and Children in America*. New York: The Free Press.

Wilson, William J. 1978. *The Declining Significance of Race: Blacks and Changing American Institutions*. Chicago: University of Chicago Press.

Wolff, Richard D., and Resnick, Steven A. 1987. *Economics: Marxian vs. Neo-Classical*. Baltimore: The Johns Hopkins University Press.

Women's Agenda. 1976a. "Women and Childcare," *Women's Agenda* (March/April 1976).

Women's Agenda. 1976b. "Women and Poverty," *Women's Agenda* (June 1976).

Wright, Erik Olin. 1978. *Class, Crisis and the State*. London: New Left Books.

Young, Iris. 1984. "Is Male Gender the Cause of Male Domination?" in Trebilcot, ed, *Mothering*. Totowa, N.J.: Rowman & Allenheld: 129–46.

Zaretsky, Eli. 1976. *Capitalism, the Family and Personal Life*. New York: Harper & Row.

Selected Bibliography

Other Works by Authors in This Anthology

Adorno, Theodor W. *Introduction to the Sociology of Music*. Trans. E. B. Ashton. New York: Seabury Press, 1973.

———. *Minima Moralia: Reflections from Damaged Life*. London: New Left Books, 1974.

———. *Negative Dialectics*. Trans. E. B. Ashton. New York: Seabury Press, 1973.

———. *Prisms*. London: Neville Spearman, 1967.

———. "The Culture Industry Reconsidered." *New German Critique*. No. 2 (Fall 1975).

———. and Horkheimer, Max. *Dialectic of Enlightenment*. New York: Herder and Herder, 1972.

———. et al. *The Authoritarian Personality*. New York: Harper & Row, 1950.

Ehrenreich, Barbara. *The Hearts of Men: American Dreams and the Flight from Commitment*. New York: Doubleday, 1983.

———. and English, Deidre. *For Her Own Good: 150 Years of Expert's Advice to Women*. Garden City, N.Y.: Doubleday, 1979.

———. Hess, Elizabeth, and Jacobs, Gloria. *Re-Making Love: The Feminization of Sex*. New York: Doubleday, 1986.

———. Piven, Frances Fox, Cloward, Richard, and Block, Fred. *The Mean Season: The Attack on Social Welfare*. New York: Pantheon Books, 1987.

Ferguson, Ann. "Androgyny as an Ideal for Human Development," in *Feminism and Philosophy,* Mary Vetterling-Braggin, Frederick A. Elliston and Jane English, eds. Totowa, N.J.: Littlefield Adams, 1977.

———. "Women as a New Revolutionary Class in the United States." In *Between Labor and Capital*. Pat Walker, ed. Boston: South End Press, 1979.

———. "Patriarchy, Sexual Identity and the Sexual Revolution." *Signs,* 7, no. 1 (Autumn 1981.)

———. and Folbre, Nancy. "The Unhappy Marriage of Capitalism and Patriarchy," *Women and Revolution*. Lydia Sargent, ed. Boston: South End Press, 1981.

———. "The Sex Debate in the Women's Movement: A Socialist-Feminist View." *Against the Current* (Sept./Oct. 1983).

———. "On Conceiving Motherhood and Sexuality: A Feminist-Materialist Approach." *Mothering: Essays in Feminist Theory*. Joyce Trebilcot, ed. Totowa, N.J.: Rowman and Allanheld, 1984.

———. "Sex War: the Debate between Radical and Libertarian Feminists." *Signs,* 10, no. 1 (Fall 1984).

———. "Pleasure, Power and the Porn Wars." *Women's Review of Books,* 111, no. 8 (May 1986).

———. *Blood at the Root: Motherhood, Sexuality and Male Dominance*. London: Unwin Hymen, forthcoming 1989.

Gorz, Andre. *Strategy for Labor*. Boston: Beacon Press, 1967.

———. *Farewell to the Working Class*. Boston: South End Press, 1982.

———. *Ecology as Politics*. Boston: South End Press, 1980.

Gramsci, Antonio. *Selections from the Prison Notebooks*. Quentin Hoare and G. N. Smith, eds. New York: International Publishers, 1971.

———. Articles in *Ordine Nuovo*. New York: International Publishers, 1920.

———. *"The Modern Prince" and Other Writings*. New York: International Publishers, 1957.

———. *Selections from Political Writings 1910–1920*. New York: International Publishers, 1977.

———. *Selections from Political Writings 1921–1926*. London: Lawrence and Wishart, 1978.

Habermas, Jurgen, *Knowledge and Human Interests*. Boston: Beacon Press, 1968.

———. *Towards a Rational Society*. Boston: Beacon Press, 1970.

———. *Theory and Practice*. Boston: Beacon Press, 1973.

———. *Legitimation Crisis*. Boston: Beacon Press, 1975.

———. *Communication and the Evolution of Society*. Boston: Beacon Press, 1979.

———. *The Theory of Communicative Action Volume I: Reason and the Rationalization of Society*. Boston: Beacon Press, 1984.

Horkheimer, Max. "Geschicte und Psychologie." *Zeitscrift fur Sozialfurschung I,* 1, no. 2, 1932.

———. *Critical Theory*. New York: Seabury Press, 1972.

———. *Critique of Instrumental Reason*. New York: Seabury Press, 1974.

———. *Eclipse of Reason*. New York: Seabury Press. 1974.

Korsch, Karl, *Marxism and Philosophy*. New York: Monthly Review Press, 1971.

———. *Karl Marx*. New York: Wiley, 1967.

———. *Schriften zur Sozialisierung*. Frankfurt: Europaische Verlagsanstalt, 1969.

Lukács, George. *History and Class Consciousness*. Cambridge: MIT Press, 1971.

———. *Tactics and Ethics*. New York: Harper & Row, 1975.

———. *Lenin: A Study on the Unity of His Thought*. New York: Schocken Books, 1970.

———. *The Historical Novel*. Boston: Beacon Press, 1962.
———. *Realism in Our Time: Literature and the Class Struggle*. New York: Harper & Row, 1964b.
———. *Political Writings 1919–1929*. London: New Left Books, 1972.
Marcuse, Herbert. *An Essay on Liberation*. Boston: Beacon Press, 1969.
———. *Counterrevolution and Revolt*. Boston: Beacon Press, 1972.
———. *Eros and Civilization*. New York: Vintage Books, 1962.
———. *Five Lectures*. Trans. Jeremy J. Shapiro and Shierry M. Weber. Boston: Beacon Press.
———. *One-Dimensional Man*. Boston: Beacon Press, 1964.
———. *Soviet Marxism*. New York: Vintage Books, 1958.
———. *Studies in Critical Philosophy*. Trans. Joris de Bres. Boston: Beacon Press.
———. *An Essay on Liberation*. Boston: Beacon Press, 1969.
———. *Negations: Essays in Critical Theory*. Boston: Beacon Press, 1968.
———. *The Aesthetic Dimension: Toward a Critique of Marxist Aesthetics*. Boston: Beacon Press.
———. *Reason and Revolution: Hegel and the Rise of Social Theory*. New York: Oxford University Press, 1941.
Mitchell, Juliet. *Psychoanalysis and Feminism*. New York: Random House, 1975.
———. *Women: The Longest Revolution*. New York: Pantheon, 1984.
———. *Women's Estate*. New York: Vintage Books, 1971.
Reich, Wilhelm. *The Mass Psychology of Fascism*. New York: Orgone Institute Press, 1946.
———. *Character Analysis*. New York: Farar, Strauss, and Giroux, 1970.
———. *Sex-Pol*. New York: Vintage Books, 1972.
———. *The Sexual Revolution*. New York: Orgone Institute Press, 1961.
Rowbotham, Sheila. *Women's Consciousness, Man's World*. New York: Penguin Books, 1974.
———. Segal, Lynne, and Wainright, Hilary. *Beyond the Fragments: Feminism and the Making of Socialism*. London: Merlin Press, 1979.
Sartre, Jean-Paul. *Anti-Semite and Jew*. New York: Schocken Books, 1965.
———. *Critique of Dialectical Reason*. London: New Left Books, 1976.
———. *The Problem of Method*. New York: Knopf, 1963.
———. *Between Existentialism and Marxism*. London: New Left Books, 1972.

Works on and by Western Marxists and Socialist-Feminists

Adler, Franklin. "Factory Councils, Gramsci and the Industrialists." *Telos*, no. 31 (Spring 1977).
Althusser, Louis. *Lenin and Philosophy and Other Essays*. New York: Monthly Review Press, 1971.
———. *For Marx*. New York: Pantheon, 1969.

———, and Balibar, Etienne. *Reading Capital*. London: Verso, 1978.

Anderson, Perry. "The Antinomies of Antonio Gramsci." *New Left Review*, no. 100 (Nov. 1976–Jan. 1977.)

———. *In the Tracks of Historical Materialism*. Chicago: University of Chicago Press, 1984.

Arato, Andrew. "Lukacs' Theory of Reification." *Telos*, no. 11 (Spring 1972).

———, and Gebhardt, Eike. *The Essential Frankfurt School Reader*. Oxford: Basil Blackwell, 1978.

Aron, Raymond. *Dialectics of Violence*. Oxford: Basil Blackwell, 1975.

Aronowitz, Stanley. *The Crisis in Historical Materialism*. South Hadley, Mass.: Praeger, 1981.

Arvon, Henri. *Marxist Esthetics*. Ithaca: Cornell University Press, 1973.

Balbus, Isaac D. *Marxism and Domination*. Princeton: Princeton University Press, 1982.

Barrett, Michele. *Women's Oppression Today*. London: Verso, 1980.

———, et al., eds. *Ideology and Cultural Production*. New York: St. Martin's, 1979.

Benjamin, Jessica. "Authority and the Family Revisited: Or, A World Without Fathers?" *New German Critique*, no. 13, (Winter 1978).

———. "The End of Internalization: Adorno's Social Psychology." *Telos*, no. 32 (Summer 1977.)

Benjamin, Walter. *Illuminations*. Hannah Arendt, ed. Trans. Harry Zohn. New York: Schocken Books, 1969.

Bernstein, Richard J. *The Restructuring of Social and Political Theory*. Philadelphia: University of Pennsylvania Press, 1978.

———. *Praxis and Action: Contemporary Philosophies of Human Activity*. Philadelphia: University of Pennsylvania Press, 1971.

Best, Michael, and Connolly, William. *The Politicized Economy*. Lexington, Mass.: D.C. Heath, 1976.

Bloch, Ernst. *On Karl Marx*. New York: Herder and Herder, 1971.

Boggs, Carl. *Gramsci's Marxism*. London: Pluto Press, 1976.

———. *Political Power and Social Movements*. Philadelphia: Temple University Press, 1987.

———, and Plotke, D., eds. *The Politics of Eurocommunism*. Boston: South End Press, 1980.

Bottomore, Thomas B., ed. *Modern Interpretations of Marx*. Oxford: Basil Blackwell, 1981.

Breines, Paul, ed. *Critical Interruptions: New Left Perspectives on Herbert Marcuse*. New York: Herder and Herder, 1972.

———. "Praxis and Its Theorists: The Impact of Lukacs and Korsch in the 1920's." *Telos*, no. 11 (1972).

Buck-Morss, Susan. *The Origin of Negative Dialectics: Theodor W. Adorno, Walter Benjamin and the Frankfurt School*. Hassocks, Sussex: Harvester, 1977.

Buci-Glucksman, Christine. *Gramsci et L'Etat*. Paris: Librairie Aetheme Fojard. 1975.

Chodorow, Nancy. *The Reproduction of Mothering: Psychoanalysis and the Sociology of Gender*. Berkeley: University of California Press, 1978.

Claudin, Fernando, *The Communist Movement: From Comintern to Cominform*. New York: Monthly Review Press, 1975.

Cohen, G. A. *Karl Marx's Theory of History: A Defense*. Princeton: Princeton University Press, 1978.

Colletti, Lucio. *From Rousseau to Lenin*. New York: Monthly Review Press, 1972.

———. *Marxism and Hegel*. London: New Left Books, 1973.

Dalla Costa, M., ed. *The Power of Women and the Subversion of the Community*, 2nd ed. Bristol: Falling Wall, 1973.

Davidson, A. *Antonio Gramsci: Towards an Intellectual Biography*. Atlantic Highlands, N.J.: Humanities, 1977.

Della Volpe, G. *Rousseau and Marx*. Atlantic Highlands, N.J.: Humanities, 1978.

Eagleton, Terry. *Criticism and Ideology: A Study in Marxist Literary Theory*. Atlantic Highlands, N.J.: Humanities, 1976a.

Eisenstein, Zillah, ed. *Capitalist Patriarchy and the Case for Socialist Feminism*. New York: Monthly Review, 1979.

Evans, Sara. *Personal Politics*. New York: Vintage Books, 1980.

Fee, T. "Domestic Labour: An Analysis of Housework and its Relation to the Production Process." *Review of Radical Political Economy*, 8, no. 2 (1976).

Feenberg, Andrew. *Lukacs, Marx and the Sources of Critical Theory*. Totowa, N.J.: Rowman and Littlefield, 1981.

Femia, Joseph V. *Gramsci's Political Thought: Hegemony, Consciousness and the Revolutionary Process*. New York: Oxford University Press, 1981.

Fiori, Giuseppe. *Antonio Gramsci: Life of a Revolutionary*. New York: Dutton, 1971.

Firestone, Shulamith. *The Dialectic of Sex*. New York: Bantam, 1970.

Fromm, Erich. *Escape From Freedom*. New York: Farrar and Rinehart, 1965.

———. *The Crisis of Psychoanalysis: Essays on Freud, Marx and Social Psychology*. Greenwich, Conn.: Fawcett Publications, 1962.

———. *Marx's Concept of Man*. New York: Frederick Ungar, 1961.

Geuss, Raymond. *The Idea of a Critical Theory*. Cambridge: Cambridge University Press, 1981.

Giddens, Anthony. *A Contemporary Critique of Historical Materialism*. Berkeley: University of California Press, 1981.

———, ed. *Positivism and Sociology*. London: Heinemann, 1974.

Goldman, Lucien. *The Human Sciences and Philosophy*. London: Cape 1969.

———. *Cultural Creation in Modern Society*. St. Louis, MO. Telos, 1976.

Goode, Patrick. *Karl Korsch*. London: Macmillan, 1979.

Gottlieb, Roger S. "A Marxian Concept of Ideology." *Philosophical Forum*, 6, no. 4 (Summer 1975.)

———. "The Contemporary Critical Theory of Jurgen Habermas." *Ethics,* 91, no. 2 (Jan. 1981.)

———. "Forces of Production and Social Primacy." *Social Theory and Practice,* 11, no. 1 (Spring 1985a).

———. "Three Contemporary Critiques of Historical Materialism." *Philosophy and Social Criticism,* 11, no. 2 (Fall 1985b).

———. *History and Subjectivity: The Transformation of Marxist Theory*. Philadelphia: Temple University Press, 1987.

Hartsock, Nancy. *Money, Sex and Power: Toward a Feminist Historical Materialism*. New York: Longman, 1983.

Held, David. *Introduction to Critical Theory*. Berkeley: University of California Press, 1980.

Heller, Agnes, ed. *Lukacs Revalued*. New York: Columbia University Press, 1983.

Howard, Dick, and Klare, Karl E. *The Unknown Dimension: European Marxism Since Lenin*. New York: Basic Books, 1972.

Hudson, Wayne. *The Marxist Philosophy of Ernst Bloch*. New York: St. Martin's, 1982.

Hyppolite, Jean. *Studies on Marx and Hegel*. New York: Basic Books, 1969.

Jacoby, Russell. "Towards a Critique of Automatic Marxism: The Politics of Philosophy from Lukacs to the Frankfurt School." *Telos,* no. 10 (Winter 1971).

———. *Dialectic of Defeat: Contours of Western Marxism*. Cambridge: Cambridge University Press, 1981.

Jagger, Alison M. *Feminist Politics and Human Nature*. Totowa, N.J.: Rowman and Littlefield, 1983.

Jameson, Frederic. *Marxism and Form: Twentieth-Century Dialectical Theories of Literature*. Princeton: Princeton University Press, 1971.

Jay, Martin. *The Dialectical Imagination*. Boston: Little, Brown, 1973.

———. *Marxism and Totality*. Cambridge: Harvard University Press, 1984.

———. "The Concept of Totality in Lukacs and Adorno." *Telos,* no. 32 (1977).

Kelly, Michael. *Modern French Marxism*. Baltimore: Johns Hopkins University Press, 1982.

Kolakowski, Leszek. *Toward a Marxist Humanism*. New York: Grove, 1968.

———. *Main Currents of Marxism,* 3 vols. New York: Oxford University Press, 1978.

Kosik, Karl. *Dialectics of the Concrete*. Boston: Reidel, 1976.

Kuhn, Annette, and Wolpe, AnnMarie, eds. *Feminism and Materialism*. London: Routledge and Kegan Paul, 1978.

Laclau, E. *Politics and Ideology in Marxist Thought*. New York: Schocken Books, 1977.

Larrain, Jorge. *The Concept of Ideology*. London: Hutchinson, 1979.

Leacock, E. B. *Myths of Male Dominance*. New York: Monthly Review Press, 1982.

Lefebvre, Henri. *The Sociology of Marx*. New York: Random House, 1968.
Leiss, William. *The Domination of Nature*. Boston: Beacon Press, 1974.
Lichtheim, George. *From Marx to Hegel*. New York: Seabury Press, 1974.
Maguire, John M. *Marx's Theory of Politics*. Cambridge: Cambridge University Press, 1978.
Malos, E., ed. *The Politics of Housework*. New York: Schocken Books, 1980.
Markovic, Mihailo. *From Affluence to Praxis: Philosophy and Social Criticism*. Ann Arbor: University of Michigan Press, 1974.
———. *Democratic Socialism: Theory and Practice*. New York: St. Martin's, 1982.
McCarthy, Thomas. *The Critical Theory of Jurgen Habermas*. Cambridge: MIT Press, 1978.
McLennan, Gregor. *Marxism and the Methodologies of History*. London: Verso, 1981.
Merleau-Ponty, Maurice. *Adventures of the Dialectic*. London: Heinemann, 1955.
Meszaros, Istvan, ed. *Aspects of History and Class Consciousness*. New York: Herder and Herder, 1971.
Millett, Kate. *Sexual Politics*. Garden City, N.Y.: Doubleday, 1971.
Mouffe, Chantal, ed. *Gramsci and Marxist Theory*. London: Routledge and Kegan Paul, 1979.
Neumann, Franz. *Behemoth: The Structure and Practice of National Socialism*, 2nd ed. New York: Oxford University Press, 1942.
New Left Review, Western Marxism. London: Verso, 1978.
Poster, Mark. *Critical Theory of the Family*. New York: Seabury Press, 1980.
Poulantzas, Nicos. *Political Power and Social Classes*. New York: Schocken Books, 1973.
———. *State, Power, Socialism*. New York: Schocken Books, 1978.
Rakovski, M. *Toward an East European Marxism*. New York: St. Martin's, 1978.
Reiter, R., ed. *Toward a New Anthropology of Women*. New York: Monthly Review Press, 1975.
Robinson, Paul. *The Sexual Radicals*. London: Temple Smith, 1969.
Rose, Gillian. *The Melancholy Science: An Introduction to the Thought of Theodor W. Adorno*. London: Macmillan, 1978.
Sargent, Lydia, ed. *Women and Revolution*. Boston: South End Press, 1981.
Schaff, Adam. *Alienation as a Social Phenomenon*. New York: Pergamon, 1980.
Schmitt, Richard. *Alienation and Class*. Cambridge: Schenkman, 1983.
Schroyer, Trent. *The Critique of Domination*. New York: George Braziller, 1973.
Sher, Gerson S. *Praxis: Marxist Criticism and Dissent in Socialist Yugoslavia*. Bloomington: Indiana University Press, 1977.
Slater, Phil. *Origin and Significance of the Frankfurt School: A Marxist Perspective*. London: Routledge and Kegan Paul, 1977.
Sohn-Rethel, Alfred. *Intellectual and Manual Labor*, Atlantic Highlands, N.J.: Humanities, 1978.

Therborn, Goran. *What Does the Ruling Class Do When it Rules?* New York: Schocken Books, 1980.

Thompson, E. P. *The Poverty of Theory*. New York: Monthly Review Press, 1978.

Thompson, John, and Held, David, eds. *Habermas: Critical Debates*. Cambridge: MIT Press, 1982.

Walker, Pat, ed. *Between Labor and Capital*. Boston: South End Press, 1979.

Wellmer, Albrecht. *Critical Theory of Society*. New York: Seabury Press, 1974.

Wright, Erik Olin. *Class, Crisis and the State*. New York: Schocken Books, 1979.

Zaretsky, Eli. *Capitalism, the Family and Personal Life*. New York: Harper & Row, 1976.